Television and the Self

Television and the Self

Knowledge, Identity, and Media Representation

Edited by Kathleen M. Ryan
and Deborah A. Macey

LEXINGTON BOOKS
Lanham • Boulder • New York • Toronto • Plymouth, UK

Published by Lexington Books
A wholly owned subsidiary of The Rowman & Littlefield Publishing Group, Inc.
4501 Forbes Boulevard, Suite 200, Lanham, Maryland 20706
www.rowman.com

10 Thornbury Road, Plymouth PL6 7PP, United Kingdom

British Library Cataloguing in Publication Information Available

Library of Congress Cataloging-in-Publication Data
Television and the self : knowledge, identity, and media representation / edited by
Kathleen M. Ryan and Deborah A. Macey.
     pages cm
  Includes bibliographical references and index.
  ISBN 978-0-7391-7957-4 (cloth : alk. paper) — ISBN 978-0-7391-7958-1 (electronic)
  1. Television broadcasting—Social aspects. 2. Self-actualization (Psychology)
  3. Television broadcasting—Influence. 4. Identity (Psychology) and mass media. I.
Ryan, Kathleen M., 1962– II. Macey, Deborah A., 1970–
  PN1992.6.T393 2013
  302.23'450973—dc23   2013003592

Printed in the United States of America

Contents

Acknowledgments

The editors would like to thank Noah Springer for his untiring and dogged work as editorial assistant for this collection.

The editors would also like to thank Alison Northridge, Lenore Lautigar, Johnny Simpson, and the staff at Lexington Books for their continuing help with this collection.

Chapter One

Introduction

Kathleen M. Ryan and Deborah A. Macey

Sitting prominently at the hearth of our homes, television serves as a voice of our modern time. The television has been dubbed an "electronic hearth," a technology which over the course of its existence has insinuated itself into "the cultural life of the public."[1] By becoming at one with (or replacing) the traditional hearth, television "embodies values extending to the founding of the nation . . . represented to be timeless and unassailable. [These values] transcend historical flux and take precedence over it."[2] The television thus becomes essential and natural—a part of our everyday lives and experience. Long before the "digital natives" of the twenty-first century emerged, there were the "television natives" of the mid-twentieth century: people who grew up without a memory of a world without television.

We are of that generation. This book—originally half-jokingly referred to as *Everything I Know I Learned from Television*—came to the editors individually, but in different places. For Ryan, the epiphany came while doing a bit of *Home Improvement* in her Colorado cottage. But it wasn't the mishaps of Tim "the Tool Man" Taylor that served as inspiration; instead, it was a gem of construction wisdom from *Gilmore Girls*' diner owner/handyman Luke Danes. He told his bumbling brother-in-law, "The screw's not going in right 'cause you got the drill on counterclockwise. It's righty-tighty, lefty-loosey."[3] That phrase ("righty-tighty, lefty-loosey") became Ryan's mantra during the remodel, used when removing cabinets, rotted subflooring or anything screwed to something else. Her husband laughed at her, but she told him, "Everything I know I learned from television."

Meanwhile Macey's connection developed over time and throughout her academic career. She always loved television and made connections with characters and narratives to explain meaning in her own life. When she started

1

teaching, Macey decided to incorporate television examples in her communication courses. She found her students enjoyed these connections as well. Early in her career *Seinfeld* was particularly useful in illustrating interpersonal communication concepts in a humorous way. In her media studies courses, *The Daily Show with Jon Stewart* has become a mainstay. As Macey discusses the need for free and independent media to support a healthy democracy, she lets Jon Stewart critique many of the media industries' shortcomings. She often jokes with her students that "everything she knows she learned from television."

While some scholars might see television as the breakdown of modern society, we believe that the messages represented on television say something important about American culture and individuals' roles in it. Those of an earlier generation may have loved Lucy and understood *Father Knows Best* as children; a later generation hung out with the *Rugrats* and embraced the heroes on a half shell. We, by contrast, waited eagerly for Miss Mary Ann (Los Angeles) or Miss Lois (St. Louis) to greet us personally from the set of *Romper Room*. At the end of *Sesame Street*, we excitedly shouted out the letter and number that had brought us the show each day before the announcer. We stared glassy-eyed at *Captain Kangaroo* or *The Flintstones* while eating morning cereal before the school day began. After school was a time to sneak in visits with the rock-and-rolling *Partridge Family*, secretly wanting braces so we could pick up radio broadcasts just like big sis Laurie. Occasionally, we tuned into ABC's *Afterschool Specials* for either an inspiring message or a bit of education. *One Day at a Time* offered not only a role model ("good" daughter Barbara, played by the spunky and pretty Valerie Bertinelli), but also a mirror to our real-life experiences: we were both raised by divorced mothers. Mary Tyler Moore made the world of television news production so glamorous that not only did one of the editors work in a small town bumbling news operation as her first job, but she also lived in a studio apartment on the top floor of an old Victorian, much like Mary Richards (a friend even noticed the similarity, making a "mixed tape" which started with the *Mary Tyler Moore Show* theme song). We wanted our MTV, loved the ditzy Mallory Keaton equally as well as the eccentric Denise Huxtable, and were twenty-somethings desperately trying to find out what our lives would be like when we became *thirtysomething*. Later, we embraced shows such as *Seinfeld* and *Friends*, which portrayed the group of friends as the new family unit. In the early twenty-first century, Sarah Jessica Parker showed us a new meaning of thirty-something (single and fabulous!), we got *Lost* in the *Supernatural* (where heroes like Buffy or Clark Kent kicked butt and lived *Charmed* lives), and a spate of smart, well-written, complicated shows both on—and more importantly—off the broadcast networks all seemed to signal that we may be heading into a new "golden age" for that old electronic hearth. And we couldn't help but wonder if we grew up with television or if television had grown up with us.

As Todd Gitlin notes, television is "the principal circulator of the cultural mainstream."[4] It can offer viewers a way to understand the rituals and norms of their own society: David Morley uses the royal Christmas broadcast in the United Kingdom as an example of how an inside-the-home media source can create "a link between the dispersed and disparate listeners and the symbolic heartland of national life . . . promoting a sense of communal identity."[5] While initially disparaged because it didn't have the same artistic trappings as film and other "high" culture, some scholars argued that it was because of its popularity that television merited study.[6] As Horace Newcomb observed, it is crucial "to recognize and understand how social life, now dependent on mass media, on popular forms of expression and entertainment, on the far-reaching lines of information afforded by new technologies, can best be taught and understood, learned and used by all citizens."[7]

Technologies like television, firmly embedded within the home "[transgress] the boundaries of the household—bringing the public world into the private—and simultaneously [produce] the coherence of broader social experience, through both the sharing of broadcast time and ritual."[8] The in-home television, as Stuart Hall observed, serves as a production site of "specific articulation(s) of language on the 'real'"; messages, ideas, and ideology are encoded at the production level, but these messages are always produced through discursive codes, which are then decoded by audiences again through culturally bound codes.[9] Hall asserted that some codes are so pervasive within a particular culture that they appeared naturalized and "conceal the practices of coding."[10] Television, it has been argued, is part of an ideological construction of what it means to be a member of a particular culture, a construction rife with power struggles and questions about the feasibility of freedom in a world where "television works to maintain or ameliorate existing social iniquities."[11]

Susan J. Douglas calls the media a "semiotic sea" in which we all swim.[12] But the sea is often murky and swirling with contradictions. Men and women both struggle with the "right" identity, as seen on TV. For men, it's a negotiation between hyper-masculinity and a type of eroticism where the male body is fetishized and idealized.[13] A similar negotiation takes place for women: should one be docile, cute and sexually pliable or tough, creative and shrewd? But as Douglas observes, the real message may be that both extremes reside in men and women: "Much of what we watched was porous, allowing us to accept *and* rebel against what we saw and how it was presented. The jigsaw pieces of our inner selves have moved around in relation to the jigsaw imagery of the media."[14]

The shows we, and the authors in this edition, cite as our influences may be largely irrelevant to you, the reader, or may not impact you in an identical manner. This lack of conformity of experience is precisely the point, according to Newcomb: "Not a medium that 'polices,' 'instructs,' 'affects' us, television present repertories—some as despicable as others are noble—and the elements we select from those offerings of meanings, belief, behavior, emotion, and performance fit variously into our experience."[15] The audience may be mired in power negotiations with the media producers,[16] but can also actively create a rich alternative to the preferred meaning, changing and manipulating the television text to better suit their own readings.[17] The old model of television as the sole arbiter of cultural identity may be outdated due to the shifting nature of technology, but nonetheless television remains relevant. It offers "a highly personalized medium of individualized, privatized consumption."[18]

It also is a form of consumption that may be tinged with nostalgia. Leah Rosenberg in this edition notes that remembering old television is "ritualized narrative action, a performative language that helps the past come alive for people" and remain an important element of our present. Instead of the much-maligned "boob tube," the authors argue that television and the stories it tells help us as individuals to understand our lives and construct a self-identity. These narratives are not simply entertainment, but powerful socializing agents that shape and reflect the world and our role in it. This book brings together a diverse group of scholars using a variety of methodological and theoretical approaches to investigate the role television plays as the voice from the hearth that frames and shapes our understanding of self and family. The essays range from audience interviews or questionnaires to authoethnographies, content analyses to textual analyses. The chapters span the life cycle, from birth to aging. The authors offer a melding of television's distant and not-so-distant past with contemporary trends in programming, from classic sit-coms to modern reality programming, television dramas to the thirty-second messages found in commercials.

The edited collection is divided into five sections. In the first, "The Electronic Hearth, or the (un)Real World," the authors explore how television has replaced the hearth of old as the center of home life. Rosenberg uses in-depth interviews to investigate how people remember the past through the act of television viewing from their childhood, while Marcelina Piotrowski looks back on her own experiences as an ex-patriot watching television from her homeland (Poland) in her adopted home of Canada. The authors argue that one way television shapes both personal and cultural memory is by how it marks time both past and future, offering a way to maintain a connection to self, friends, family or even a country left behind. While both authors investigate the notion of the past, there is a tension between Rosenberg's conception of nostalgia and Piotrowski's use of television to both anchor her to the present and learn about her forgotten homeland. Rosenberg's elegant analysis demonstrates the sincere pleasure people get from past television shows, enabling them to remember specific times and spaces (often long forgotten) in relation to television viewing. The viewing thus becomes what Rosenberg calls a "narrative action." Television, while often dismissed as a passive or unproductive pursuit by the interviewees, was revealed to actually provide not only serious pleasure but also a way to keep in touch with and interpret the past. For Piotrowski, television isn't a source of actual memories, but rather a way to fill a "lack" either in her own life (the remembered firsthand knowledge of her homeland, Poland) or in her parents' lives (the lack of the Polish community from "home"). She uses the concept of spectatorship to explain how she (and her parents) negotiated this lack: "a socially, historically and economically determined process that produces meaning through the encounter of a visual text, a human person, a social circumstance, a family, a space, geographic location, and so on. The spectator as a person not necessarily exists prior to these encounters, but is formed through the encounters that comprise multiple and fluid connections."

Part two, "Father (and Mother) Knows Best," begins the life cycle, looking at how television works as a pseudo-parent: echoing and at times replacing the in-home parental role models. From women comparing their own birth narratives to ones learned from reality television (Hall) to television's (often not-so) idealized portrayal of mothers (Betancourt) and fathers (Staton), the authors in this section explore how our concepts of a "good" family life can be shaped by television narratives. Jennifer Hall begins the section, looking at the role of television birth narratives in shaping how women develop expectations for how their own pregnancies should evolve. In her interviews with women who have had high-risk pregnancies, she discovers that television both leads to expectations by the women in the circumstances surrounding their child(ren)'s birth as well as frustrations that their pregnancy and birth experiences don't follow the television "norm." Andrée Betancourt's chapter on television mothers is next, looking specifically at the mothers as seen on the HBO series *The Sopranos* and *Six Feet Under*. Her self-reflexive chapter explores how the series, and the companion books the series spawned, offer lessons in motherhood, both demonstrating how these fictional characters attempt to negotiate the somewhat tricky world of a stay-at-home mom in a post-feminist world. The notion of fatherhood is taken up by David Staton, who investigates its representation in the AMC programs *Mad Men*, *Breaking Bad*, and *The Walking Dead*. The consistent marker in the three programs (aside from their broadcast on AMC), is the male lead's use of a sartorial accoutrement—the hat. The three fathers in question each wear hats, and Staton argues that the presence of the accessory reveals a split in the characters' personalities. Far from a cultural sign with a myriad of potential readings, for these fathers the hat spells authority—and the absence of it creates a man adrift, uncertain of his own role and his own masculinity.

In the third section, "Family Ties," the authors investigate television's role in shaping how we communicate family values, both inside and outside of the home. Ellen E. Stiffler, Lynne M. Webb and Amy C. Duvall look at how our own family relationships influence an individual's appreciation of a character in contemporary family-based comedies. Contrary to past research in other generations, their survey of twenty-first-century millennials finds that the amount of television viewed has little impact on how individuals evaluate potential role models on television. Instead, it was the individual's home-instilled values that led him or her to determine which characters best represented each's worldview and value system. Jingsi Christina Wu and Brian McKernan use an analysis of online chat boards for the series *The Real Housewives of New York City* to determine how viewers define norms for parenting and family life. They argue that using the audience's own voice via the boards reveals "diverse and potentially surprising ways" the audience uses the show not to "passively internalize all the ideological messages embedded in these programs" but rather use the show to make sense of their own parenting choices and family lives. Amanda S. McClain analyzes the tortuous family/business relationship found in *Keeping Up with the Kardashians*. She argues the series espouses complicated, and contradictory, values. On the one hand, the family embraces the "do anything for fame" ethic that seems to permeate contemporary society; on the other, they also embrace the notion that family trumps all. As McClain notes, "The Kardashians embody the contradictions present within us all—theirs are intimate and familiar, yet extreme and larger than life."

The authors in the fourth section, "The Facts of Life," consider the mediated evolution as an individual moves from childhood to adulthood. Susan G. Kahlenberg begins the section by looking at advertisements aimed at "tweens" (roughly ages eight to twelve) on the children's cable channel Nickelodeon. Through a content analysis of ads, she found that the world represented to children is a highly gendered place, with boys and girls for the most part operating in separate spheres (boys play outside the home, girls play within the home or in traditional "feminine" activities; boys compete against each other, girls work together toward a goal or work independently). Even though Nickelodeon has a "kids first" message and would appear through its programming to promote "girl power," the ads shown on the channel "are strategically and consistently imbued with gender-role stereotypes that may influence children's cognitive, attitudinal, and behavioral tendencies." Cynthia J. Miller and A. Bowdoin Van Riper investigate how the rocketmen children's programs during the Cold War era (specifically the 1950s) embraced notions of heroism, bravery and good citizenship, and, through the sidekick character each show had, helped young boys to learn what it meant to be a man in the post-World War II world. Robin Redmon Wright turns her attention to the early 1960s version of the British television series *The Avengers*, and uses extensive interviews with viewers to argue that the female lead of Dr. Cathy Gale was (as one of the producers noted) "the first emancipated woman on television," a role which would lead viewers (and fans) to reevaluate the role of women in British society. In the final chapter in the section, Tanja N. Aho looks at MTV's often-dysfunctional and certainly bumpy road to maturity as seen in shows like *Teen Mom* and *16 and Pregnant*. In a compelling and innovative Foucaultian-based analysis, Aho argues that the shows function as a way for the state (in this case television producers and cable channels) to regulate the self in terms compatible with neoliberal capitalism. But, as she points out, the model is complicated by the fact that even with various controls in place, the teens still manage to talk back, offering agency to the young mothers and their boyfriends, and demonstrate their "rejection of [the series'] claims to truth."

In the final section, "As Not Seen on TV," the two authors (Michael Johnson Jr. and Deborah A. Macey) look at what had for many years been an invisible population on American television: older men and women. Johnson argues that the relative invisibility of gay characters over forty, especially those of color, sends a message to audiences that those demographics simply don't matter—not simply to advertisers, but also to community members. He notes that while gay men and lesbians may appreciate the younger characters seen on television, a more inclusive representation will offer validation to all gay and lesbian Americans in "their ability to obtain recognition" and "pursue 'full membership' into American society through their media consumption practices." Macey explores the fascination with ninety-year-old Betty White in the midst of a culture that is youth obsessed, arguing that White's popularity is based in part on her characters' embodiment of ancient archetypal goddesses. Macey also asserts that over White's long career neither she nor the characters she plays challenge mainstream ideology, making White less threatening to the status quo, and thus more likeable. Finally, Macey notes that White's success is bolstered by the intertextuality of new programming on a network created out of nostalgia for past television experiences.

In recent years, the non-broadcast networks have been staking out a ground recognizing the link between audience and identity that the authors in this edition explore. "Brace yourself" (Showtime), the programmers say, because the electronic hearth is "more than you imagined" (HBO). While the message is most direct at ABC Family ("a different type of family") and Lifetime ("your life, your time"), these two outlets are not the only ones to emphasize that the tales television weaves are important to viewers. As AMC so elegantly states, "story matters." Far from simply catchy promotional slogans designed to promote a corporation, these phrases can also be descriptors of our own negotiation of self. Television is a place to "live out loud" (Oxygen) and "watch what happens" (Bravo). There is room in this exploration for the very funny (TBS), for characters (USA) and drama (TNT), and for a place to make yourself at home (Hallmark). The learning goes far beyond the treacly "very special" episodes found in family sit-coms in the 1980s. Instead, television reflects our reality and helps us to sort out what it means to be a twenty-first-century man or woman.

Notes

1. Cecelia Tichi, *Electronic Hearth: Creating an American Television Culture* (New York: Oxford University Press, 1992), 7.

2. Tichi, *Electronic Hearth,* 43.

3. *Gilmore Girls*, "Fight Face," directed by David Palladino, first broadcast September 20, 2005 on WB.

4. Todd Gitlin, *Watching Television: A Pantheon Guide to Popular Culture* (New York: Pantheon Books, 1985), 3.

5. David Morley, *Home Identities: Media, Mobility and Identity* (New York: Routledge, 2000), 106.

6. See Bonnie J. Dow, *Prime-Time Feminism: Television, Media, Culture and the Women's Movement Since 1970* (Philadelphia: University of Pennsylvania Press, 1996); Horace Newcomb, ed., *Television: The Critical View*, 7th ed. (New York: Oxford University Press, 2006).

7. Newcomb, *Television,* 8.

8. Morley, *Home Identities,* 3.

9. Stuart Hall, "Encoding/Decoding," in *Media and Cultural Studies: Key Works*, ed. Meenakshi Gigi Durham and Douglas M. Kellner, rev. ed. (Malden, MA: Blackwell Publishing Ltd., 2001), 167.

10. Hall, "Encoding/Decoding," 167.

11. Newcomb, *Television,* 364.

12. Susan J. Douglas, *Where the Girls Are: Growing Up Female with the Mass Media* (New York: Random House, 1994), 301.

13. Roger Horrocks, *Male Myths and Icons* (New York: St. Martin's Press, 1995), 170.

14. Douglas, *Where the Girls Are,* 9.

15. Horace Newcomb, "Reflections on TV, *The Most Popular Art*," in *Thinking Outside the Box: A Contemporary Television Genre Reader*, ed. Gary R. Edgerton and Brian G. Rose (Lexington, KY: University of Kentucky Press, 2005), 35.

16. Matt Briggs, *Television, Audiences and Everyday Life: Issues in Media and Cultural Studies* (Maidenhead, Berkshire, England: Open University Press, 2009).

17. See Jonathan Gray, Cornel Sandvoss, and C. Lee Harrington, eds., *Fandom: Identities and Communities in a Mediated World* (New York: New York University Press, 2007); Henry Jenkins, *Textual Poachers: Television Fans and Participatory Culture* (New York: Routledge, 1992).

18. Graeme Turner and Jinna Tay, eds., *Television Studies After TV: Understanding Television in the Post-Broadcast Era* (New York: Routledge, 2009), 2.

Part One:

The Electronic Hearth, or the (un)Real World

Chapter Two

The Way We Were:
Ritual, Memory, and Television

Leah A. Rosenberg

Mapping the different kinds of pleasure viewers receive from television contributes not only to further understanding this complex sentiment in relation to media usage, but also in developing a richer sense of how memory, media, and self operate in the context of pleasurable viewing. Lara, when asked about both what and how she viewed TV when she was younger, recalled that every afternoon after school she went home and immediately turned on the television. Both she and her brother watched TV with what Lara described as "tremendous frequency." For at least four hours a day she enjoyed a range of shows. Lara and her brother often took half-hour turns watching their individual shows, but sometimes would watch together, sharing a deep appreciation for shows like *Cheers* and *Perfect Strangers*. It was apparent from her facial expressions, hand gestures, and the occasional brief explanation of a particular show that television viewing was a deeply pleasurable activity for her.

For Lara and the seventeen other women and men I interviewed about watching television, the familiar and taken for granted activity was a meaningful and even extraordinary aspect of their youth. It was extraordinary not necessarily because of the quality of what they viewed or how they viewed it, though without a doubt both directly influenced their experiences, but because the pleasure they felt watching television (either alone or with others) stood out in their memories and was frequently described as special and distinct from other daily activities they enjoyed. Recalling details about gritty suspense dramas like *The Fugitive* (ABC 1963-1967) or rehashing the comedy styling of

11

Alf (NBC 1986-1990) was a way in which people produced an understanding of their past and present. Structured and open-ended interview questions conducted with a near equal number of men and women representing three separate age cohorts (twenty to thirty; thirty to forty; and fifty to sixty) illuminated their past TV viewing practices. Their responses reveal how television influences their memories about family and self.

Discussing the past in the context of television is a specific type of "narrative action," to borrow from Michel de Certeau.[1] The memories they shared about how and what they watched on television can be understood as a complex process, whereby stories are told about stories that in turn structure more stories.[2] De Certeau notes that stories traverse, organize and regulate places effectively linking them together and making itineraries out of them.[3] Accordingly, every story is essentially a travel story; thus narratives about television and narratives as told by television can function metaphorically as a modality of transport that assists in the process of recalling past places and people, and of course back to a time when TV viewing was a serious pleasure. It is a narrative action confirming what memory scholars already know about the archeology of individual and collective memory.[4]

This chapter examines the role of television in people's everyday lives, arguing that people often approach television in a manner that allows them to construct and reconstruct personal histories. Its focus is less on the textual content of any one show and more about detailing the experiences of what watching television means and still means to people as they were growing up. For those interviewed, growing up was usually defined and identified as three discrete, though by no means rigid, categories consisting of childhood, adolescence, and adulthood (which they tended to mark as beginning when they went off to college). In addition to using television reception studies, which has called into question assumptions of audience passivity and challenged the veracity of the "couch potato" label frequently assigned to TV viewers, and memory studies for illuminating the connection between cultural memory and media, this chapter also borrows from ritual studies as a way of taking into account the TV practices of ordinary media users. A concentration on the ritualization of television viewing effectively aids in distinguishing ritual from non-ritual viewing and encourages a more nuanced examination into what people bring to television and what they take away from it.

Both time and resources were contributing factors in the size and scope of the sample. However, since a key goal of the interviews was to explore the intersection of memory, ritual, and watching television, a smaller sample also allowed for longer, detailed responses about the intersection of these components. I sought to understand how television contributes to the ways in which the participants discuss meaning and memory of their life experiences. In some respects this is a continuation of research done by television scholars, whereby a diverse number of factors are considered from age to gender when thinking about active audiences. All interviewees have had some college education, many possessing an M.A. or higher. While education level might not be representative of the broader population, the participants' responses illuminate a real connection between television and the meaning(s) of memory and self. Future research might explore how education influences the ways audiences decode their viewing experiences.

Part of a larger project exploring people's attitude and approach to viewing news and non-news television, this chapter is comprised of three sections, each one seeking to address significant themes or patterns gleaned from interviews. The first addresses people's attitudes and feelings toward a number of shows they watched, focusing on the pleasures of television viewing, as well as what constitutes ritualized versus non-ritualized viewing. The second examines how viewing is a ritual practice that aids in the production and reproduction of past time and place. The last section is concerned with how people understood television as shaping and influencing family relationships, friendships, and a sense of who they once were.

Serious Pleasure

The men and women interviewed discussed how pleasurable it was for them to watch television when they were younger. They commonly and frequently used words such as "loved," "enjoyed," and "fun" to describe their feelings about watching television. Some answered the follow-up question, asking for an explanation about the kinds of shows they used to watch, with a great deal of enthusiasm. Without hesitation they went into details about the appeal of *The Muppet Show* (CBS 1976-1981), for example, which Robert recalled being "bonkers" about, or the silliness of Bugs Bunny's antics that Lance, another interviewee, claimed he was "wild" about. Indeed, Lance enjoyed Bugs Bunny cartoons so much that he remembered being "extremely annoyed" when the Bugs Bunny holiday special was interrupted due to breaking news that Ronald Reagan had been shot. For older participants like Alice and John, thinking back to shows like *Winky Dink and You* (CBS 1953-1957) and *Lassie* (CBS 1954-1973) made them chuckle. Regardless of the genre, what participants emphasized most was how pleasurable it was for them to watch television in their youth. Even Melissa, the one interviewee who claimed having neither a current nor past interest in television, could recall how much she enjoyed watching *Little House on the Prairie* (NBC 1974-1982), although it was framed, as an extension of her love for the book series written by Laura Ingalls Wilder.

In using the term "pleasure," I evoke what religious studies scholar Julie Byrne refers to as a commonsense definition. According to Byrne pleasure is "simply a person's sense of satisfying desire."[5] While desire is a complicated concept, what is most pertinent about it for the purpose of this discussion is that "desire holds the place of human agency, that tangled assemblage of forces that constitute us, from the midst of which we move and are moved."[6] Past work on television viewing and audience attitudes has also raised pleasure as an important and relevant sentiment;[7] however, little work has been done on investigating the ritual usage of television as a way of recalling one's personal past and as a means of summoning both past and present feelings of pleasure, joy, and satisfaction. Indeed, interviewees' discussions on television make clear that their pleasures, tastes, and values are directly connected to their emotional lives.[8]

When interviewees were asked to recall television shows from their youth, pleasure was embodied through a range of gestures such as smiling or chuckling, and narratively both in general terms and in the occasional retelling of specific episodes or shows they used to watch. For example, Louisa, a fifty-year-old university lecturer and department director, in recalling how much she enjoyed viewing with her brothers and father what she referred to as "spy stuff" from the 1960s, smiled wistfully. With her voice raised slightly she then exclaimed, "*I Spy*, *Get Smart*, and *The Man from U.N.C.L.E* were great! I wanted to see the Bond movies, but they failed the Catholic Decency Standards." When asked what it was she enjoyed about these types of shows she replied, "It was the action, the adventure, and the cute male actors!" Louisa added that even today she still likes the spy stuff and that the James Bond movies are some of the only ones she and her husband will actually watch in a theater. In addition to the attractive male leads and thrilling story lines, viewing these types of shows was also an enjoyable way for her to spend time and connect with the male members of her household. Similarly, Melissa remembered liking CBS's *Gunsmoke,* which aired 1955 to 1975, for two reasons: because of the time she got to spend with her father and "the man was handsome and his son was cute! What can I say—I was only nine or ten at the time!"

Generally speaking, there was nothing especially exceptional about the time participants spent with their families watching television. In fact, one aspect of viewing together people seemed to most appreciate centered on what a seemingly mindless, yet enjoyable, activity it was for them. Sociologist Ron Lembo outlines viewing practices and typologies of television usage, which are essential for understanding how television viewers often engage in mindful and meaningful viewing strategies. He writes, "When watching television, people participate in an oftentimes complex social world, one in which they routinely exhibit varying levels of mindful and emotional involvement with television and other people as well."[9] While I do not disagree with Lembo (quite the contrary), he neglects to address what a pleasurable activity television viewing can be precisely because people are engaged in what they interpret to be a mindless activity. In other words, for some interviewees the understanding that they were doing something unproductive fueled the pleasure of their viewing.[10] Moreover, some of the pleasure they felt (sometimes a guilty-pleasure) seemed to stem directly from the way they defined their viewing as having a passive quality to it.

The threat or danger television viewing might have had on people's productivity was perceived as real. Lance, a graduate student in his thirties, along with a number of other participants, recalled how his viewing was limited to a few hours a day because his parents were concerned about him wasting too much time in front of the television. He added, "If I have kids I'll probably limit their viewing to two hours as well just to keep with tradition I guess." Regardless of his parents' vigilant attitude against wasting time, Lance managed to take full advantage of his allotted two hours a day as his responses revealed how much he loved the long-running British TV series *Doctor Who* (BBC 1963-1989), repeatedly remarking that he had a *Doctor Who* "fetish," how he was a "dedicated" *Doctor Who* viewer, and, further into the interview, that the show was one of his favorites. Margot, a language student in her early twenties, recalled not being allowed to watch anything except programs approved by her father because viewing television took time away from her homework. She and her brother were only permitted to watch what she called "educational television." In a society that readily subscribes to the Protestant ethic of hard work, watching television, even within the confines of regulated and limited viewing, can be understood as a kind of quiet, but pleasurable, rebellion against a relentless cultural attitude regarding the central importance of industriousness and productivity.

Television viewing was also regarded as a delightfully antisocial activity. Just as it was a way of being together and sharing time with each other, people also spoke of shows they would watch without their family, and the sense of pleasure they felt engaging in a kind of private enjoyment. Denise, a health technician in her late twenties, recalled watching "a lot" of television when she was younger, nearly five to eight hours a day. A great number of these hours were spent viewing alone, indulging in her love of such shows from the 1980s and early 1990s such as *The Fresh Prince of Bel Air*, *Family Ties*, and *Silver Spoons*, series her father, a retired military veteran, and mother would not normally watch. Several participants laughed in a manner that seemed to suggest such shows were too silly to be watched with others. For example, Julia, a 33-year-old graduate student, looking faintly embarrassed, discussed watching the soap opera *Santa Barbara* (NBC 1984-1993) but quickly added, "It was only for a brief time," explaining that she gave up on the serial when she was in high school, preferring instead to watch music videos on MTV in the privacy of her bedroom.[11]

Sociologists Lembo and Andrea Press have each emphasized in their work on television reception how those they interviewed often characterized their viewing as having a ritual dimension to it. However, neither their participants nor they themselves ever explicitly define what they mean by ritual, which tended to be integrated in larger discussions of routine and practice.[12] While media scholars Daniel Dayan and Elihu Katz use the work of anthropologist Victor Turner to discuss how viewings of live broadcasts of historic events have become "world rituals," their work does not address the ritualization of ordinary or everyday television viewing, nor has it ever made explicit what they mean by the phrase "world rituals."[13] Therefore, I turn to ritual studies scholar Catherine Bell for a more nuanced and detailed understanding of ritual.[14] As Bell and other scholars have stressed, rituals need not be connected to the extraordinary or sacred. They can occur within a number of contexts for various reasons, and they do not necessarily involve either intricate or complex actions. She writes, "An even simpler example might contrast the routine activity of buying some regularly used article of clothing for a spouse or a child (such as gym socks) and the ritualized version of buying a similar or different article (argyle socks) and giving it as a gift."[15] Ritualization (the term is intentionally evoked) she argues, is interpreted in terms of practice and is a way of acting that draws attention to the way in which some social actions strategically distinguish themselves in relation to other ones.[16]

For interview participants, viewing specific shows, regardless of whether they were broadcast daily, weekly, or even just once a year (such as the annual showing of the movie *The Wizard of Oz*), constituted a ritualization of their television viewing. This was due in part to the manner in which they viewed certain shows that was qualitatively different from their usual engagement with TV. Ritualized viewing meant that their attention was more focused, expectations of an emotional return was higher in comparison to non-ritual viewing, and all other activities tended to decrease. Rob's recollection of watching the sitcom *Alf*, which centered on the adventures of a cat-eating alien who resided with a suburban, middle-class, white family, is an excellent example of ritual viewing. Now in his mid-twenties, his discussion of the show revealed how Alf was more than just a routine part of his weekly viewing. In addition to anticipating its scheduled appearance, he also spoke of his affection, love, and even admiration of the main character, Alf, who was extraterrestrial extraordinaire in his eyes. When his beloved weekly ritual viewing of it was interrupted by a speech given by President Reagan, he distinctly remembered being "really mad!" Rob laughed as he recounted this story, but the disruption of Alf was a disruption not simply to his routine viewing, but to a show that was consciously set apart (from other shows) and considered special. His expression of irritation and the fact that he remembered this incident many years later was evidence of how seriously Rob took this show and reflected his commitment to the pleasure of television.

In addition to pleasure, recalling shows also made some feel a sense of nostalgia and even loss, such complex emotional expressions that highlight how personal and meaningful TV viewing can be that it sometimes encourages a sense of mourning or melancholia. Lara discussed how the sitcom *Cheers* (NBC 1982-1993) was closely associated with feelings about who she once was and how her life "used to be." In particular, whenever she heard the theme music to *Cheers* it made her feel sad and contemplative because she directly equated the end of the show with the end of a period of her life. She explained:

> Sometimes when I hear the theme song to *Cheers* it's everything I can do not to cry. I remember loving that show and watching it with my brother. When I was a kid I would hear the theme song from the other room and come running in! I e-mailed him [her brother] a couple of weeks ago reminding him of how much

we liked that song and loved *Cheers* and he wrote back saying that he could devote a whole dissertation to discussing how that song makes him feel. When the show ended, I felt like a part of my life ended as well . . . a part of my life when I felt happy quite often.

In Robert's case, his feelings of nostalgia regarding *The Muppet Show* were connected more to the actual characters themselves and how their personalities and actions appealed to, as well as reflected, aspects of his own thoughts and feelings. Recalling two Muppets in particular, he explained:

> I think the appeal of *The Muppet Show* for me was the wide range of personalities presented. Some of which have the realistic dimensions that helped the audience relate to them. I mean Kermit is a complex character trying to keep the show on track while problems keep coming up. He has sort of a fun side where he enjoys what is going on around him and then there's this melancholic side to him like when he's singing "It's Not Easy Being Green." Even Fozzie-the-Bear struggled with trying to write funny jokes even though his jokes were typically really stupid.

Along with the obvious pleasure *The Muppet Show* gave him, his comments are also about his strong identification with Kermit and Fozzie trying their best even if they do not always succeed and, perhaps even personally importantly for Robert, the ability to laugh at and enjoy oneself even when success does not come or come easily. The narrative excerpts of both Lara and Robert speak to a sense of longing for the past and of missing a period in their lives when familiar and beloved TV characters entertained them and gave them a sense of pronounced pleasure and happiness.

Time, Place, and the Persistence of Memory

In addition to sentiments of pleasure and longing, the workings of both individual and collective memory in relation to TV viewing were also found in a wide range of genres from sitcoms to late night variety shows. Recalling old television shows is a ritualized narrative action, a performative language that helps the past come alive for people. The powerful appeal of bringing a television past into the present speaks to the growing popularity of cable channels such as Nick at Night or its spinoff niche-network TV Land, both of which air a myriad of old television shows from *The Donna Reed Show* (ABC 1958-1966) to *Mork and Mindy* (ABC 1978-1982). More recently ME-TV (Memorable Entertainment Television, launched 2010) and Antenna TV (launched 2011) became national networks carrying classic sitcoms, dramas, and classic commercials from the 1950s through the 1980s. Additionally, there have been a number of movie remakes of popular American television shows such as *Miami Vice* (2006) and *The A-Team* (2010).

A number of scholars argue that memory and history are vulnerable to the fast pace of life and the acceleration of media images;[17] however, recalling television shows is a practice people engage in order to anchor themselves in the swirl of the past. Television has not been traditionally thought of as an object that sustains or even creates memories; in fact, it has been actively critiqued for doing the opposite.[18] However, Steven Anderson argues "that since its inception, American television has sustained an extremely active and nuanced engagement with the construction of history and has played a crucial role in the shaping of cultural memory."[19]

One way television shapes both personal and cultural memory is by how it marks time both past and future. Or as Alice explained, "Television watching is a way of marking time. It's like a song in the sense that shows act as place markers during the day or throughout your life." Shows psychically located people in the specifics of past time and space. For example, a good many participants remembered not only the exact name of shows they watched, but how old they were (I was either nine or ten, I was in high school), as well as actual show times (every evening at 6:00, afternoons around 3:00), and where they watched (living room, den). In Rob's case, television viewing was linked to a season. He explained, "I remember watching a lot of television in the summer. School was out, I was one of the only kids on my block, and there was nothing else to do."

Days of the week were also frequently mentioned: "I loved Saturday morning cartoons!" and "Every Sunday, I would watch *60 Minutes* with my father. It was our tradition, our time together." They discussed viewing as part of their daily routine: "I would come home from school and watch a lot of cartoons," "I went to bed earlier than my siblings because I was youngest, but they [her parents] used to let me stay up with them to watch *The A-Team* (laughter)." Even participants who did not watch a lot of television when they were younger such as John, a scientist now in his late fifties, could still recall watching cartoons in the morning before going off to school. Growing up on a dairy farm, time spent viewing was something he enjoyed especially after a 4:00 a.m. wake-up in order to milk the cows. It was a considerably more pleasurable way of filling the time between less fun activities like school and milking.

While time and place together established the situational context in which interviewees viewed, viewing in turn helped establish a sense of time and place. Alice remembered being the first family on her block to own a television, which was placed in the living room. While it is possible viewing was either a frequent or occasional collective neighborhood experience, what she recalled was how her family enjoyed watching entertainment programs such as *The Ed Sullivan Show* (CBS 1948-1971), as well as the nightly news, together. Viewing together at night in their living room helped establish a sense of time and reinforced the living room as a shared, familial place. In contrast, Rob and Julia remember receiving their own television sets when they were teenagers around the time when they entered high school. Both spoke of watching in the solitude of their bedrooms, which meant there was a pronounced shift from television watching as a family activity, as well as an emphasis on watching shows other members had no interest in watching. Julia mentioned that "after I got my own TV set, we never watched television together in the same way as when there was just the one small set in the living room. Occasionally we would still gather together and watch a movie someone rented." Rob noted how he enjoyed watching what he understood to be "his" shows, staying up much later than his parents in order to watch shows like *The X Files* or *The Late Show with David Letterman* and other late night television.

Religious scholar Jonathan Z. Smith's work explicates place, ritual, and the emergence of meaning.[20] Smith argues that ritual is first and foremost a mode of paying attention and a process of marking interest; place is a fundamental component of ritual because it directs attention.[21] This issue of place and ritual seems especially important when it comes to discussing the personal and cultural significance of how place is constructed, along with the physical placement of television sets in people's home. In Smith's analysis, it is human beings who direct ritual and thus the transformation of space into place.[22] It was both the ritual and non-ritual practice of television viewing day in and day out that aided in the transformation of the space of their living rooms, dens, or basements into places of enjoyment and pleasure, attitudes that may have differed if the exact same spaces were being used to host relatives, for example.

In terms of time, weekend viewing took on a more pronounced ritual dimension for most participants. The weekend was often loose and unrestricted in terms of parental oversight, and it was also when ritualized viewing frequently occurred for a number of participants—that is, their mode of viewing was characterized by a special kind of attention. Watching Saturday morning cartoons was a ritual that distinguished the weekend from other days and parents themselves recognized the importance of this distinction. For example, Susan, a mother of four, currently feels that monitoring what her children watch and how much they watch is an important part of looking after their well-being. However, on weekends she "lets them loose" and they get to watch cartoons and other shows all morning. Weekend viewing for all participants now in their late twenties and thirties was often a means of contrasting their childhood TV viewing from the news or other more serious viewing they associated with becoming or being adults.

As children they immersed themselves in their viewing in a manner different from the way they did so during a typical week when homework, bedtime, or chores competed with their TV viewing. A sense of mundane, normal, or regulative time was temporarily suspended and they focused their viewing in a way that reflected the symbolic importance of weekend television viewing, which was not bounded by the usual daily obligations and responsibilities. American history professor Mark Carnes in discussing the function of ceremonies and rituals in his work on fraternal orders in the American Victorian era notes that such rituals were about conjuring a world that offered solace from real life.[23] Interviewees recalled how as children they immersed themselves in a world of cartoon rabbits, frustrated coyotes, and heroes wearing brightly colored tights. It was a way of embracing pleasure as well as a strategy for resisting the demands of everyday life. Additionally, weekend TV viewing was a form of emotional expressiveness that helped symbolize, for participants, what was perceived to be the delightful and special condition that constituted childhood. Fraternal ceremonies and the pastime of watching Saturday morning cartoons function in remarkably similar ways. Both are responses to shifting life conditions, be it disruptions in the larger social order during the nineteenth century, or the start of more serious interaction for children in a world that had begun to extend beyond boundaries of the home. Both types of ceremonies offered grown men and small children alike a sense of reassurance and refuge in a changing and sometimes seemingly unstable world. And perhaps even most important, they offered participants what sociologist Paul Connerton stresses is an important aspect of rites, a sense of value and meaning in their lives.[24]

The Way We Were

While a number of interviewees discussed how television brought their families together, this does not imply that families were or became emotionally close just because they were spatially close, gathered if you will, around the television. Although older respondents in their fifties and sixties stressed how watching television as a family was an activity they looked back on with some fondness, others commented less on the particularities of any warm familial memories, remembering that it was simply inconceivable to watch alone. As Scott put it, "In my family you did not just go and turn on the television by yourself." Moreover, as people got older they often stopped watching with their families and began watching more with siblings and friends or by themselves. Younger interview participants in their twenties rarely mentioned watching non-news television with their families. Regardless of the gradual shifts in viewing, for most, watching television was a meaningful and substantive way, especially when they were younger, of connecting with family members and friends. However, viewing was not an entirely neutral or conflict-free experience, as Melissa had little to no choice over what to watch and Alice's viewing was restricted to educational shows only. Moreover, some respondents, like Scott, recalled how much their mothers disliked television and maintained strict control over access to the television. The memories people had of the shows their parents watched and the shows they themselves watched all helped produce a sense of family and in some instances marked family-time, but family in connection to TV viewing was not always understood as entirely pleasurable.

At times, watching together was an experience parents consciously chose for interviewees. While some of this was structural, especially for older participants since there were fewer show selections when they were growing up, it also had as much to do with people's attitudes regarding family time. For example, growing up in the mountains of North Carolina, watching television was something Alice and her family did together. "In those days you had to wait until the shows came on, but when it came on it stayed on. The television was always on in our house. My mother was alone sometimes and I think she liked the sound on." Alice then went on to reminisce about watching what she called "cowboy shows" such as *Roy Rogers* (NBC 1951-1957) and *Bonanza* (NBC 1959-1973). Similarly, Louisa watched with her father and brothers, enjoying both cowboy shows and spy shows. It is possible that for Louisa, watching these types of shows was a way of relating her interests in adventure and espionage stories to her father and brothers' appreciation of them. Melissa recalled how she would watch *Little House on the Prairie* with her mother and *Gunsmoke* with her father. Her comments revealed that there was a fairly limited viewing democracy in her home and, perhaps as a result, the outcome was one that actually reinforced family togetherness. "Television viewing, like dinner time in my household (the one I grew up in and the one that I am parent of now), is a family time. We watched whatever my parents (mostly my dad) wanted to watch or we didn't watch at all."

Jerry, a reference librarian, remembered that he and his sister would sometimes go with their mother to visit her friends on Saturday night. "On those nights we got to stay up late and watch *Saturday Night Live (SNL)*. I loved that show for its subversive humor." What is so interesting about this narrative excerpt is that it captures Jerry's memories of *SNL* in relation to where he watched it (at his mother's friend's house), who he watched it with (his sister), the context in which they watched (his mother spending time with her friends), and finally, how he felt about watching it (he loved it). In a deceptively simple statement about childhood TV viewing, Jerry revealed a great deal about memories, feelings, and the state of his closest relationships at that time.

Margot recalled growing up in a regimented house where television was considered a waste of time even though her father, who worked for the New York City Transit system, would often find abandoned television sets, bring them home, and repair them. Her father was especially strict, demanding that she and her younger brother do two things and two things well: study hard and help around the house. "Certain educational shows were allowed, but nothing frivolous like cartoons! For those, I went over to a friend's house to watch. I loved them. I think I told my parents I was going to go study." Lying to her parents was a subtle but explicit way of resisting her father's authority and asserting herself within limits, as well as assuaging her desire to watch "fun" television. For Margot and Melissa, what they could (or could not) watch on TV effectively helped set the tone for how leisure time was spent and social relationships were forged or severed. In contrast, both Lara and Denise were allowed to watch completely unfettered by adult supervision, meaning there appeared to be few if any restrictions placed on their viewing. They watched a wide variety of shows daily, often for hours on end. Lara watched as much with her brother as by herself; however, Denise and Rob, both some of the youngest interviewees in their mid-twenties, frequently watched by themselves.

In the homes of older interview participants in their fifties and sixties, such as Alice, John, and Louisa, television viewing was understood solely as a family activity. While this might have been due partly to the limited number of channels from which to choose (or a limited number of sets in a household), it had more to do with the fact that viewing was both understood and experienced primarily as a social activity rather than an individual pursuit. They each interpreted television as a kind of social technology that was fit into their daily schedule and was first and foremost a way of spending time together that was consistently meaningful and remembered fondly. This is not to discount how much they enjoyed certain shows, but rather to stress the sociality of their viewing. Although younger, Scott, too, recalled that watching television alone, without permission, was simply not allowed. Shaking his head he added, "If either my brother or I just turned on the television without permission . . . whew. She would've . . . I don't know what she would've done." In his household, it seemed to have less to do with sociality and more to do with other issues: productivity (as previously discussed), an attitude toward television that it was a time waster, and an overt display of parental control. This is also evidenced by the fact that both he and his brother were allowed to watch as much news programming as they wished because their mother understood the news to be educational and therefore productive viewing. Louisa recalled that television was social and restricted. For example, dinner was a time when her family talked about their day, looked up words in the dictionary, and even discussed news events. "We did not watch television during dinner. My parents felt that dinner was a time for talking. But after dinner we would watch together." John noted, "We never watched by ourselves. We had a big family so that may explain some of it, but you just didn't watch by yourself. It was a group activity."

For a number of participants, thinking back to television they used to watch was a way of remembering who they were and also what was going on in their lives. Before being interviewed, some had never thought about the television they used to watch, like Susan, a university lecturer in her early forties, who during the interview was reminded of the wide range of television genres such as game shows, *The Wonderful World of Walt Disney*, and "Let's see . . . I really liked *The Partridge Family* and *The Brady Bunch*. I watched *The Partridge Family* pretty regularly. You know, I haven't thought about these shows in ages!" For Jerry, also in his early forties, the process of recalling shows like *Sanford and Son* and *Get Smart* became meshed with thinking about and feeling a sense of his earlier or younger life. Discussing how some television shows made him feel while offering an analysis of what they offered him, he stated, "I really liked *Sanford and Son*. I grew up in Nevada and that show offered me a view of African-American life, which was interesting." Growing up in the suburbs of Nevada as a young, white male did not offer Jerry many opportunities to encounter ethnically diverse social groups; nevertheless, television afforded him a glimpse into the lives of people he rarely had the chance to interact with. Although this view was fictional, it helped broaden his understanding and fueled his imagination about what life was like for people in other places.

In some respects, television appears to function similarly to music as interviewees recalled characters, story lines, and theme music as a way of producing a personal biography of their lives, a means of remembering who they once were, and also as a way of identifying themselves as members of a generation, many who share similar memories and feelings about particular shows.[25] Of course some television shows go into syndication or are released on DVD, effectively allowing members from different generations to enjoy shows no longer aired (even in syndication). Recounting television viewing from their youth helped interviewees reconstruct a sense both of themselves at a certain age and of the relationships they held with those around them (like Lara and her brother's special connection to *Cheers* or the Saturday nights Jerry spent with his sister watching *SNL*), demonstrating how people link text and context in their quest for personal and collective meaning.

Unlike previous assumptions about television and memory, this chapter furthers the claim that people remember through and with television, not in spite of it. The concern that television is a threat to memory is part of an ongoing cultural preoccupation with the erosion of memory in the face of new technologies.[26] However, I have argued that remembering through television enabled people to recall past time, place, identity, and social relationships. In order to make further sense of this process I paid close attention to ritual, using it as a lens to take into account a range of TV practices. Interviewees discussed the pleasure shows gave them in a manner that reveals how important television is for people in the shaping of their past.

Notes

1. Michel de Certeau, *The Practice of Everyday Life* (Berkeley: University of California Press, 1988), 115.

2. This is very similar to Walter Benjamin's concept of mémoire voluntaire/involuntaire (stories get stuck in our brains and become a part of our memories/identities). See Walter Benjamin, "On the Image of Proust," in *Walter Benjamin Selected Writings Volume 2, Part 1, 1927-1930*, ed. Michael W. Jennings, Howard Eiland, and Gary Smith (Cambridge: Harvard University Press, 2005), 237-247.

3. de Certeau, *Everyday Life*, 115.

4. Steven Anderson, "History TV and Popular Memory," in *Television Histories: Shaping Collective Memory in the Media Age*, ed. Gary R. Edgerton and Peter C. Rollins (Lexington: The University Press of Kentucky, 2001), 23.

5. Julie Byrne, *O God of Players: The Story of the Immaculata Mighty Macs* (New York: Columbia University Press, 2003), 5.

6. Byrne, *O God of Players*, 9.

7. Ien Ang, *Watching Dallas: Soap Opera and the Melodramatic Imagination* (London: Routledge, 1989); C. Lee Harrington and Denise Bielby, *Soap Fans: Pursuing Pleasure and Making Meaning in Everyday Life* (Philadelphia: Temple University Press,

1995); Ron Lembo, *Thinking Through Television* (Cambridge, UK: Cambridge University Press, 2000).

8. David Hesmondhalgh, "Audiences and Everyday Aesthetics: Talking About Good and Bad Music," *European Journal of Cultural Studies* 10, no. 4 (2007): 508.

9. Lembo, *Thinking Through Television*, 29.

10. See Janice Radway, *Reading the Romance* (Chapel Hill, University of North Carolina Press, 1984) for her discussion on the societal value placed on work rather than leisure time. See also Max Weber, *The Protestant Ethic and the Spirit of Capitalism* (Los Angeles: Roxbury Publishing Company, 1996) for further discussion on the influence of Protestantism on the social, economic, and cultural attitudes of American life.

11. Julia's feelings of what could be interpreted as guilt over watching the soap opera *Santa Barbara* fit with David Gauntlett and Annette Hill's findings that people "feel guilty about watching or enjoying material which they suspected was indecent or moronic; and for imposing programmes on people who were not keen to watch them, in shared spaces." David Gauntlett and Annette Hill, *TV Living: Television, Culture and Everyday Life* (London: Routledge, 1999), 139.

12. See Lembo, *Thinking Through Television*.

13. Daniel Dayan and Elihu Katz, *Media Events: The Live Broadcasting of History* (Cambridge: Harvard University Press, 1992).

14. Catherine Bell, *Ritual Theory, Ritual Practice* (New York: Oxford University Press, 2009), 67.

15. Bell, *Ritual Theory*, 91.

16. Bell, *Ritual Theory*, 90-91.

17. Richard Terdiman, *Present Past: Modernity and the Memory Crisis* (Ithaca, NY: Cornell University Press, 1993); Andreas Huyssen, *Twilight Memories: Marking Time in a Culture of Amnesia* (New York: Routledge, 1995); Pierre Nora, *Realms of Memory: Rethinking the French Past* (New York: Columbia University Press, 1997-2000).

18. Stephen Heath, "Representing Television," in *Logics of Television: Essays in Cultural Criticism*, ed. Patricia Mellencamp (Bloomington: Indiana University Press, 1990), 279; Mary Ann Doane, "Information, Crisis, Catastrophe," in *Logics of Television: Essays in Cultural Criticism*, ed. Patricia Mellencamp (Bloomingon: Indiana University Press, 1990), 226-227.

19. Anderson, "History TV and Popular Memory," 20.

20. Jonathan Z. Smith, *To Take Place: Toward Theory in Ritual* (Chicago: The University of Chicago Press, 1987).

21. Smith, *To Take Place*, 103.

22. Smith, *To Take Place*, 28.

23. Mark C. Carnes, *Secret Ritual and Manhood in Victorian America* (New Haven: Yale University Press, 1989), 33.

24. Paul Connerton, *How Societies Remember* (Cambridge: Cambridge University Press, 1989), 33.

25. Tia DeNora, *Music in Everyday Life* (Cambridge: Cambridge University Press, 2000).

26. See Marita Sturken, who writes, "Throughout history, the most prominent characterization of memory has been the idea that it has been in crises. Memory has been seen to be threatened by technology since ancient times. Indeed, Plato saw the development of writing itself as a threat to individual memory." Marita Sturken, *Tangled*

Memories: The Vietnam War, the AIDS Epidemic, and the Politics of Remembering (Berkeley: University of California Press, 1997), 17.

Chapter Three

Becoming-Spectator: Tracing Global Becoming through Polish Television in a Canadian Family Room

Marcelina Piotrowski

The spectator does not have a stable relationship to television. I have been becoming a spectator of television, and particularly Polish television shows and films on video/DVD, for over twenty years now. It is this constant phase of becoming, morphing, adjusting and dancing with what television is and what it does, particularly in family life and in the context of migration, that I trace my own becoming-spectator. Becoming-spectator uses Gilles Deleuze and Felix Guattari's[1] conceptual framework of becoming as a process that is based on difference, multiplicity and different temporal dimensions. Spectating is an activity that constantly changes in purpose and composition. While showing what it means to become spectator, I also trace the lifecycle of becoming Polish through television in the context of global migration. By outlining how the duration of living in a foreign country, age and generational difference affect television-viewing practices, I wish to illustrate a complex narrative that shows how the concept and affect of national identity and the identity as spectator continue to evolve.

After emigrating from Poland in 1989, my family viewed Polish shows and films on television in Canada. For my parents, these were acts of maintaining culture and language and identifying with their memories of Poland. For me, they were acts of learning what it meant to be Polish and the negotiation of how to identify with Polish beliefs and behaviors. Viewing television is how I became Polish. While the shows have usually been apolitical and comedic,

27

viewing television through the lens of immigration and identity has, for me, opened up micropolitical investigations into the process of becoming-spectator.

Written through an autobiographical account, into which I interweave my parents' voices, I describe my experiences with television as a form of pedagogy that has been, and continues to be, a significant influence in shaping my sense of identity as a Polish-Canadian. This experience of becoming-spectator indicates that the spectator does not have a stable relationship to television. The purpose of this chapter is to show how television has contributed to a transformed practice of spectatorship, from one that identifies spectatorship as lack (of national identity) to one which celebrates the productive power of multiple national identities: a spectatorship of multiplicity. As part of writing a trans-generational narrative, it was important for me to capture the narrative of becoming-spectators for my parents. Both my parents continue to live in New Westminster, a suburb of Vancouver. Their television viewing habits have changed significantly through the twenty odd years we have been here, and through many conversations they have shared their narratives of immigration, family life and the role that television played within and through these domains. I will try to reflect their words and capture the emotions that they have shared with me as part of writing this chapter. At times I paraphrase, and at times I will weave their stories into mine using italics.

I will start off by introducing Deleuze and Guattari's concept of becoming, which emerged in their book *A Thousand Plateaus: Capitalism and Schizophrenia*.[2] Presenting a conceptual framework early on in the chapter is meant to do two things. It situates this chapter about television, family and migration within a discussion of identity and subjectivity, or in other words, how we understand the concept of "self." It also allows me to provide the reader with an orientation to my approach. This chapter is about a transformation of the changing nature of spectatorship. Looking at it through the lens of becoming means realizing that there is no goal to becoming-spectator, in the sense that being reflective or critical might epitomize a "good" spectator. Such a project would be opposed to the spirit of becoming. Instead, becoming invites us to look at identity not as a state to transform, but as a compilation of juxtaposing, conflicting and simultaneous processes that are productive through their difference.

The following sections of the chapter outline some of my reflections on the difference of nationality as observed on television, and the nationality-in-between of a teenager growing up in a Polish-Canadian community. Polish communities outside of Poland's geographic boundaries often refer to themselves as Polonia, a collective of émigrés who sustain Polish culture by way of gatherings, churches, folklore celebrations, festivals and stores specializing in Polish produce. I trace the process of becoming a spectator by juxtaposing the image of myself as a part of the Polonia in Canada, and my practice of looking at "real" Polish people through television. My struggle as a teenager to place myself within Polish nationality became a spectatorship of lack: the perception of simultaneously not recognizing, or lacking an image of myself as part of "real" Poland, missing language skills, as well as lacking the framework to juggle multiple national identities.

I describe becoming-spectator through a global and transgenerational narrative of the changing patterns of viewing Polish television in my family over twenty years, interweaving my parents' voices with my own analysis. While my parents' viewing frequency of Polish television declined, Polish television has remained a steady staple in my new family nucleus as a woman married to a Polish immigrant. This change in spectating is a transformation toward a spectatorship of multiplicity of increased language abilities in both Polish and English over time, and a growing historical awareness which has enabled me to embrace the conservative and generative aspects of Polish television viewing alongside Canadian identity.

This chapter adds to the body of literature that describes how issues of migration and national identity are highlighted in media practice. Becoming-spectator is a literal and figurative concept that shows that identity both influences and is shaped by television viewing practices. Of course the economic and technological aspects of media sharing have an enormous influence on access to ethnic media. Streamed video and peer-to-peer file access by sharing torrents of data are unique situations that did not exist twenty years ago, at which time access to Polish television required borrowing or renting video home system tapes (more commonly known as VHS tapes), and required a special excursion to a video rental shop, where the selection was limited.

De-subjecting the Spectator

Becoming is a continuous and generative transformation based on influences/ encounters. It is a way of looking at the self as emergent. Becoming lacks a subject in itself and questions the possibility of a self-determined subject.[3] Deleuze and Guattari provide a series of examples, such as becoming-woman, becoming-animal, becoming-other, to illustrate how external, discursive and constantly fluctuating parameters determine what woman, animal and other are.[4] Becoming is therefore a project to de-subject identity from the labels that precede them as a subject—a woman, a national, native in a way that excludes the possibility of their transformation and unique instance. Identity is a becoming, not a being or something that can be attributed to oneself. While subjectivity or identity cannot be attributed to oneself, it is also not an inherited state; instead it is concerned with alliance.[5]

I was particularly drawn to the concept of becoming because it challenges the progressive notion of things getting better over time, one in which growth is based on growing-up, filling-out, maturing or saturating. This is often found in discourses of maturing as an individual or a family acclimatizing in its process of immigration. Becoming, however, does not recognize any pre-conceived or idealized destiny point. It does not see an end to the process of transformation, or being. Growth is not an overcoming of lack, in the psychoanalytic sense, where being is a state that an individual desires.[6] Becoming is an *and*, not a lack, because change is not a shedding of an old identity or incapacity. Instead, to look at identity through becoming, means to consider its newness in each moment and encounter.

As extended into the realm of visual media culture, becoming-spectator allows us to consider the transformation and generative fluidity of encounters and changes that influence a person's participation with television culture. It is an invitation to consider spectating as a socially, historically and economically determined process that produces meaning through the encounter of a visual text, a human person, a social circumstance, a family, a space, geographic location, and so on. The spectator as a person does not necessarily exist prior to these encounters, but is formed through the encounters that comprise multiple and fluid connections. Becoming-spectator is an eternal undefined state of spectatorship that changes and morphs in nature based on the complex relationship that the viewer assumes in relation to social, temporal, spatial, affective and political circumstances and events.

No spectator uniformly or consistently relates to visual media or a practice such as watching television. In this context, becoming-spectator is the encounter people have with television content that is based on a series of socio-historic, temporal, geographical, affective circumstances. The spectator becomes differently each time through a negotiation of differences that matter at that specific moment. It is also the approach that there is no single characteristic that can claim to define a predictable spectating practice. The concept of becoming-spectator is important to understanding the role of television as a source of pedagogy. The pedagogical aspect is not only in the content, and what it teaches about society, yet in the context of the content within a set of the everyday domestic as an important dimension in understanding how people make meaning based on the shows they see.[7]

Television viewing is much more than the relaxation or "unplugging" at the end of the day when examined in the context of migration; it is a key dimension of the social interaction that contributes to the development of a sense of identity(ies) in immigrant families. Approaching television viewing through the concept of becoming has changed my view of nationality as a hereditary component of identity. Instead, I began to approach nationality as an encounter that happens through the circumstances and relationships that frame television viewing, particularly in the context of television and immigration.[8]

Family, Migration, and Spectatorship

Immigration is marked by waves of immigration, number of immigrants in the new country of residency, socioeconomic status, and the origin and destination location of immigration, all of which affect the desire and degree to which immigrants continue to relate to their country of origin.[9] Immigration and media have a long relationship. Media representations of immigration and immigrants and the stereotypes they build up or change over time provide an example of one of these relationships. Many migrant communities began creating media to share common experiences and provide representation to their own stories. This relationship is often referred to as diasporic, ethnic or minority media, and refers to the media productions or media outlets created by immigrants.[10] Another type of relationship is on the way immigrants use media to maintain ties to their country of origin.[11]

Diaspora has been a term that was typically used for non-white migrant groups, particularly those that are displaced from their home country or those that maintain a minority status in their new country of residence. However, the term has expanded in meaning to include those migrants who self-identify with not being able to easily assimilate, even if they are Caucasians, coming to live in a predominantly Caucasian nation.[12] The idea that capacity for immigrant assimilation is only determined by the factor of the color of one's skin, is clearly challenged. Examples of this include the difficulty of the assimilation experienced by the large quantities of Polish people who migrated to the UK after Poland entered the European Union in 2004 and Polish people became legally permitted to work and reside in the UK. The ability or desire to assimilate is in this instance not necessarily determined by color, but on the volume of immigrants in a given community, language barriers and particularly the type of work that is possible for these immigrants and hence their socio-economic status.[13]

Immigrants, while often forming a community, not all perceive their identity to be characterized by that community. Some Polish people reject the diaspora identity, as they perceive the diaspora to embody the values of the country they decided to escape from. While living in a country with new values, new immigrants in a "diaspora" often continue to judge themselves and others according to the old values. Those who wish to embody new values or lead lifestyles that are considered "alternative" to those that are traditional often do not use the term diaspora in relation to themselves.[14] Immigration does not come with a stabilization point where the immigrant is able to mark the point when he or she is no longer an immigrant. There is no stage of immigration where that resemblance of "local" has been reached. Instead, what changes is the proportions of attachment, disattachment, enchantment, and imagination of a sense of nationality of the country of origin and the new country. Similarly, becoming-spectator is the ongoing re-creation of oneself within and through the space of media practice, such as television viewing. Television provides a social and historical framing for the family's current circumstance, and its relationship to its country of origin and its new country of residency.

This process has largely revolved around my family life, and as an extension to television viewing in the family home. In the next paragraphs I wish to engage the readers in a narrative about my reflections on the experiences of viewing television as an immigrant child as I see it now. My parents decided

that our immediate family (my brother, parents and I) would emigrate from
Poland in 1988. This was a period in Poland in which the Solidarity movement
was well under way, but the promise of the demise of Communism was still
farfetched. We migrated through Germany, living there for several years while
awaiting sponsorship to Canada, and eventually found our way to Vancouver.

My experience of viewing television over the past twenty years has
morphed from a spectatorship of lack to a spectatorship of multiplicity.
Spectatorship of lack is one in which the viewer defines her practice of looking
and spectating as a searching for a recognizable identity that can be assumed, or
looking for a representation of her identity, essentially a validation through
representations. Early on, viewing television involved recognizing my own
inability to match the representations of the Polish people I saw on television. It
involved finding myself between two spaces of a child and youth without a
strong sense of identity to either Poland, where I was too young to perceive a
national subjectivity, or Canada, where I was not-yet feeling Canadian. It
involved a lack of a stable national identity and a practice of viewing that was
based on my own comparison to representations of nationality. This stage of
not-quite, no-longer, and not-yet then morphed to one where identity became a
production, a generative dimension that included these instable states. This has
changed to a spectatorship of multiplicity, where viewing is new each time
based on connections and circumstances rather than the consumption of
television by a private individual.

The general trend in my own becoming-spectator over the past twenty years
has been a transition from the frustration of the juxtaposition of different
identities available to me in my daily surroundings in Canada and the identities
available on television, to the enjoyment of the possibilities this juxtaposition
offers and recognizing no need to make it whole. I have recognized that viewing
television has both a conservative function and a generative one. It is
conservative because it encourages and celebrates a process of recognizing
oneself in a culture, but it is also generative, because each encounter spells the
possibilities for a new becoming. More than anything, television viewing has
taught me to reflect on my own relations to identity as well as to the way
relationships influence the uptake of media, and how media in turn give shape to
familial interactions.

What began for me as an interest in the role that television has played in our
family home throughout our process of immigration to Canada, has morphed
into thinking about identity in different ways. One is that identity is an
encounter, characterized by becoming. The other is that identity is a process of
acquiring and amending oneself within the identities available. Thinking about
this now, many years after immigration had begun, I have come to the
realization that early on, my awareness of identity was limited to thinking within
the possible positions I felt were afforded to me at the time. For me, these years
were characterized as an identity gap, or as being stuck in the in-between of
nationality as observed versus nationality as lived. Part of this involved looking
at television and participating in the culture of a spectatorship of lack.

Becoming-Spectator: 1991

My parents, brother and I arrived in Vancouver, Canada, in 1991. Leisure time, for me, rarely included watching television. Under the premises of an immigrant's work ethic, the time that was available to me beyond school or part-time work as a teenager was time that could be used for something productive. When I was a teenager, viewing television was perceived by my parents to be a waste of time that did not seize the opportunity of personal growth afforded through the immigration process, the opportunity to be something or someone that one could not be before. I embraced this approach myself, allowing little of my free time after school to be devoted to watching television. Whether that meant using the time on something like reading a book or vacuuming the house, this personal labor, which was in some form always encouraged of me by my parents, was partly filling out of myself, as a productive immigrant. On this same pathway, the television, which was located in the family room, afforded a space of familial gathering around another type of productivity that disguised itself as leisure. That productivity was one of nationality. Television was a waste of time and simultaneously a source of education. It disguised itself as leisure, but was productive as a source of national pedagogy. More so, it was an education about national culture and the process of acquiring a national identity.

Early on as a child, watching television often meant watching Polish television, and particularly Polish movies and sitcoms that we rented from stores. It was possible to view live television through one of the multiple Polish channels. We could have had a satellite dish, but, generally, my parents thought the infrequency with which we watched television did not warrant that extra cost for a new immigrant family. Plus, interestingly, TV Polonia, a channel created for Polish people living outside of Poland, was perceived to be too immigration-focused by my parents. In the early years, right after we arrived in Canada, my parents viewed very little English-language television, while I, as a child, do remember watching English-language cartoons after school and on Saturday mornings. During days off around holidays such as Easter and Christmas we engaged in television marathons, viewing television and particularly Polish movies, which for my father was a time of *a common family experience of living the past together.*[15] In the early 1990s, this repertoire usually started when my mother drove to Surrey, a suburb of Vancouver, to a Polish deli, which doubled as a video rental store. She would return from the Polish deli with an assortment of Polish delicacies, pierogi, and several VHS tapes. At times my father would borrow Polish films from acquaintances who had traveled to visit Poland and had returned with the latest movies on VHS tapes.

When I asked my parents how they felt about our customary television sit-downs they described that watching television as a family allowed them to fulfill their responsibility to be our cultural education. Perhaps even more so, television became a focal point for coming together and being a Polish family. My mother said,

We still felt very, very Polish. We did not speak any or very little English, and everything outside of the walls of our house seemed foreign and strange. Watching television allowed us to re-create a mini-Poland. Television gave us an incredible sense of comfort and safety. We had no ability to converse with the outside world, to take care of ourselves linguistically, discursively. We became a four-person Poland.

As a child I was not aware of this nationality. It was not until I entered my teenage years when I became aware of nationality.

At times we viewed films that my parents would consider to be core curriculum, historical films based on classic literature, such as *Pan Wolodyjowski (Colonel Wolodyjowski,* 1969)[16] or *Potop (The Deluge,* 1974),[17] or *Jak rozpętałem drugą wojnę światową (How I Started World War II,* 1969)[18] and a television series *Czterej pancerni i pies (Four Tank Men and a Dog,* 1966-1970).[19] My parents remembered these films as core curriculum pieces that provided a sense of a common past to those who felt their lives were upheaved during Communism. Watching these classics and wartime serials on television was more than a historical lesson; it was a legitimate source and form of education.

I was six years old when my family emigrated from Poland. My parents facilitated a learning of nationality that I had never experienced directly, and the physical transition from one continent to another intensified their sense of responsibility to ensure the acquisition of cultural capital[20] and, therefore, national capital. I certainly do not remember having an awareness of what nationality or nation was from those days. Growing up in a Communist Poland meant living between the space of Communist sanctioned propaganda, the omnipresence of the Catholic Church as a centralizing family value, and the growing presence of the Solidarity movement. Yet to me, as a child, the notion of being present in a national or historically important time was completely missing. It was perhaps of this that my parents write of the need to create a space for learning the yet unknown and to have the ability to return to these moments with a different sense of history.

There was a strong sense of responsibility to ensure that you (children) did not miss out on anything you do not yet know. We felt that we needed to make up for the education you would miss; to ensure a cultural and linguistic capital that you would have received there would be available to you. We also felt that film was a way to ensure you (our children) would continue to be interested in Poland on an ongoing basis, and therefore maintain that relationship not only to the country, but also to us (my parents), in the future.

My mother in particular felt a strong sense of responsibility not to lose anything by leaving. She said, *We had to be the school.*

As a teenager living in Canada, I began to form an image of what Poland and Polish people were like, without ever having been old enough to be aware of the experience of nationality. People who aspire to a sense of nationality form imagined communities,[21] because they are said to hold an idealized image of an affinity, without direct contact with most of the people they consider fellow citizens. I cannot quite pinpoint a characteristic of this sense of nationality, but only that there was a unity in struggle, in their identity, a wit to self-reflect and for self-satire in the context of social unrest. As we particularly watched drama, comedy, or historical dramatic films, and rarely children's stories, I do not remember having any particular child or teenager that I aspired to be. I did not necessarily have an aspiration to mirror any characters or aspire for anything I saw in particular. Instead it was a longing to relate in the commonality of the experience.

There are approximately twenty million Polish people living outside of Poland, and approximately one million in Canada.[22] Not only does Polonia refer to a group of people that contribute to a Polish community (as explained above), but it is also a word to describe a sense of cultural identity that is based on Polish nationality intertwined with a newness. Polonia is at once a state of constant reproduction of Polish identity—it re-creates itself wherever it goes, in churches, picnics, theaters, festivals, and at family dinners—and simultaneously it is a Polish identity in flux, based on new circumstances and experiences. I therefore not only had an image of Poland, I also had an image of myself as part of Polonia. Perhaps this was because I participated quite extensively as a child and teen in Polonia. This ranged from being a part of the Polish Scouting Association in Canada as a child, then dancing as a teenager in Polonez, a folk dance group that existed in the community and performed at various local festivals, and also attending Polish Catholic Church. Despite this, as a teenager I had two mirrors without the original image, and perceived that to be able to understand myself as part of Polonia, I needed to engage with the original images of the *real* Poland.

When I was a little bit older, I watched television series from the 1970s and 1980s with my family like *Alternatywy 4* (*4 Disjunction Street*, 1983)[23] that used satire to depict every day in communist life through the narratives of several neighbors in a high-rise building, at number 4 on Disjunction Street. Films like *Rejs* (*A Trip Down the River*, 1970),[24] and *Miś* (*Teddy Bear*, 1980)[25] were considered classic viewing for Polish people and often infiltrated the texts and dialogues of young people. My father liked to pick films and shows that he remembered to be enjoyable, although in his own words he was often disenchanted that *they were no longer what I remembered them to be, as my thinking had changed a bit since the eighties.* In the 1990s, the practice of enlivening the dialogues, jokes and slangs from movies from the late communist and early capitalist beginnings, and appropriating the scenarios and meanings of fiction, can be described as textual poaching, a practice that became important among the youth of the Polonia community.[26] The use of television texts was a way to relate to an experience that we had difficulty in knowing directly.

My parents believed that television was a trigger for us to start a conversation. Even during the middle of watching a Polish film, we would often stop the tape, because the children wanted to know something, why something was said. For me at the time, the lack of understanding of the slang meant that I could not indulge within the excitement of understanding television and film texts, even though, for example, teenagers who were slightly older than I began to appropriate these texts and use them to express their belonging to a culture and transposing television texts into situations in daily life. As a teenager, television/film and my inability to practice this type of textual engagement, was a measure of comparison of my Polishness to others, and a lack of Polish identity based on a lack of spectatorship skills. I perceived the nature of my spectatorship to be lacking in the skills of textual leveraging, where the ability to recite and play with words demonstrates the strength of one's cultural and therefore national capital. I extended my spectatorship of lack to my lacking sense of nationality. When I traveled to Poland as a teenager, I had the sense that if I had acquired more "cultural capital" through poaching television texts, I would have an easier time assimilating.

The struggles through which adolescents go as part of identity development have been compared to transnational migration and the identity struggles contained in this process.[27] Yet adolescence is a stage, at least from a developmental and psychological perspective, that most people get out of. I do not get the sense that migration is a stage I will ever get out of, although it is an exciting process of becoming. It is important to consider television's role in migration over generations and in terms of its socio-historic context to both the country of immigration and emigration. Poland itself has been marked by the need to constantly redefine itself in its struggle against invasive kingships, Russian and German tanks, communist propaganda, and now capitalist laissez-faire. Growing up means getting to know history through different sources, and being able to imagine oneself as a component of historical moment.

Communism itself, to my generation, is an abstraction that we lived through from stories told by our parents and viewed on television. The children born in Poland from the late 1970s and 1980s are all, in a way, spectators and consumers of communist stories. All of our "memories" of Communism are not memories, but experiences gained from conversations and encounters with television throughout childhood, adulthood and every stage in between. These visual texts are our reminders of the mere traces we remember as children from those times, such as the ticket-based lineups to pick up food from the grocery store, the scarcity of clothing, or the civil war. In early phases of immigration, my parents' relationship to television was nostalgic longing for a vacuumed space: *We left Poland—but we wanted to be there, we wanted Poland to be better. We wish we could be there, but we also didn't want to be there any longer. It was nostalgia for a place that we wish existed.*

The mark of the Polonia condition appeared to me to be nostalgic about all Polish things and an ongoing desire to lament about the difficult immigrant existence, lament how much better life could have been in Poland than it is in this new nation. For my mother, the burst to nostalgia was one where use of Canada and Canadians as the 'other' was no longer possible and being Polish needed to find itself within the possibility of other linkages. In Svetlana Boym's words, nostalgia is "a longing for a home that no longer exists or has never existed. Nostalgia is a sentiment of loss and displacement, but it is also a romance with one's own fantasy."[28]

My personal interpretation of the Polonia condition therefore consisted of three parts: a boasting about the bravery of taking on the migrant life, the complaining about the hardships on this migrant path, and the simultaneous lamenting and celebration of the irrevocability of this transition. Simultaneously, the other part of this condition is marked by boasting about the break with Poland and the inability to any longer fully relate to the Polish people in Poland, and that way of life. It is marked by a renewed sense of becoming as an assembled narrative of previous and new. Of her relationship to Polish people living in Poland, and the new narratives of the Polish television post-Communism, my mother said,

> We don't know one another any longer. I tried to transport myself into the 'new Poland' and to try it, but it did not reflect the reality I know. I did not understand it. I feel being in Canada has made me open to life, to others, etc., but the shared reality was different with the Polish people in Poland.

Becoming-Spectator: The New Poland

It was in the mid-to-late 1990s that several things started to happen to our familial experiences of watching Polish television. As a family we continued to view comedies such as *Kiler* (*The Killer*, 1997)[29] and *Nic Śmiesznego* (*Nothing Funny*, 1995),[30] which depict narratives of characters who presented a disenchantment with the true opportunities that were afforded in the new Poland when it became capitalist. There was a rupture to nostalgia. As we became teenagers, my parents would rent fiction that depicted life in the first decade of capitalist years, yet quickly would become dismayed. The films of the later half of the 1990s created a transformation. The language became much more vulgar, and increasingly my parents began to feel disenchanted with viewing Polish films and television, observing a dramatic and rapid sexualization and violence in the content and language. The passage of time also allowed my parents to be more comfortable in English, and it was in the early 2000s when it could be said that my parents stopped watching Polish movies.

My brother and I were both growing up and moving away from home, and the whole concept of our parents' responsibility to use television to supply access to the culture we may have encountered in Poland became less and less valid. At the same time, my parents' becoming included acquisition of the English language, a component that they attribute to enjoying Canadian television, and feeling that Polish television was not needed as a source of safety. My mother explained,

*We tried watching television in English early on, but could not identify
ourselves with the plots. After a few years of being in Canada, we started to
enjoy watching television in English and American movies. English television
started to make sense and we started to understand and feel comfortable, and
be inquisitive about culture in Canada. The feeling of safety afforded through
the viewing of Polish television was no longer as necessary. Through watching
English television in Canada, I have learned to feel emotionally safe in this
country.*

When I asked my mother whether she still felt the need to watch Polish
television or movies in the late 1990s and 2000s, she articulated the need to
continue her personal historical becoming, one that was based on linkages that
could emerge between her own experience and the new cultural and discursive
possibilities. *Would you want to continue watching WW II and Communist
movies thirty, forty, fifty years after it happened? We needed to get over it*, she
said. In my adult life, however, my return to Polish television changed
significantly. Whereas my parents feel they cannot identify with actors,
language and narratives in the majority of shows and films today, I feel I can
connect more to the actors now, because they live in post-communist Poland,
which has increased transglobal cultural and communication flows and is united
in similar current global, political and economic problems.

I began to relish the ability to find meaning in multiple cultures by being
able to relate more closely to the texts as I grew up. To continue my trans-
generational narrative of changing patterns of viewing Polish television in my
family over twenty years, I transport myself to 2004. One of the significant
changes in my family life was the influx of the presence of the so-called new
Poland in my life when I met my current husband, a Polish immigrant who
moved to Canada in 2004, the same year that Poland became a nation of the
European Union. While my parents might have referred to the post-communist
Poland as the new Poland, to me the "new Polish" people whom I meet in
Canada are the post-EU integration migrants. While my parents' viewing
frequency of Polish television declined, the influx of this new-Poland has meant
that Polish television has regained its status as an old means to traverse a new
stage of my becoming Polish, and hence becoming-spectator. While I had
always spoken Polish at home with my parents, living with someone who is
closer in age to myself has infused my Polish language with more contemporary
vocabulary. I began to enjoy Polish television and find new pleasure in
understanding myself as a Polish-Canadian with the ability to enjoy and traverse
multiple national identities.

Moving from a unit of four in which the selection of what we would watch
was determined largely without me, to my own family unit in which this choice
is largely in my hands, or in discussion with just my husband, I still choose
Polish shows, usually acquired, borrowed or downloaded in some way through
the Internet. This means that as long as I have Polish television available, shows
that I have acquired by borrowing from other users online or from our friends in
the Polish community, these shows win out over the more easily available

English-language television shows available on cable. Immediately after my husband and I started living together, Polish television provided me with the language to engage in a new family practice, one through which I could learn to engage closer to my husband's recent reality.

I often indulge in Polish movies with my husband, feeling that they are a way to celebrate the root of our similar culture, in light of each of us having different narratives of upbringing and migration. Although I have been in Canada for over twenty years now, I watch significantly more Polish television now than I did with my parents in 1991 and in the early years of immigration. I find myself at the intersection of a comfortable sense of being sufficiently assembled into my own Canadian sense of place, yet being in the productive space of multiplicity where I can find intellectual and emotional stimulation from having a sense of multiple nationalities. The whole experience of becoming-spectator involves various connections, which include the geographical site of emigration and immigration, what other historical events accompany those memories, and the very exchange of ethnic media materials that is often determined through the relationships that bring immigration into the foreground (such as newly met immigrant friends or spouses) or backgrounds.

Cinema after 1989, the year in which Poland defeated communist rule, was concerned with the "small narrative" or the banal scenario of the everyday. This type of cinema was largely disinterested in history or its deconstruction.[31] In comparison, I find that television shows and films made after Poland entered the European Union in 2004, depict Polish people's lives within contemporary situations, often by traveling abroad for work, or referring to the changing reality of living in Poland post-EU entry, in a highly reflective tone. These themes enable me to understand immigrant reality in the new millennium, and reflect on its differences to the 1990s. For example, I found myself to be especially attracted to television shows such as *Londyńczycy* (*The Londoners*, 2008-2009),[32] which focuses on the core experiences of a group of different Polish immigrants living in London.

Rydzewska has argued that television abroad, and in this case in the UK, has attempted to represent the increasing influx of Polish immigrants to the UK; it has done so with presenting them with relatively minor and subdued roles.[33] The high-end television drama *Londyńczycy* highlights a series of narratives of adults in their twenties and thirties encountering different types of immersion in UK culture. It probes the redefinition of Poland and Polish identity within the new contemporary circumstances of Poland's integration in the European Union, suggesting that Polish people wish to identity themselves as citizens of the New Europe.[34] The micronarratives of the Polish Londoners enable me to be a spectator of the process of migration, a process I directly experience, but feel I did not have enough reflective 'vision' to see myself as part of it, being only a child during the time my family emigrated from Poland.

My husband and I first learned about the show *Londyńczycy* through our mutual Polish-Canadian friends, who emigrated from Poland to Canada more recently than we did. Our mutual perception of the show was that it provided a realistic glimpse into contemporary immigration in Europe, yet that somehow our immigration was different. Personally, it taught me yet another version of nationality, one that is elected, not defaulted, through one's parents' choice, but chosen through migration as young adults. I imagined myself as part of that Polish nationality, but instead of not being able to relate, I found pride in being a hybrid nationality, through which I can still associate with other narratives such as that of the immigrants' struggle. In other words, the difference in waves of immigration generations (based on the year of migration) and location of immigration destinations makes a difference in the experience of television as a factor in learning, maintaining or disassociating nationality.

We also see shows that highlight Polish immigrants who have been non-residents for multiple years, but who return to Poland. This is the case of the multi-season show called *Rancho* (*The Ranch*, 2006),[35] which started in 2006, in which the key protagonist is a thirty-year-old Polish-American woman called Lucy. Lucy returns to Poland after living in the United States for many years to settle in a small countryside town after she receives a small ranch in an inheritance. Lucy highlights the work that time imprints in the shape of foreign accents, acquired American habits, and different concepts of community. As a show, *The Ranch* highlights the ability of Poland to try to imagine itself as part of a global and therefore dispersed citizenship. What I find particularly intriguing is the possibility that a show like *The Ranch* also suggests that Polish spectators are interested in knowing what it might be like to be looked at and observed by from a foreigner's perspective, such as Lucy. It attests to the interest in the globally networked and complex nature of spectator where the connections between viewers are broadened outside of the framework of geographic proximity.[36]

From late 2008 to today, there has been proliferation of high-profile films that address issues of Poland during communist times. Nations, like individuals, encounter their reflective phases on becoming based on new experiences, welcoming a resurgence of film and television that revisits history in the context of current circumstances, passage of time, and perhaps, quite literally, the regeneration of generations: the concept that younger generations might be interested in returning to "take a look" at what they experienced as children. It appears as though the intense awareness of Poland globalization, in the context of its entry into the European Union, has sparked a sense of looking at Poland retrospectively. Films like *Mała Moskwa* (*Little Moscow*, 2008),[37] *Rewers* (*The Reverse*, 2009),[38] *Różyczka* (*The Rose*, 2010),[39] *Czarny Czwartek* (*Black Thursday*, 2011),[40] *80 Milionów* (*80 Million*, 2011)[41], and *Wszystko co Kocham* (*All That I Love*, 2010)[42] exemplify a return of contemporary films addressing the interpersonal politics and organized struggles of daily life between the 1960s and 1980s in Poland. The popularity of this genre of films and the fact that many of them received multiple awards in Poland and internationally set a tone of the resurrection of explicit political and historical reflection in Poland.

Perhaps my own reflective thinking about the role of family life in influencing television habits is driven by these recent reflective films. Becoming is therefore a way of self-understanding in which we begin to conceive of ourselves as comprised of difference and emergence. This element of connectivity, as the emergence of new habits of looking, is a multiplicity, which Deleuze and Guattari suggest "has neither subject nor object, only determinations, magnitudes, and dimensions that cannot increase in number without the multiplicity changing in nature."[43] My current narrative, one through which I have been thinking about media spectatorship through Deleuze and Guattari's concept of becoming-spectator, is a consideration that inquires differently about affective looking. It is more than an inquiry, a reception study, into the "feelings" of recipients and how they interpret television content. It considers that viewers do not exist; they constantly become. Becoming-spectator, therefore, situates the viewer in complicated temporal and generational contexts and starts from the position that this practice and desire of viewing is one that always morphs.

When we embrace the concept of becoming in this way, it is inconceivable to consider identity as a process through which we acquire labels and identify with pre-determined categories, or be spectators who spectate predictably. Becoming is "not content to proceed by resemblance and for which resemblance, on the contrary, would present an obstacle or stoppage." The whole concept is non-representational, and "becoming can and should be qualified as becoming-animal even in the absence of a term that would be the animal become." Instead of seeking to resemble and situate one's identity against pre-conceived categories, such as citizen, immigrant, child, youth, and migrant, identity becomes comprised of encounters that include oppositions and different configurations of these terms, in which the meanings of these are negotiated within geographical, situational, temporal and affective circumstances.

Notes

1. Gilles Deleuze and Félix Guattari, *A Thousand Plateaus: Capitalism and Schizophrenia* (Minneapolis: University of Minnesota Press, 1987).
2. Deleuze and Guattari, *A Thousand Plateaus*.
3. Deleuze and Guattari, *A Thousand Plateaus*, 238.
4. Deleuze and Guattari, *A Thousand Plateaus*.
5. Deleuze and Guattari, *A Thousand Plateaus*, 238.
6. Gilles Deleuze and Félix Guattari, *Anti-Oedipus: Capitalism and Schizophrenia* (Minneapolis: University of Minnesota Press, 1983).
7. David Morley, *Family Television: Cultural Power and Domestic Leisure* (New York: Routledge, 1986).
8. When I write about 'watching television' I am not only including viewing the shows and movies available on cable television, but also the experience of watching rented and downloaded shows on television, which with today's technology advances becomes a mere screen to view all sorts of moving images from whatever device is plugged into it.

9. Karim Karim, *The Media of Diaspora* (London: Routledge, 2003).

10. Mark Deuze, "Ethnic Media, Community Media and Participatory Culture," *Journalism* 7, no. 3 (2006): 262-280, doi: 10.1177/1464884906065512.

11. Russell King and Nancy Wood, *Media and Migration: Constructions of Mobility and Difference* (London: Routledge, 2001).

12. Karim, *The Media of Diaspora.*

13. Ayona Datta, "'This is Special Humour:' Visual Narratives of Polish Masculinities in London's Building Sites," in *After 2004: Polish Migration to the UK in the "New" European Union,* ed. Kathy Burrell (London: Ashgate, 2009): 189-210.

14. Bogusia Temple, "Diaspora, Diaspora Space and Polish Women," *Women's Studies International Forum* 22, no. 1 (1999): 17-24.

15. All italicized text is from interviews conducted with my mother and father throughout June 2012 by phone. I indicate between my mother's and father's voices where appropriate.

16. *Pan Wolodyjowski (Colonel Wolodyjowski),* directed by Jerzy Hoffman (1969; Zespol Filmowy Kamera), VHS.

17. *Potop (The Deluge),* directed by Jerzy Hoffman (1974; A.P. Dovzenko Filmstudio & PRF Zespol Filmowy), VHS.

18. *Jak rozpętałem drugą wojnę światową (How I Started World War II),* directed by Tadeusz Chmielewski (1969; PRF Zespol Filmowy), VHS.

19. *Czterej pancerni i pies (Four Tank Men and a Dog),* directed by Andrezej Czekalski and Konrad Nalecki (1966-1970; Poland), VHS.

20. Pierre Bourdieu, "Forms of Capital," in *Handbook of Theory of Research for the Sociology of Education,* ed. John Richardson (New York, NY: Greenwood Press, 1986), 241-258.

21. Benedict Anderson, *Imagined Communities: Reflections on the Origin and Spread of Nationalism* (London: Verso, 1983).

22. According to the 2006 Census Canada there are 984,565 people in Canada who claim to have Poland as their ethnic origin.

23. *Alternatywy 4 (Disjunction Street),* directed by Stanisław Bareja (1983; Centralna Wytwórnia Programów i Filmów Telewizyjnych Poltel), VHS.

24. *Rejs (A Trip Down the River),* directed by Marek Piwowski. (1970; Studio Filmowe Tor), VHS.

25. *Miś (Teddy Bear),* directed by Stanisław Bareja (1981; Studio Filmowe Perspektywa), VHS.

26. Textual poaching refers to a practice of appropriating cultural texts. The term was first used by Michel de Certeau, and developed by Henry Jenkins in the context of fan culture.

27. Meenakshi Gigi Durham, "Constructing the 'New Ethnicities': Media, Sexuality, and Diaspora Identity in the Lives of South Asian Immigrant Girls," *Critical Studies in Media Communication* 21, no. 2 (2004): 140-161, doi: 10.1080/0739318041000168804 7.

28. Svetlana Boym, *The Future of Nostalgia* (New York, NY: Basic Books, 2001), xiv.

29. *Kiler (The Killer),* directed by Juliusz Machulski (1997; Studio Filmowe Zebra), DVD.

30. *Nic Śmiesznego (Nothing Funny),* directed by Marek Koterski (1995; Kinoplex-Silesia), DVD.

31. Ewa Mazierska, *Polish Postcommunist Cinema* (Bern: Peter Lang Publishing, 2007).

32. *Londyńczycy (The Londoners)*, directed by Maciej Migas, Konrad Piwowarski and Wojciech Smarzowski (2008-2009; Telemark), DVD.

33. Joanna Rydzewska, "'Great Britain, Great Expectations': The Representation of Polish Migration to Great Britain in Londyńczycy / Londoners," *Critical Studies in Television* 6, no. 2 (2011): 127-140.

34. Rydzewska, "Great Britain."

35. *Rancho (The Ranch)*, directed by Wojciech Adamczyk (2006-2013; TVP), DVD.

36. The scope of this chapter, however, does not allow me to delve extensively into the areas of technology or political economy of how the television and film industry has evolved over the past few decades.

37. *Mała Moskwa (Little Moscow)*, directed by Waldemar Krzystek (2008; Polska, Skorpion Art Film), DVD.

38. *Rewers (The Reverse)*, directed by Borys Lankosz (2009; SyrenaFilms), DVD.

39. *Różyczka (Little Rose)*, directed by Jan Kidawa-Błoński (2010; Monolith Films), DVD.

40. *Czarny Czwartek (Black Thursday)*, directed by Antoni Krauze, (2011; Kino Świat), DVD.

41. *80 Milionów (80 Million)*, directed by Waldemar Krzystek (2010; Kino Świat), VHS.

42. *Wszystko Co Kocham (All That I Love)*, directed by Jacek Borcuch (2010; ITI Cinema), DVD.

43. Deleuze and Guattari, *Capitalism and Schizophrenia*, 8.

Part Two:

Father (and Mother) Knows Best

Chapter Four

As Seen on TV: Media Influences of Pregnancy and Birth Narratives

Jennifer G. Hall

The black and white thirty-second commercials feature mothers engaged in the most basic of mothering tasks such as bathing a chubby infant in the sink or rocking a yawning, curly-haired infant in the nursery. The sounds in the commercial are soft music combined with the sweet giggles and sighs of the adorable baby, closing with the tag line, *Having a Baby Changes Everything.* This Johnson & Johnson commercial epitomizes what could be considered a cultural ideal of motherhood—that having a child means a life full of tender and joyous moments.

George Gerbner's Cultivation Theory proposes that the messages sent by the mass media shape the public's perception and belief concerning reality.[1] Commercials such as the example above are just one of the ways that women and even young girls begin to develop expectations about what pregnancy, childbirth, and motherhood will be like. Women learn from the women around them as they talk to and observe their own mothers, aunts, sisters, friends, and neighbors during their pregnancies and after. Women can also read books, magazine articles, and scour the Internet for information. Even more subtly, women learn and develop expectations from the television and movies they consume.

It can be argued that media have created a societal narrative as to how pregnancy and birth should progress, what a woman should experience and feel, and how mothers should relate to their new infants. Certainly variations of this tale exists as women differ in their actual birth experience ranging from being assisted by a midwife at home to being admitted to the hospital for a scheduled C-section. However, there is a general script these stories follow which has given rise to several criticisms. The story begins with an overriding perception that motherhood is and should be a woman's ultimate goal.[2] This promotes the ideal of the purely unselfish mother who would do anything and everything for her offspring as well as the notion that there is instantaneous bonding and joy upon the birth of the infant. This narrative does not allow for a woman to be tired, stressed, or confused when their new infant enters the world.

Other criticisms of both fictional and actual accounts of pregnancy and childbirth are the reliance of medical interventions, the equating of a fast delivery with a good delivery, and the inclusion of a happy ending despite any complications that present themselves.[3] Through television and other media, women learn what pregnancy should be like and develop an idea of what childbirth will entail.

Media Usage by Pregnant Women

Bronny Handfield, Sue Turnbull, and Robin Bell explain that with the medicalization of childbirth and the modernization of the American family, few women have directly observed a birth and instead must rely on media representations to learn what occurs.[4] Additionally, media representations, both fictional and non-fictional, have become an important source of information for women. A study of women who gave birth in 2005 found that 68 percent of the women regularly watched reality programs that focused on pregnancy and childbirth. This helps explain the popularity of programs such as The Learning Channel's *A Baby Story,* which quickly became one of its highest rated programs when it was introduced in 1998.[5] In another study, 33 percent of pregnant women indicated books were a primary source of information, while only 16 percent named their physician as a primary source.[6] Diony Young argues that as women rely more and more on media for information, it becomes increasingly important to be aware of media content and how women use the media to inform their understanding of pregnancy and childbirth as well as their medical decisions.[7]

In addition to shaping perceptions of reality, it is also possible that media narratives influence and shape the stories individuals tell. The act of creating and telling a story about pregnancy and childbirth is of integral importance for most women who experience pregnancy. Because narrative is central to the way people think and speak[8] it predominates illness, disease, and health experiences including how people make sense of those experiences.[9] Through narratives, individuals are able to piece together the multiple aspects of their illness or health-related experience and make connections among seemingly random events.[10] Barbara Sharf and Marsha Vanderford explained that narrative sense-making is especially powerful because it proceeds after events have taken place, which means that "storytellers can interpret events, ascribe meanings, justify actions, and make links in retrospect that are less likely to be discerned when the narrator experiences events in real time."[11] Pregnancy narratives provide a way for women to reflect on and make sense of their experience.

These narratives also assist women as they transform into the role of mother and help them make sense of the many physical and emotional changes that accompany pregnancy.[12] Narratives allow individuals to cast themselves in a new way and talk about their new roles in relation to their previous experiences. Pregnancy and birth narratives can be cathartic and healing if the birth was traumatic or was not what women expected.[13] The act of telling and sharing one's story can help individuals to reflect on and understand the negative events. Finally, sharing these stories also can create a connection between the teller and the listener, providing a common link among women who have experienced pregnancy, labor, and birth.

High-Risk Pregnancies

Because of this important role of pregnancy and birth narratives, it is important to understand how narratives in the media may shape and influence those stories. A special concern surrounds women who experience a high-risk pregnancy with complications or give birth prematurely. Factors that place women in the high-risk category and at greater risk for preterm labor are being under age seventeen, being older than thirty-five, having diabetes, having high blood pressure or the development of preeclampsia, kidney problems, certain clotting disorders, being pregnant with multiples, or having an incompetent cervix.[14] Navigating any pregnancy can be difficult and stressful, as women must make decisions about their prenatal care, medical procedures, and childbirth as well as negotiate their changing identities and relationships.[15] The process becomes even more stressful when there are complications. A woman is often fraught with uncertainty and must make decisions regarding her health and the health of her unborn child(ren).[16] High-risk pregnancies and premature births vary drastically from the norm, and few of these women's experiences match up to the predominate narrative. It is therefore imperative to examine the sense-making processes of these women as well as the potential narrative influences on their sense-making.

Cultivation Theory

Existing work on media and media effects offers a lens through which to explain the potential influence of the media on pregnant women's stories. As previously mentioned, the Culitivation Theory, first introduced by Gerbner in the 1960s, explains how media consumption contributes to our understanding of reality.[17] Gerbner's initial research found that television watching contributed to viewers' perceptions of violence and crime and led them to overestimate the risk of being a victim of violent crime.[18] Although early cultivation work focused on television watching in general and specifically the impact of violence on television, more recent work has looked at specific types of programs such as television news.[19] Research even shows specific cultivation effects such as the impact of patient satisfaction among people who regularly watch *Grey's Anatomy*.[20]

One explanation for the cultivation theory is the narrative nature of media accounts. Because narratives are central to the way humans think about and make sense of the world they are easy to process.[21] Additionally, when reading or viewing a narrative, individuals can become so immersed in the story that they are transported into it. During transportation individuals are less resistant to persuasion and more likely to adopt the ideas presented by the narrative.[22]

These wonderings lead to the following research questions. First, how do women use media during their high-risk pregnancies? Although studies indicate that women do use media related to pregnancy, we do not know how they use the media in terms of how they find media, their consumption behaviors, and how they assess the media they consume. Secondly, how do they incorporate the stories they see or read into the stories they tell? The stories women tell play an instrumental role in helping them to make sense of a traumatic event and in understanding their role as the mother of a premature infant, so it is therefore imperative to explore how media representations of pregnancy and childbirth influence their stories.

Methodology

To answer the questions posed by this study, in-depth semi-structured interviews were conducted. An interview methodology was selected because interviews are "well suited to understand the social actor's experience and perspective."[23] Interviews are a technique that "aids researchers in our attempts to describe and understand the unique experiences of others."[24]

Participants

Participants for this study were women who experienced a high-risk pregnancy with the threat of preterm labor or birth as labeled by their physician, women who experienced preterm labor, and/or women who gave birth prematurely (i.e., a gestation of less than thirty-seven weeks). This included any woman with diabetes or gestational diabetes, women diagnosed with an incompetent cervix, and women pregnant with two or more infants.

Sampling Strategy

Participants were recruited using a purposive sampling technique, which is most appropriate for this uniquely personal topic and merits attention to these women's demanding schedules.[25] Purposive sampling is "intentionally selecting, in a non-random fashion, subjects who are likely to be able to furnish needed information."[26] This sampling strategy enabled me to recruit women with a rich variety of pregnancy and birth experiences. For example, after interviewing several women who had twins or more infants, I actively recruited more women who had single births in order to gain more perspective on how having a multiple birth compared to the experience of having a single birth. Through purposive sampling I also was able to talk with women whose child(ren) had been born at a variety of gestational ages, providing insight into how the experience of premature birth is influenced by the gestational age at which a child is born.

In addition to directly contacting participants to request an interview, announcements were sent to local mothers' groups and mothers of multiples groups. Some of the groups forwarded the request to their list-serves as well. Requests were also posted on message boards in on-line support groups for high-risk pregnancies.

Initially, fourteen interviews were conducted. After reviewing the information gathered during this initial set of interviews, questions were modified. For example, during the initial interviews I found that direct questions, such as please give me an example of a story that influenced a decision you made, were difficult for women to answer on the spot. In subsequent interviews I asked women more general questions, such as tell me where you went for information when you had to make a decision, or what did your friends tell you about what you should do while you are pregnant.

A total of forty-seven interviews were conducted. Interviews lasted between thirty-five and ninety-five minutes. The number of participants allowed for a variety of responses as well as the repetition of key themes and ideas. Recruitment of participants ceased when theoretical saturation was reached. Theoretical saturation is reached when "we cease to be surprised by what we observe or we notice that our concepts and propositions are not disconfirmed as we continue to add new data."[27] After forty-seven interviews were conducted it was evident from the field notes that the same themes were continually arising and recruitment ceased.

Demographics

All of the women who were interviewed were white.[28] Of the forty-seven women, nine had singletons, twenty had twins, seventeen had triplets, and one had quadruplets. One mother started her pregnancy with quintuplets but reduced the pregnancy to triplets, and one started with quadruplets and reduced to twins. Twenty-five of the pregnancies were spontaneous and twenty-two of the women had some kind of fertility assistance ranging from the use of the ovulation inducing drug chlomid to invitro fertilization (IVF). The ages of the women ranged from twenty-four to forty-three. The time that had passed from the woman's high-risk pregnancy ranged from three months to twelve years. The gestation at which the women's child(ren) were born ranged from twenty-three to forty weeks. Three of the women had experienced more than one high-risk pregnancy.

Findings

As women talked about what they had seen it became apparent that television and other media depictions of pregnancy, birth, and motherhood had given them expectations of what pregnancy and birth would be like and that their own stories rarely looked like the stories they saw. This was a source of frustration and many times sadness. The interviews also revealed that some women sought out as much information as possible while others preferred to take the less is more approach to information gathering. Women were often critical of the media available to them and expressed the desire to have more options and more stories available. Finally the interviews showed that no matter how women felt about the media they consumed, their own stories were greatly influenced by what they had watched and read about pregnancy.

Media for Information

As prior research has indicated, many women used media as a source of information. Almost every woman recalled at least one television show or program she had watched about pregnancy, and often women had watched multiple programs. Cynthia, mother of twins, described how she began watching *A Baby Story* and similar shows regularly once she was pregnant. She explained that she was most interested in watching programs about twins. Other mothers shared how they would search for television programs about twins, triplets, and high-risk pregnancies, as these stories rang more true to their experiences than programs that depicted typical pregnancies. With the invention of digital recording devices such as TiVo or the DVR, women were able to enter search terms such as triplets or NICU to find and record programs with storylines similar to their own.

Amy W., mother of twins, was a great example of how women actively sought out information by watching programs such as *A Baby Story*, and learning more about the birthing process:

I think I found them more comforting than stressful. I don't know, just for me it seems, to think about how all of the birthing stuff goes down, it just gives me comfort. It's like, okay, I have seen it. It gives me just a little more insight on what's going to happen so that I wasn't in complete shock when, you know . . . I sort of could have, you know, an idea of what to expect, you know, if confronted with whatever. But usually they don't have the horrible ones on TV. You know, it's usually the regular, the normal.

Amy initially watched the shows because it was her first pregnancy and she wanted some idea of what was to come. When she experienced complications in her pregnancy and went into labor prematurely the programs no longer had prepared her and she had a difficult time comparing her experiences to those she had seen on television.

Another key source of information for women was books. The most commonly mentioned book was *What to Expect When You are Expecting* by Arlene Eisenberg, Heidi Murkoff, and Sandee Hathway. On the *New York Times* bestseller list for over eight years, countless women have used this book to guide them through their pregnancies. For women pregnant with multiples, the most common book they mentioned was *When You're Pregnant with Twins, Triplets, or Quads: Proven Guidelines for a Healthy Multiple Pregnancy* by Dr. Barbara Luke and Tamara Eberlein. Women expressed mixed feelings about the book. Some women believed it was an excellent guide, followed all the recommendations, and credited following the guidelines with their more positive outcomes. Other women disliked the book and felt as if some of the recommendations, such as eating five thousand calories a day, were unrealistic. Still other women were put off by the blunt discussion of the possible complications of a multiple pregnancy and felt the book placed tremendous pressure on them to have a great outcome such as those featured in the book.

Astrid, mother of triplets, was one of the women who liked Dr. Luke and Eberlein's book. She explained, "The 'Doctor Luke' *[sic]* book was very informative. It opened my eyes quite a bit to what could be." For her, the stories of very premature infants with severe complications helped her to understand what the risks of early delivery were and strengthened her resolve to do anything in her power to ensure a good outcome. Another mother, Ambrosia, talked about one of the most powerful images in the book, which was a page that featured the footprints of infants born at each week of gestation. "They show you these pictures of the babies at twenty-four weeks, like their head size and their foot. And you are like, okay, I don't want that to be me." Several other women mentioned the foot image and the stories they read of extremely premature infants as a driving force to stay on strict bed rest and follow all of their doctors' orders in an attempt to prevent their own stories from featuring such tiny and premature infants.

For some of the women who experienced more rare complications or pregnancies with higher order multiples, books and television were one of the few places where they could find stories about situations like their own.

Christine spoke about watching the popular program, *Jon and Kate Plus 8*. As a parent of triplets she had an added interest in how this family tried to raise their two sets of multiples. She explained that although she did not particularly enjoy or admire the family, she did appreciate seeing a depiction of family life that more closely resembled her own. She explained, "I do watch *Jon and Kate Plus 8*. I—sometimes get annoyed by it. Sometimes, I don't know, sometimes it kind of helps validate me sometimes." This show represented one of the few stories she saw on television that somewhat mirrored her own life and experiences and even though she did not particularly like the show she still watched for the sense of connection and familiarity. The program normalized her own experiences as she observed another family whose life was even crazier and more chaotic than her own.

Another mother of triplets had a slightly different reaction to the reality program. Jenny, mother of triplets and a singleton, also talked about watching *Jon and Kate Plus 8*. "Like, I watch *Jon and Kate* and I just sit there and think, oh my god, how does she do it? Because I'm like, I'm ready to pull my hair out now. I cannot imagine. I cannot imagine having six and the two older." She was also in awe of the many trips and outings that they were able to take. "And then I see the places they take them and that was great. They live in a much bigger city and there is much more to do. But I'm thinking, I wouldn't be taking my three to any of those places. Because you think, there is too much to get into and they're going to get lost."

In this case the program was setting up expectations for Jenny of what life with multiples should be like, but rather than identifying with what she saw, she compared her own experiences and found her story to be lacking. Further discussion did bring up the issue of the money the show generated and some of the help the family received that was not featured on air, which allowed the family to participate in so many opportunities. Other mothers discussed how popular reality programs and news featuring multiples gave an inaccurate picture of the risks and challenges of having multiples. They pointed to shows such as *Jon and Kate Plus 8* or the national fascination with Nadeya Suleman, dubbed the "octomom," a California woman who gave birth to octuplets in 2009, as examples of stories that did not characterize the true nature of having multiples and the risks associated with higher-order multiple births. Much of the focus of the programs was on what they described as the cute factor and crazy antics of several babies, but rarely did the issues of developmental delays, health conditions, and the stress of the experience on the mother and the family come up. They also complained that many of the programs did not detail the behind the scenes help families had such as nannies, cleaning services, volunteers, and financial assistance. More than one of the mothers of triplets who was interviewed mentioned that others assumed they were showered with free gifts from companies when, in reality, the most women reported getting was a case of free formula and a box of diapers.

Avoiding Media

Several of the women who gave birth to premature infants went through a period where they tried to avoid hearing or reading stories about other women who had given birth to full term infants. The success or happy stories of others dredged up feelings of bitterness and envy. The happy stories often stood in stark contrast to the women's experiences, so they tried to avoid them altogether in order to minimize their bitter and envious reactions. For example, some of the women described turning off television programs when a full term infant was depicted, as it was too hard to see someone else's happiness, ideal delivery, or healthy infants. Women avoided stories about infants who did not need time in the NICU because they were too hard to hear and dredged up feelings of envy and grief.

Michelle, a mother of triplets, described how she was selective in what kinds of television programs she watched, such as *A Baby Story*. When asked if she watched these kinds of programs, she replied, "Not while I was pregnant, not like, and especially when it was something scary." Jenny, mother of triplets, explained, "I tried hard not to research it too well." Jenny actively tried to avoid information about all of the complications of a triplet pregnancy. Nancy, mother of twins, also struggled with infertility and hated watching programs filled with pregnancies and infants. She found that even after she became pregnant, she still did not want to watch shows such as *A Baby Story*:

> Yeah, I mean when I was in the hospital on bed rest for two weeks. The only channels they had were like the local TV channels and like the baby channels and I was like I don't want to see a C-section, I don't want to see—I'm pretty grossed out anyway. I don't like it and I had never watched those shows because of the whole infertility thing. I kind of just pushed that out of my mind.

For both these women the reality of having a caesarean (or C-section) and potential complications were too real, and television programs depicting painful and stressful deliveries were not entertaining or soothing, but instead just one more source of stress. This brings to light an interesting tension that many women found between wanting to be informed and being critical of media programs for not showing more pregnancies with complications, and also not wanting to be confronted with frightening story lines and images.

Some women found themselves turning off television programs if they were upsetting. Catt, the mother of surviving triplets, explained how she started to turn off programs such as *A Baby Story* because of her strong emotional reaction to the stories she saw. Surviving triplets is the term used to describe situations when one or two of a set of triplets passes away in utero or after birth. She was very upset about the loss of one of her triplets during her pregnancy and her time on bed rest. Because of her pregnancy complications, she knew her remaining two surviving triplets would be born early and spend time in the NICU. She explained why she turned the programs off, "When I went on bed rest, I couldn't watch them, I got very angry at them, and it made me sick, like sick to my stomach to watch them because they were all happy and wonderful, and they had the rainbow." The programs she was watching depicted the norm, and the images she saw and the stories they told reminded her of just how different her experience was. Many women spoke with resentment that their own experiences did not have happy storybook endings, but instead their stories were more like tragedies or dark dramas.

Dissatisfaction with Media

As women's pregnancies progressed and they gave birth, many began to view media more critically. Christine, mother of triplets, talked about watching *Bringing Home Baby*, with her husband during her pregnancy and while her daughters were in the NICU. *Bringing Home Baby* is a program that follows families for the first forty-eight hours after their infants come home from the hospital. As Christine contemplated what it would be like to bring her three infants home she found herself examining the stories she saw with a critical eye: "Yeah I know, after the girls were born. I remember my husband and I, we were watching one show, it's *Bringing Home Baby*, and they had like the woman and husband and the woman's parents were there. And it was like, you people need four adults to care for one baby? You know, isn't that pathetic?"

In this case, Christine's story differed from the norm she often saw on television and, rather than making her feel bad about her own experience, it made her question the authenticity and accuracy of the programs on television. She wondered if the shows made infants look so difficult to care for the drama effect rather than telling the true story. It also angered her that no television programs were discussing how hard it is to have infants sick and in the NICU, unable to come home. The more she watched, the less she trusted the television programs as a source of reliable information.

Women were also critical of the books they read in terms of their discussion of birth and its complications. Many of the women spoke somewhat negatively about *What to Expect When You're Expecting*. Although the book has been criticized by some for being too alarmist in its coverage of the many possible complications of pregnancy/delivery and promoting paranoia, women who experienced complications found the book lacked the detail they wanted and needed. Mary, mother of a singleton, remarked that only two pages at the back of the book discussed preeclampsia, rather than an entire chapter. After she was diagnosed with preeclampsia, the book was no longer useful to her.

When it came to pregnancies with multiples, some women complained about the lack of useful books, as they had a hard time applying the information, advice, and stories to their own situations. Kelli, mother of twins, explained her disappointment with the available books on twin pregnancies. She explained:

I looked in the book *Pregnancy for Dummies* and I looked and there is like a page or a paragraph and they would just say the most idiotic things like, oh, it is pretty much the same as having one. You just have two, and I am like, no, clearly whoever wrote that did not have multiple children. The *What to Expect When You are Expecting* book made me mad. It just would say it was just like having one but you have two, or three, or four. And I'm like no, honestly this is not helping, it is not just like having another.

Other mothers echoed the sentiment that those giving them advice and information about raising multiples, raising preemies, or even coping with a high-risk pregnancy often had no direct experience and seemed out of touch. The narrators' credibility was questioned as women placed a much higher value on direct experience than education or titles.

Influence on Stories

Despite women's critiques and avoidance of media, it was evident that media had strongly shaped the stories they told about their pregnancy and birthing experiences. When talking about their experiences of having a high-risk pregnancy or having a premature infant, women often talked about what they had missed out on and what was lacking. Jana, who had two high-risk pregnancies, described what she felt she had missed:

I have talked to other people who have had kind of difficult pregnancies and they all say the same thing. You do feel kind of robbed of the story of your pregnancy, especially with your first pregnancy. Everything is supposed to be new and wonderful and exciting and you get to plan all of this and the baby shower is supposed to be wonderful and it is supposed to be this kind of fun-filled exciting time, and that is sort of clouded over by your concern for your children and your children's health and your own. And you kind of just feel a little bit robbed of that experience. You know that you have seen *Baby Story* or you have heard from your friends, you've seen the pictures on their blog in the hospital, of them delivering the baby and holding the baby right away.

The stories she had heard or read had set up expectations for her of what being pregnant and having a baby would be like. When those expectations were not met her story included an element of loss. She and other women she knew who had experienced high-risk pregnancies felt robbed of an experience they wanted and that they should have experienced.

One of the moments or scenes that women most often referred to was the moment after birth when a mother is handed her newborn and immediately starts the bonding process. Women had seen this moment in movies and on television, and many had dreamed about the moment when they would meet their children. Women described lying on the operating table waiting to hear a cry to ensure their babies were breathing, but being unable to do anything more than glance at their infants. Most of the women never had those moments, as their premature infants were whisked away after birth to receive immediate medical attention. Some of the women were not able to hold their children for days or even weeks, until each infant's medical condition had stabilized. For example, Carrie, mother of triplets, described her children's birth, "I was definitely not prepared for the lack of connection. First, the amount of drugs pumped into me following my C-section was crazy. I was out of it for a while, and then I did not even see them for about sixteen to eighteen hours after the birth. It is also hard when you have to ask permission to hold your own baby or told you can or can't come hold your baby."

Repeatedly women described how they had missed out on this key bonding moment and how they had struggled to bond with their new infants who most often were in isolettes in the NICU. Because they had seen it so often, many women believed and felt as if the first moments after birth were critical to the bonding process and therefore the stories they told were full of disappointment, concern, and at times bitterness. One described visiting her infants in the NICU and feeling guilty because she knew she was supposed to love them, but she had a hard time feeling like they were even hers. She commented that she often felt like she was just visiting some babies in the NICU and she struggled to feel a strong maternal bond.

As women tried to make sense of their experiences they compared their experiences and themselves to the stories they had seen and read about. Women were not always aware of this comparison, but many of them were as they specifically talked about how what happened to them did not match what they saw depicted in the media. For example, Megan, mother of twins, described how watching programs such as *A Baby Story* or *Bringing Home Baby* was difficult because she was envious of the way the husbands on the programs acted toward their wives and infants. She saw the images of husbands doting on their wives and crying at the delivery and hoped her husband would do the same, when in reality he got faint during the delivery and had to leave the room and then went home to sleep the first night because he was feeling tired. She described it, "I was just alone in a room with these two kids and was just so sad." She and her husband had never discussed what she wanted him to do post delivery, but from watching shows she just assumed that he would eagerly take on the role of excited new dad. As she told her own story about her delivery she focused on what had not occurred and how her husband had not acted, rather than what did occur.

Analysis and Implications

The interviews revealed that media, particularly television programs and books, were an important way in which the women learned about pregnancy and delivery. Even if they did not watch documentary-type programs that depicted pregnancies and births, women still were exposed to a variety of images of pregnancy and motherhood through entertainment programs, movies, magazines, and advertisements. These media portrayals often contained depictions of the ideal mother, one who sacrifices all for her offspring and feels an overwhelming joy and love for her children. Due to their constant media exposure, many of the women, especially those who were first-time mothers, had definite ideas about what their experiences should and would be like. They had high expectations of pregnancy and motherhood and spent a lot of time anticipating the joyous moments of motherhood they so frequently saw. This is consistent with cultivation theory as women's attitudes and beliefs about motherhood were strongly shaped by their media consumption.

With such a narrow set of expectations, many women whose pregnancies and births do not conform to the norms are bound to be disappointed. Even though they critiqued the stories, they used them as benchmarks to understand their own experiences. Because these media outlets were very influential in shaping the stories women told, women need access to alternative stories about motherhood and the journey to becoming a mother. These alternative depictions should include mothers who struggled with the early months of motherhood for a variety of reasons including postpartum depression, poor maternal health, or poor infant health. Particularly, women need stories about women who struggled, but over time were able to progress into their roles as mothers. Women need access to stories about women who nursed, who could not nurse, and about women who chose not to nurse to illustrate the many options available. Women also need stories about different types of labor and deliveries.

It is interesting that women in high-risk situations were critical of the lack of information regarding pregnancy complications because books, such as *What to Expect When You are Expecting* have been criticized by some physicians and women for being too alarmist and unnecessarily frightening to pregnant women.[29] Perhaps for women who experience pregnancies without complications these critiques are justified, but for women who experience complications, the books they read did not contain enough information about complications and risks.

The women's critiques point to a need for books and television programs that meet their informational needs. One of the key themes that arose from the interviews was that a high-risk pregnancy was very different than a typical pregnancy. Therefore, women need information that addresses their complications and concerns. This should include information about premature infants, the NICU, as well as the emotional aspects of having a high-risk pregnancy or having a premature infant. Access to more realistic stories will help prepare women for situations they might be facing as well as justify and normalize their experiences. One suggestion would be to publish a book co-authored by a high-risk pregnancy specialist and a mother or mothers of premature infants. The mothers' perspective could help address the emotional and logistical concerns of women. Another way would be to request outlets such as TLC or Discovery Health to show more variation in the types of stories they cover about multiple births, such as via letters to or comments posted on the channel/program websites. Reporters who cover sensational multiple births such as quintuplets or sextuplets should also be briefed by doctors and other medical personnel about the general risks and financial costs of higher order multiples and include these issues in their stories or articles.

Women have a wide variety of resources for learning about pregnancy, childbirth, and early motherhood. Television and books are ways that women can actively and passively learn and develop expectations and ideas about pregnancy and childbirth. Media often promote an ideal story and when a woman's story varies from that ideal, she often struggles to reconcile those differences. Providing access to more varieties of stories and experiences may serve to expand societal understandings of the many possibilities of pregnancy, childbirth, and motherhood.

Notes

1. George Gerbner, "On Defining Communications: Still Another View," *Journal of Communication* 16, no. 2 (1966): 99-103; George Gerbner, "Toward 'Cultural Indicators': The Analysis of Mass Mediated Public Message Systems," *AV Communication Review* 17, no. 2 (1969): 137-148.

2. Susan J. Douglas and Meredith W. Michaels, *The Mommy Myth: The Idealization of Motherhood and How It Has Undermined Women* (New York: Free Press, 2004); Nikki Shelton and Sally Johnson, "'I Think Motherhood for Me Was a Bit Like a Double-Edged Sword': The Narratives of Older Mothers," *Journal of Community & Applied Social Psychology* 16, no. 4 (2006): 316-30.

3. Kimberly N. Kline, "Midwife Attended Births in Prime-Time Television: Craziness, Controlling Bitches, and Ultimate Capitulation," *Women and Language* 30, no. 1 (2007): 20-29; Madonne M. Miner, "'Like a Natural Woman': Nature, Technology, and Birthing Bodies in Murphy Brown," *Frontiers: A Journal of Women Studies* 16, no. 1 (1996): 1-17; Theresa Morris and Katherine McInerney, "Media Representations of Pregnancy and Childbirth: An Analysis of Reality Television Programs in the United States," *Birth: Issues in Perinatal Care* 37, no. 2 (2010): 134-40.

4. Bronny Handfield, Sue Turnbull, and Robin J. Bell, "What Do Obstetricians Think About Media Influences on Their Patients?" *Australian & New Zealand Journal of Obstetrics & Gynaecology* 46, no. 5 (2006): 379-83.

5. Christine Champagne, "Rattles and Ratings," *Advocate*, no. 788 (1999): 107.

6. Eugene R. Declercq, Carol Sakala, Maureen P. Corry, and Sandra Applebaum, "Listening to Mothers II: Report of the Second National U.S. Survey of Women's Childbearing Experiences," *Childbirth Connection 2006*, accessed November 10, 2012, http://www.childbirthconnection.org/pdfs/LTMII_report.pdf.

7. Diony Young, "Childbirth Education, the Internet, and Reality Television: Challenges Ahead," *Birth: Issues in Perinatal Care* 37, no. 2 (2002): 87-89.

8. Walter R. Fisher, "Clarifying the Narrative Paradigm," *Communication Monographs* 56, no. 1 (1989): 55-58; Walter R. Fisher, "Narration as Human Communication Paradigm: The Case of Public Moral Argument," *Communication*

Monographs 51, no. 1 (1984): 1-22; Walter R. Fisher, "The Narrative Paradigm: An Elaboration," *Commuincation Monographs* 52, no. 4 (1985): 347-67.

9. Lars-Christer Hyden, "Illness and Narrative," *Sociology of Health and Illness* 19, no. 1 (1997): 48-69.

10. Arthur P. Bochner, "It's About Time: Narrative and the Divided Self," *Qualitative Inquiry* 3, no. 4 (1997): 418-38; Arthur P. Bochner, "Narrative's Virtues," *Qualitative Inquiry* 7, no. 2 (2001): 131-57; Arthur Frank, *The Wounded Storyteller* (Chicago: The University of Chicago Press, 1995).

11. Barbara Sharf and Marsha Vanderford, "Illness Narrative and the Social Construction of Health," in *Handbook of Health Communication*, ed. Teresa L. Thompson, Alicia M. Dorsey, Katherine I. Miller, and Roxanne Parrott (Mahwah, NJ: Lawrence Earlbaum, 2003), 17.

12. Sarah J. Brubaker and Christie Wright, "Identity Transformation and Family Caregiving: Narratives of African American Teen Mothers," *Journal of Marriage and Family* 68, no. 5 (2006): 1214-28; Lou-Marie Kruger, "Narrating Motherhood: The Transformative Potential of Individual Stories," *South African Journal of Psychology* 33, no. 4 (2003): 198-204; Graziella Fava Vizziello, Maria Elisa Antonioli, Valentina Cocci, and Roberta Invernizzi, "From Pregnancy to Motherhood: The Structure of Representative and Narrative Change," *Infant Mental Health Journal* 14, no. 1 (1993): 4-16.

13. Cheryl Tatano Beck, "Pentadic Cartography: Mapping Birth Trauma Narratives," *Qualitative Health Research* 16, no. 4 (2006): 453-66; Vizziello et al., "From Pregnancy to Motherhood," 4-16.

14. Denise M. Chism, *The High-Risk Pregnancy Sourcebook* (Los Angeles, CA: Lowell House, 1997); Vizziello et al., "From Pregnancy to Motherhood," 4-16; Barbara Luke and Tamara Eberlein, *When You're Expecting Twins, Triplets, or Quads* (New York: Harper Collins, 2004).

15. Avi Besser and Beatriz Priel, "Trait Vulnerability and Coping Strategies in the Transition to Motherhood," *Current Psychology* 22, no. 1 (2003): 57-72.

16. Lisa McDermott-Perez, *Preemie Parents: Recovering from Baby's Premature Birth* (Westport, CT: Praeger, 2007).

17. Gerbner, "On Defining Communications."

18. McDermott-Perez, *Preemie Parents*; Daniel Romer, Kathleen Hall Jamieson, and Sean Aday, "Television News and the Cultivation of Fear of Crime," *Journal of Communication* 53, no. 1 (2003): 88-104.

19. Jeff Niederdeppe, Erika Franklin Fowler, Kenneth Goldstein, and James Pribble, "Does Local Television News Coverage Cultivate Fatalistic Beliefs About Cancer Prevention?" *Journal of Communication* 60, no. 2 (2010): 230-53; Helena Bilandzic and Rick W. Busselle, "Transportation and Transportability in the Cultivation of Genre-Consistent Attitudes and Estimates," *Journal of Communication* 58, no. 3 (2008): 508-29.

20. Jennifer B. Gray, "Interpersonal Communication and the Illness Experience in the Sex and the City Breast Cancer Narrative," *Communication Quarterly* 55, no. 4 (2007): 397-414.

21. Rashmi Adaval and Robert S. Wyer Jr., "The Role of Narratives in Consumer Information Processing," *Journal of Consumer Psychology* 7, no. 3 (1998): 207-45.

22. Emily Moyer-Guse and Robin L. Nabi, "Explaining the Effects of Narrative in an Entertainment Television Program: Overcoming Resistance to Persuasion," *Human Communication Research* 36, no. 1 (2010): 26-52; Bilandzic and Busselle,

"Transportation and Transportability," 508-29; Melanie C. Green and Timothy C. Brock, "The Role of Transportation in the Persuasiveness of Public Narratives," *Journal of Personality and Social Psychology* 79, no. 5 (2000): 701-21.

23. Thomas R. Lindlof and Bryan C. Taylor. *Qualitative Communication Research Methods*, 2nd ed. (Thousand Oaks, CA: Sage, 2002).

24. Christine W. Stage and Marifran Mattson, "Ethnographic Interviewing as Contextualized Conversation," in *Expressions of Ethnography: A Novel Approach to Qualitative Methods*, ed. Robin P. Clair (Albany, NY: State University of New York Press, 2003), 97-105.

25. Richard E. Boyatzis, *Transforming Qualitative Information* (Thousand Oaks, CA: Sage Publications, 1998).

26. Craig A. Mertler and C. M. Charles, *Introduction to Educational Research*, 5th ed. (Boston, MA: Pearson Education, 2005).

27. Lindlof and Taylor, *Qualitative Communication*, 129.

28. The homogeneity of the race of women interviewed most likely is correlated to the areas where women were recruited, which were central Indiana and central Ohio.

29. Lynn Andriani, "'What to Expect' Readies for a Rebirth," *Publishers Weekly* 255, no. 11 (2008): 8.

Chapter Five

All About My HBO Mothers: Talking Back to Carmela Soprano and Ruth Fisher

Andrée E. C. Betancourt

In May 2008 I presented at a conference called "*The Sopranos*: A Wake." As a doctoral student who had recently passed my exams and been awarded a dissertation fellowship, I was free as a bird to enjoy the proceedings. I even took a Sopranos tour with other conference-goers. The highlight was a visit to Satin Dolls, the location used for filming the strip club, Bada Bing!, where Tony Soprano had an office. Fellow scholars awkwardly wandered around sneaking peeks at the dancers. I bought a souvenir tank top for myself and a T-shirt for my spouse, who had introduced me to *The Sopranos* on one of our first dates in 2003. Fast forward to May 2009, I had successfully defended my dissertation, and my baby bump would soon outgrow my Bada Bing! tank top. My spouse had relocated for my doctoral program so it was my turn to move, from the Gulf Coast to the East Coast, for his career. The timing of our due date led me to accept a freelance consulting opportunity and stay home with our newborn while continuing my research program as an independent scholar. Having planned to follow in the footsteps of my mother, a professor, I had never even considered an arrangement other than leaving my child with childcare providers five days per week. Her reply to my question "Did you ever want to be a stay-at-home mom?" was "No, but I wished I could have hired a stay-at-home mom to take care of you." Even if my mother had wanted to sacrifice her career to stay home and care for us full time, it was not an option financially. She returned to her undergraduate studies days after my birth, and was back in her office working

full-time very shortly after each of her four subsequent births. She remembers
the tension between motherhood and her career that marked these transitions. I
have very early childhood memories of her jumping rope late at night in an
effort to stay awake so that she could study. I grew up with the understanding
that in order to be a mother with a career, I would have to depend on full-time
childcare. That is what I witnessed the women around me having to do.

My undergraduate studies at a women's college provided a foundation in
feminist theory that I further developed during my graduate studies. The work of
French feminist Julia Kristeva prepared me a bit for the abject experiences of
birth and breastfeeding. The primary discourse among my academic colleagues,
however, was about equal opportunities for women outside of the home. No one,
including myself, planned to be a stay-at-home parent. If we had the option of
maternity leave, it might be abbreviated due to the ticking tenure clock. There
was no discussion about the logistics of situations such as juggling the work of
being a stay-at-home mother while also working from home on paid freelance
assignments and the unpaid research necessary to stay current in one's academic
field. Betty Friedan, an alumna of my undergraduate institution, Smith College,
wrote *The Feminine Mystique*. A critique on stay-at-home motherhood, it is
arguably "the founding document of the second wave of feminism."[1] Stacy
Gillis and Joanne Hollows explain that following Friedan's book, "the idea that
an investment in domestic life is contrary to the aims of feminism has structured
much feminist debate and the figure most closely associated with the
domestic—the housewife—often operates as the feminist's 'other.'"[2] Recent
issues of the *Smith Alumnae Quarterly* demonstrate that the controversy
surrounding the value of stay-at-home motherhood remains alive in third-wave
feminist debates. In response to an alumna's claim that stay-at-home mothering
does not make the world a better place, one woman wrote: "Right now being
home with my children is my 'unique contribution to this world' partly because
our family cannot justify the cost of childcare so that I can work, and partly
because I see that my job now is to be a mom."[3] Responding to the problematic
"Mommy Wars" that rage on and present a "false conflict," Amy Allen argues
that the practice of mothering presents a "dilemma that theorists delight in
deconstructing" yet "must nevertheless still be negotiated in practice in the here
and now, within our existing social and cultural world."[4] Elizabeth Paré and
Heather Dillaway explain that "ultimately, all forms of parenthood and paid
work are intertwined in lived experience, and we may need to reconceptualize
more than one set of identities and activities to truly capture the daily lives of
women, men, and children."[5] On call around the clock, and armed with a breast
pump and breast pads, I would no longer be free as a bird at academic
conferences. For that matter, it would become a novelty to go to the bathroom
without holding a baby or having a toddler tag along like one of Tony Soprano's
wild ducklings. Fervently in search of answers about how to negotiate the
challenges and sacrifices demanded by stay-at-home motherhood, even if it was
only a temporary and hybrid work situation for me, I turned on the television
and tuned into two televisual mothers.

This chapter examines lessons learned from these two memorable HBO mothers, Carmela Soprano of *The Sopranos* and Ruth Fisher of *Six Feet Under* (*SFU*), and talks back about the ways in which their roles are used to voice concerns surrounding contemporary motherhood. It does so through focusing on how the series' official publications *Entertaining with the Sopranos: As Compiled by Carmela Soprano* and *Six Feet Under: Better Living Through Death* showcase these mothers and the processes and products of their domestic labor.[6] Employing feminist and critical cultural theory, this essay uses these companion books to frame how the two mothers are depicted on screen. It demonstrates how their experience with issues, ranging from identity to sacrifice to isolation, reinforces or problematizes contemporary criticisms of stay-at-home motherhood. David Lavery writes, "like the series that 'inspire' them, TV tie-in books can sometimes be 'quality' offerings, wonderfully imaginative extrapolations that become for those who read them instrumental factors in how serious viewers 'read' the show."[7] Lavery references Umberto Eco on cult objects in his assertion that "only quality companion books" such as the earlier *Sopranos* companion books, along with the *SFU* book, "hail readers as 'adepts of the sect', inviting them to exhibit all the care and imagination with which they watch, to immerse themselves in an expanded, broadened, deepened—in time and space—multimedia diegesis, existing now in print and on screen."[8] As television series continue to capitalize on the popularity of companion books, media scholars seeking to better understand the expanding cultural impact of these programs must consider these important hybrid sites. While companion book reviews can be useful, we must critically engage these texts as seriously as we consider the television series that birth them. These books freeze, reflect, and reframe images that we have seen in motion on screen and dialogue that we have heard or imagined, inviting us to access the subject matter at a different pace and from new angles. The repetition of subject matter from the series found in the companion books is punctuated by the new content introduced by each medium, a process that potentially interrupts previous readings in productive ways. Through close textual analysis of select examples from *Entertaining* and *Better Living*, I attempt to demonstrate the dynamic relationship between screen and page.

The following two sections focus primarily on one of the mothers and approach her through a theme that marks her mothering: Carmela and entertaining, and Ruth and mourning. I include autoethnographic passages to situate myself as a scholar-fan, daughter, and mother in an attempt to negotiate my relationships with these characters and their mothering styles. Carmela and Ruth are primarily stay-at-home mothers, and much of their time is spent in their respective domestic spheres caring for their families. They struggle with the sacrifices that they make in order to stay at home for their families. They are married to men whose absence, literal and emotional, causes profound unhappiness, increases their parental responsibility, and complicates their roles as mothers. Both women engage in some type of work outside of the home at certain points in their series, and face unexpected obstacles. As white, middle-class, heterosexual women, they lead privileged lives. Carmela can be described as *nouveau riche*, upper middle class. They demonstrate, however, that regardless of status, motherhood can be difficult work and stay-at-home motherhood presents unique challenges. These women are not the feminist role models that my own mother has been for me, yet I turn to them, because Ruth, like Carmela, whose "choices and actions" are described by Janet McCabe and Kim Akass as "seemingly at odds with feminism," potentially "push us into new directions for a feminist television criticism in the post-feminist age."[9]

Much scholarship has been published about the highly popular, critically acclaimed, award-winning television series *The Sopranos* and *SFU*. Contributors to the anthology *Quality TV: Contemporary American Television and Beyond* refer to *The Sopranos* and *SFU* as benchmarks for "quality" television.[10] The definition of the term "quality" television continues to be debated. Sarah Cardwell explains that "American quality television programmes tend to exhibit high production values, naturalistic performance styles, recognised and esteemed actors, a sense of visual style created through careful, even innovative, camerawork and editing, and a sense of aural style created through the judicious use of appropriate, even original music."[11] Because both shows are big-budget cable television programs with approximately one-hour-long episode slots, the characters Carmela and Ruth are given significant development and narrative authority. *The Sopranos* spanned six seasons (86 episodes). Robin Nelson, referencing Akass and McCabe on the generic hybridity of *The Sopranos*, explains that its "mix of gangster movie, soap opera, and psychological drama . . . plays self-consciously and intertextually with the various contributing discourses and plays them against each other to produce complex seeing."[12] *SFU* had a smaller following and spanned five seasons (63 episodes), though the popularity of creator Alan Ball's current *True Blood* HBO series is likely to attract new viewers to his older show. Jane Feuer explains that *SFU* "reeks of a European art cinema heritage in combination with a more televisual tradition of quality lifted from the miniseries of Dennis Potter also the more serialised tradition of American quality television."[13] Given each program's respective popularity, *The Sopranos* and *SFU* will live on in the imaginations of viewers and serve as important cultural references for future generations.

Carmela Soprano and Entertaining Motherhood

I don't know how to cook very well as it was not one of the things that my professor mother taught me. She did buy a very basic cookbook for me before I left for college that included directions for boiling water. Between her academic career and being a single mother of three during the majority of my childhood, she did not have much time to spend in the kitchen. A first-generation college graduate born to a Mexican-Belizean immigrant mother and an orphaned father (possibly of Italian heritage), her world lacked the material comforts enjoyed by

Carmela Soprano. However, like Carmela she is Roman Catholic, she has a rich connection to her familial roots outside of the United States, and she is an author. Her books feature psychological research instead of the kind of items found in Carmela's book such as family recipes, fish and food poisoning, or napkin folding. Carmela's mothering heavily involves cooking and entertaining for her family, and the book *Entertaining with The Sopranos: As Compiled by Carmela Soprano* showcases her methods for entertaining and a number of her recipes, as well as tips she collected from "family" members, both blood relations and those connected to her through (sometimes bloody) Mafia ties. Each of the ten chapters focuses on a category of gatherings ranging from rituals such as baptisms, that welcome one into a community, to events, such as wakes, that honor those who have passed away.

The book is a ripe text, written by Allen Rucker, a film school friend of *Sopranos* creator David Chase, and features recipes by Michele Scicolone.[14] Like the series, it invites cultural critique, particularly on the theme of production and consumption and the ways in which Carmela, as leading lady, frames the domestic labor of mothering through the lens of entertaining. In other words, Carmela's book offers a behind-the-scenes look at the processes of production and consumption involved in domestic labor, with a focus on the work of entertaining, work that she finds essential to her role as a stay-at-home mother and homemaker. Gillis and Hollows propose that feminists "need to explore new ways of thinking about the role of domesticity in social, economic and cultural life that neither simply condemn domesticity as a site of oppression and boredom nor simply celebrate domesticity as an expression of feminine virtue."[15] Carmela does not identify as a feminist, yet her character reveals the tension of the condemnation/celebration binary identified by Gillis and Hollows, and in doing so problematizes simplistic renderings of domesticity and stay-at-home mothers. Throughout the series and in *Entertaining*, there are a number of explicit examples in which characters condemn or celebrate Carmela's domestic role, depending on the circumstance. In doing so, these characters' reactions to her stay-at-home mothering, particularly those of her spouse and children, send mixed messages. A psychiatrist she visits condemns her role based on the "blood money" that supports it; however, during Carmela's confession in the Catholic parish they attend, her priest dismisses the condemnation and in turn continues to benefit from the Sopranos' monetary support. Carmela's pursuit of real estate work reflects her desire to provide for herself and her children if need be, as well as a desire to be a professional outside of the home. Her career choice, however, maintains intersections with domesticity through her building of a spec house, and the challenging process involves working with and dependence upon family members including her husband and her father. Carmela's relationships with other women in the series, some who work outside of the home, including wives and widows of her husband's Mafia associates, reveal ways in which she negotiates her privilege and power. In terms of domesticity, Carmela is difficult to pin down as either a celebratory or a condemnable figure, and her character demonstrates a complexity that requires us to move beyond traditional, dualistic interpretations of stay-at-home mothers.

Becoming Home"made": Carmela's "Job" as Mafia Wife, Mother, and Hostess

Carmela, the fictional character, characterizes *Entertaining* as a "commercial venture," and though she credits her husband for the idea and features content that she solicited from a number of other people, she retains narrative authority.[16] Her narrative highlights her less privileged roots; for example, she recounts her parents' "football wedding" in the 1940s "when no one in the Italian-American community at that time had any money."[17] In the introduction to the Graduation Parties chapter, Carmela describes graduations as "momentous" events, particularly for families like her own "where college was not traditionally an option."[18] On screen we learn that she attended Montclair State University, but dropped out and married young to Anthony "Tony" Soprano, a second-generation New Jersey wise guy who rises from capo to acting boss over the course of the series. She has two children with him, Meadow and Anthony Jr. (A.J.). Lisa Cassidy explains that Carmela's "traditional marriage . . . rendered her financially and emotionally dependent on a violent and duplicitous husband."[19] Cassidy notes that when Carmela separates from Tony in the finale of Season four (they reunite at the end of the fifth season) her daughter Meadow's response is "God, Mom! How could you eat shit from him all those years?"[20] *Sopranos* creator David Chase asserted in a post-series interview that "Meadow may not become a pediatrician or even a lawyer, but she's not going to be a housewife-whore like her mother. She'll learn to operate in the world in a way that Carmela never did. It's not ideal. It's not what the parents dreamed of. But it's better than it was. Tiny, little bits of progress—that's how it works."[21] McCabe and Akass emphasize that while the younger, Ivy-League educated Meadow has options, Carmela's "are closing down," revealing "the uncomfortable dilemma—a television character unable to blow the whistle on approved scripted cultural performances that praise particular models of female achievement and normalcy because there is no language within her representation to articulate it."[22] Carmela may not have the language to "blow the whistle," but her "will-to-empowerment" problematizes labeling her as a victim or "housewife-whore."[23] It manifests itself in the pieces of resistance that Carmela serves to those who get in her way, and *Entertaining* offers tasty samples of her no-nonsense style that makes her character so attractive on screen.

In her introduction to *Entertaining*, "a labor of love" and "the work of dozens of people, all close family and friends," Carmela's notes that Tony "successfully argued that such a commercial venture was a logical extension of [her] main 'job,' that of wife, mother, and amateur hostess."[24] By placing the term "job" in quotations Carmela emphasizes the complex relationship between domestic labor and the familial role of wife and mother. Throughout the book, she continues to highlight the domestic labor involved in various tasks, labor that sometimes requires sacrifices such as missing the very rite of passage that is being celebrated. The first chapter, "Welcome to the Family: Baptisms, Communions, and Confirmations," opens with a description of Carmela's own baptism. Her mother, "a devout Catholic," stayed home and missed the ceremony in order to cook rice balls for the potluck that followed in the church basement.[25] As Lynn Spigel writes: "women's household work presented a dilemma for the twin ideals of family unity and social divisions, since housewives were expected to perform their distinctive productive functions but, at the same time, take part in the family's leisure time pursuits," a conflict that can be traced back to "Victorian domestic ideology."[26] The tips that Carmela offers in *Entertaining* for negotiating this conflict involve doing extensive preparation. Should unexpected issues arise, she explains that the hostess must attempt to deal with them or have others lined up to do so. In the series there are events for which she depends on others to help with the "dirty" work. She sometimes employs hired help such as Charmaine Bucco, her professional-caterer friend, who she thanks in the first chapter of *Entertaining*. When questioned by Charmaine's husband, Artie, as to why she does not regularly hire someone to help with cooking, Carmela's surprising reply is that she has never thought of that; and she adds that they do not like strangers in their house. This makes sense considering Tony's role in the Mafia, and marks Carmela's character as unique in terms of possessing the means to hire domestic laborers but having to do the work herself. She explains to Artie: "Call me old-fashioned, but I think cooking is one way—maybe the best way—of communicating to my family that I love and care for them."[27]

Entertaining offers examples that demonstrate the entanglement of work and family, especially for homemakers whose family produces much of their work and consumes the fruits of their often "invisible" labor, in some cases with little or no recognition of or appreciation for the processes involved. In the fourth season finale episode, a particularly nasty argument between Carmela and Tony erupts and provides an example.[28] As he criticizes Carmela's privileged role as homemaker in an attempt to defend his unfaithfulness, she shouts: "Who the fuck wanted it like this? Who the fuck pissed and moaned of just the idea of me with a fucking real estate license?" and Tony responds: "Well, you sit back for twenty fucking years all you did was fiddle with the air conditioning and fucking bitch and complain!" As Tony attempts to justify his adulterous lifestyle as part of the "deal" that goes along with his business that she married into, he points to Carmela's materialism as evidence of her acceptance. She asserts, "You really don't hear me, do you? You think for me it's all about things," to which he replies, "No I forced all this shit on you. What you really crave is a Hyundai and a simple gold heart on a chain." Tony reveals his lack of recognition of Carmela's domestic labor as actual work, and she in turn reminds him of his resistance to her pursuit of work outside of the home. Kristyn Gorton argues that "Carmela continually plays with her role as first wife of the Mafia family, vacillating between enjoying the power it affords her and, at other times, realizing that she is trapped within it."[29] When Carmela kicks Tony out of the house after receiving a phone call from one of his ex-mistresses in this episode, he brings up their children as a reason she should not. In doing so he attempts to define for her what good motherhood should entail: accepting a spouse's adulterous behavior in order to keep one's family together. Exhibiting her agency she proceeds with the separation, though she later reconciles with Tony on her own terms.

In Carmela's afterword she asserts that the labor of entertaining is not graded like a test, yet she contradicts this assertion in various instances that describe the potential price of failure, ranging from embarrassment to discomfort to death: "a perfectly good spaghetti pie with an unintended crust of candle wax"; dinner party guests "on opposite sides of the gun-control issue"; and on a more serious note, "pool drowning"—something her own son risked in his botched suicide attempt.[30] As Spigel argues, "once the home is considered a workplace, the divisions between public/work and domestic/leisure become less clear."[31] Carmela asserts that "planning a menu and setting a table in a delightful way for a party of twelve is no more 'work' than gardening or owning a pleasure boat."[32] In placing the term "work" in quotations, and offering examples associated with taming land and navigating water, she attempts to make the art and practice of entertaining more accessible to readers who are perhaps less comfortable than she is working inside the home. Successful gardening and boating, however, usually require some work, whether nurturing plants so that they may bloom or charting a safe course through stormy weather. Carmela's materialism in part influences her support of her husband's Mafia leadership, support that she believes God punishes her for with ovarian cancer (her diagnosis turns out to be a non-cancerous thyroid problem).[33] As she escapes into her well-stocked kitchen and lavishly entertains guests in a well-kept home, we find that, along with Carmela's guilty conscience, a high price is often paid by her children, whose blooming is challenged and safety compromised.

Carmela and the F Word

Carmela is credited with 52 of the 3,539 instances where the word "fuck" is heard in *The Sopranos*, yet the "f" word that many of us wanted to hear more from her is "feminism," a dirty word in her book.[34] Why turn to *Entertaining* for a better understanding of the domestic labor involved in mothering when the book can be dismissed as the product of a privileged fictional character who explicitly rejects the label of feminist? There are instances in which Carmela's actions speak otherwise. For example, she confides in her friend Rosalie Aprile that she "wants to have an equal relationship with her husband when it comes to the financial stability of their family."[35] Lisa Cassidy uses the term "antifeminist" to describe Carmela, who she views as a "salon-pampered homemaker who presides over the furniture suites and window treatments of the Soprano mini-mansion," yet argues that "Carmela uses feminist care reasoning in her moral deliberations."[36] A scene in which she delivers a ricotta-pineapple pie to a woman in order to secure a Georgetown University recommendation letter for Meadow is one of Cassidy's favorite examples of "Carmela using care reasoning while being intimidating and tough" versus upholding "the stereotype of a yielding, self-sacrificing deferential woman that care ethics might at first glance be said to valorize."[37] Referencing Leslie Heywood and Jennifer Drake's research on third-wave feminism, McCabe and Akass argue: "what makes Carmela Soprano so pleasurably compelling is how she gives representation to the paradox defining contemporary womanhood, 'shaped by struggles between various feminisms as well as cultural backlash against feminism and activism.'"[38] Included among the reasons that McCabe and Akass, citing Joan Williams, identify as making feminism problematic for Carmela is the sentiment that "feminism abandons them once they embrace traditional roles as homemaker, 'just a housewife' rather than wage earner—an alleged separation between the public world of the labor market and the private space of domesticity and childrearing."[39]

In their essay on how female narrative authority is negotiated by Carmela and other women in *The Sopranos*, Kim Akass and Janet MaCabe assert that the female characters "know how media representation of the gangster works, a knowledge that is played out between women as receivers of media texts and gangsters as products of them."[40] Akass and MaCabe argue that as spectators "denied direct access to the sites of male action," Carmela and other female characters are positioned to identify "the gap that exists between fictional gangsters and their real-life selves living normal lives in the suburbs. In so doing, [Carmela and other women in the series] use that knowledge to their advantage." *Entertaining* is important in that it allows Carmela's character to serve as the producer of a media text that riskily capitalizes on this very gap by offering its audience a peek at the "real-life" selves of gangsters while craftily giving a bold between the lines nod to readers hungry for the "fictional selves." In contrast to traditional books on entertaining that sugar coat life, Carmela directly acknowledges that "all families have problems," offering marital separation and rebellious children as examples.[41] I find Carmela's classism, homophobia, and racism repulsive and agree with Cassidy's assertion that her "child rearing practices reinforce traditional gender roles,"[42] something I attempt not to do. *Entertaining* reminds us, however, that there is a lot more to Carmela than meets the eye and troubles feminist attempts to dismiss her as just a privileged stay-at-home mom known to sport serious "bling." Carmela is also attentive to the potential enjoyment of domestic labor. I appreciate her closing remark that entertaining involves "staging an event and entertaining *yourself*," and as she snappily reminds us: "No one is sticking a gun to your head. If you don't want to go to the trouble, don't."[43] I breathe a deep sigh of relief, and save her intimidating New Jersey cheesecake recipe for another day.

Mothering and Mourning with Ruth Fisher

My toddler got his hands on my copy of *Six Feet Under: Better Living Through Death* and the book fell open to a photograph of two empty armchairs and a coffee table topped with a box of tissue and catalogs of caskets and flower arrangements. Pointing at this image of a room in Fisher and Sons funeral home where clients decide what to do with their loved ones' remains, my son resolutely said "hotel." One of the greatest challenges of parenthood has been figuring out how to teach my children about death. Though we did not grow up in a house that was also a family business funeral home in Pasadena, California, as did Ruth Fisher's three children, my mother took my siblings and me to the funerals of loved ones when we were young and was always open about the topic of death. Instead of going to an empty home after school, my siblings and I often rode the city bus to my mother's office at the university psychology clinic. While she worked, we entertained ourselves in the playroom that had a two-way mirror for observation, and we even starred in a few instructional videos. We enjoyed being hooked up to the biofeedback machines that my mother used in her research. We served as subjects for her graduate students who needed practice administering psychological tests, and we became seasoned interpreters of Rorschach inkblots. My eldest brother and I would go on to earn psychology degrees. Years later, my spouse-to-be introduced me to *Six Feet Under* at the same time as my *Sopranos* introduction. I greedily consumed all of the episodes I had missed, and I eagerly awaited new ones. We learned a lot about each other through our shared reactions to the series and their focus on topics such as death. All four of his grandparents had passed away when he was young. I had not experienced the death of a close family member and was haunted by *SFU's* treatment of death and grieving.

In the introduction to the *SFU* companion book, series creator Alan Ball reflects on his earliest experiences with death, including asking his mother what would happen to him when she and his father died. Though she comforted him with reassurance that "nothing like that would happen to him for a very long time," when Ball was thirteen his older sister was killed in a car accident while she was driving him to his piano lesson.[44] On the surface, Ruth Fisher as a stay-at-home mother and my professor mother do not have much in common, but like Ball's mother, they both lost a child. One of my younger brothers passed away unexpectedly at age twenty-two due to a previously unknown heart condition. As Ball writes, "Death *is* life: an epic, primal force that terrifies and fascinates us, gives our experience meaning, and ultimately consumes us."[45] *Six Feet Under* introduces us to a fictional family intimate with grief. As the matriarch, Ruth's role as stay-at-home mother is complicated by the fact that her home is shared with the family funeral business. After years of watching his father, Nathaniel, work on dead bodies, Ruth's youngest son, David, joined the family business at age twenty. Before my toddler abandoned the *SFU* companion book and wandered off to play with his own puzzles, he flipped through the book and looked concerned as he silently gazed at the image of a troubled Claire, Ruth's youngest child, sitting alone on a sofa. If my toddler could read, he would have noted that the caption to the image of Claire is a first season quote from her mother: "You wake up one day and your baby's stolen a foot. Where have I been?"[46] That is a good question.

Where has Ruth Fisher been and what might we learn from her adventures in mothering? Her teenage daughter leaves a corpse's foot in her boyfriend's locker in revenge for his telling his friends that she sucked his toes. The foot belongs to Fisher and Son's client who was dismembered by an industrial dough mixer while cleaning it. Unlike other families who have ping-pong tables or preserve collections in their basements, the Fisher family has corpses and a collection of cremated remains in theirs. The boundaries between private and public, professional and familial, domestic space and workplace are blurred throughout the series, often creating betwixt and between places and spaces in which magical realism blossoms through exchanges between the living and the dead. As Ruth and her family navigate their lives between the deaths of Ruth's husband and her eldest son, Nate, that bookend the series, the invisibility of labor, both domestic and that of the death care industry, is made visible, and boundaries in the Fisher home and business are revealed as fluid. Ruth is portrayed as a character who has always grappled with motherhood, a struggle that intensifies as she faces new challenges of widowhood, grandmotherhood, and the death of an adult child.

Better Living is marketed as "a history of the Fishers and their extended family. From Nate and David's childhood to the disappearance of Lisa Kimmel [Nate's first wife], major events and daily routines are revealed through the character's personal photographs, correspondence, and memorabilia."[47] The book is packaged in a red and white semi-transparent plastic case that ghosts the book cover image, an image created by artist Gregory Crewdson that was used to promote Season three. Echoing David Lavery, I found that the protective book cover lends a family scrapbook feeling to the edition, as does the colorful exposed spine of the book.[48] Referencing two well-known works quoted as transitional epigraphs in the book, Lavery asserts that *Better Living* is "the *Bhagavad-Gita* or *Tao Te Ching*" of companion books.[49] In the cover image, Nate, Claire, David, and Keith (David's partner) sit at the kitchen table that is topped with a meal presumably cooked and served by Ruth who, standing and dressed in her apron, frames the right side. Brenda (Nate's second wife) frames the left side. Frederico, a Fisher and Son's employee, is the only character who returns the viewer's gaze. He sits on the kitchen counter, and dressed in his mortician apron creates a visual association between his and Ruth's behind-the-scenes labor that in discrete ways puts food on the Fisher's table. The bottom and lower sides of the frame are filled with strikingly colorful roses and other flowers that appear to be growing out of the floor. Serving as a family photograph, the image captures the magical realism aesthetic of the series while evoking the bittersweet scent of funeral flowers that viewers may imagine always lingers in the Fisher home.

Holiday Letters

Better Living, while not a book compiled by Ruth Fisher in the way that *Entertaining* is framed as Carmela's "commercial venture," contains, using creator Alan Ball's description, "relics—albeit fictional ones left behind by fictional characters" who to him "are very real."[50] Many of these relics are the type of objects, such as school photos and Valentine's cards, traditionally saved by parents, and in particular by mothers, whose domestic labor more typically includes assembling family albums and scrapbooks. In their research on scrapbooks and memory, Tamar Katriel and Thomas Farrell found that "in the engagement of younger children with scrapbooks, the figure of 'the Mom' looms large as either the stimulus or an active collaborator in the practice of assembly."[51] My own mother pokes fun at holiday family photo cards, particularly those from people she does not know well. She finds them irritating and tiring since she feels guilty throwing away pictures of other people's children after displaying them for an obligatory period. In showcasing picture "perfect" families, along with annual letters, they communicate a sense of achievement. Imperfect or not, these relics are work, that like the everyday documenting of family, more often falls on mothers. *Better Living* features two annual Christmas letters and a holiday letter written by Ruth that mark her becoming a mother to two, then three children, and, finally, a grandmother.

In the first Christmas letter, Ruth writes about her husband's return from Vietnam and three-year-old Nate's play, sassing, and favorite food. Only then does she briefly turn the spotlight on herself, and does so modestly. She mentions that after courses in "decoupage, crocheting, and leather tooling, to name a few, and for better or worse, the house is now filled with [her] handiwork."[52] In the same "breath," she announces her pregnancy, and shares news of her great aunt's death with a grateful nod to an extended family member's homemade burnt sugar cake (presumably served at the wake). Ruth's world is a mix of new life, death, and bittersweet dessert. Though she narrates the letters, her husband's name appears first in the closing. Ruth's 1983 letter is written in rhyming verse, and celebrates the arrival "from Heaven" of her daughter Claire, "a princess, sweet and fair."[53] Her 2002 holiday letter is much simpler, as it does not detail a rosy family like the previous. It serves as a birth announcement and features only three sweet sentences and a photograph of her new granddaughter, Maya, and is signed "Peace, the Fishers."[54] Kim Akass argues that Maya's birth "seems to offer Ruth an opportunity to relive the part of her life that she so obviously mourns," yet after incidents in Season three such as Ruth feeding Maya peanut butter without first finding out about possible allergies, her daughter-in-law "reveals how the ideology of motherhood has completely changed."[55] Akass emphasizes that in addition to the challenge of "re-insert[ing] herself into society" as a widow, Ruth discovers "that she can no longer rely on the now outdated mothering skills that have carried her through her key role in life."[56] Members of a mothers' group I belong to, a mix of primarily stay-at-home moms including some of who find ways to stay active in their pre-motherhood professions, can empathize with Ruth. We continually express exasperation at how difficult it is to keep mothering skills up to date, and one member recently alerted us to a major change in pediatricians' approach to children's food allergies. In the series, Ruth is portrayed as isolated to some extent from the outside world and not Internet savvy, making it all the more difficult for her to stay current with mothering practices.

"Motherhood is the Loneliest Thing in the World"

Arranged in chronological order, the objects in *Better Living* provide clues to Ruth's "Where have I been?" question, and present a prehistory for series viewers. Ruth's wedding invitation is followed by correspondence between her and Nathaniel during his service in Vietnam. Ruth's first letter to her husband opens with a critical reference to her six months pregnant young body: "I'm glad you don't have to see me like this . . . I'm so huge! Your mother says it looks like I'm hiding a twenty-pound turkey under my apron."[57] Ashley Sayeau writes that "the fear of having missed opportunities, or let other lives pass you by, contributes to the show's melancholy tone," and offers as an example Ruth's confession to Claire in Season three that at age nineteen: "I got pregnant the first time I'd ever had sex. It changed my life forever" and led her to "wonder how life would have been different"[58] In the subsequent episode Claire, who is nineteen, finds out that she is pregnant by her boyfriend Russell and chooses to have an abortion, which Janet McCabe describes as her "turn[ing] not to the discourse of motherhood (Ruth) but to one of female resistance (Brenda) for help. Knowing what is best for her, she remains haunted by her decision."[59] It is only with Nate's death and Claire's move to New York in the final season that Ruth, approximately forty years after becoming a mother, is released from the everyday duties of mothering. She takes the opportunity to move in with her sister and a close friend, women portrayed as more free spirited than her. The flash-forwards of the series finale reveal that Claire marries but never has children, and that Ruth opens the Four Paws Pet Retreat in Topanga Valley.[60]

In Season two Ruth discovers The Plan, a self-empowerment seminar with the motto "You are the architect of your life." She ultimately abandons The Plan, but her involvement proves to be cathartic in terms of confronting those, living and dead, who have abused her, treated her poorly, or taken her for granted. *Better Living* features an image of a binder with literature from The Plan, and some of Ruth's infamous lines from the third episode of Season two including: "You want me to complain. All right then, fuck this. Fuck you. Fuck my dead husband. And my lousy children with their nasty little secrets."[61] Kristyn Gorton explains that Ruth troubles the "sentimental idea" that "a woman is not truly a woman until she is a mother" by expressing "a deep sense of regret at being *just* a mother and that her children, who are expected to provide this sense of purpose, are, in actuality providing a sense of unbalance and frustration."[62] After her husband dies in the first episode of the series, rather than serving as the picture perfect mother, Ruth confesses her own nasty little secret to her children.[63] Shattered, her guilt and grief force the admission of a long-standing affair with her hairdresser, revealing that her marriage was unfulfilling and further complicating her children's grieving processes. Her subsequent attempts throughout the series at securing a satisfying romantic relationship lead her to marry George Sibley, a geology professor who had six previous marriages. Nate follows in his mother's footsteps when he pursues an affair with George's daughter, Maggie, his stepsister, in the final season of the series. In this instance, Nate confesses his own "nasty little secret" to his pregnant wife in order to tell her that he wants a divorce, an option that Ruth did not pursue with her first husband.[64] We can only imagine the reasons Ruth did not, as the narrative leaves this open. Her character recalls *Feminine Mystique*-era homemakers who have felt trapped in terms of not having skills to support themselves working outside of the home; or those who have thought that a divorce would create greater problems for them and their children than it would solve. Ruth's second husband, George, initially hides his mental illness from her. This, along with Ruth's efforts to take greater control over her life, leads her to end their marriage though they maintain a close relationship.

There are newspaper clippings of advice columns in both *Entertaining* and *Better Living* from Carmela and Ruth's early days as young brides. Carmela suggests that readers pin her clipping of the Dear Happy Homemaker column to their bulletin boards, explaining that it is what helped her "understand the art of hostessing."[65] The Dear Phyllis column has a very different tone as Ruth is more concerned with surviving than entertaining, and it suggests possible postpartum depression. She voices what she hides from her husband, including her in-laws, rejection of her, and asks if she should be honest with him: "[Nathaniel] had just received his draft notice. . . . Now I feel like I'm trapped in a cage. I know it's horrible, but I feel like my baby boy is my jailer. When he cries at night, sometimes I take an extra second to get out of bed."[66] Her "worry about [her] baby boy being in the presence of so much death" clearly disturbs her. Ruth's anonymous reaching out to a stranger for advice demonstrates her isolation and exhaustion from the labor of caring for a baby alone full time while her absent husband is at "Tan Son Nhu Air Base [t]olling away in the mortuary . . ." without Ruth "there to greet [him] with a kiss at the top of the stairs when the work is done."[67] Ruth's work at home as a mother, on the other hand, is never done. The "presence of so much death" intensifies several decades later, as Nathaniel is killed in his car by a bus in the pilot episode of the series.[68] She, now grieving, is once again left alone to care for her teenage and adult children. In the series finale Ruth offers to help her newly widowed daughter-in-law with her baby and confides that, "If my experience is anything to go by, motherhood is the loneliest thing in the world."[69]

Family Photographs

Akass poses the question, "If the narrative of *Six Feet Under* can be defined as liminal, with each episode beginning with a death and ending with a burial, could it not be argued that Ruth's position within the narrative represents another kind of liminality: that of the middle-aged post-menopausal mother with adult children?"[70] Drawing on Michelle Boulous Walker, Akass argues "that Ruth's narrative finds her negotiating her way through uncharted territory while offering us an innovative subject position which allows the 'unrepresentable to emerge from the patriarchal restrictions of representation.'"[71] *Better Living* perhaps best captures Ruth's liminality with a photograph shot in 2003 by Claire that is juxtaposed with Ruth's 2002 holiday letter. In Claire's black and white portrait, Ruth, dressed in an apron and holding a dish towel in her left hand, gazes back at the viewer. Her other hand and the towel are blurred, creating a sense of movement, of busy, nervous energy, yet her expression is still and strong. She stands in front of the sink, and the overexposed window behind her ghosts the top of her head, part of her face, neck, and upper body. It is as if she is "betwixt and between" worlds, and as the reader opens to this page, Maya smiles joyfully at her grandmother Ruth from the holiday letter photograph on the opposite page. The click of Claire's camera connects the three generations. As a teenage artist, negotiating issues of identity and independence, Claire's family members in particular become the object of her familial gaze. She documents both the everyday mundane practices of life in a funeral home as well as the more unusual, in which case the boundaries between the Fisher home and business erupt forth in the form of human blood in the kitchen sink.[72] Like Carmela and Meadow's relationship, the mother-daughter relationship of Ruth and Claire portrayed throughout the series demonstrates the existence of greater opportunities for the younger generation. Both born in the early 1980s, Meadow and Claire are nevertheless depicted as having their share of challenges, including being misunderstood by their mothers.

A photograph of Keith and David in bed that appears in *Better Living*, a couple of pages after Ruth's portrait, features his lines "Keith's got a lot of anger issues he inherited from his father and I've got a lot of doormat issues I inherited from Mom."[73] His "doormat" mother, however, was assertive in her instructions for David and Nate's babysitter as demonstrated in the 1975 letter found in *Better Living*: "Don't let them talk you into riding bikes in the driveway."[74] Ruth did not have a chance to read the French feminists at college, a desire she had that she shares with Claire in Season two.[75] Her mothering practices are at times problematic from feminist perspectives. Nevertheless, her struggle to care for and better understand her children, while also focusing on her own needs for a change, offers a fresh perspective on the challenges of mothering, especially while mourning. Ashley Sayeau asserts, "The few moments when Claire and Ruth actually connect are some of the most moving of the entire series."[76] The exchange between mother and daughter in the series finale as Claire leaves home and moves to New York captures the bittersweetness of the empty-nesting process. As Ruth hugs Claire, she says, "I pray you'll be filled with hope for as long as you possibly can," and Claire responds, "Thank you for everything and thank you for giving me life." Ruth tells her, "You gave me life," to which Claire exclaims, "Oh my God, I don't wanna go!"[77] All of the *SFU* characters deal with grief in distinct ways. Ruth holds court often in the kitchen through mothering. Whether feeding, scolding, or comforting them, her children and grandchildren are the lives that balance the death that surrounds her, marking the death of Nate as especially tragic. Many of us did not want to let go of the Fisher family and mourned the end of the show, but as the series tagline and soundtrack title remind us: "Everything ends."

The TV Dinner Party

Growing up, my siblings and I ate our share of TV dinners on nights when my mother was busy after a long day of teaching, research, and clinical practice. A native New Orleanian, on special occasions she would take the time to make classics such as crawfish étouffée. She learned to cook pot roast from my paternal grandmother, who has eleven children. She left it up to her mother to teach us to cook Belizean favorites such as shark empanadas, though I have yet to attempt these family recipes on my own. We did not have cable television, and I do not remember any stay-at-home role models from the programs we watched as a family such as *The A-Team*, *Magnum, P.I.*, or *Miami Vice*. I do remember that when we lived in Miami my mother was approached by a casting agent who offered her an appearance on *Miami Vice*. To our great disappointment, she declined since between us and her career she had her hands full. My mother is eligible to retire now, but she continues to work full-time as a professor and psychology clinic director. She looks forward to spending more time with her children and grandchildren after she retires. In the meantime, though she did not appear on *Miami Vice*, we still have opportunities to watch her on television when local news stories feature her as a psychology expert. My mother's path is very different from the paths taken by the characters Carmela Soprano and Ruth Fisher. I have yet to meet a television character who portrays the range of challenges my professor mother has faced for more than three decades in her attempt to balance mothering and an academic career. However, studying Carmela and Ruth reminds me of the ways in which I often take my mother for granted and fail to recognize the invisible labor of her mothering. Some of this "invisible" work is made visible in the narratives of *The Sopranos* and *Six Feet Under* and in the pages of *Entertaining* and *Better Living*, yet there are a number of instances in which it remains behind the scenes. In *Entertaining*, Carmela acknowledges the work of parenting in her explanation that hosting a graduation party for one's child is not only about honoring the graduate, but also oneself.[78] These characters also invite me to question how I frame the labor of mothering for my own children, and how to encourage dialogue about the televisual representations of parenting that they consume.

A home cooked meal by Carmela and Ruth would be a delicious experience. In terms of mothering, I imagine it could leave a bad aftertaste, because as entertaining as each can be, their parenting skills often leave much to be desired. It would also leave me hungry for even more complex contemporary televisual mother role models. Not perfect mothers, because motherhood is an imperfect role for anyone and in the quest for perfection in mothering, both mother and child often become lost. Watching season after season, episode after episode of Carmela and Ruth, the repetition of their domestic labor reminds me that a mother's work is never done, and too often it is not recognized. While it can be enjoyable to escape into the fictional worlds of these series, let us not forget the importance of seeking out oral histories from actual mothers, caretakers, and domestic laborers who do not make it to the screen. We have much to learn from their struggles, and it is not always useful to hide our own, though sharing them risks stigmatization in cultures, including the academy, that continue to undervalue mothers in and outside of the home. In her auto-ethnographic solo performance about being a mother and a tenure track professor, "Mamafesto! Why Superheroes Wear Capes," Deanna Shoemaker acknowledges that her performance "feels dangerous," explaining that "colleagues have quietly warned me to 'be careful about the tree I'm barking up,' to make sure this work isn't seen as my primary research so that I won't be marginalized or reduced to the 'mommy track.'"[79] We can continue to silence discourse about the "daily, mundane, invisible, unpaid labor" of mothers and other caretakers in academia and beyond, or we can embrace Shoemaker's perspective: "Academic careers have become oversized, and the expectations only seem to be going up. Doesn't this hurt the quality of life for ALL of us?"[80]

The Brooklyn Museum, home to Judy Chicago's controversial installation *The Dinner Party*, describes the work as "an important icon of 1970s feminist art" that "comprises a massive ceremonial banquet, arranged on a triangular table with a total of thirty-nine place settings, each commemorating an important woman from history."[81] Jane Gerhard explains that "despite its popularity *The Dinner Party* was met with considerable criticism from art professionals, who dismissed it as craft, and by feminists, who criticized it as essentialist and Eurocentric."[82] While we might learn from Chicago's mistakes, and create a more inclusive TV themed Dinner Party featuring diverse televisual mothers, television programs will certainly not solve all of the problems that contemporary mothers face, including those faced by mothers without the most basic resources. The representations of mothers on popular series such as *The Sopranos* and *Six Feet Under*, however, demonstrate that mothering in the Mafia or funeral home presents unique challenges from which we might learn more about motherhood in relation to entertaining, mourning, as well as a host of other issues. We must embrace companion books, such as *Entertaining* and *Better Living*, as important texts with potentially powerful roles in our processes of interpretation. The ways in which fans (including scholar-fans) consume series through them must receive greater critical consideration. The relationship between series' websites and companion books also calls for further study. This essay focused on lessons learned about stay-at-home motherhood via a reading of *The Sopranos* and *Six Feet Under* through the companion books. There is much more to learn from Carmela and Ruth, as well as from the other mothers in both series. The inspiration for *The Sopranos* was David Chase's own mother, who he explains had a lot in common with Tony Soprano's mother, Livia.[83] The representation of fathers in these series also invites further study. The fathers on *SFU*, for example, include one who continues to interact with his children after he dies, a widower with a young daughter, a queer interracial male couple who adopt two sons, and a Latino father with two sons. Elizabeth Paré and Heather Dillaway call for "those shaping the issue in the public realm to alter their conceptualization of motherhood, fatherhood, and paid work" and "for feminist and family scholars . . . to further document the realities of parenting and work and the continuum of identities and behaviors falling under each."[84] In responding to this call, it is important to also address the role that televisual representations play in shaping these conceptualizations and documentation practices.

Diana Davidson writes, "Contemporary motherhood contains more choices than motherhood in the early 1960s," the decade during which Ruth became a mother, "but it is still a difficult identity to negotiate on personal and political levels."[85] A recent Gallup analysis showed that "stay-at-home moms report more depression, sadness, anger," and that "low-income stay-at-home moms struggle the most."[86] This suggests that "for those who choose to stay home, more societal recognition of the difficult job stay-at-home mothers have raising children would perhaps help support them emotionally" and that "increasing employer-sponsored or other types of subsidized and low-cost child care may be a means to help create more choices for mothers," including those who stay home out of economic necessity rather than by choice.[87] Carmela became a mother in the 1980s and is more concerned with charger plates and comfort food than I will ever be, and for Ruth Fisher "motherhood is the loneliest thing in the world." Audience members will continue tuning into these mothers because we can learn from their successes and failures, strengths and weaknesses. Carmela and Ruth demonstrate limitations of the domestic environments that they occupy while also revealing that there is a lot more to their lives than cooking and cleaning, domestic labor that continues to be taken for granted in problematic ways. Perhaps with some practice, even those of us not raised to spend much time in the kitchen can find it empowering to master the bittersweet burnt sugar cake that comforted a pregnant, grieving Ruth or Carmela's infamous ricotta-pineapple pie.

Notes

1. Patricia Bradley, *Mass Media and the Shaping of American Feminism, 1963-1975* (Jackson, MS: University Press of Mississippi, 2003), 3.

2. Stacy Gillis and Joanne Hollows, eds., *Feminism, Domesticity and Popular Culture* (New York: Routledge, 2011), 1.

3. "Smith Voices," *Smith Alumnae Quarterly* 98, no. 4 (2012): 3.

4. Amy Allen, "'Mommy Wars' Redux: A False Conflict," *New York Times*, May 27, 2012, http://opinionator.blogs.nytimes.com/2012/05/27/the-mommy-wars-redux-a-false-conflict.

5. Elizabeth R. Paré and Heather E. Dillaway, "'Staying at Home' versus 'Working': A Call for Broader Conceptualizations of Parenthood and Paid Work," *Michigan Family Review* 10, no. 1 (2005): 66-87.

6. Allen Rucker, *Entertaining with the Sopranos: As Compiled by Carmela Soprano* (New York: Warner Books, 2006), hereafter referred to in the essay as *Entertaining*; Alan Ball and Alan Poul, eds., *Six Feet Under: Better Living Through Death* (New York: Pocket Books, 2003), hereafter referred to in the essay as *Better Living*.

7. David Lavery, "Read Any Good Television Lately? Television Companion Books and Quality TV," in *Quality TV: Contemporary American Television and Beyond*, ed. Janet McCabe and Kim Akass (London: I.B. Tauris, 2007), 229.

8. Lavery, "Read Any Good Television," 236. Lavery's essay "incorporates and expands upon an earlier review of *Buffy the Vampire Slayer* and *Sopranos* companion books in *Television Quarterly*, 2001: 89-92." The essay was presumably written before the publication of *Entertaining with the Sopranos*.

9. Janet McCabe and Kim Akass, "What has Carmela Ever Done for Feminism?: Carmela Soprano and the Post-Feminist Dilemma," in *Reading The Sopranos: Hit TV from HBO*, ed. David Lavery (London: I.B. Tauris, 2006), 39-55.

10. Janet McCabe and Kim Akass, eds., *Quality TV: Contemporary American Television and Beyond* (London: I.B. Tauris, 2007).

11. Sarah Cardwell, "Is Quality Television Any Good? Generic Distinctions, Evaluations and the Troubling Matter of Critical Judgment," in *Quality TV: Contemporary American Television and* Beyond, ed. Janet McCabe and Kim Akass (London: I.B. Tauris, 2007), 26.

12. Robin Nelson, "Quality TV Drama: Estimations and Influences Through Time and Space," in *Quality TV: Contemporary American Television and* Beyond, ed. Janet McCabe and Kim Akass (London: I.B. Tauris, 2007), 46.

13. Jane Feuer, "HBO and the Concept of Quality TV," in *Quality TV: Contemporary American Television and Beyond*, ed. Janet McCabe and Kim Akass (London: I.B. Tauris, 2007), 145.

14. Mark Lawson, "Mark Lawson Talks to David Chase," in *Quality TV: Contemporary American Television and Beyond*, ed. Janet McCabe and Kim Akass (London: I.B. Tauris, 2007), 218.

15. Gillis and Hollows, 8.

16. Rucker, *Entertaining*, 4.

17. Rucker, *Enertaining*, 42.

18. Rucker, *Entertaining*, 25.

19. Lisa Cassidy, "Is Carmela Soprano a Feminist?: Carmela's Care Ethics," in *The Sopranos and Philosophy: I Kill Therefore I Am*, ed. Richard Greene and Peter Vernezze (Chicago: Open Court, 2004), 97.

20. Cassidy, "Is Carmela Soprano a Feminisit?", 106.

21. "Sopranos Creator Takes on Angry Fans," *Entertainment Weekly*, October 17, 2007, http://www.ew.com/ew/article/0,,20152845_2,00.html.

22. McCabe and Akass, "What has Carmela Ever Done," 53.

23. McCabe and Akass, "What has Carmela Ever Done," 40.

24. Rucker, *Entertaining*, 4.

25. Rucker, *Entertaining*, 7.

26. Lynn Spigel, *Make Room for TV: Television and the Family Ideal in Postwar America* (Chicago: University of Chicago Press, 1992), 91.

27. Allen Rucker, *The Sopranos Family Cookbook: As Compiled by Artie Bucco* (New York: Warner Books, 2002), 55.

28. *The Sopranos*, "Whitecaps," directed by John Patterson, first broadcast December 8, 2002 by HBO.

29. Kristyn Gorton, "'Why I Love Carmela Soprano': Ambivalence, the Domestic and Televisual Therapy," *Feminism & Psychology* 19, no. 1 (2009): 130.

30. Rucker, *Entertaining*, 12, 93, 72; *The Sopranos*, "The Second Coming," directed by Timothy Van Patten, first broadcast May 20, 2007 by HBO.

31. Spigel, *Make Room*, 74.

32. Rucker, *Entertaining*, 199.

33. *The Sopranos*, "Amor Fou," directed by Timothy Van Patten, first broadcast May 13, 2001 by HBO.

34. *"The Sopranos*: Trivia," *Internet Movie Database*, 1990-2012, http://www.imdb.com/title/tt0141842/trivia (accessed September 17, 2012).

35. Gorton, "Why I Love Carmela Soprano," 129.

36. Cassidy, "Is Carmela Soprano a Feminist?," 97, 106.

37. Cassidy, "Is Carmela Soprano a Feminist?," 106.

38. McCabe and Akass, "What has Carmela Ever Done," 40-41.

39. McCabe and Akass, " What has Carmela Ever Done," 41.

40. Kim Akass and Janet McCabe, "Beyond the Bada Bing!: Negotiating Female Narrative Authority in *The Sopranos*," in *This Thing of Ours: Investigating The Sopranos*, ed. David Lavery (New York: Columbia University Press, 2002), 151.

41. Rucker, *Entertaining*, 2.

42. Cassidy, "Is Carmela Soprano a Feminist?," 97, 106.

43. Rucker, *Entertaining*, 199.

44. Alan Ball, "Introduction," in *Six Feet Under: Better Living Through Death*, ed. Alan Ball and Alan Poul (New York: Pocket Books, 2003), 5.

45. Ball, "Introduction," 5.

46. Ball and Poul, *Better Living*, 142-43; *Six Feet Under*, "The Foot," directed by John Patterson, first broadcast June 17, 2001 by HBO.

47. Ball and Poul, *Better Living*, back cover.

48. Lavery, "Read Any Good Television Lately?," 235.

49. Lavery, "Read Any Good Television Lately?," 234.

50. Ball, "Introduction," 5.

51. Tamar Katriel and Thomas Farrell, "Scrapbooks as Cultural Texts: An American Art of Memory," *Text & Performance Quarterly* 11, no. 1 (1991): 3.

52. Ball and Poul, *Better Living*, 33.

53. Ball and Poul, *Better Living*, 80.

54. Ball and Poul, *Better Living*, 166.

55. Kim Akass, "Mother Knows Best: Ruth and Representations of Mothering in *Six Feet Under*," in *Six Feet Under: TV to Die For*, ed. Kim Akass and Janet McCabe (London: I.B. Tauris, 2005), 117-18.

56. Akass, "Mother Knows Best," 118.

57. Ball and Poul, *Better Living*, 16.

58. Ashley Sayeau, "Americanitis: Self-help and the American Dream in *Six Feet Under*," in *Six Feet Under: TV to Die For*, ed. Kim Akass and Janet McCabe (London: I.B. Tauris, 2005), 98.

59. Janet McCabe, "'Like, Whatever': Claire, Female Identity, and Growing Up Dysfunctional," in *Six Feet Under: TV to Die For*, ed. Kim Akass and Janet McCabe (London: I.B. Tauris, 2005), 133.

60. *Six Feet Under*, "Everyone's Waiting," directed by Alan Ball, first broadcast August 21, 2005.

61. Ball and Poul, *Better Living*, 134-35.

62. Kristyn Gorton, "Domestic Desire: Older Women in *Six Feet Under* and *Brothers and Sisters*," in *Feminism, Domesticity and Popular Culture*, ed. Stacy Gillis and Joanne Hollows (New York: Routledge, 2011), 97.

63. *Six Feet Under*, "Pilot," directed by Alan Ball, first broadcast June 3, 2001 by HBO.

64. *Six Feet Under*, "Ecotone," directed by Daniel Minahan, first broadcast July 31, 2005 by HBO.

65. Rucker, *Entertaining*, 4.

66. Ball and Poul, *Better Living*, 22.

67. Ball and Poul, *Better Living*, 19.

68. *Six Feet Under*, "Pilot."

69. *Six Feet Under*, "Everyone's Waiting."

70. Akass, "Mother Knows Best," 110.

71. Akass, "Mother Knows Best," 111.

72. *Six Feet Under*, "Parallel Play," directed by Jeremy Podeswa, first broadcast June 27, 2004 by HBO.

73. Ball and Poul, *Better Living*, 169.

74. Ball and Poul, *Better Living*, 46.

75. *Six Feet Under*, "I'll Take You," directed by Michael Engler, first broadcast May 19, 2002 by HBO.

76. Sayeau, "Americanitis," 104.

77. *Six Feet Under*, "Everyone's Waiting."

78. Rucker, *Entertaining*, 28.

79. Deanna Shoemaker, "Mamafesto! Why Superheroes Wear Capes," *Text & Performance Quarterly* 32, no. 2 (April 2011): 194.

80. Shoemaker, "Mamafesto," 194.

81. "The Dinner Party by Judy Chicago," Brooklyn Museum, 2004-2011, http://www.brooklynmuseum.org/exhibitions/dinner_party (accessed September 17, 2012).

82. Jane Gerhard, "Judy Chicago and the Practice of 1970s Feminism," *Feminist Studies* 37, no. 3, (2011): 615.

83. Lawson, "Mark Lawson Talks to David Chase," 187-88.

84. Paré and Dillaway, "'Staying at Home,'" 82.

85. Diana Davidson, "'A Mother Like You': Pregnancy, the Maternal, and Nostalgia," in *Analyzing Mad Men: Critical Essays on the Television Series*, ed. Scott F. Stoddart (Jefferson, NC: McFarland and Co., Inc., 2011), 152.

86. Elizabeth Mendes, Lydia Saad, and Kyley McGeeney, "Stay-at-Home Moms Report More Depression, Sadness, Anger, But Low-Income Stay-at-Home Moms Struggle the Most," *Gallup*, May 18, 2012, http://www.gallup.com/poll/154685/stay-home-moms-report-depression-sadness-anger.aspx.

87. Mendes, Saad, and McGenney, "Stay-at-Home Moms Report."

Chapter Six

Mad Hatters:
The Bad Dads of AMC

David Staton

Whether we are donning a power tie or dressing down, looking sharp or looking the part, when we wear clothes, and even when we don't, we are communicating. Call it a fashion statement or non-verbal communication, largely we consciously craft a persona, a public image whereby our clothes do the talking. Often, these sartorial selections are laden with messages and shaped by context; sign and signified become malleable by design. Clothing's intent, representation and reception are not always easily decoded.[1]

Except when it's old hat.

In the 1951 short story, "Clothes Make the Man," Richard Matheson writes:

> "They used to come to him," he recalled, "all of them. There he'd sit in his office with his hat on his head, his shiny shoes on the desk. Charlie! they'd scream, give us an idea. He'd turn his hat once around (called it his thinking cap) and say Boys! cut it this way. And out of his lips would pour the damnedest ideas you ever heard. What a man!"[2]

Charlie's authority, cleverness and intelligence are embodied in his hat/"thinking cap." As the story (one of many such allegories sharing the same title) unfolds, Charlie loses his identity via his fixation on his attire. He is defined by his outerwear. In particular, he is defined by his hat—absent which he becomes inert—as it fully informs his inner self.

Charlie is all stylish sizzle and, as it turns out, no substance. Readers likely are not surprised to learn Charlie is an advertising man. While he sells ideas and ideals to people, his biggest commodity is his dressed up, über-charming self. His hat allows him to be cloaked in bravado and without it, or without the notion of it, he is not himself. Wrote Matheson: "'Things got bad after that,' he went on. 'Without a hat, Charlie couldn't think. Without shoes, he couldn't walk. Without gloves he couldn't move his fingers.'"[3]

Nearly sixty years removed from the fabulist fantasies of Matheson, TV viewers met a modern-day interpretation of Charlie. His name is Don Draper and he is the protagonist of cable television's critically acclaimed AMC channel program, *Mad Men*. He is an ad man, practicing his craft in New York of the 1960s. And, as with Matheson's creation, Draper's distinctive identity marker is his headwear; it speaks to his authority, to his confidence, to his manhood, his essence. But, absent the haberdashery—away from the workplace and his cohort and colleagues—his persona is altered. He is home and he is dad—a hatless head of household and a changed man.

Mad Men is joined on AMC by two other critical and popular successes—*Breaking Bad* and *The Walking Dead.* These shows also feature fathers as lead characters, Walter White and Rick Grimes, respectively, whose psychic apparatus[4] and public presentations are shaped by what they rest atop their heads. Grimes wears a traditional lawman's hat (he is/was a sheriff) and White sports a black porkpie. And, as with Charlie and Don Draper, they too have altered presences when in the face of absence (the hat). It is part and parcel of their makeup, their uniform to the world.

As this chapter will demonstrate, for this TV trio the power of the hat is so all encompassing, that no room exists for negotiation of its meaning. The power of the hat is transformative (clothes make the man) and that is beyond question—it is the authority of the male. This generally flies in the face of pop culture and sociological analysis of fashion, as well as semiotics, that suggest fashion—and its meanings—comes and goes (the fashion cycle) or that the production of meaning evolves from an ever-evolving culture. As Fred Davis writes in *Fashion, Culture and Identity,* there is high social variability in the signifier-signified relationship: "In the symbolic realm of dress and appearance, however, 'meanings' in a certain sense tend to be simultaneously more ambiguous and more differentiated than in other expressive realms. . . . Meanings are more ambiguous in that it is hard to get people to interpret the same clothing symbols in the same way; in semiotic terminology, the clothing signs signifier-signified is quite unstable."[5] And, while these theories are well reasoned and valid works by significant scholars, they don't neatly adequately address the AMC trio's dress.

For instance, Malcolm Barnard in *Fashion as Communication* scoffs at the notion that meaning of an item of apparel can be internal, "this is not a very sophisticated position to argue,"[6] or external, "there are numerous problems."[7] The characters in these TV dramas would likely sneer, convincingly, at such suggestion. For them, the hat sends an absolute message—authority—and the audience unequivocally knows that message: respect this authority. They likely would offer a similar askance glare at influential media critic John Fiske's notion that the meanings of pop culture items, including fashion, are open.[8]

The ideas of Roland Barthes, as put forth in *Rhetoric of the Image* and *Myth Today*,[9] which ascribe denotative and connotative properties to objects and representations of objects, might rate a slight tip of the hat from Don, Walt and Rick. A clothing item might vary in its form, but as far as what *their* hats connote, there's little room for negotiation. Stuart Hall's encoding and decoding philosophy, especially the cultural theorist's inclusion of the hegemonic code (preferred meaning), likely would hold similar appeal for this group.[10] These men are in charge and they'd prefer it stay that way. When they're not in charge—hatless—things (can and often do) go awry.

From a communications examined viewpoint, the metamorphosis that occurs when Don, Walt and Rick are behatted is best lensed through the eyes of the social semiotician Theo Van Leeuwen. In *Introducing Social Semiotics*,[11] he points to an inventory of rules governing semiotic regimes ("the ways in which the uses of semiotic resources are governed in specific contexts").[12] Van Leeuwen poses a few key questions by which those regimes are defined. They include: "How is control exercised and by whom? How is it justified? Whenever there are rules, the question 'why?' can arise 'Why must we do this?' Or: 'Why must we do this in this way?' . . . What happens when people do not follow the rule? What sanctions are attached to deviance?"[13]

Van Leeuwen, while still allowing for negotiated meanings, identifies categories or regimes of semiotic systems, which include, notably, personal authority. Personal authority is exercised by people in positions of power who see no need to justify their actions. "If we were to ask them why—'Why does this rule exist?' 'Why must I do this?'—the answer would be, 'Because I say so.' It is the rule of the 'dictate' and hence the dictator."[14]

Van Leeuwen establishes two semiotic regimes that act as corollary to personal authority: expertise and role models. In these systems, the rhetorical query, "Why do we have to do it this way?" would likely be met with the response, "Because XXX said so." In this case, XXX is an influential person or a person with expertise. For the purposes of this chapter, personal authority, expertise and role model are embodied by the hat wearers, Don, Walter and Rick. Or, as Neil Steinberg writes in *Hatless Jack*, "No matter what society you examine, in any era, anywhere in the world, ninety-nine times out of a hundred, the guy with the biggest, most expensive hat is boss."[15]

The aforementioned AMC programs (*Mad Men, Breaking Bad, The Walking Dead*) unfold in different eras, yet the headwear's intent—contrary to ephemeral traditional fashion dictates—remains constant, inviolable. *Mad Men,* which wrapped its fifth season in summer of 2012, began airing in 2007; its first season was set in 1960. Viewers met the dapper Don Draper, the creative head of Sterling Cooper, a Madison Avenue ad agency. With chiseled, movie star looks, he is crafty, confident, cocky and every bit a ladies' man. His business uniform almost always includes a short-brimmed fedora, and while he is quite polished at hat etiquette and well mannered with regard to general public decencies, his fidelity away from work is far less refined. Though married, he will fall into bed at the drop of a hat, and often does. And, as viewers discover early on, there is mystery surrounding Don's true identity, things he'd rather keep under his hat.

Walter White is the lead character in *Breaking Bad,* which unfolds in contemporary time—all visual and verbal cues suggest the action unfolds in present day—in the desert Southwest: Albuquerque, New Mexico, to be precise. The series, which debuted in January 2008, introduces viewers to Walter, a high school chemistry teacher who, in the first episode, receives a diagnosis of advanced lung cancer. As a desperate ploy to pay medical bills and leave his family a nest egg for financial stability, the teacher, employing his knowledge of chemical properties, begins to manufacture methamphetamine. It's complicated. As Walter's health and personal world spin wildly out of control, he reshapes, or builds, a separate identity as a drug dealer. In this world, he is the highly successful Heisenberg. Heisenberg's signature item of apparel is a black porkpie hat. When the mild-mannered Walter cloaks himself in the business uniform of Heisenberg, he is cold, calculating and capable of heinous acts.

The Walking Dead character Rick Grimes is a sheriff in a Georgia community, sometime in the near future. Time in this AMC drama, which debuted on Halloween in 2010, is a little difficult to pinpoint as the action takes place in a post-apocalyptic America inhabited by zombies. Rick is the leader of a group of survivors united by a singular focus to simply stay alive; the zombies are incessantly attacking, incessantly hungry and incessantly growing in numbers. Though he doesn't physically appear threatening—or overpowering— Rick is nonetheless accorded deference and respect because of the ubiquitous presence of his sheriff's hat. It gives him body, substance, command, authority.

There are others who wear head coverings in *The Walking Dead* but Rick is the only one to wear a proper hat. A definition might clarify this point; hats have brims that extend all the way around and generally have shaped crowns. Symbolically, this can be read as offering full protection or shelter to the wearer and serves as a signifier of authority, expertise, status. Two other characters, Glenn and Shane (Rick's nemesis), wear baseball caps. Glenn, and his cap, can be interpreted as youthful (he even wears it brim forward like a Pee Wee league baseballer), while Shane, Rick's former partner on the sheriff's force, sports an ominous ball cap, suggesting fracture from the group—it's emblazoned with a police logo. And Dale, the survivors' sage figure, sports a floppy, bucket hat; like Dale, it is well worn.

From the outset, Rick's hat is central to his essence. A Stetson Roper, its rich brown felt is set off by gold campaign cords and the seven-point star forming the King County Sheriff's badge. In the program's debut episode Rick wakes up in a hospital bed clad only in a clinical gown, recovering from gunshot injuries viewers learn he suffered in a shootout.[16] He is thoroughly disoriented and dazed. What he finds—a new world order that includes zombies—furthers his sense of dislocation. In short order, he escapes the hospital, is "greeted" by a young survivor with a shovel smack to the face who, once he regains consciousness, fills him in on what he's missed during his indeterminate period of convalescence. Rick's first order of business is to retrieve weapons and supplies from the sheriff's office—and his hat.

Considering the plight of humankind to which Rick has awoken, he fares quite well; fighting zombies, making plans, beginning his quest to reunite with his wife (Lori) and son (Carl). And, he soon does all of these things. But then, he loses the hat.

In a moment of questionable judgment that involves a strong likelihood of the loss of his stature in the survivor's community and, more importantly, jeopardizes lives, Rick decides to go back to the site of his loss—Atlanta— ostensibly to retrieve a cache of weapons. Really, this is a quest for something more. In Season one's fourth episode, "Vatos," survivor Glenn says to Rick, "Admit it, you only came back to Atlanta for the hat." "Don't tell anybody," Rick responds.[17]

Reunited with his Stetson Roper, Rick is restored, rejuvenated, and so is (the new) law and order. There is a moral authority, an imperative, to protect and serve when the hat is donned. There is, in a word, power, and Rick swells with it. He is a benevolent protector, justified in his decisions in this new world of good and evil, of black and white. In his son Carl's eyes, he is a hero, near mythic.

The Rick character personifies Van Leeuwen's semiotic regimes of role model. The survivors are followers, almost childlike, albeit, at times, sassy, questioning children. They do things at Rick's behest because he appears thoughtful, concerned and considerate, or parent-like. His responses appear reasoned, rational. Though his approach seems democratic, he has followers because what he says goes. His word and integrity are absolute, though the pesky Shane tries to dilute his authority. There are repercussions when his decisions are questioned or not followed. By profession, he is a lawman, after all, and has agency to carry out justice.

He is the hegemonic male, as explained by Rebecca Feasey in *Masculinity and Popular Televison*: "The hegemonic male is said to be a strong, successful, capable and authoritative man who derives his reputation from the workplace and his self esteem from the public sphere. . . . This model of masculinity is said to be the ideal image of the male against which all men are judged, tested and qualified."[18]

Rick, in fact, rarely leaves his role as a lawman, wearing his workplace identity—not on his sleeve, but on his head—and behaving accordingly. So, when his Stetson is removed, one might reasonably expect a transformation. Such expectations are realized in the program's second season, which debuted on AMC in October 2011.

As the season's story arc progresses, Carl suffers an accidental gunshot wound and his injuries are extensive. The band of survivors alights on a quaint farmhouse refuge where Carl is tended to. He gradually gains his strength, and halfway through the season's fourth episode, "Cherokee Rose,"[19] the boy awakens (a mirroring of his father's stirring in the series' debut episode).

In a tender father-son moment, Rick places his sheriff's hat on Carl.

Carl: Hey, I'm like you now. We've both been shot. Isn't that weird?
Rick: Yeah, I think your mother would rather hear we got the same eyes. So let's keep that between us. Since you're in the club now, you get to wear the hat. Didn't you know? We'll pad the rim tomorrow so it sits better.
Carl: Won't you miss it?
Rick: Maybe you'll let me borrow it from time to time.

As Carl drifts to sleep, Rick places his sheriff badges in a drawer. One he has removed from his hat, the other from his shirt. The camera lingers on the image of the twin stars, a dull gleam in the wardrobe drawer. And, like the stars of Gemini, Rick's persona is twinned.

By season's end, the authoritative lawman and what remains of his group are on the run. He has become untethered, lawless, without moral anchor or hat. Shane is dead by his hand: "I wanted him dead. I killed him," he tells his wife, Lori.[20] (When Lori and Shane thought Rick dead, they formed a survival pact and had an affair. She is now pregnant and the child may or may not be Shane's.) Absent of his father's attentions, Carl wanders recklessly from dangerous moment to treacherous encounters. In the same episode, any pretense Rick has accorded his group of equality is laid bare. "If you're staying, this isn't a democracy anymore," he says. It's half desperation—he is afraid the group is irreparably splintered following their dramatic and violent exit from the farmhouse—and full, unhinged threat. Though he loudly asserts his authority, it no longer seems apparent nor is visible.

Breaking Bad's Walter White is also a different person with a hat. The mildly geeky but affable high school teacher and devoted family man is a sympathetic figure, one viewers can root for. Not so when he transforms into his alter ego, Heisenberg, with the porkpie hat perched atop his head. This bit of dress-up escapism—though taken far too far—is initially understandable. Walt has terminal cancer; his wife, Skyler, is in the late stages of pregnancy; his son, Walt Jr., has cerebral palsy; and Walt is a vastly overqualified (he was part of a Nobel-nominated research team) middle-aged man who is making less than $50,000 a year. It's depressing business but, when he becomes Heisenberg, he is all business—drug business.

Heisenberg is, from the outset, Walt's antithesis: a violent man, devoid of emotion, who issues ultimatums. The alter ego's initial, explosive appearance, in which he blows apart a drug den, comes in Season one, episode six, "Crazy Handful of Nothing."[21] His signature hat is not present when he introduces himself to Tuco, the regional drug runner he wishes to impress. However, his visage is radically redefined. He is gaunt and, for the first time, completely bald, the after-effects of his chemotherapy treatments. Following the explosion, Walt/Heisenberg returns to his vehicle, his obscenely ugly Pontiac Aztek,[22] and grunts animal-like; his body vibrates orgiastically—he (Heisenberg) has won this face-off and done something Walt could never imagine.

At a followup meeting in the subsequent episode, "A No-Rough-Stuff-Type Deal,"[23] the black porkpie debuts. Walt/Heisenberg deftly puts it on, fingering it and spinning it like a showman before resting it atop his crown. His sidekick and literal partner in crime, Jesse, shoots him a look before slipping into a knit, watchman's cap and dark glasses. (As with *The Walking Dead,* there are other characters in this drama who wear head coverings—the hipster chullo is ubiquitous—but **no one** wears a hat like Heisenberg.)

Heisenberg's product, a particularly potent, blue-hued strain of the drug methamphetamine, becomes increasingly popular. And, too, Walt comes increasingly to revel in the persona of Heisenberg. As the drama has unfolded over the course of four seasons (the fifth began in the summer of 2012), Walt has slowly edged closer to embracing a full-time Heisenberg persona. In earlier appearances, Heisenberg seems almost bemused by his growing reputation and concomitant respect; it's an identity he's playing around with.

By the time a Heisenberg *narcorrido* (a Mexican folk ballad tribute to drug smugglers) is written—complete with a flashy music video featuring a Heisenberg lookalike[24]—Walt has full buy-in for this character he has created. And though he keeps the identity secret from his family, it is for them, he continually tells himself, that Heisenberg exists; he must provide for his family, family is everything. And nothing is off limits, including murder. People die at the hands of Heisenberg and at his behest. But Walt's insistent default refrain is "Everything I do, I do for family." Walt's convictions align with Van Leeuwen's further description of the semiotic regime of personal authority: "It may well be that the powerful person operates on the basis of principles rather than on the basis of whims, but those whose actions are being regulated have no way of knowing this," he writes.[25]

In Season five's debut episode, "Live Free or Die," there is an aural and visual echo of Van Leeuwen's written account of the sort of response someone so fully invested in their personal authority typically gives to one who questions that authority. When Mike, a menacing amalgamation of assassin-grandfather-mob guy-cop asks Walt/Heisenberg how he can be sure an intricate ploy he has implemented to cover up a crime has worked, the chilling response is, "Because I say so." In an ensuing scene, his weaselly lawyer is trying to abandon his client: "We're done when I say we're done," Walt/Heisenberg coldly tells him, his face inches from the counselor.[26] In both cases, Walt/Heisenberg receives no comment, no resistance.

The transformation from Walt to Heisenberg is symbolically completed when Walt ceases to hide the alter ego. He's become cocky and quite possibly, because of his inflated ego, careless. Or, in this schema of semiotic regime, he simply doesn't care—he is beyond question. In "Fifty-One" (a reference to Walt's birthday and chronologically one year removed from his cancer diagnosis), Walt and his son are at a mechanic's shop, retrieving the aforementioned Aztek, which has undergone some extensive repairs.[27]

When Walt opens the door to the Aztek, Heisenberg's dark porkpie is resting on the passenger seat. The camera—from Walt's vantage—lovingly caresses the hat, pulling back from it in a sensuous, slow motion glide, moving from soft focus object to something Walt sees clearly. In rapid succession, he sells the non-stylish, but extraordinarily reliable, Aztek to the mechanic for $50. "Dad, are you crazy?" Walt Jr. asks. By way of answer, his father virtually anoints himself with the hat, admiring his be-hatted visage in the rear view mirror. He replaces the Aztek with a sleek, black sedan for himself and a red sports coupe for Walt Jr. Father and son park the new rides in the driveway and, grinning maniacally at one another, rev their engines. Walt's impulse control, and seemingly the last vestiges of his former self, has evaporated. He is not crazy; he is Heisenberg.

Mad Men's Don Draper also takes on a new identity—that of Don Draper. The devilishly handsome Madison Avenue advertising executive was once just another grunt in an Army helmet in the Korean War; he was Dick Whitman, a bit of a nervous Nellie with no small amount of psychological baggage. When the opportunity arose—Dick accidentally started an explosive fire—he switched identities with his commanding officer, Lieutenant Donald Draper, who was killed, his body burned beyond recognition in the blaze.

From the series' first episode, "Smoke Gets in Your Eyes,"[28] Don uses the hat, typically a somber, gray fedora, to cloak himself in his businessman's identity. Rarely is he seen in the workplace and its environs (the endless smoke-and-martini business meals) without it and seldom is he seen in any recreation or family setting with it. There is, at this time, proper hat etiquette,[29] and Don follows these rules and the "Guy Code" with rigor. When the rules change or are violated, or the setting/context differs, the usually cool Don becomes out of sorts; psychologically, he becomes the damaged Dick Whitman: his mother was a prostitute who died during his childbirth, and his father was a dour and violent drunk.

Don's workplace charm, calculatedly detached demeanor, and hat are checked at the door when he returns from the hulabaloo of Manhattan to his Westchester County home. In an oft-repeated scene—so common it is as mundane as the lived experience—Don arrives home from work to find his children, Sally and Bobby, eating dinner while his wife, Betty, smokes and drinks hers. Don removes his hat and with it his cool objectivity; a chink in the armor is revealed, and confidence and competence, as father, as husband, are compromised.

In one of many revealing scenes that unfold at the informal dining room table, Bobby is playing with a toy robot during meal time.[30] In so doing, he spills a drink on his sister. "Don, do something!" Betty yells. In turn, Don picks up the robot and smashes it violently against the wall. "Is that what you wanted?" he jabs at Betty. As they take their dispute upstairs to their bedroom, it becomes violent; Betty strikes at Don and he pushes back.

In another tense homefront interaction,[31] Don looks on as Bobby and Gene, Betty's infirm father, open a box of war "trophies" Gene took during combat in WW I. One of these items is similar to a Prussian helmet and Bobby tries it on. Don, who as Dick Whitman wore an Army bucket, quickly tells his son to remove the hat. "War is bad, Bobby." "Maybe, but it makes a man of you," his father-in-law, Gene, responds. Don tries to discourage Gene, who is egging on the encounter. Then to Bobby he says, "There was a man in that hat. Bobby, it's a dead man's hat. Take it off!" Don is well familiar with wearing another's hat and it *has* made a man of him. That truth hits uncomfortably close.

Home is not the manageable space of the advertising agency. This is not the place where Don compiles neatly billable hours. These are not employees he can willfully dismiss nor abstract ideas he can corral. He is not girded in his businessman's uniform nor his assumed identity, and solutions are neither neat nor simple. People, especially little people, question his authority and raise questions in him he can't answer; questions that bring him back to Dick Whitman. "Did your daddy get mad?" asks Bobby. "We have to get you a new daddy," he concludes to a dumbstruck Don.[32] In another, Sally says to her father, "Tell me about the day I was born."[33] In these instances, the usually fearless and flawless Don—the idea man—is without gravity.

At work there is someone—and usually that someone is attractive and of the opposite sex—to assist in such matters. That someone organizes your day, screens or shields you from distraction. That someone fetches ice for cold drinks, orders meals in, services every manner of need. That someone takes your hat, gives it a delicate primp and hangs it up for you.

At the agency, Don is the golden child who, in the eyes of his peers, has it all. He is to be envied and emulated and, as such, he neatly fits Van Leeuwen's semiotic systems of expertise and role model. Not only is Don admired for his performance at work, he's well respected for his performance in bed. He's experienced and rewarded in both areas. For all the tumult in his personal life—the life without the hat—he is a principled man and that also accords him admiration and respect. Men buy him drinks; women grant him sexual favors.

When Don tries to bring the hat—and his personal authority and professionalism—to his home, he cannot bridge the gulf. In one telling scene,[34] fedora perched atop head, he sits alone in his apartment (he is now separated from Betty) at a typewriter trying to construct a break-up letter. There's a germ of an idea here for him to develop and deliver, just like an ad campaign. But, he can't. "Dear Allison," the letter begins. "I wanted you to know I'm very sorry. Right now my life." And there it ends; he is at a loss for words. He pulls the paper from the typewriter, crumples it and tosses off the fedora. The sense of dislocation—work at home, home at work—finds him neither here, nor there.

For Don, Walt and Rick, the hat is a shaping force, a tightly held marker of self identity visually presented to others. So closely are their identities aligned with the message of their respective hats, it governs their lives, successes and failures. If their identity is in any way fluid, it is only in the sense that they differentiate between work (hat on) and home (hat off, generally)—or try to.

Each of these men is successful in their respective professions, and to one degree or another they build things. Rick is building a new world (though it appears it won't be a democratic one); Walt/Heisenberg is building a drug empire; Don is building and rebuilding a top-notch advertising agency. Building relationships and a home life is another matter entirely. The absolute authority and identity offered by the hat, which accords warmth, security and protection to the center of thought, ideas and intelligence, afford no such shelter in matters governed by the heart.

On that front, the three men appear to have lost their moorings, (if not their souls or minds), their spouses and their offspring. Don has shared custody of his children and, for his lifestyle, they are more bother than blessing. Offering the kids food, money and TV viewing are Don's parental go tos. Walt has slipped so far into his Heisenberg persona that he is now watching the hyper-violent *Scarface* and reciting dialogue with his teen son and infant daughter.[35] He shares much more of a nurturing father-son bond with Jesse, his crime cohort. In one episode,[36] Walt tearfully and lovingly calls his son (Walt Jr.) Jesse. Rick, in giving Carl his hat, ceded parental authority and with his disregard for personal safety, he places Carl, his wife and his unborn child in the likely position of life without a father/husband.

And which—the heart or the hat—will win out? Or perhaps 'Who will win out?' is a better question. Writes the sociologist-come-cultural theorist Richard Sennett at the conclusion of his essay, "Street and Office: Two Sources of Identity," "my argument therefore comes down to this: you can do without authority in your sense of place, you cannot do without it in your sense of work."[37]

Most of us would likely take exception to this assertion. Don, Walt and Rick would likely agree. But they should know, at the close of Matheson's "Clothes Make the Man," Charlie lost the girl and everything else: "They tell me Charlie is getting weaker. Still in the hospital. Sits there on his bed with his grey hat sagging over his ears mumbling to himself. Can't talk, even with his hat on."[38]

Notes

1. As Malcom Barnard notes in *Fashion as Communication*, 2nd ed. (London and New York: Routledge, 2002), 32, in discussing Saussurean structuralism "it will hardly be surprising if different readers from different cultural backgrounds produce different meanings or readings of texts. Nor will those different readings be seen as evidence of communicative failure; they are only to be expected on the semiotic model."

2. Richard Matheson, "Clothes Make the Man," *Worlds Beyond* 1, no. 3 (February 1951): 84.

3. Matheson, "Clothes," 86.

4. Sigmund Freud, in *The Ego and the Id*, trans. Joan Riviere (London: Hogarth Press and Institute of Psycho-analysis, 1927), held that psychological makeup is a construct of relational parts called the id, ego and super ego. Additionally, in *Dream Psychology* (New York: MacMillan, 1900), Freud contends the hat is a stand-in for male genitals.

5. Fred Davis, *Fashion, Culture and Identity* (Chicago: University of Chicago Press, 1992), 8-9.

6. Barnard, *Fashion as Communication*, 79.

7. Barnard, *Fashion as Communication*, 80.

8. Fiske advances his ideas of open, or polysemic, readings in a number of publications, including *Television Culture* (London: Methuen, 1987) and *Reading the Popular*, 2nd ed. (New York: Routledge, 2011).

9. Roland Barthes, *Image-Music-Text* (New York: Noonday Press, 1977) 32; Roland Barthes, *Mythologies* (New York: Farrar, Straus and Giroux, 1972), 109.

10. Stuart Hall, *Representation: Cultural Representations and Signifying Practices* (London, Thousand Oaks, New Delhi: Sage and Open University, 1997), 166-67.

11. Theo Van Leeuwen, *Introducing Social Semiotics* (London and New York: Routledge, 2005).

12. Van Leeuwen, *Introducing*, 285.

13. Van Leeuwen, *Introducing*, 53.

14. Van Leeuwen, *Introducing*, 53.

15. Neil Steinberg, *Hatless Jack; The President, the Fedora, and the History of an American Style* (New York: Plume, 2004), XVI.

16. *The Walking Dead*, "Days Gone By," directed by Frank Darabont, first broadcast October 31, 2010 by AMC.

17. *The Walking Dead*, "Vatos," directed by Johan Renck, first broadcast November 21, 2010 by AMC.

18. Rebecca Feasey, *Masculinity and Popular Television* (Great Britain: Edinburgh Press, 2008), 2-3.

19. *The Walking Dead*, "Cherokee Rose," direected by Bill Gierhart, first broadcast November 6, 2011 by AMC.

20. *The Walking* Dead, "Beside the Dying Fire," directed by Ernest Dickerson, first broadcast March 18, 2012 by AMC.

21. *Breaking Bad*, "Crazy Handful of Nothing," directed by Bronwen Hughes, first broadcast March 2, 2008 by AMC.

22. In 2007, *Time* magazine named the Aztek one of the worst cars of all time; the following year the *Daily Telegraph* dubbed it number one in a poll of the "100 Ugliest Cars of All Time."

23. *Breaking Bad*, "A No-Rough-Stuff-Type Deal," directed by Tim Hunter, first broadcast March 9, 2008 by AMC.

24. *Breaking Bad*, "Negro y Azul," directed by Félix Enríquez Alcalá, first broadcast April 19, 2009 by AMC.

25. Van Leeuwen, *Introducing*, 54.

26. *Breaking Bad*, "Live Free or Die," directed by Michael Slovis, first broadcast July 15, 2012 by AMC.

27. *Breaking Bad*, "Fifty-One," directed by Rian Johnson, first broadcast August 5, 2012 by AMC.

28. *Mad Men*, "Smoke Gets in Your Eyes," directed by Alan Taylor, first broadcast July 19, 2007 by AMC.

29. *Mad Men*, "For Those Who Think Young," directed by Tim Hunter, first broadcast July 27, 2008 by AMC. In Season two's debut episode, two brash young men in overcoats and hats share an elevator with Don. They are carrying on a vulgar conversation about a particular sexual exploit, and an older woman joins them, entering the lift on another floor. As the conversation continues, and the woman becomes visibly uncomfortable, Don boils over. "Take your hat off!" he grittily commands the men.

When they don't, Don forcefully removes one of their hats and shoves it in the gape-faced man's hands.

30. *Mad Men*, "Three Sundays," directed by Tim Hunter, first broadcast August 17, 2008 by AMC.

31. *Mad Men*, "The Arrangements," directed by Michael Uppendahl, first broadcast September 6, 2009 by AMC.

32. *Mad Men*, "Three Sundays."

33. *Mad Men*, "Out of Town," directed by Phil Abraham, first broadcast August 16, 2009 by AMC.

34. *Mad Men*, "The Rejected," directed by John Slattery, first broadcast August 15, 2010.

35. *Breaking Bad*, "Fifty-One."

36. *Breaking Bad*, "Salud," directed by Michelle MacLaren, first broadcast September 18, 2011 by AMC.

37. Richard Sennett, "Street and Office: Two Sources of Identity," in *On the Edge: Living with Global Capitalism*, ed. Will Hutton and Anthony Giddens (London: Jonathan Cape, 2000), 175-190.

38. Matheson, "Clothes," 87.

Part Three:

Family Ties

Chapter Seven

Family Communication and Television: Viewing, Identification, and Evaluation of Televised Family Communication Models

Ellen E. Stiffler, Lynne M. Webb, and Amy C. Duvall

Viewers expect televised families to represent the changing lifestyles and values in our culture, and such a match between families on television and actual families may facilitate realistic programs to act as socializing agents for both parents and children.[1] However, "television has been and remains clearly out of sync with the structural characteristics of real world families," contend James Robinson and Thomas Skill.[2] Television exposes viewers to specific socially constructed views of reality and cultivates ideas about family life.[3] Furthermore, heavy viewers of television are more likely to accept the televised families as typical models of family interaction in the real world.[4] Perceived realism, heavy exposure to television, and limited real-world experience can lead to altered perceptions of family events in the real world.[5]

Given these findings, a next logical step in the research on television and family communication is to explore the relationships between viewers' family communication patterns, television viewing patterns, identification with a favorite family television character, and the evaluation of the television character's family communication efficacy. To examine this topic, we undertook a study about family communication environment, media portrayals of families on TV, social learning theory, cultivation theory, and role modeling.

Review of Literature

Ritchie and Fitzpatrick defined family communication environment (FCE) as "a set of norms governing the tradeoff between informational and relational objectives of communication."[6] The FCE can influence both the amount of time spent with the media and the types of content preferred.[7] The family communication patterns (FCP) typology, based on the parents' conversation and conformity orientation,[8] is consistent with the notion that a family's communication style can influence how people use and interpret the media.[9] The current study investigated how FCE influences the amount of time spent with television, viewers' identification with favorite television characters, and the evaluation of the characters' family communication efficacy.

McLeod and Chaffee[10] developed the concept of FCP to describe the role of the family environment as an influence in children's media use. Parents and children mutually construct the FCE;[11] social behaviors learned in this environment influence children's' attitudes and behaviors in many ways.[12] Ritchie[13] revised McLeod and Chaffee's original instrument[14] and renamed the two dimensions: conversation orientation and conformity orientation. Conversation-orientation (i.e., concept orientation) assesses the extent to which parents encourage children to develop and express their opinions and ideas. Conformity orientation (i.e., socio-orientation) assesses the extent to which parents encourage children to pursue relational objectives through acceptance of parental attitudes, values, and beliefs.

Previous research has employed the FCP and revised family communication patterns (RFCP) instrument to examine media habits and uses,[15] such as modeling social behavior of characters and problem solving communication witnessed on TV.[16] Koerner and Fitzpatrick maintained that a family's communication serves as a cognitive processing template that influences both what content viewers employ to make interpretations and how they interpret that content.[17] Viewers employ their FCE to make sense of what they see on TV by utilizing their own family as a comparison group when interpreting TV episodes.[18]

Across a diverse group of multiple studies, researchers agreed that family portrayals on TV may serve as a basis for models in understanding family communication.[19] Family communication researchers have moved beyond a concern for the representation of a traditional, positive model of families to address issues such as misrepresented family configurations, unhealthy sibling relationships, and work-family stresses. However, scholars remain concerned about misrepresentations: Skill and Robinson concluded that the families on television, between the 1950s and 1990s, did not proportionally represent the American family configurations described by the U.S. Census data.[20] For example, Skill and Robinson concluded that two-parent families were consistently underrepresented on TV shows; further, single-parent families were overwhelmingly portrayed as headed by widows or widowers—a portrayal inconsistent with census data. Heintz-Knowles asserted that television's representation of work and family as completely separate entities may be sending misleading messages to viewers.[21] While other concerns could be raised, the issues listed above serve as examples of misrepresentations that viewers may see on TV shows where families are prominently featured, hereafter referred to as family TV programs. The current study continues this line of research by investigating viewers' perceptions of the family communication behaviors portrayed in family TV programs.

Theoretical Background

Our study is predicated on the notion that viewers may learn social behaviors and roles by observing television. This assumption is consistent with both social learning theory and cultivation theory. Social learning theory explains that people, especially children, can learn vicariously through the observation of both real-life and mediated models.[22] Social learning is a commonly embraced theoretical perspective to explain attitudes about family life.[23] The television provides behavioral models that viewers may perceive as "normal" or "ideal" within families; the repetitive presence of these images increases the likelihood that they will be learned.[24] For this reason, it is appropriate to study viewers' favorite television programs, as they are likely viewed on a recurring basis.

Cultivation theory purports that experiences viewers observe on television shape their expectations for real-life experiences.[25] The more time people spend watching television, the more likely they perceive the world around them in terms of televised images, values, portrayals, and ideologies.[26] Television functions as a major socializing agent by exposing viewers to recurrent images and representations over long periods of time.[27] Heavy viewers of television programming are more likely to conceptualize the world in ways that closely resemble televised images than more objective measures of social reality.[28]

Television not only reflects society but also provides us with collective models of how families behave.[29] It serves as the most common and consistent learning environment for our nation and much of the world.[30] Swan noted that reports released by the mid-1980s found that television had become a major agent of socialization for American children.[31] The National Institute of Mental Health concluded that television viewing had important influences on viewers' conceptions of social reality.[32] Researchers acknowledge a need to examine the impact of media on the family, specifically to what extent viewers use TV portrayals of family life in their own daily routines.[33]

Variables and Relationships

Following a social learning perspective, modeling of observed behavior is most likely to occur when positive, desirable family models are present (i.e., role models). A role model is "someone who demonstrates the appropriate behavior for a specific role or relationship with another person."[34] Role models can demonstrate both positive and negative behaviors that may be observed, learned, and even modeled.

Mass media figures can serve as role models.[35] Television characters are distinct as role models in that they have the potential to reach mass audiences and serve as role models for large numbers of people. Weber suggested "Role Model Television" as a means of influencing children in a positive way by presenting realistic, positive context for both children and parents.[36] Family TV programming has been a staple on American television networks for many years; hence, it is reasonable to conclude that characters on family programs may serve as role models of family communication behaviors.

Although FCE may influence viewers' choices and perceptions of family communication portrayed on television, few researchers have examined "the influence of a child's actual family models on the impact of television's stereotypic portrayals."[37] Thus, we offer an original model (displayed in Figure 7.1) depicting FCE's influence on television viewing patterns (heavy/light), identification with television characters, and viewers' evaluations of their favorite characters' communication efficacy. The model depicts seven relationships among four distinct variables.

Family communication environment refers to individuals' perceptions of communication and control within the family. Ritchie's family communication dimensions, conversation and conformity orientation, were employed to assess FCE.[38] Previous research ties FCE to viewers' responses to the mass media. In brief, a family's style of communication can influence the extent and type of effects television has on viewers.

Viewing patterns refers to the average number of hours people spend watching television. Given the many research findings related to viewing patterns,[39] it was appropriate to assess its influence on FCE and evaluations of characters' communication efficacy. Please note that the association between TV viewing patterns and FCE was the only previously tested relationship examined in our study.

Identification is the viewer sharing the television character's perspective and vicariously participating in the character's experiences when viewing.[40] Identification with television characters, hereafter called simply identity, is an important mediating factor in the media effects process, including the interpretation of media content and learning that comes from exposure.[41] One primary factor in identification between observer and model is perceived similarity.[42] Research has documented the importance of identification in mediating television's effect on viewers, especially gender identification.[43] Therefore, we examined identification as a mediating variable between the FCE and evaluations of characters' family communication efficacy.

Figure 7.1: Model of variables and relationships

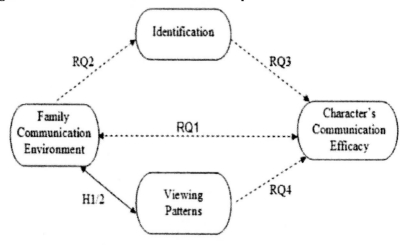

Note: the dashed lines indicate original research questions and relationships. The solid lines represent hypotheses and relationships being retested.

Character's communication efficacy refers to the extent to which viewers rate their favorite character as enacting effective family communication behaviors. Individuals learn how to communicate and how to perceive communication in the family.[44] However, media research documents that parents and children believe television images represent what is "normal," "right," and "acceptable behavior" within families.[45] Viewers may rely heavily on communication strategies they see portrayed on television, specifically those involving conflict.[46] Both home and media can act as powerful influences on socialization, especially for developing adults.[47] Modeling of observed behavior is most likely to occur when desirable family models are present.[48] However, viewers may seek effective family communication models in the media when they perceive a positive model is absent from their own family communication environment. Therefore, we examined individuals' evaluations of their favorite television character's family communication efficacy in relation to their FCE to discover if mutual influence existed. To this end, we posed the following research questions:

Research Question 1: What is the relationship, if any, between viewers' family communication environments (in the family of origin) and their evaluation of a favorite television character's family communication efficacy?

Research Question 2: What is the relationship, if any, between viewers' family communication environment (in the family of origin) and identification with a favorite character on television?

Research Question 3: What is the relationship, if any, between viewers' identification with a favorite television character and the evaluation of the characters' family communication efficacy?

Research Question 4: What is the relationship, if any, between television viewing patterns (heavy versus light viewers) and their evaluations of favorite television characters' family communication efficacy?

The FCE may help people interpret televised content, but also serve as predictors of the amount of time people spend with television. Conformity orientation is positively related to total television viewing, and high conformity individuals preferred programs that express conformity-oriented values.[49] As family communication patterns correlate with time spent with television, it is important to consider some of the research that documents a distinct effect for heavy viewers of television.

Previous researchers reported a positive relationship between television viewing and holding the opinion that being single is a calamity, having a family is admirable, and most families are large in number.[50] Additional research documented that attitudes and behaviors portrayed frequently on television were positively correlated with television viewing frequency, including the prevalence of divorce[51] and interpersonal mistrust.[52] Based on these previous findings, we formulated the following hypotheses:

Hypothesis 1: A conformity-oriented family communication environment is positively related to a heavy television viewing pattern.

Hypothesis 2: A conversation-oriented family communication environment is negatively related to heavy viewing patterns.

Methodology

Participants

The convenience sample consisted of 336 undergraduate students enrolled in the freshman-level communication course at a large, public university in the southeastern United States. Participants (Ps) ranged in age from seventeen to forty-nine years (M=19). The sample included 61 percent female and 39 percent male Ps. Most Ps self-reported as Caucasian-Americans (88.7 percent), although the sample included African-Americans (5.4 percent), Asian-Americans (3.0 percent), Native-Americans (2.4 percent), and Latino-Americans (1.8 percent). Nearly 90 percent of the Ps described themselves as full-time students; only 3.3 percent reported financial responsibility for children.

Instruments

Family communication environment. The revised family communication patterns (RFCP) instrument[53] assessed perceived parental conversation orientation and perceived parental conformity orientation via five-point Likert scales across twenty-six items. We conducted a principal axis factor analysis using Varimax rotation that revealed the two expected dimensions of family communication: conversation and conformity orientations—factors consistent with past research using RFCP and FCP with the exception that two of the items did not load strongly on either dimension and thus were omitted from future analyses. Our Chronbach alpha of 0.93 for conversation orientation and 0.84 for conformity orientation compared favorably with previous research reporting Chronbach alpha scores ranging from 0.76 to 0.92.[54]

The frequency distribution of both FCP dimensions revealed that the data clustered around the mean. Therefore, unlike the typical median split, we grouped the sample by dividing the standard deviation by two and then adding and subtracting that number from the mean to ensure a sufficient number of Ps in each group for meaningful interpretation of subsequent analyses. Consequently, the 106 P scores at or below 43.31 were considered low conversation, and the 108 P scores of 54.18 and higher were considered high conversation. The 122 Ps falling in the middle of the distribution with an "average" score were eliminated from further analyses. We employed the same procedure to categorize Ps into high or low conformity groups. The 107 Ps with a score of 22.79 and lower were considered low conformity; the 100 Ps with a score of 29.49 and higher were considered high conformity. The number of Ps dropped from the conformity dimension was 129. Ps' scores were categorized into the appropriate family type: laissez-faire, protective, pluralistic and consensual.

Viewing patterns. We employed Shrum, Wyer, and O'Guinn's procedures to determine the amount of time they spend with television during an average week.[55] We asked Ps to indicate the number of hours of television they watched during each of four time periods (6 a.m.-noon, noon-6 p.m., 6 p.m.-midnight, and midnight-6 a.m.) for both an average weekday (Monday–Friday) and weekend day (Saturday–Sunday). The questionnaires were silent on the issue of whether the television programs were watched online or in front of a traditional television set; Ps were free to include any kind of viewing they elected to include in the measure. We multiplied the weekday response by five and the weekend response by two and added these products to create the total-TV-viewing-hours-per-week measure. Dividing the total-TV-viewing-hours-per-week by seven created the variable, average TV viewing hours per day. Finally, dividing the average TV viewing hours per day by four gave an appropriate score for a six-hour time period; we used this score to classify Ps into high or low viewing categories. We created the groups splitting the scores into three segments of approximately 30 percent each, which provided a sufficient number of Ps in the high and low groups for meaningful interpretation of subsequent analyses. We devised the three groups by halving the standard deviation (1.02 / 2 = 0.51) and subtracting or adding that amount to the mean. Thus, we considered the 117 Ps with a score of 2.35 or lower as light viewers and the 97 Ps with scores of 3.37 and above as heavy viewers. The 122 Ps with mid-range scores were not included in subsequent analyses involving the variable "viewing patterns."

Identification. Eyal's measure of identification with media characters scale[56] assessed viewers' identification with their favorite television character from a family-based program. Ps' responses to the seventeen items ranged from strongly disagree (1) to strongly agree (5). To examine the structure and reliability of the measure, we performed a principal axis factor analysis with Varimax rotation. Two factors emerged in the analysis analogous to Eyal's findings: absorption/self-awareness and empathy/perspective taking. We dropped two items that did not meet the minimum loading requirement (0.50 or above and were separated by at least a level of 0.30 from other factors). Thus, the identification measure used in this study consisted of ten items (five items for absorption/self-awareness and five items for empathy/perspective taking). Although Eyal reported a Chronbach alpha of 0.88 for the overall measure,[57] we assessed the reliability of the two identification factors individuals; the analyses yielded a Chronbach alpha of 0.86 for absorption/self-awareness and 0.93 for empathy/perspective taking. Ps' responses were summed and averaged to indicate viewers' level of identification.

Character's communication efficacy. Caughlin's family communication standards[58] measured Ps' perceptions of effective communication behaviors in their favorite character's family. Caughlin's forty-one items factored into ten family communication standard categories associated with family satisfaction: openness, maintaining structural stability, expression of affection, emotional/instrumental support, mind reading, politeness, discipline, humor/sarcasm, regular routine interaction and avoidance. The stem used for items in the scale was "My character . . ." The Ps responded to the forty-one items on five-point Likert scales ranging from strongly disagree (1) to strongly agree (5).

We subjected the forty-one items to a principal axis factor analysis with Varimax rotation, as this was the first time Caughlin's scale was used with television characters. Five items did not meet the minimum loading requirements of 0.50 with a clear separation between factors (0.30 or more). Nonetheless, analyses with our data produced the same ten factors. Caughlin reported Chronbach alpha scores for measures of family communication standards ranging from 0.74 to 0.95.[59] We calculated Chronbach's alpha scores of 0.87 for openness, 0.92 for expression of affection, 0.86 for mind reading, 0.87 for support, 0.86 for politeness, 0.80 for discipline, and 0.83 for humor.

Procedure

The survey webpage opened with an explanation of the research project. After the Ps indicated agreement to the procedures, a short demographic questionnaire appeared, followed by a series of questions about their favorite family TV show and favorite character in that show. The remaining three instruments (i.e., RFCP, the television viewing instrument, identification measure) appeared in counter-balanced orders. After the measures, Ps were debriefed, thanked for their participation, and offered the opportunity to provide identifying information to award extra credit. A pretest of the instruments and procedures with a convenience sample of ninety-two undergraduate students resulted in minor modifications to the questionnaires.

Results

Preliminary Analyses

Given that television programs are designed to appeal to narrow population segments,[60] any study of characters on a genre of television programs would want to examine the influence of viewer demographics on interpretations of such programming. Therefore, we conducted a series of independent t-tests to assess potential differences between Ps with diverse demographic characteristics (i.e., age, sex, ethnicity, financial obligation for children, work status and primary guardian for family-of-origin) across the variables on interest. The analyses revealed multiple significant differences by sex. Therefore, we divided the sample by sex for most subsequent analyses. A parallel set of t-tests revealed significant differences by ethnicity in conformity orientation and absorption/self-awareness. However, the size of the "all other" group (N=49), when considered independently from "Caucasians" and further divided by sex, was too small for most statistical analyses. Consequently, all subsequent analyses related to conformity orientation or absorption/self-awareness included only Caucasian Ps (N=286).

Additionally, the analyses revealed significant differences for family-of-origin household type groups (two-parent families versus all other) and for work status groups (full-time students versus all other) across discipline and interaction time. Thus, we divided the sample into "two-parent household" and "all other" for further analyses involving discipline, and we divided the sample by "full-time students" and "all other" for further analyses concerning interaction time.

Next, we examined the frequency distribution for each variable of interest to assess normalcy of the distributions. The variables of openness, humor, and support failed to display normalcy. We conducted nonparametric analyses with these variables (i.e., Spearman's rho analyses). For subsequent analyses with all other variables, we conducted parametric analyses to test the queried relationships and where appropriate to discover the type of association that best described each relationship (i.e., linear, quadratic, cubic, and/or exponential).

Primary Analyses

Research Question 1 queried the relationship between FCE and the evaluation of a favorite character's communication efficacy. A series of curvilinear analyses for male Ps revealed no significant findings. However, analyses revealed significant correlations for females concerning conversation orientation and three factors of evaluation of a favorite character's family communication efficacy. As female Ps' conversation scores moved toward the high or low end of the scale, their evaluations of a favorite character's family communication involving mind reading ($F_{quadratic}$=6.62, $p \leq 0.001$) and meeting regularly with family members ($F_{quadratic}$=4.06, $p \leq 0.01$) were more favorable. Conversely, as the female Ps' conversation scores increased, their evaluations of a favorite character's avoidance of personal topics with family members were less favorable ($F_{exponential}$=4.72, $p \leq 0.005$).

To increase power, the nonparametric correlations were computed for the total sample (males plus females). The Spearman's rho calculations yielded evidence of a significant linear relationship between (a) conversation orientation with openness (p=0.14, p^2=0.02, p<0.009) as well as (b) conversation orientation with emotional and instrumental support (p=0.28, p^2=0.08, p<0.000). No other significant relationships were found for conversation orientation and efficacy evaluations.

We only included data from Caucasian Ps in the multiple curvilinear analyses concerning conformity orientation and the evaluation of a favorite character's family communication efficacy. Again, analyses with male Ps yielded no significant results. For female Ps, the analyses revealed significant relationships between conformity orientation and four factors of characters' communicative efficacy: avoidance of personal topics ($F_{linear}=6.65$, $p \leq 0.01$), mind reading ($F_{quadratic}=4.67$, $p \leq 0.01$), avoidance of hurtful topics ($F_{linear}=4.46$, $p \leq 0.05$), and politeness ($F_{quadratic}=3.08$, $p \leq 0.05$). These findings suggested that as Ps' conformity orientation scores moved to opposite ends of the spectrum, their efficacy evaluations involving empathy and perspective taking, mind reading and politeness became more favorable. As expected, evaluations of a character's avoidance of both personal and hurtful topics became more favorable as conformity orientation scores increased.

Research Question 2. Multiple curvilinear analyses assessed the relationship between FCE and identification with a favorite television character. The analyses revealed significant relationships for both males and females: as female Ps' conversation orientation increased, their ability to identify with a favorite character's absorption/self-awareness increased ($F_{linear}=6.77$, $p \leq 0.01$). Conversely, as males' conformity orientation increased, their identification with characters' absorption/self-awareness increased ($F_{linear}=7.54$, $p \leq 0.01$). The analyses revealed no significance relationships between FCE and a character's empathy/perspective taking.

Research Question 3. A series of curvilinear analyses assessed associations between identification with a favorite character and the evaluation of the character's family communication efficacy. We divided Ps into two groups based on household type (i.e., two-parent household vs. all other) for analyses involving empathy/perspective taking and discipline. We also divided Ps into two groups based on work status (i.e., full-time student vs. all other) for analyses involving empathy/perspective taking and interaction time. Virtually all analyses resulted in significant relationships, indicating that Ps' identification with a favorite television character was associated with evaluations of that character's family communication behaviors.

Research Question 4. A series of independent-samples *t*-tests tested for differences between high versus low viewers' evaluations of favorite television characters' family communication efficacy. Only one significant result emerged: high versus low viewing females differed in their evaluation of favorite characters' communication efficacy on the dimension of discipline.

Hypothesis 1: T-tests tested for differences in the *conformity* scores of high versus low viewers. The analyses yielded non-significant results ($t_{male}=-0.36$, $p=0.72$; $t_{female}=-1.72$, $p=0.09$).

Hypothesis 2: T-tests tested for differences in the *conversation* scores of high versus low viewers. The analyses yielded non-significant results (t_{male}=1.24, p=0.22; t_{female}=0.17, p=0.87).

Discussion

Based on the above described results, we revised the original model, creating two distinct models displaying the confirmed relationships, one for male and one for female Ps (see Figures 7.2 and 7.3). These results provide five insights into how viewers perceive the family communication behaviors of potential role models in TV programs.

1. In our study, high versus low viewing patterns were not directly related to how viewers evaluated potential role models viewed on TV, nor to FCE or identification. In our study, communication efficacy evaluations were linked with Ps' family communication backgrounds and/or identification with the character rather than directly with amount of viewing. Our finding that amount of television use is unrelated to FCE is inconsistent with previous research.[61] This inconsistency may be attributed to our unusually rigorous definitions of high versus low television viewing patterns versus the typical median split to define groups. Given that our results represent a more rigorous test for differences between high and low viewers, perhaps our results more accurately represent reality. Further, many past studies with contradictory results were published more than twenty years ago. Perhaps the current generation of young adults employs somewhat different viewing patterns that vary with conformity scores.

2. Our Ps' FCE scores were directly associated with identity with potential televised role models; however, the specific patterns of association differed for male versus female Ps: as males' *conformity* orientation scores increased, their identification with characters' absorption/self-awareness also increased. Conversely, as females' *conversation* orientation scores increased, their identification with media characters' absorption/self-awareness increased. Our results are consistent with past research that proposes sex as a basic motivator for content choice as adolescents seek models with which they can identify.[62]

3. In our findings, for female Ps only, FCE also was directly related to evaluations of televised role models. This relationship seems reasonable given past research suggesting that families not only provide instruction in how to approach the world but also specifically predict social uses of media.[63] Krcmar advocated family communication as a moderator between viewing and interpretation of television content.[64]

Figure 7.2: Revised model of confirmed relationships for male participants.

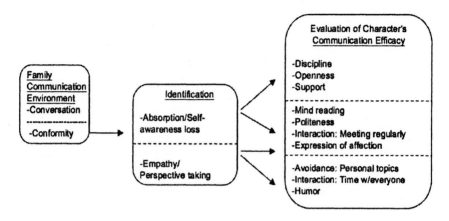

Figure 7.3: Revised model of confirmed relationships for female participants.

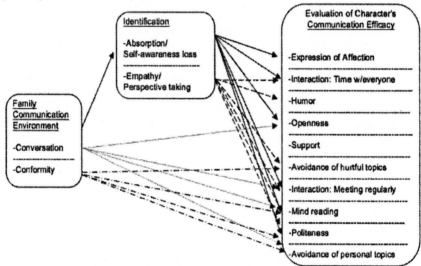

Note: The variety of solid and dashed lines used in this model are used only to identify the different variables: they do not indicate varying types of relationships.

Barbato, Graham, and Perse reported a direct link between individuals' conversation—or conformity-orientation and their motives for other communication.[65] Our analyses revealed a significant relationship only among female Ps—a finding also in line with past research documenting differences in the ways males versus females watch and interpret television content.[66]

4. In our study, identity with a television character was associated with evaluations of that character's family communication efficacy. This finding could prove valuable to television producers. The more viewers identify with a particular character, the more favorably they evaluate that character's behavior. A favorable evaluation, in turn, could increase the likelihood that the viewer would want to continue observing the model, thereby increasing the show's overall ratings. If producers use this information to conceive characters with which viewers can easily identify, they may increase the program's chances for success.

5. Significant differences between male versus female scores emerged across multiple variables and associations. Such sex differences are consistent with previous research documenting the importance of gender identification in mediating television's effect on viewers.[67]

Theoretical Implication of the Findings

Cultivation theory served as a theoretical basis for this study and provides viable explanations for its findings. It posits that the more time viewers spend watching TV, the more likely they are to perceive the world around them in terms of the values and ideologies that emerge from the screen.[68] Males and females prefer different types of programming; indeed, females are more likely to enjoy family-based programming.[69] Thus, cultivation theory would argue that males versus females are influenced across time by the different types of television programming that they watch. Our results, consistent with the above cultivation-theory-based explanation, provides additional support for the notion that males and females may respond differently to what they see on television and thus explain sex-based differences in viewer identification and efficacy evaluations of TV characters.

Further, cultivation theory is appropriate for discussing the differences in associations between identification with and evaluation of a character's communication efficacy by gender. As mentioned previously, males and females are likely to watch and respond to different types of programming based on their perceptions of the world around them. Thus, television may "cultivate" specific gender perspectives, which explains why males and females would identify with and evaluate their favorite characters somewhat differently.

Social learning theory provided an additional theoretical basis for the study and also provides viable explanations for its findings. Social learning theory is based on the assumption that people can acquire social behaviors through observation of others.[70] The theory purports that similarity between the viewer and role model will influence whether or not televised behaviors are modeled;

therefore, it is reasonable to presume that individuals would look to models of a similar sex for socialization information. Consequently, viewers' identification with and evaluation of these models would likely be linked to their sex, and they would subsequently look for models who they perceive to be similar in gender.

Further, the basis of social learning theory, or social cognitive theory, suggests a relationship between FCE and identification,[71] a relationship confirmed in our study. The theory acknowledges that the extent to which viewers learn from and imitate media characters is influenced by viewers' identification with characters.[72] The viewer identifies with a certain character for very specific reasons, and that reason, such as FCE, also may determine how the viewer evaluates the character's family communication efficacy.

Limitations and Suggestions for Future Research

There are multiple limitations to our study. First, the nonrandom sample of college students contained Ps homogenous in geographic location and ethnic background, thus limiting the generalizability of the findings. Second, the identification measure we employed was introduced to media research within the last decade,[73] and we were the first researchers to employ Caughlin's ten dimensions of family communication[74] in a third-person evaluation and with media characters. While our measures produced impressive reliability figures, continued validation in future studies would lend credence to their assessments.

Our findings indicate a need for future studies. Our results suggest a symbiotic relationship between (a) perceptions of FCE and identification with media characters and (b) identification with media characters and evaluations of characters' family communication efficacy. Future research could explore the relationships through an experimental design to provide media and family communication researchers with an advanced understanding of the direction of influence among the variables. Results would be useful to scholars and television producers alike in that they could aid in the development of television programming that would be both attractive to mass audiences and educational in terms of functional family communication. Further, multiple theoretical explanations were offered for the findings; future studies could examine which theoretical explanations best comport with reality.

Conclusions

Despite its limitations, our study contributes to the discipline's knowledge base in six ways: (1) It provides an initial look at the relationships between the variables of interest—the variables surrounding identification and modeling of television characters' family communication behaviors. (2) The study provides initial evidence of a number of relationships depicted in an original path model. (3) Our study confirms previous findings regarding conversation orientation and television viewing patterns.[75] (4) It provides further reliability and validity for the revised family communication patterns instrument, the character identification scale, and the television viewing instrument. (5) It offers initial reliability data and validity for using Caughlin's ten family communication standards[76] with media families. (6) Finally, it provides a warrant and meaningful direction for future research.

Notes

1. Barbara J. Wilson, "The Mass Media and Family Communication," in *Handbook of Family Communication*, ed. Anita L. Vangelisti (Mahwah, NJ: Erlbaum, 2004), 563-91.

2. James D. Robinson and Thomas Skill, "Five Decades of Families on Television: From the 1950s through the 1990s," in *Television and the American Family*, ed. Jennings Bryant and J. Alison Bryant, 2nd ed. (Mahwah, NJ: Erlbaum, 2001), 161.

3. Nancy Signorielli and Michael Morgan, "Television and the Family: The Cultivation Perspective," in *Television and the American Family*, ed. Jennings Bryant and J. Alison Bryant, 2nd ed. (Mahwah, NJ: Erlbaum, 2001), 333-51.

4. George Gerbner, Larry Gross, Michael Morgan, Nancy Signorielli and James Shanahan, "Growing Up with Television: The Cultivation Perspective," in *Media Effects: Advances in Theory and Research*, ed. Jennings Bryant and Dolf Zillmann, 2nd ed. (Mahwah, NJ: Erlbaum, 1994), 17-41; Signorielli and Morgan, "Television and the Family," 333-51.

5. Audrey J. Weiss and Barbara J. Wilson, "Children's Cognitive and Emotional Responses to the Portrayal of Negative Emotions in Family-Formatted Situation Comedies," *Human Communication Research* 24, no. 4 (1998): 584-609.

6. L. David Ritchie and Mary Anne Fitzpatrick, "Family Communication Patterns: Measuring Intrapersonal Perceptions of Interpersonal Relationships," *Communication Research* 17, no. 4 (1990): 524.

7. Steven H. Chaffee, Jack M. McLeod, and Charles K. Atkin, "Parental Influences on Adolescent Media Use," *American Behavioral Scientist* 14, no. 3 (1971): 323-40; Steven H. Chaffee and Albert R. Tims, "Interpersonal Factors in Adolescent Television Use," *Journal of Social Issues* 32, no. 4 (1976): 98-115; James Lull, "Family Communication Patterns and the Social Uses of Television," *Communication Research* 7, no. 3 (1980): 319-34.

8. L. David Ritchie, "Family Communication Patterns: An Epistemic Analysis and Conceptual Reinterpretation," *Communication Research* 18, no. 4 (1991): 548-65.

9. Marina Krcmar, "The Contribution of Family Communication Patterns to Children's Interpretations of Television Violence," *Journal of Broadcasting and Electronic Media* 42, no. 2 (1998): 250-54.

10. Jack M. McLeod and Steven H. Chaffee, "The Construction of Social Reality," in *The Social Influence Process*, ed. James T. Tedeschi (Chicago: Aldine-Atherton, 1972), 50-59.

11. Melissa N. Saphir and Steven H. Chaffee, "Adolescents' Contributions to Family Communication Patterns," *Human Communication Research* 28, no. 1 (2002): 86-108.

12. Li-Ning Huang, "Family Communication Patterns and Personality Characteristics," *Communication Quarterly* 47, no. 2 (1999): 230-33.

13. Ritchie, "Family Communication Patterns," 548-65.

14. McLeod and Chaffee, "The Construction," 50-59.

15. Erica W. Austin, "Exploring the Effects of Active Parental Mediation of Television Content," *Journal of Broadcasting and Electronic Media* 37, no. 2 (1993): 147-58; Chaffee et al., "Parental Influences," 323-40; Chaffee and Tims, "Interpersonal Factors," 98-115; Krcmar, "The Contribution," 250-54; Lull, "Family Communication Patterns," 319-34.

16. Lull, "Family Communication Patterns," 319-34.

17. Ascan F. Koerner and Mary Anne Fitzpatrick, "Toward a Theory of Family Communication," *Communication Theory* 12, no. 1 (2002): 70-91.

18. Krcmar, "The Contribution of Family Communication Patterns," 250-54.

19. Kelly F. Albada, "The Public and Private Dialogue about the American Family on Television," *Journal of Communication* 50, no. 4 (2000): 79-109.

20. Thomas Skill and James D. Robinson, "Four Decades of Family on Television: A Demographic Profile, 1950-1989," *Journal of Broadcasting and Electronic Media* 38, no. 4 (1994): 449-64.

21. Katharine E. Heintz-Knowles, "Balancing Acts: Work-Family Issues on Prime-Time TV," in *Television and the American Family*, ed. Jennings Bryant and J. Alison Bryant, 2nd ed. (Mahwah, NJ: Erlbaum, 2001), 177-206.

22. Albert Bandura, *Social Learning Theory* (Upon Saddle River, NJ: Prentice-Hall, 1977).

23. Lawrence H. Ganong and Marilyn Coleman, "Effect of Family Structure on Family Attitudes and Expectations," *Family Relations* 33, no. 3 (1984): 425-32.

24. Albert Bandura, *Social Foundations of Thought and Action: A Social Cognitive Theory* (Englewood Cliffs, NJ: Prentice-Hall, 1986).

25. George Gerbner, "Cultural Indicators: The Third Voice," in *Communications, Technology, and Social Policy*, ed. George Gerbner, Larry Gross, and William H. Melody (New York: Wiley, 1973), 555-73.

26. George Gerbner, Larry Gross, Michael Morgan, and Nancy Signorielli, "The 'Mainstreaming of America': Violence Profile No. 11," *Journal of Communication* 30, no. 3 (1980): 10-29; Nancy Signorielli and Michael Morgan, *Cultivation Analysis: New Directions in Media Effects Research* (Newbury Park, CA: Sage, 1990).

27. Signorielli and Morgan, "Television and the Family," 333-51.

28. George Gerbner and Larry Gross, "Living with Television: The Violence Profile," *Journal of Communication* 26, no. 2 (1976): 173-99.

29. Signorielli and Morgan, "Television and the Family," 333-51.

30. Signorielli and Morgan, "Television and the Family," 333-51.

31. Karen Swan, "Social Learning from Saturday Morning Cartoons," in *Social Learning from Broadcast Television*, ed. Karen Swan, Carla Meskill, and Steven DeMaio (Cresskill, NJ: Hampton, 1998), 87-112.

32. National Institute of Mental Health, *Television and Behavior: Ten Years of Scientific Progress and Implications for the Eighties, Vol 1. Summary Report* (DHHS

Publication No. ADM 82-1195; Washington, DC: U.S. Government Printing Office, 1982).

33. Judith P. Van Evra, *Television and Child Development*, 3rd ed. (Mahwah, NJ: Erlbaum, 2004); Ellen Wartella and Nancy Jennings, "New Members of the Family: The Digital Revolution in the Home," *Journal of Family Communication* 1, no. 1 (2001): 59-69.

34. John Jung, "How Useful is the Concept of Role Model? A Critical Analysis," *Journal of Social Behavior and Personality* 1, no. 4 (1986): 528.

35. John L. Caughley, *Imaginary Social Worlds: A Cultural Approach* (Lincoln, NE: University of Nebraska Press, 1984); Jung, "How Useful," 525-36; Mary K. Pleiss and John F. Feldhusen, "Mentors, Role Models, and Heroes in the Lives of Gifted Children," *Educational Psychologist* 30, no. 3 (1995): 159-69; Charles E. Schaefer, *How to Influence Children* (New York: Van Nostrand Reinhold, 1978).

36. Bill Weber, "We Need Better TV Role Models for Kids," *Television Week,* June 28, 2004: 10.

37. Van Evra, *Television and Child Development*, 113.

38. Ritchie, "Family Communication Patterns," 548-65.

39. Jennings Bryant, Rodney A. Carveth, and Dan Brown, "Television Viewing and Anxiety: An Experimental Investigation," *Journal of Communication* 31, no. 1 (1981): 106-19; Rodney Carveth and Alison Alexander, "Soap Opera Viewing Motivations and the Cultivation Process," *Journal of Broadcasting and Electronic Media* 29, no. 3 (1985): 259-73; Gerbner et al., "The Mainstreaming," 10-29; Robert P. Hawkins, Suzanne Pingree, and Ilya Adler, "Searching for Cognitive Processes in the Cultivation Effect," *Human Communication Research* 13, no. 4 (1987): 553-77; Michael Morgan and Heather Harr-Mazar, *Television and Adolescents' Family Life Expectations,* unpublished manuscript (Annenberg School of Communications, University of Pennsylvania, Philadelphia, 1980); Thomas C. O'Guinn and L. J. Shrum, "The Role of Television in the Construction of Consumer Reality," *Journal of Consumer Research* 23, no. 4 (1997): 278-94; L. J. Shrum, "Psychological Processes Underlying Cultivation Effects: Further Tests of Construct Accessibility," *Human Communication Research* 22, no. 4 (1996): 482-509; L. J. Shrum, Robert S. Wyer, and Thomas C. O'Guinn, "The Effects of Television Consumption on Social Perceptions: The Use of Priming Procedures to Investigate Psychological Processes," *Journal of Consumer Research* 24, no. 4 (1998): 447-58.

40. Cynthia Hoffner and Joanne Cantor, "Perceiving and Responding to Mass Media Characters," in *Responding to the Screen: Reception and Reaction Proce*sses, ed. Jennings Bryant and Dolf Zillmann (Hillsdale, NJ: Erlbaum, 1991), 63-101.

41. Albert Bandura, Dorothea Ross, and Sheila A. Ross, "Transmission of Aggression through Imitation of Aggressive Models," *Journal of Abnormal and Social Psychology* 63, no. 3 (1961): 575-82; Jonathan Cohen, "Defining Identification: A Theoretical Look at the Identification of Audiences with Media Characters," *Mass Communication and Society* 4, no. 3 (2001): 245-64; Eleanor E. MacCoby and William C. Wilson, "Identification and Observational Learning from Films," *Journal of Abnormal and Social Psychology* 55, no. 1 (1957): 76-87.

42. Phillip J. Decker and Barry R. Nathan, *Behavior Model Training: Principles and Training* (New York: Praeger, 1985); Jung, "How Useful," 525-36; Charles R. Owens and Frank R. Ascione, "Effects of the Model's Age, Perceived Similarity and Familiarity

on Children's Donating," *Journal of Genetic Psychology* 151, no. 3 (1991): 341-57; Brian Wilson and Robert Sparks, "'It's gotta be the shoes': Youth, race, and sneaker commercials," *Sociology of Sport Journal* 13, no. 4 (1996): 398-427.

43. Bandura et al., "Transmission of Aggression," 575-82; Aimee Dorr, "II. Television and Affective Development and Functioning: Maybe this Decade," *Journal of Broadcasting* 25, no. 4 (1981): 335-45; L. Rowell Huesmann, Leonard D. Eron, Monroe M. Lefkowitz, and Leopold O. Walder, "Stability of Aggression over Time and Generations," *Developmental Psychology* 20, no. 6 (1984): 1120-34; Byron B. Reeves and Mark M. Miller, "A Multidimensional Measure of Children's Identification with Television Characters," *Journal of Broadcasting* 22, no. 1 (1978): 21-86.

44. Jerome Bruner, *Acts of Meaning: Four Lectures on Mind and Culture* (Cambridge, MA: Harvard University Press, 1990).

45. Albada, "The Public," 79-109.

46. Rebecca Dumlao, "Tapping into Critical Thinking: Viewer Interpretations of a Television Conflict," *Studies in Media and Information Literacy Education* 3, no. 1 (2003), doi: 10.3138/sim.3.1.001.

47. Erica W. Austin and C. Leigh Nelson, "Influences of Ethnicity, Family Communication, and Media on Adolescents' Socialization to U.S. Politics," *Journal of Broadcasting and Electronic Media* 37, no. 4 (1993): 419-35.

48. Bandura, *Social Foundations*.

49. John D. Abel, "The Family and Child Television Viewing," *Journal of Marriage and the Family* 38, no. 2 (1976): 331-35; Roy L. Moore and George P. Moschis, "The Role of Family Communication in Consumer Learning," *Journal of Communication* 31, no. 4 (1981): 42-51.

50. Morgan and Harr-Mazar, *Television and Adolescents' Family Life*.

51. Carveth and Alexander, "Soap Opera," 259-73; Shrum, "Psychological Processes," 482-509.

52. Gerbner et al., "The Mainstreaming," 10-29.

53. Ritchie and Fitzpatrick, "Family Communication Patterns," 523-44.

54. Mary Anne Fitzpatrick and L. David Ritchie, "Communication Schemata within the Family: Multiple Perspectives on Family Interaction," *Human Communication Research* 20, no. 3 (1994): 275-301; Koerner and Fitzpatrick, "Toward a Theory," 70-91.

55. Shrum, Wyer, and O'Guinn, "The Effects," 447-58.

56. Keren Eyal, "Measuring Identification with Media Characters" (paper presented at the annual meeting of the National Communication Association, Miami Beach, Florida, November 2003).

57. Eyal, "Measuring Identification."

58. John P. Caughlin, "Family Communication Standards: What Counts as Excellent Family Communication and How Are Such Standards Associated with Family Satisfaction?" *Human Communication Research* 29, no. 1 (2003): 5-40.

59. Caughlin, "Family Communication Standards," 5-40.

60. Task Force on Television Management, Nielsen Media Research, "Independent Task Force on Television Measurement Report," last modified March 21, 2005, http://ebookbrowse.com/task-force-on-television-measurement-report-pdf-d18751968.

61. Abel, "The Family," 331-35; Austin, "Exploring the Effects," 147-58; Chaffee et al., "Parental Influences," 323-40; Chaffee and Tims, "Interpersonal Factors," 98-115;

Krcmar, "The Contribution," 250-54; Lull, "Family Communication Patterns," 319-34; Moore and Moschis, "The Role," 42-51.

62. Robyn Ridley-Johnson, June E. Chance, and Harris Cooper, "Correlates of Children's Television Viewing: Expectancies, Age, and Sex," *Journal of Applied Developmental Psychology* 5, no. 3 (1984): 225-35.

63. Austin, "Exploring the Effects," 147-58; Chaffee et al., "Parental Influences," 323-40; Chaffee and Tims, "Interpersonal Factors," 98-115; Kremar, "The Contribution," 250-54; Lull, "Family Communication Patterns," 319-34.

64. Krcmar, "The Contribution," 250-54.

65. Carole A. Barbato, Elizabeth E. Graham, and Elizabeth M. Perse, "Communicating in the Family: An Examination of the Relationship of Family Communication Climate and Interpersonal Communication Motives," *Journal of Family Communication* 3, no. 3 (2003): 123-48.

66. Mildred M. Alvarez, Aletha C. Huston, John C. Wright, and Dennis D. Kerkman, "Gender Differences in Visual Attention to Television Form and Content," *Journal of Applied Developmental Psychology* 9, no. 4 (1988): 459-75; Leonard D. Eron, "Age Trends in the Development of Aggression, Sex Typing, and Related Television Habits," *Developmental Psychology* 19, no. 1 (1983): 71-77.

67. Bandura et al., "Transmission of Aggression," 575-82; Dorr, "II. Television," 335-45; Huesmann et al., "Stability of Aggression," 1120-34; Reeves and Miller, "A Multidimensional Measure," 21-86.

68. Gerbner et al., "The Mainstreaming," 10-29; Signorielli and Morgan, *Cultivation Analysis*.

69. James E. Sneegas and Tamyra A. Plank, "Gender Differences in Pre-adolescent Reactance to Age-Categorized Television Advisory Labels," *Journal of Broadcasting and Electronic Media* 42, no. 4 (1998), 423-34; Van Evra, *Television and Child Development*; T. H. A. Van der Voort, *Television Violence: A Child's Eye View* (Amsterdam: North Holland, 1986).

70. Bandura, *Social Learning Theory*.

71. Albert Bandura, "Social Cognitive Theory and Exercise of Control over HIV Infection," in *Preventing AIDS: Theories and Methods of Behavioral Interventions*, ed. Ralph J. DiClemente and John L. Peterson (New York: Plenum, 1994), 25-59.

72. Albert Bandura, "Social Cognitive Theory of Mass Communication," *Media Psychology* 3, no. 3 (2001): 265-99.

73. Eyal, "Measuring Identification."

74. Caughlin, "Family Communication Standards," 5-40.

75. Austin, "Exploring the Effects," 147-58; Chaffee et al., "Parental Influences," 323-40; Chaffee and Tims, "Interpersonal Factors," 98-115; Kremar, "The Contribution," 250-54; Lull, "Family Communication Patterns," 319-34.

76. Caughlin, "Family Communication Standards," 5-40.

Chapter Eight

Reality Check:
Real Housewives and Fan Discourses on Parenting and Family

Jingsi Christina Wu and Brian McKernan

In June 2012, the popular reality television series *Real Housewives of New York City* (*RHNYC*) returned for its fifth season with a bang. The premiere featured an explosive argument between show veterans LuAnn and Ramona.[1] *RHNYC* is itself a spinoff of the incredibly successful Bravo TV Real Housewives franchise, which began with *The Real Housewives of Orange County* (*RHOC*) in 2006. After *RHOC*'s success, producers quickly rolled out several spinoff series featuring women from such diverse locales as Atlanta, Beverly Hills, Miami, New York City, New Jersey, and Washington D.C. *RHNYC* debuted in 2008 and featured five new housewives, which the show's marketing hyped as members of New York City's elite social class, including LuAnn, Ramona, Jill, Bethenny, and Alex.

At the start of the first season of *RHNYC*, LuAnn, or "the Countess," was married to Count Alexandre de Lesseps. The show features many segments with LuAnn reminding others of her nobility or providing unsolicited instructions to the other housewives on proper etiquette. Ramona is an energetic businesswoman who is quick to share her opinion, which often results in heated arguments with other cast mates. Ramona's husband, Mario, owns a flourishing jewelry business. Jill helps run her second husband Bobby's successful family business. Jill often assumes a parental role on the show, offering other housewives sage business and personal advice. Alex is a graphic designer and lives in Brooklyn with her husband, Simon, who works in the hotel industry. The show often features Alex and Simon eagerly preparing for major social events and many of the other cast members often derogatorily describe the pair as social climbers. Bethenny is the only cast member to not be married or have children. Many of Bethenny's scenes focus on her own attempts at starting a business or family and other housewives giving her relationship advice.

After the departure of Bethenny and what many considered to be a lackluster Season four, the producers drastically changed the roster, with LuAnn and Ramona being the only original cast members still on the show at the start of Season five. LuAnn and Ramona have always had somewhat of a tense relationship, most notably when LuAnn supported the opposition in Ramona's quarrel with Jill. However, the show usually focused on feuds between other housewives during the first four seasons. This all changed in the Season four finale.[2] During a one-on-one conversation with LuAnn, Ramona called her a "weekend mom." According to Ramona, LuAnn cared more about her new romantic partner and social life than being the proper parent her two children need. To support her claims, Ramona not so subtly alluded to the disciplinary problems her children have recently experienced, including a party involving underage drinking at LuAnn's home. In contrast, Ramona insisted that she always places her own daughter's needs and happiness first. LuAnn took extreme offense to Ramona's accusation that she was a bad parent. It is important to note that all of the housewives with children espouse themselves as parents first and foremost. Thus in her criticism, broadcast on national television, Ramona called into question LuAnn's authenticity and integrity, particularly in regards to LuAnn's personal parenting priorities. LuAnn was especially outraged that Ramona brought up the behavior of her children. Indeed, one of the reoccurring themes across the entire *Real Housewives* franchise is that the behavior of children is off limits, even though all the programs frequently feature segments with the housewives and their children. Consistent with this overarching theme, LuAnn insisted that Ramona leave her children out of their feud.

This argument between LuAnn and Ramona carried into the Season four reunion and Season five picked up right where the reunion left off. In the beginning of Season five, LuAnn continued to seek an apology from Ramona, because as she repeatedly insisted, people are not supposed to tell others how to be a parent.[3] Ramona refused to apologize, much to LuAnn's frustration. The feud between these two housewives has become one of the show's primary plotlines, making proper parenting one of the show's most prominent themes. Indeed, as we show in this chapter, the LuAnn versus Ramona feud is simply the most explicit manifestation of the deep thematic emphasis the entire franchise places on parenting and domestic life. This chapter examines how parenting and family relation themes have been present in *RHNYC* from the start of the series and explores how audience members use the show to help define their own understandings of parenthood and family life. We argue that reality television and the online communities that form around it provide a space for viewers to reflect upon their real-life situations and reach deeper understandings of the social world. We document how the housewives' frequent supply of (often unsolicited) parenting tips and the show's general emphasis on the family lives of these reality personalities serve as major topics of discussion in online forums. In these online exchanges, forum posters assess the housewives' parenting techniques and family life as well as share their own family experiences and advice. We argue that this interaction with the show and other viewers plays an important role in viewers' own understandings of what constitutes a "good" parent and spouse.

Reality Television: False Sense of Reality?

In the field of reality television, two things have remained relatively constant over the past two decades: the programs still enjoy massive popularity and academics criticize the genre as a dangerous form of escapism and false reality. Scholars operating from this critical orientation assert that reality TV serves as a vacuous form of entertainment that capitalizes on its audience's unhealthy craving for a voyeuristic glimpse into others' lives;[4] it serves as an ideological tool that promotes neoliberal ideals and a consumerist mentality;[5] and it instills audiences with dangerous stereotypes related to race, gender, and sexuality.[6] Although these critical works are certainly insightful and voice legitimate concerns, they predominantly draw their conclusions from textual analyses of reality television content, largely ignoring how audiences actually interpret these texts in their own life situations and use them in the construction or maintenance of their own identities. For example, in his critique of makeover reality television, John McMurria argues that these shows reinforce neoliberal ideals, such as home ownership, corporate benevolence, and individual volunteerism, and evade fundamental social inequalities in their portrayals. He points out that the commercial makeover reality TV format often celebrates corporate charity, and "more fully integrates philanthropy with corporate branding and product marketing."[7] At the same time, the programs also encourage individuals to take charge of their self-improvement and volunteer their efforts to help other citizens. McMurria's major concern is that these programs end up boosting private business interests rather than encourage substantive structural policy interventions by the state.

McMurria provides a powerful critique of the reality television format. However, his findings offer no insight into the actual encounter between the television text and the audience's reception. Applying a similar political economy perspective, Nicole Cox and Jennifer Proffitt fill the gap by looking at how online audiences critically interpret depictions of a consumerist lifestyle on the *Real Housewives* franchise.[8] Although Cox and Proffitt extend beyond the critical perspective's traditional emphasis on textual analysis by examining fan comments on the cast blogs hosted by Bravo, they tend to impose their critical interpretations on the audience discourses. The crux of their argument asserts that the show does not encourage serious conversations amongst fans because the official Bravo website for the show predominantly promotes consumerist values. The authors find that viewers tend to negotiate the value of consumerism in the happiness of one's life rather than directly reject it. In contrast to such perspectives held by McMurria, Cox and Proffitt, a growing body of scholarly literature emphasizes how audiences often exhibit a high level of critical agency in their engagement with television programs.[9] We argue that such perspectives provide a much more nuanced and comprehensive understanding of how an audience interacts with reality television and thus a stronger grasp of reality television's role in the contemporary social world.

Reality Check: Construction of Critical Discourses Around Reality Television

Contrary to the critical perspective that tends to ignore actual audience experiences, other scholars recognize that reality television viewers do not necessarily condone the cast's behavior or buy into all the program's ideological messages or preferred readings. Such recognitions trace back to the argument made by audience reception studies that the media experience possesses the capacity to provide audience members with a powerful platform for social bonding and critical reflections on one's own life. These works insist that audiences have the critical agency to reject preferred reading of media texts. Such audience reception research finds that common media experiences help audience members build interpersonal relationships,[10] audience members are not all influenced by media texts in the exact same way,[11] and they are often not so susceptible to the hidden messages uncovered by insightful critical scholars.[12]

Similarly, in the field of reality television studies, Annette Hill aptly notes that scholars should not make assumptions about how audiences actually interpret such media texts, especially how they are passively manipulated by corruptive messages in reality television.[13] This argument is supported by Alice Hall's empirical work that finds the predominant viewing experience for many audience members is feeling better about themselves when the cast behaves badly, or relating to the cast when they overcome obstacles and succeed.[14] Moreover, Hall finds that "the more outlandish doings of reality program cast members . . . function as conversational currency" more than role models.[15] In other words, instead of passively receiving bad influence from reality television, viewers talk with themselves and others about the cast's behaviors, in the process of which they define their own standards and principles. These viewing experiences provide viewers with a safe space separate from their own reality to figure out what they would do in similar situations, and especially how they would not repeat the same mistakes.

Leigh Edwards suggests, "reality TV opens a fresh chapter in TV's long-running love affair with the family . . . [as it] grapples with the postmodern family condition."[16] She points out that viewers who are also parents often reflect on their own parenting through such media experiences and further argues that reality TV provides a fodder for public debate about family values. This chapter seeks to examine such viewer engagements in more detail through their online discussions.

Online Community Around *Real Housewives of New York City*

To examine viewers' reception of *RHNYC*, we conducted a close textual analysis of online discussions on the first season of *RHNYC* from the online forum Television Without Pity (TWoP), a popular reality television fan forum purchased by the Bravo unit of NBC Universal in 2007.[17] As Bravo also produces the *Real Housewives* franchise, we were particularly interested to see how audience members criticize the show on its official site and grapple with the *RHNYC* forum manager's diligent moderating.

Interestingly, although TWoP promotes "snark" as the site's core principle ("spare the snark, spoil the networks"), which would make it seemingly safe to assume that the site encourages a certain degree of sarcasm and critical viewpoint on the part of posters, the forum devoted to Bravo's own production clearly tries to exercise strict moderation in the name of "network executive." The top of every forum page includes the following warning about what the site considers to be inappropriate discussion topics: "Do not post to discuss yourself, other TV shows, other websites, the general state of the economy, your sociopolitial analysis of the fashion industry, etc. Your posts should be directly about the show." This is followed by a long list of "don'ts" that specifically states that posts should only focus on the show and posts touching on broader social issues risk being deleted by the moderator. As a result, we found a large number of posts missing from the forum discussion at the time of sampling, including a plethora of comments posted roughly around the time when episodes two to five aired. On March 10, 2008, "network executive" posted an announcement, "Closed for a bit. This really doesn't bode well," before the forum was reopened to comments on April 3, 2008, which spanned episodes two to five of Season one.

In January 2011 we collected all the posts on the forum published during the twenty-four-hour period after Bravo's original broadcast for episodes one, six, and seven of Season one, leading to a sample of 487 posts. After gathering the sample, we conducted a deep textual analysis of the audience's discussion by utilizing an inductive, iterative coding framework. More specifically, both authors read through the sample and took note of posts that extended beyond the show to talk about such broader topics as family, class relations, and the economy. We chose to focus on the theme of family in the interest of this chapter and practiced coding small subsets of the sample (usually around fifty posts) to make sure we agreed on the definition of this theme. After each round of practice, we re-read the posts together and discussed our disagreements. In the third round, we practiced coding on 100 posts and reached intercoder agreement at Krippendorff's *alpha* coefficient of 0.7752. Then the second author finished coding the rest of the sample and compiled all posts that touched on the topic of family for deeper analysis of patterns in the fan discourses. In this chapter we quote excerpts of these online posts verbatim, including spelling and grammatical errors.

In our sample, one of the most recurring topics to appear in forum discussions pertained to family and related issues. In particular, we noticed that audience attention was directed to two areas of contemporary family life. One area pertains to parenting in terms of commendable as well as improper parenting behaviors. The other area takes up other contemporary family relation issues, such as remarriage and gender roles. Below we provide a thick description of how *RHNYC* facilitated its audience's reflection on parenthood and family relations.

Fan Discourses on Parenthood

For the TWoP online community, one of the most prominent topics of conversation focused on describing how the NYC housewives' own emphasis on the importance of family or family matters is one of the most appealing elements of the show. In fact, several discussants specifically explained that they enjoyed *RHNYC* more than the original series set in Orange County simply because the New York housewives appeared to be better parents. Many posters explained that they found it refreshing, as one poster noted, "to see these women genuinely enjoying their spouses and kids."[18] For example, one discussant wrote: "I appreciate *RHNYC* because I can watch it without becoming apoplectic the way I do when I watch certain other housewives. Most of the NY women are pretty good parents as opposed to their CA counterparts."[19]

Similarly, a different discussant explained: "Overall, I much prefer the NYC women to the OC women. Despite their flaws, they all seem like good people and would never do something as dispicable [*sic*] as airing your kid's drug problems in order to better present yourself."[20] In these discussions on family matters, conversations primarily focused on identifying proper parenting strategies or appropriate parental behavior. Many posters claimed that the NYC housewives appeared to be better parents because they devoted more attention to their children and tended to shelter them from the camera. However, discussants also regularly criticized the NYC housewives for behavior they considered to be inappropriate or irresponsible for parents. For example, numerous posts considered the manner in which LuAnn's children interacted with the family's staff as a direct result of LuAnn's flawed parenting. The forum considered a particular scene in which LuAnn's son ordered their housekeeper to walk the dog to be especially problematic. The first poster to raise this concern wrote:

I really don't like the way LuAnn's son interacted with Rosana their housekeeper. Although it was a short interaction (telling Rosana that she would have to walk the dog), it was very dismissive and demanding. Even though it is likely Rosana would have to care for the dog anyway, I don't think it's appropriate for a child (and anyone for that matter) to be so disrespectful of another person. He should have asked and been much more respectful. I imagine there will be more instances like this throughout the season.[21]

In responding to this initial post, multiple discussants blamed LuAnn for her son's behavior. For example, one post explained: "Agreed. If the parents know what they're doing, they will actually MAKE the kids look after the dog, cause we all know thats [sic] a nice way to teach responsibility. So if Rosana ends up doing everything, they're really doing their kids a disservice. We all know how spoiled kids end up."[22] In this post, the discussant criticized LuAnn for not only missing the chance to teach her kids responsibility, but also possibly spoiling the kids by making their helper do everything. In prefacing this argument with "If the parents know what they're doing," the discussant constructed rules for good parenting.

Similarly, a follow-up post stated: "I find LuAnn to be the prettiest and most full of her self of all the wives. The way she looks down her nose at 'the help' is a true indicator to me that she has no true grace or class. I don't care how many faux titles she has. And it looks like she passed the attitude on to at least one of her kids."[23] Interestingly, this post started with both a compliment and a harsh critique in one sentence, which is quite representative of the online discussion in general. The viewers could marvel at the grandeur of the cast's abodes, the beauty of their clothing, or other excitements in their social life, but they did not shy away from criticism when the housewives' behaviors invited disagreements. In that sense, although LuAnn liked to emphasize her Countess title and prided herself on being a woman of class and sophistication, the way she interacted with "the help" did not win her respect among many viewers. Furthermore, as these examples illustrate, the manner in which LuAnn's son interacted with the help was connected to scenes on the show where LuAnn herself treated the staff disrespectfully. In other words, her son's behavior was understood as a direct result of LuAnn's terrible parenting. Setting bad examples for their children constituted one of the primary critiques about bad parenting from online discussants.

On a somewhat lighter note, many posts used scenes from the show to discuss how parents and adults in general should act in front of children. For example, several posters were disgusted at the manner in which Ramona conducted herself during her daughter's prom, going as far as to describe her as "dirty dancing." These posters considered such behavior to be entirely unbecoming of a parent, embarrassing for the child, and interpreted it as a desperate move on Ramona's part to appear "cool" in front of her daughter's friends. For example, one post disdainfully explained: "She's totally THAT mom trying so hard to be 'cool' to her kid's friends that I'm sure she's way more permissive than she should be. For reference, see Amy Poehler's character in 'Mean Girls.'"[24]

Other posts claimed that Ramona must be delusional if she believes that her daughter's friends love her. They also expressed concern that if Ramona is so desperate to be liked by her daughter and her friends then she probably lets them get away with troubling behavior. These posters chastised Ramona for placing her own interest in having fun and looking cool over her primary responsibility as a parent to properly raise her daughter.

Alex and Simon's lifestyle, including the condition of their house, is another popular topic of discussion that the forum connected to the issue of proper parenting. During the sixth episode of the show, Alex invited Bethenny over to their house even though the house was currently under renovation. The scene opened with Bethenny entering the house through the bottom floor, which according to many posts appeared to be in horrible condition. In commenting on the current state of their house, numerous posts criticized Alex and Simon for raising their children in such a poorly maintained home, which was especially unacceptable given how much money they spent on other luxury products in their efforts to raise their own social status. For example, one post explained: "OMG Alex and Simon are pathetic. They spend 10,000 on that hideous dress but let their toddlers run around in that rat trap! I always thought it was suspect that they only showed them in their bedroom."[25]

Similarly, two additional posts wrote:

Alex, stop spending money on clothing and fix up that house. At least put some floors in so the kids don't get splinters. She's so concerned with where the kids attend school but can't be bothered to make their home (the place where the kids spend most of their time, at least at this age) comfortable?????[26]

I was apalled [sic] at Alex and Simon's house. Perhaps they should quit worrying about forcing the boys to speak French, and concentrate more on providing with them a safe place in which to live.[27]

As these examples illustrate, discussants did not just ridicule Alex and Simon for having a home in poor condition. They treated the house's terrible condition as a reflection of Alex and Simon's inability to serve as proper parents. Moreover, discussants regularly criticized Alex and Simon for being more concerned about spending their wealth in pursuit of climbing the social ladder than devoting their resources to providing their children with a safe home. In this sense, the forum found Alex and Simon to be inferior parents.

To be fair, not all the discussion focused on scenes from the show revealing the housewives to be bad parents. In certain instances forum participants praised the housewives for behavior they considered to be appropriate parenting techniques. For example, both the first and the sixth episodes of the season sparked a large debate on the forum over Alex and Simon's insistence that their children learn French. Some discussants treated this behavior as just another illustration of Alex and Simon's vanity. These posters explained that French is a high-class language with limited practical use. Consequently, Alex and Simon's selection of French was simply another attempt by the pair to appear more sophisticated than they are. However, many other discussants applauded Alex and Simon's efforts at teaching their children a foreign language. For instance, in support of Alex and Simon, one post explained: "I have no issue with them wanting their children to learn another language. I find it commendable; especially in the USA were very few native Americans bother to learn another language as opposed to our counterparts in Europe and elsewhere who on average speak 2 or more language [sic] outside their native tongue."[28]

This post and other similar posts considered learning multiple languages to be a valuable asset in the contemporary world, and thus by encouraging their children to learn French, Alex and Simon were acting as good parents should. Other posts, however, argued over the choice of French versus other more "practical foreign languages" for the kids to master. In response to another viewer's explanation that "English and French are international languages," the following post speculated that Alex and Simon chose French in another desperate attempt to add more class to their image rather than provide their children with a valuable educational and professional resource:

Yep, I know . . . but so are Chinese, Russian, Spanish and Arabic. I was just curious as to why they chose French as the second language for their children. French has a cache [sic] that other languages don't have and I guess I never understood why. I'd think that Spanish would be a much more practical choice, but obviously having money precludes one from having to be practical—as evidenced by dropping six figures on clothing from that one shop in St. Bart's.[29]

According to this viewer, parents should be more practical and choose a foreign language that their children will most likely need to use in their personal life and career. For similar reasons, many viewers equated the choice of French with being "pretentious."[30]

Furthermore, while supporting Alex and Simon's desire for their children to speak a second language, some participants criticized the particular manner in which Alex and Simon were trying to teach their children French. For example, expressing frustration with Alex and Simon's particular techniques, one discussant stated:

Note to Alex and Simon—if you want the children to speak French, you should speak French to each other. The children will communicate with you in response. But your speaking in French might limit your reality TV appeal. God forbid. ITA. Relying on the au pair (who is limited in how many hours she can work, IIRC) to speak French or Latin or whatever so that your kid can learn a foreign language is ridiculous. Kids (or adults for that matter) learn by practicing. Since Alex and Simon both speak French (according to them at any rate), they should be speaking French to Francois and Johan as much as possible. If they want their kids speaking another language, they need to be more proactive. It isn't enough to hire someone to do it. Gawd, this is reminding me of The Nanny Diaries.[31]

A later poster supported this claim, writing:

And I'm really trying to understand Alex and Simon (Simon really) with this desire for Johan and Francois to speak French. As someone noted, the best thing for them to do is to speak to the children in French (and to speak to each other in French). Like any language, you learn by hearing it for a long while. The speaking piece comes later. However, it seems that Simon and Alex (and to some extent based on what we've seen), are trying to formally teach these boys, what with "Limonade, Francois," and "en français, Francois; en français, Francois" (which began to hurt my ears after awhile) and the au pair trying to get them to repeat the numbers in French while sitting at the dinner table. If you want to teach them to count in French, start counting when you're walking up or down the stairs, counting each step along the way. It would seem more natural that way, anyway.[32]

As these posts illustrate, this discussion of Alex and Simon's choice to teach their children French served as a starting point for a broader discussion on proper or effective language learning techniques in particular and the value of education in general. Overall, the NYC housewives were credited for the importance they place on their children's education, reflected in the following comment: "I gotta say I do like that, unlike the OC loons, there was again talk of education being important."[33]

In evaluating the housewives as parents, forum discussants defined what it means to be a good parent. According to these discussions, a good parent must serve as a role model in their interactions with others and teach their children to treat others respectfully regardless of their social status. Moreover, as the posters' criticisms of Alex and Simon's social aspirations and Ramona's childish behavior at her daughter's prom demonstrate, a good parent must also devote as much energy and attention as possible to properly raising their children and should absolutely not place their own pleasure over their children's interests. Finally, a good parent should equip their children with the skills they need to be successful in the twenty-first century, including teaching them a second language, but for the right reasons. In general, these posters constructed an image of a completely selfless and model parent, willing to do anything for their child's future well-being.

Fan Discourses on Family Relations

Our analysis indicates that *RHNYC* not only provides viewers with a chance to reflect on what it means to be a good parent, but also inspires viewers to share their own thoughts on some of the most prominent issues facing families in the twenty-first century, such as divorce and re-marriage. The fact that many Real Housewives families include family members from previous marriages prompts many of the online posters to discuss how family members should appropriately navigate such relationships. In addition, forum discussants also critically examined couple dynamics on the show and discussed how to have a healthy relationship with one's life partner.

One specific storyline that attracted a lot of attention on the forum is the interactions between Jill's husband, Bobby, and her fourteen-year-old daughter from a previous marriage, Allison. Jill has been married to Bobby for seven years, yet many posters characterized the relationship between Bobby and Allison as awkward. Many posters noted that Jill was trying too hard to push the two closer together and wondered whether her efforts would work after such a long time. One of the most talked about scenes happened during the first season after Jill took her daughter to an expensive detox center for Allison's weight struggles. During this scene, Jill pushed Allison to give Bobby a hug to show her appreciation. Many posters expressed discomfort over this awkward exchange. For example, one poster wrote:

> And, I HATED the bit where the daughter has to go and hug/kiss her stepfather like a trained dog—Ewwwww! It was obvious that he was just as uncomfortable as she was. He even shifted his attention to the little girl in the room (don't know who she belonged to—maybe his granddaughter?) saying "aren't YOU cute", just so he wouldn't have to react to his stepdaughter's hug. Maybe it was because he wasn't used to the cameras, but after 7 years of stepfatherhood, you'd think he'd not be so ill at ease with the girl.[34]

This comment represented a common sentiment among the posters that Jill should stop trying to force Bobby and Allison to express affection toward one another if either one of them feels uncomfortable doing so. While some understood her desire to make her husband get along with her daughter, others argued that Jill should not artificially push the two together and risk making them feel even more uncomfortable than they already were.

On that note, some viewers pointed out that the relationship between stepparents and stepchildren is often much worse than that between Bobby and Allison. One post expressed this sentiment by comparing Bobby and Allison's relationship to that of a different stepparent-stepson pair from *RHOC*. This commentator explained: "I agree with earlier poster about Ally and Bobby. Be happy they tolerate each other and there isn't any animosity there (it isn't like Tamra's son and husband in RHOOC [*sic*])."[35] In referencing the OC housewife Tamra's struggle to end the constant confrontations between her then husband in earlier seasons (whom she recently divorced) and her son from a previous marriage, this post touched on a major obstacle facing more and more families today. As divorce rates increase, second marriages and other arrangements become an obstacle that many families have to address. In that sense, watching the real housewives struggle on the reality show provides a platform for the viewers to explore such issues.

Parent-children interactions were not the only focus of forum conversations on family dynamics. Posters generally expressed a strong interest in discussing and evaluating how each housewife interacted with her husband or significant other. In doing so, these posters constructed or reiterated their own understandings of what constitutes a healthy relationship between romantic partners. Perhaps not surprisingly given our previous examples (and the name of the site), most posters expressed their definition of a healthy relationship through criticism. Based on the forum exchanges, there is clearly a lot about the way the housewives interacted with their partners (and vice versa) on the show that forum members did not appreciate.

Much of the posters' criticism targeted the way housewife Alex and her husband Simon acted towards one another. The posters found them to be far too involved in each other's lives and often described their interactions as obsessive. For example, several posters voiced disgust over one particular scene from the show in which Simon helped Alex pick out some new wardrobe items. During the scene, Simon was quite vocal about which clothes and accessories he thought looked best on Alex. Many discussants found Simon's involvement in Alex's wardrobe shopping to be problematic and even somewhat creepy. One poster wrote:

> And Simon's commentary upon his wife trying on clothes was beyond weird. I've tried on clothes with men before and they look bored and begrudgingly hold your purse for you. Any ongoing commentary consists of "are you done yet? can we go now? why does it take you so long?"[36]

Similarly, a different commentator explained: "Simon treats Alex like the Barbie doll his dad never let him have."[37] These two commentators were not alone in disapproving of Simon and Alex's behavior during this scene. As these examples illustrate, many posters used traditional conceptualizations of gender norms to define what they consider to be appropriate behavior. According to this logic, Simon is a male and thus should not take so much pleasure in clothes shopping or even express interest in his wife's wardrobe choices in general. The online discussants further suggested that Simon's passion in fashion, not just in his wife's wardrobe but also in his own, could put his sexuality in question. In doing so, the discussants constructed their gender associations. According to such critiques, shopping and fashion are exclusively in the realm of women or homosexual men.

In addition, discussants treated the shopping scene as emblematic of Alex and Simon's co-dependent relationship. Commentators frequently criticized the pair for not being able to separate for even a single moment and noted that this severe co-dependency led the two to participate in activities not suited for a husband and wife, such as Alex's clothes shopping, or Jill's girls-only party. Moreover, discussants criticized Alex and Simon for having no individual personalities, opinions, or hobbies beyond constantly being with each other. For example, one poster jokingly predicted that the first season would end with "Alex and Simon, magically morphing into one being by the end of the season . . . the great shopping superpower Aleximon."[38] On a related note, a different poster wrote: "Couples who can't stand to spend some time apart and have their own identity truly need help."[39] These examples help illustrate how posters actively defined the criteria for a healthy relationship by criticizing the housewives on the show. There appears to be a general agreement amongst the posts we examined that a healthy romantic relationship must still allow enough space for each partner to preserve his or her own individuality and autonomy.

Discussion

In her work, Leigh Edwards points out that reality television documents America's transition from a traditional "modern nuclear family" model to that of a "postmodern family."[40] While there are more diverse arrangements across households, reality television features "family in crisis." Edwards argues that we no longer have a single standard for what is the best way to parent, the most effective route to a healthy relationship, or the most successful strategy to build a parents-children bond. Instead, she finds that reality shows both challenge and reaffirm traditional values, oftentimes resolving them into a liberal pluralistic message. In other words, each family can be different; therefore, there is no universal path to a happy family.

Consistent with Edwards' work, we find that the audience reception of *RHNYC* both confirms traditional family values, such as providing proper shelter and serving as a good role model for one's children, and touches on topics related to the "postmodern family" condition, such as maintaining individuality in relationships and dealing with re-married family relations. Although the forum discussants largely expressed conservative opinions about how to parent and fairly traditional views about gender expectations, they embraced new family models and shared their understandings through a critical stance on the cast behavior.

Contrary to dominant perspectives about the effect of reality television on its audience, we find that audience members do not passively internalize all the ideological messages embedded in these programs. Discussants on the forum we examined were not primarily interested in discussing the show's portrayal of a lavish New York lifestyle. Instead, posters used the show as a platform to discuss parenting and family issues. We arrive at this finding by letting the audience's own voice guide our research, which serves as a testament to the value of an empirical examination open to the diverse and potentially surprising ways in which audience members make sense of television shows. We strongly urge future works to combine critical insights with more empirically grounded examinations into audience activities. Although it makes an interesting discussion about how "real" the "real housewives" are, it is equally interesting, if not more, to see how the viewers use the show in their own construction of parenting and family life.

Notes

1. *The Real Housewives of New York City*, "A New New York," written by Scott Dunlop, first broadcast June 4, 2012 by Bravo.

2. *Real Housewives of New York City*, "Burlesque is More," written by Scott Dunlop, first broadcast July 14, 2011 by Bravo.

3. *The Real Housewives of New York City*, "A New New York."

4. Lemi Baruh, "Publicized Intimacies on Reality Television: An Analysis of Voyeuristic Content and Its Contribution to the Appeal of Reality Programming," *Journal of Broadcasting & Electronic Media* 53, no. 2 (2009): 190–210.

5. John McMurria, "Desperate Citizens and Good Samaritans: Neoliberalism and Makeover Reality TV," *Television & New Media* 9, no. 4 (2008): 305-32.

6. Angela Cooke-Jackson and Elizabeth Hansen, "Appalachian Culture and Reality TV: The Ethical Dilemma of Stereotyping Others," *Journal of Mass Media Ethics* 23, no. 3 (2008): 183-200.

7. McMurria, "Desperate Citizens and Good Samaritans," 309.

8. Nicole Cox and Jennifer Proffitt, "The Housewives' Guide to Better Living: Promoting Consumption on Bravo's The Real Housewives," *Communication, Culture & Critique* 5, no. 2 (2012): 295–312.

9. Mark Andrejevic, "Watching Television without Pity: The Productivity of Online Fans," *Television & New Media* 9, no. 1 (2008): 24-46; Henry Jenkins, *Convergence Culture* (New York: New York University Press, 2006).

10. Nancy Baym, *Tune in, Log on: Soaps, Fandom, and Online Community* (Thousand Oaks: Sage, 2000).

11. Henry Jenkins, *Convergence Culture: Where Old and New Media Collide* (New York: New York University Press, 2006).

12. Janice Radway, *Reading the Romance* (Chapel Hill: University of North Carolina Press, 1984.)

13. Annette Hill, "Fearful and Safe: Audience Response to British Reality Programming," *Television & New Media* 1, no. 2 (2000): 193-213.

14. Alice Hall, "Perceptions of the Authenticity of Reality Programs and Their Relationships to Audience Involvement, Enjoyment, and Perceived Learning," *Journal of Broadcasting & Electronic Media* 53, no. 4 (2009): 515-31.

15. Hall, "Perceptions of the Authenticity," 527.

16. Leigh Edwards, "Reality TV and the American Family," in *The Tube Has Spoken: Reality TV and History*, ed. Julie Taddeo and Ken Dvorak (Lexington, KY: The University Press of Kentucky, 2011), 126.

17. Josef Adalian, "Bravo Nabs Popular TV Website," *Variety*, March 13, 2007, http://www.variety.com/article/VR1117961063?refCatId=14 (accessed July 1, 2012).

18. Post #373.

19. Post #1022.

20. Post #965.

21. Post #390.

22. Post #391.
23. Post #415.
24. Post #443.
25. Post #958.
26. Post #1019.
27. Post #1027.
28. Post #1052.
29. Post #379.
30. Post #373.
31. Post #1015.
32. Post #1020.
33. Post #398.
34. Post #397.
35. Post #383.
36. Post #422.
37. Post #404.
38. Post #410.
39. Post #425.
40. Edwards, "Reality TV," 124.

Chapter Nine

Keeping Up with Contradictory Family Values: The Voice of the Kardashians

Amanda S. McClain

Since its first appearance in 2007, the TV program *Keeping Up With The Kardashians* has immensely grown in popularity, raking in profit and fame for the family. The series averages more than three million viewers per week.[1] Indeed, it is the highest-rated series ever on the cable *E!* network; its fifth season debuted with over 4.5 million viewers and ended with 4.7 million viewers tuning in for the season finale, a record for *E!*.[2] Additionally, 1.1 million women ages eighteen to thirty-four watched the season six finale, setting an *E!* channel record for that particular demographic.[3] As further evidence of the Kardashian popularity, 10.5 million viewers watched the two-part special *Kim Kardashian's Fairytale Wedding.*[4]

Moreover, the Kardashian family commands a "branding empire that includes fashion boutiques, fitness videos, credit cards, a best-selling fragrance, skin care products and a self tanner."[5] The family has endorsement deals with PerfectSkin, Tropicana Juicy Rewards, and Quick Trim, along with a myriad of other companies.[6] The three older sisters jointly own three Dash clothing boutiques, one each in L.A., Miami, and New York City. Mom Kris Jenner manages the entire extended family, including son-in-law Lamar Odom, a professional basketball player, earning 10 percent of each member's income for her work.[7] Other ventures include clothing, jewelry, and shoe lines, fragrances, calendars, and various other endorsements. The list of merchandise seems to grow daily, and includes a new store in Las Vegas, Kardashian Khaos.[8] As a *New York Times* article noted, "ultimately, what Ms. Kardashian and her sisters create and sell are products based on their own image, and not much of it is particularly distinctive from the standard uniforms of Southern California nightclubs."[9] This chapter seeks to understand what significances reside within this image, through a discourse analysis of the series that established them as household names.

Much has been written about *Keeping Up With The Kardashians* in the popular press. An article in *Entertainment Weekly* noted that the show adheres to a tried and true sitcom formula: "Whereby lapses in judgment or boneheaded mistakes lead to nutty conclusions and hurt feelings that get resolved with confession, discussion, apology, and hugging."[10] The same article called it a "conventional family sitcom, once you get past the booze, bleeped language, and bawdy sex talk."[11] Ted Harbert, president and CEO of Comcast Entertainment Group, called the show "a modern-day *Eight is Enough.*"[12] Are these claims correct? Is the show an innocuous family-friendly sitcom-esque show? While this may be at least partially true, the themes within the series controvert this supposition. This chapter interrogates the popular press's family-friendly claims by a systematic exploration of values depicted on the popular and provocative show. Investigation of television helps illuminate contemporary societal norms. Through a discourse analysis, this chapter determines that throughout the first season of *Keeping Up With The Kardashians* contradictory values of family/business, beauty/unhappiness, intimate/transgressive, and sexuality/conservatism are endorsed. Moreover, throughout these dichotomous values, an emphasis exists on contravention of traditional gender roles.

Theoretical Framework and Methodology

As John Fiske noted, television helps shape, reflect, and maintain culture. Television is a "cultural agent," a "provoker and circulator of meanings."[13] Moreover, Fiske asserts that television attempts to "make meanings that serve the dominant interests in society."[14] Thus, meanings reinforce the existent social structure, firmly establishing the status quo as "unchallengeable and unchangeable."[15] Therefore, the prevalence of television and the socializing role it occupies in American culture necessitate its study.

Within television, dominant social meanings are produced and reinforced through repetition. Television "delineates the terrain within which meanings may be made and proffers some meanings more vigorously than others."[16] This foremost set of meanings corresponds with dominant ideology. The dominant ideology in contemporary America supports the extant cultural, economic, and institutional status quo.

Characters on television manifest prevailing ideology. Moreover, televised "real" people and their inherent ideals may be more important than fictional characters. The familiarity of the banal everyday tasks visible on reality TV engenders an "intimate relationship between participant and viewer."[17] This results in a fame based upon the shared normality of the participant and viewer.

This intimate relationship warrants even more intense scrutiny of reality TV participants and their characteristics. The audience is asked to accept the people on reality TV as average, normal people, as "us." Thus, the values and ideals embodied within the reality TV participants may have more significance and importance than values inherent within fictional characters.

Not only does television reproduce contemporary dominant ideologies;[18] it also "reflect[s] long-established cultural stereotypes of masculinity and femininity."[19] Television functions as a socializing agent, teaching young audience members behavior norms, conspicuously in relation to gender.[20] Women are encouraged to be sexual, feminine, and passive, as corresponds to cultural feminine ideals, yet then objectified for these qualities.[21] Reality television is "particularly strong in reinforcing traditional views of women and what makes women desirable."[22] Given this context, the Kardashian family's popularity within television and other media indicates an important element of popular culture to investigate.

Discourse analysis is an ideal methodology for television analysis. This technique consists of searching for patterns and themes within a text or groups of texts.[23] Discourse creates the world as we understand it.[24] Moreover, while systems of knowledge are explicated and supported through discourse, how we communicate creates and maintains our social identities as well.[25] As Michel Foucault elucidated, the concept of discourse also refers to institutionalized power disparity, or the naturalizing of structural inequality.[26] With these inherent markers in mind, discourse "may be characterized as a portion of speech, either verbal or written, generally advocating a particular point of view, and often used to position authority."[27] Put simply, the study of discourse examines not only how our world is created and understood, but also how individuals understand themselves, others, and relationships. This particular discourse analysis permits an examination of a televised contemporary family; the values they abide by, how they maintain relationships, and the family's social identity.

For this analysis I watched for recurring patterns and themes, both in the program's narrative aspect and in characters' behavior. I particularly noted how they interacted with each other, the verbal language used, and emotional moments. As Hill notes, audiences consuming reality TV tend to look for emotions, believing these to be truthful.[28] Correspondingly, other research finds that reality TV participants use emotion to convey sincerity and authenticity.[29] For this analysis, I watched all eight episodes of the first season of *Keeping Up With The Kardashians*. Each was approximately twenty-two minutes long. In total, several contradictory values were illustrated overtly and implicitly over the course of the season.

Discussion

Keeping Up With The Kardashians follows the blended Kardashian/Jenner family, focusing on mom and stepfather Kris and Bruce Jenner, and Kris's adult children, Kim, Kourtney, Khloe, and Rob Kardashian. Kris and Bruce's tween daughters, Kendall and Kylie Jenner, also appear. Various boyfriends and friends pop in and out, notably Kourtney's boyfriend, Scott Disick, and in later seasons, Khloe's husband, Lamar Odom. Each show typically features some sort of family or business dilemma, and often a conflation of both.

Family/Business

Typically, reality television reinforces cultural stereotypes, including the male/female, public/private sphere dichtomy. Televised women generally remain in the domestic sphere, caring for home and children, while men have worthwhile public-sphere careers.[30] The Kardashians challenge this assumption. In the first episode, Kris explains the twofold family/business value by explaining her role in the family: "I'm the mom and Kim's manager."[31] Her very role as a self-described "momager" conflates family and business principles. When Kim was asked to appear on the Tyra Banks talk show, with the caveat of necessarily discussing a pornographic recording in which she appeared, Kris explained: "When as I first heard about Kim's [sex] tape, as her mother I wanted to kill her. But as her manager, I knew I had a job to do and I really just wanted her to move past it."[32] Each role has dissonant expectations and beliefs. A mother might bemoan her daughter's behavior, scolding her judgment; a manager must attempt to exploit the situation to her client's benefit.

In the second episode Kim discusses her mother's recent rash of mistakes in managing Kim's career.[33] While Kris considers herself a hands-on manager, working for two clients, her daughter and her husband," Kim notes, "I need her to pay attention and really focus on what's going on." As a prank, Khloe (operating at Kim's behest to "teach Mom a lesson") tells her mother that Kim may be firing her as manager. Kris immediately overreacts, changing her outgoing answering machine message to say that callers have reached "Kim Kardashian's former manager. If you'd like to get a hold of my ungrateful daughter, you can call her on her personal and private cell phone, which is . . .". By the end of this episode, in true television fashion, everyone realizes that family is paramount. Additionally, Kim learns a lesson about the amount of work her mother truly performs as her manager, signifying the value conflict between business and family. Kim says to her mom, "I love you and I don't want anyone else as a manager but you." The heart-to-heart conversation Kim and Kris have about her professional performance occurs while Khloe and Kourtney yell and roughhouse in the background, highlighting the physical merging of business and family.

Another factor that highlights the conflation of the business and mother roles is the setting of many business discussions: the home. The home is traditionally a feminine private sphere, free from public sphere commercial decisions. However, the Kardashians determine many career decisions at home. When Kris and Bruce, Kim's stepfather, discuss Kim posing for *Playboy*, this professional conversation is conducted in the kitchen of their house, while Kris bakes dessert.[34] The roles of businesswoman and mother are blended through both setting and actions.

That Kris is the momager is never forgotten; it appears frequently on the program. For example, in episode eight, Khloe asked, "Why is Kim Mom's screensaver?" Kourtney answered, "Because Mom gets 10 percent."[35] These off-handed comments are woven into dialogue throughout the season.

Kris is much more frequently depicted in a business role, even within the home, than performing motherly duties. These duties, such as carpooling and buying school supplies, are delegated to stepfather Bruce. The role of mother is usurped by the managerial duties. The contradictory values of mother and manager coexist, with managerial characteristics dominating.

Beauty/Unhappiness

On reality TV, the primary female beauty characteristics are youth, whiteness, thinness, surgical alteration, and hypersexuality.[36] *Keeping Up with The Kardashians* reifies these qualities, while complicating the issue of beauty norms through the depiction of another duality: beauty and unhappiness. The first words of the very first episode are this exchange.

Kim: "I'm starving."
Khloe: "Don't you have a photo shoot tomorrow? Stop eating."
Kris then whispers to Khloe: "I think she has a little junk in the trunk. The jiggles."

Other family members laugh in the background, implicitly bolstering the idea of beauty requiring a svelte figure.[37]

In another telling instance, in episode four, after Kim decides to pose for *Playboy*, Kris instructs her to "go run around the block," and as Kim exits, Kris yells "cardio, cardio, cardio, cardio, cardio."[38] Examples of this type are myriad throughout the show; they emphasize physical appearance norms, while sowing insecurity, jealousy, and family discord.

The Kardashian women represent almost a caricature of femininity and the female form. This is illustrated through lengthy hair extensions, an hourglass figure exaggerated through tight, fashionable designer clothing, sky-high heels, huge eyes encircled with dramatically heavy makeup, and darkly tanned skin. The Kardashian sisters epitomize a level of physical appearance that most people cannot possibly achieve. The at-home audience views them barely working to achieve this beauty, endorsing the message that by the work depicted, this beauty is attainable. However, unseen labor exists: exercising, dieting, and, frequently, cosmetic surgery. What the audience does witness promotes the goal of perfection, seemingly achievable through the little work actually portrayed. The Kardashians perform the "work of being watched," the labor of having their lives recorded for which they receive payment.[39] Like the majority of people appearing on television, they simply exist resplendent in their beauty, without the audience seeing the majority of preparation involved. While the Kardashian family members seemingly embrace their full-figured curves, their discourse indicates a preference for the societal norm of a lithe shape. In tandem with the beauty message within the show is the idea that beauty does not equal happiness or confidence.

In a symptomatic sequence, while preparing for Tyra Banks's talk show, Kim has false eyelashes applied, her hair professionally styled, and tries on several outfits and pairs of high heels. Simultaneously, she confesses her anxiety about appearing on the show, demonstrating her humanity. Kim's superficial appearance is an accomplishment that takes a team of people, several hours, and thousands of dollars, with apparently little work actually done by her. Paradoxically, after all this beauty pampering, insecure and nervous, Kim looks into the camera and says tearfully, "I wish my sisters were here."[40]

Kim's unhappiness juxtaposed with her physical appearance exemplifies a conflict: beauty norms and the supposed happiness of being considered good-looking, contrasted with the pressure of the aforementioned norms and celebrity.

The show also stresses a perfect body image while paying lip service to the idea that everyone should be happy with his or her natural appearance. The perfect body image is emphasized through body-image anxiety present throughout program discourse and through a prominence of visual nudity. Additionally, fans of the show may be aware of the family's endorsement of a line of appetite suppressants, which also highlights the importance of bodily perfection.

There are dual messages present. The overt message is that appearance is extremely important and beauty is attainable with money. Anyone can look like a Kardashian by buying Kardashian-designed clothes, spraying Kardashian-endorsed perfume, and mimicking their make-up choices. The implicit message is that even unrealistic perfection does not guarantee contentment.

Intimate/Transgressive

Throughout the first season, the intimacy of the family is illustrated repetitively. However, their closeness is transgressive, too close, breaking traditional taboos and standards, particularly those related to sex. This is undoubtedly related to the daughters' sexual images, necessarily discussed with their dual mother/manager.

An episode titled "Remembering Dad" demonstrates their closeness. It focuses on the family's commemoration of Robert Kardashian, Senior, the patriarch of the Kardashian family. In particular, Khloe has difficulties with her anger and sadness related to his death. Through editing and dialogue, this episode associates his death with Khloe being arrested for drunk driving. The family joins together to eulogize their father and help Khloe with her issues. In this episode, Khloe must contend with two judgmental fathers. Kris provokes Khloe asking, "What would Dad think of this?" referring to Robert Kardashian, Sr.; Khloe must also face her stepfather Bruce's disapproval of her arrest. The episode ends with a montage of home movies of Robert Kardashian, Sr.[41] Their collective grief over this loss bonds the individual family members into a cohesive unit.

Yet this intimacy infringes on typical familial limitations. In an example illustrative of the boundary-breaking nature of their close-knit relationships, Kim's anniversary gift for Bruce and Kris is a stripper pole. This gift shatters American parent/child relationship and familial sexuality norms. Later, twelve-year-old Kylie finds Kim showing the gift to anniversary party guest Robyn Anton, founder of the female burlesque/pop group Pussycat Dolls. Kim and Robyn watch in surprise as the pre-teen sexily dances and slides up and down the pole. The hi-jinks end when Bruce strolls into the room, reprimands Kim, and carries a yelling Kylie out of the room.[42] The stripper pole may be a funny gag gift for parents, albeit a risqué one, but it also shows the family's nonchalance about sexuality and sex. While Bruce, the conservative voice of reason, deems that the stripper pole is an inappropriate plaything for Kylie, it still exists in their house, representative of the high level of sexual talk prevalent in their household. This demeaning of the significance of sex has visible results in oldest sister Kourtney's supposedly unplanned pregnancy. During Kourtney and Scott's Season one pregnancy scare in the episode titled "You Are So Pregnant Dude," Khloe decrees, "These bitches better be smart and use a condom."[43] Seemingly not learning from this incident, Kourtney later refers to her Season four pregnancy as welcome, yet accidental.[44]

In the same episode as the stripper pole incident, during Kris and Bruce's anniversary party, Kendall and Kylie play at bartending, mixing drinks and dancing behind the bar.[45] Mom Kris asks the pre-teens, "Do you really think it's appropriate that you're behind a bar . . . while we're having a party?" Later in the episode, at the anniversary party, Khloe's toast to her stepfather includes, "Thank god you had a vasectomy a couple years ago!" as everyone watching laughs.

The family seemingly has no restrictions on behavior. Kris breaches the normal demarcation lines between family and non-family members as she intrudes on her daughter Kourtney's relationship. Kris apparently has no inhibitions telling Kourtney's boyfriend that he is too young for her, not ready to settle down, and intimates that he cheats on her. Later, Khloe explains to her mother, "It's none of your business and I don't think it's appropriate for you to say that. You need to stay out of people's personal lives." Kris notes, "But in this family, that's not how it rolls. We make it our business to know what's going on." This is humorously paired with Khloe then stating to the camera, "I know mom is hiding something from us and I am going to get to the bottom of it."[46] The lack of parent/children boundaries is part of the show's appeal, as audience members may watch to see which taboos will be broken.

Sexual/Conservative

The show also exhibits a paradox of conservative family-first values with an image of overt sexuality. While the sisters often appear explicitly sexualized in popular media, verbal discourse of the show emphasizes conservative values, such as fidelity, stability, and marriage. Whereas Kim earned fame from her supposedly privately-filmed pornographic recording, on the show she is hesitant and dubious of posing for *Playboy*. Kim's initial reaction to the magazine's offer is incredulity, and she wants to turn down the offer.

> Kris convinces her, "They really really really really want you. Wouldn't it be fun?"
> Kim protests saying, "Ever since the sex tape scandal, I have to be really careful about how I'm perceived."
> Kris asserts, "I think it would be an awesome experience for you, if nothing else. On top of all that, it's a ton of money."
> Kim objects, "People are going to say, ohhhh, all she's good for is taking her clothes off. Can she do anything else?" [47]

After debating whether or not to say yes, Kim decides to pose for the magazine with the caveat that she will not be photographed fully nude, saying, "In the end, I'm sticking to what I believe and not taking it off." *Playboy* is unhappy with the resultant images and requires more skin to be shown.

Kim equivocates, "I'm really conflicted. They're unhappy with the shoot and want me to show more skin and I'm not sure if that's something I really want to do." She eventually acquiesces.

Despite Kim's doubtful and insecure portrayal, once in front of the *Playboy* camera again, she sexily poses, arches her back, and appears almost fully nude, bare save for strands of pearls.

Kim's superficial concern about her sexualized image, when anyone can buy her pornographic video, is extremely ironic. Moreover, she capitalizes on her body, posing practically nude for magazines, calendars, and other merchandise, and often appears in public provocatively dressed. This contradiction between vocalized conservative values and outward image may provoke fascination and is perhaps cultivated to make Kim appeal to both men (who may appreciate her figure) and women (who possibly may appreciate her verbal value system). Kim has created an image that is both the Madonna and whore. This image exemplifies many powerful media messages present within popular culture. As scholars Jhally and Katz noted, two cultural imperatives coexist within media for women: "sexuality is everything" and "good girls don't."[48]

Moreover, while superficial overt sexuality standards (such as skimpy clothing and nudity) are often considered negative in real life (although oft celebrated in media), on the show these norms are depicted as neutral, if not positive. However, these sexuality norms may be dangerous, as evidenced by the family's attempts to shield Kylie and Kendall from them. On a telling occasion, one of the little girls entered the kitchen while Kourtney, Khloe, Kim, and Kris were perusing Kim's images from the *Playboy* shoot. Rob carried the little girl out of the room, saying, "We don't want to see."[49] The family acknowledges the younger girls should be protected, while the older sisters exploit their sexuality in order to earn fame and monetary rewards.

Gender Role Contravention

With Kris as the income-generating manager, Bruce takes on the traditionally female role of caregiver. Bruce completes errands, looks after the two youngest daughters, and generally runs the household. In episode two, Kris noted, "Thank god for Bruce. I couldn't do it all and take care of the little girls without him." While ostensibly appreciated, like many off-screen women, his voice is often unheard on the program, or unheeded. Later in that same episode, he asked Kris, "Would you like my opinion? You would?" She answered, "Depends on what it is."[50]

Not only does Bruce represent the established wifely role, he is also the voice of conservative values. The family is often afraid of his moralistic disapproval. In episode three, *Girls Gone Wild* movie series founder Joe Francis calls from prison, requesting that the Kardashians become spokesmodels for his high-end bikini line. He offers to fly them to his beach-front mansion in Puerto Vallarta, Mexico for a photo shoot, to which they readily agree. When asked if she's told Bruce about the photo shoot, Kris demurs, saying, "No, he's really conservative. He's gonna have a problem that you guys are posing in bikinis" and "I just don't want him to get upset one more time."[51]

Later, Kris says in her personal narrative to the camera: "Bruce and I have a great marriage and a great dynamic. But sometimes things just work out better if he doesn't know every single detail." This recurs again and again; when the family knows Bruce won't like a decision, they try not to tell him about it until the last possible moment, which results in drama-filled scenes. Bruce is the voice of prudence, which often results in the family laughing at him and his disgust with them. The roles of the typical patriarchal family are reversed; Bruce is ignored, while the women in the family dictate the norms by which the family abides. This is another example of how *Keeping Up With The Kardashians* challenges the standard reality TV conventions of white men being depicted as powerful and dominant and women as reliant upon men.[52] Here, the Kardashian domestic norms upend traditional reality television standards.

Upon finding out about the bikini shoot, Bruce flies to Mexico, confronting his wife about lying to him. He contends, "Probably the most important thing in my life is protecting these girls. You know, you see what happened with Kim and her sex tape, they really have to watch what they're doing because just a little thing can get totally blown out of proportion."[53]

When he arrives at the photo shoot, Kris is embarrassed that he's there, not sad or regretful that she lied by omission. When asked why she didn't tell him about the shoot, Kris calls him conservative and Bruce responds, "The high road is always the good road, isn't that amazing?" Ultimately, while Bruce can express his unhappiness and dismay, he has no agency. He often states his dissenting opinion, which the family then scorns. The family ostensibly is afraid to tell him things and incur his wrath; why is unclear, as they simply disregard him anyway. When Kim elects to pose for *Playboy*, Bruce says, "Pretty scary when I'm the only one to vote no on Kimberly doing *Playboy*. I mean, she's got a sex tape out, and now she's doing *Playboy*? Please, this is your daughter."[54] In this family, father may know best, but no one pays him any attention.

Conclusion

Throughout the dichotomies present within the show there are emphases on sexuality and women's conflicted roles. The Kardashians utilize sexuality, normalizing body and beauty ideals. Concurrently, while venerating sexual imagery, they endorse conservative sexuality norms and are depicted as neither promiscuous nor immoral. Nudity and debauchery are not conjoined on the program. Any negative behavior, such as drunk driving, reaps severe emotional repercussions.

The sexual images of the women on the show help reinforce certain conventional beauty, body, and fashion ideals. They help define femininity and celebrity, setting unrealistic expectations that even they seemingly cannot achieve. The lack of attention on the show given to exercise and diet promotes that idea that anyone may attain a seemingly perfect body. However, the lack of satisfaction Kim expresses about her body complicates the strengthening of beauty exemplars; rather, the norm is seemingly constant frustration, a theme with which many viewers likely empathize. While body ideals are vaunted, none of the sisters ever appear content, despite their celebrity and beauty.

Another duality present throughout the season is the public/private spheres and the roles of women and men in the home. Kris runs her management business from her home, merging the public and private spheres. The two fusions (business/family, public/private) result in a unique value system for the Kardashians. What other families may regard as off-limits, such as sexuality and public nudity—integral components of Kim's image—are very much a part of their televised home life. Moreover, *Keeping Up With The Kardashians* subverts traditional gender roles. Kris is most frequently framed in a business light, illustrating her fruitful techniques of managing Kim's career. While women traditionally care for children and run households, Kris has seemingly allocated these duties to her husband. Moreover, Kris seems to make all the decisions in the family (pertaining to business and family), while Bruce's opinion is disregarded.

Within reality TV as a genre, women are frequently depicted negatively.[55] In this sense, *Keeping Up With The Kardashians* bucks this trend, providing a role model for entrepreneurial women. Not only is Kris an entrepreneur, but her daughters are as well. Many of the shows' scenes take place in Dash, the sisters' co-owned clothing store. The women within the show refute the stereotype that sexy women are not smart.

The Kardashians blur boundaries that are distinct in typical households. There are no clear demarcations in any of the dichotomies discussed here. The syntheses of family and business, permissible and objectionable sexual behavior, and traditional male and female gender roles result in a complex web of right and wrong. In *Keeping Up With The Kardashians* the only ideal clearly elucidated is a reliable and clichéd sitcom moral, the importance of family.

However, this study only examines the first season of *Keeping Up With The Kardashians*. In future seasons of the show, the values discussed here may change as the show gains or ebbs in popularity or attempts to move its story line forward. Moreover, as the Kardashian family nature is impulsive and unpredictable, future events may alter the contradictory ideals.

Nevertheless, this investigation sheds light upon how conventional mediated messages may be evolving; not every televised familial relationship necessarily adheres to hackneyed stereotypes of men and women's expected behavior. Women no longer need to be the Madonna or the whore; they can be both. Moreover, men are no longer the inevitably dominant partner and family leader; out of the realm of reality TV, new paradigms may be emerging.

Undeniably, television analysis helps illuminate contemporary societal norms. These norms are not simple or easily definable, on-screen or off-screen. The Kardashians embody many conflicting values; doubtlessly these all influence and mimic the world we live in. The original query posed earlier within this chapter asked which values are represented with *Keeping Up With The Kardashians*. The answer is that the values are sundry and multifaceted: conventional and alternative, sexual and smart, and close-knit and too close for comfort. The Kardashians embody the contradictions present within us all— theirs are intimate and familiar, yet extreme and larger than life.

Notes

1. Sofia Fernandez, "E!'s 'Keeping Up With the Kardashians' Hits Ratings High," *Hollywood Reporter*, September 9, 2011, http://www.hollywoodreporter.com/ live-feed/es-keeping-up-kardashians-hits-231695.

2. Jeff Jensen, "Naked Ambition," *Entertainment Weekly*, September 3, 2010, 42-46; Daphne Merkin, "The Wild Bunch," *The New York Times*, December 4, 2010, http://tmagazine.blogs.nytimes.com/2010/12/04/the-wild-bunch.

3. Fernandez, "E!'s 'Keeping Up With the Kardashians' Hits Ratings High."

4. Stephanie Goldberg, "Kim Kardashian, Kris Humphries: Are you surprised?" *CNN.com*, November 1, 2011, http://www.cnn.com/2011/11/01/showbiz/celebrity-news-gossip/kim-kardashian-kris-humphries-divorce/index.html.

5. Eric Wilson, "Kim Kardashian Inc." *The New York Times*, November 17, 2010, http://www.nytimes.com /2010/11/18/fashion/18KIM.html?emc=eta1.

6. Kevin O'Leary, "Sisters Torn Apart," *US Weekly*, August 23, 210, 42-47.

7. Ani Esmalian, "Lamar Odom's New Manager: Mama Kris Jenner," *Holly Scoop*, October 13, 2010, http://www.hollyscoop.com/lamar-odom/lamar-odoms-new-manager-mama-kris-jenner_25399.aspx.

8. Jeff Jensen, "Naked ambition," 42-46.

9. Eric Wilson, "Kim Kardashian Inc."

10. Jeff Jensen, "Naked ambition," 46.

11. Jeff Jensen, "Naked ambition," 43-44.

12. Jeff Jensen, "Naked ambition," 44.

13. John Fiske, *Television Culture* (London and New York: Methuen, 1987), 1.

14. John Fiske, "The Codes of Television," in *Media Studies: A Reader*, ed. Paul Marris and Sue Thornham (New York: New York University Press, 2000), 220.

15. Fiske, *Television Culture*, 36.

16. Fiske, *Television Culture*, 16.

17. Su Holmes, "'All You've Got to Worry About is the Task, Having a Cup of Tea, and Doing a Bit of Sunbathing': Approaching Celebrity in Big Brother," in *Understanding Reality Television*, ed. Su Holmes and Deborah Jermyn (New York: Routledge, 2004), 111–35.

18. Stuart Hall, "Encoding/Decoding," in *Media and Cultural Studies: Key Works*, ed. Meenakshi Gigi Durham and Douglas M. Kellner, rev. ed. (Malden, MA: Blackwell Publishing, 2001), 163-173.

19. Julia Wood, *Gendered Lives: Communication, Gender, and Culture*, 9th ed. (Boston: Wadsworth Cengage Learning, 2011), 272.

20. Gaye Tuchman, Arlene Daniels, and James Benet, eds., *Hearth and Home: Images of Women in Mass Media* (New York: Oxford University Press, 1978).

21. Sut Jhally and Jackson Katz, "Big Trouble, Little Pond: Reflections on the Meaning of the Campus Pond Rapes," *Umass*, Winter, 2001, 26-31.

22. Wood, *Gendered Lives: Communication, Gender, and Culture*, 265.

23. Norman Fairclough, "Critical Analysis of a Media Discourse," in *Media Studies: A Reader*, ed. Paul Marris and Sue Thornham (New York: New York University Press, 2000), 308-325.

24. Malcolm Sillars and Bruce Gronbeck, *Communication Criticism: Rhetoric, Social Codes, Cultural Studies* (Prospect Heights, Ill.: Waveland Press, 2001).

25. Fairclough, "Critical Analysis of a Media Discourse."

26. Michel Foucault, *Archaeology of Knowledge* (London: Tavistock, 1972).

27. Amanda McClain, *American Ideal: How American Idol Constructs Celebrity, Collective Identity, and American Discourses* (Lanham, MD: Lexington Books, 2011).

28. Annette Hill, "Big Brother: The Real Audience," in *Television: The Critical View*, ed. Horace Newcomb, 7th ed. (New York: Oxford University Press, 2007), 471-485.

29. McClain, *American Ideal.*

30. Charlotte Brunsdon, Julie D'Acci, and Lynn Spigel, introduction to *Feminist Television Critism*, ed. Charlotte Brunsdon, Julie D'Acci, and Lynn Spigel (Oxford: Clarendon Press, 1997), 1-19; Jennifer Pozner, *Reality Bites Back* (Berkeley, CA: Seal Press, 2010).

31. *Keeping Up With The Kardashians*, "I'm Watching You," directed by Chris Ray, first broadcast October 14, 2007 by E!.

32. *Keeping Up With The Kardashians*, "I'm Watching You."

33. *Keeping Up With The Kardashians*, "Managing Mom," directed by Chris Ray, first broadcast October 21, 2007 by E!.

34. *Keeping Up With The Kardashians*, "Birthday Suit," directed by Chris Ray, first broadcast November 4, 2007 by E!.

35. *Keeping Up With The Kardashians*, "The Price of Fame," directed by Chris Ray, first broadcast December 2, 2007 by E!.

36. Pozner, *Reality Bites Back.*

37. *Keeping Up With The Kardashians*, "I'm Watching You."

38. *Keeping Up With The Kardashians*, "Birthday Suit."

39. Marc Andrejevic, *Reality TV: The Work of Being Watched* (New York: Rowman & Littlefield Publishers, Inc., 2004).

40. *Keeping Up With The Kardashians*, "I'm Watching You."

41. *Keeping Up With The Kardashians*, "Remebering Dad," directed by Chris Ray, first broadcast November 11, 2007 by E!.

42. *Keeping Up With The Kardashians*, "I'm Watching You."

43. *Keeping Up With The Kardashians*, "You Are So Pregnant Dude," directed by Chris Ray, first broadcast November 1, 2007 by E!.

44. David Caplan, "Kourtney Kardashian Agonized Over Whether to Keep Her Baby," *People*, August 19, 2009, http://www.people.com/people/article/0,,20298807,00 .html.

45. *Keeping Up With The Kardashians*, "I'm Watching You."

46. *Keeping Up With The Kardashians*, "I'm Watching You."

47. *Keeping Up With The Kardashians*, "Birthday Suit."

48. Jhally and Katz, "Big Trouble, Little Pond."

49. *Keeping Up With The Kardashians*, "Birthday Suit."

50. *Keeping Up With The Kardashians*, "Managing Mom."

51. *Keeping Up With The Kardashians*, "Brody in the House," directed by Chris Ray, first broadcast October 8, 2007 by E!.

52. Dwight Brooks and Lisa Hebert, "Gender, Race, and Media Representation," in *Handbook of Gender and Communication*, ed. Bonnie Dow and Julia T. Wood (Thousand Oaks: Sage, 2006), 297-317; Wood, *Gendered Lives: Communication, Gender, and Culture*, 265.

53. *Keeping Up With The Kardashians*, "Brody in the House."

54. *Keeping Up With The Kardashians*, "Brody in the House."

55. Pozner, *Reality Bites Back.*

Part Four:

The Facts of Life

Chapter Ten

The Selling of Gender-Role Stereotyping: A Content Analysis of Toy Commercials Airing on Nickelodeon

Susan G. Kahlenberg[1]

Nickelodeon, arguably one of the most commercially successful cable television networks, has been the top-rated children's cable network for the past sixteen years.[2] In 2011, the *Nickelodeon* network yielded $3.95 billion in fourth-quarter earnings for its multimedia parent company Viacom,[3] accounting for an estimated 25 percent of Viacom's advertising revenue.[4] According to Nielsen ratings, *Nickelodeon* averaged 952,000 viewers in the first quarter of 2012 and was rated number one among daily viewers aged two to eleven.[5]

Kids television has become big business. Youth marketer James McNeal refers to children as a "three-on-one-market":[6] they have their own money to spend, strongly influence family spending patterns, and have the most market potential for establishing brand loyalty. A case in point: "eight to twelve-year-olds spend $30 million of their own money each year and influence another $150 billion of their parents' spending."[7] With children exposed to approximately forty thousand ads on television alone in a year, this chapter will focus on how commercials on *Nickelodeon* have the potential to strongly influence its viewers.[8]

Sarah Banet-Weiser examines the relationship among children, citizenship, and consumerism. She argues that political rhetoric on *Nickelodeon* inculcates in children a sense of belonging and respect through watching its hip, cool, humorous, and anti-adult based programs.[9] *Nickelodeon* brands itself as a liberating alternative to family and social contexts where children face rules and oppression. This "us-versus-them"[10] brand identity appeals to youth because it denounces any traits of being a "green vegetable network," one that parents want their children to watch because of its educational benefit. Simultaneously,

Nickelodeon successfully dual markets itself to adults by spotlighting its original TV series that are educational, diverse, and cast progressive female leads in programs such as *iCarly, As Told by Ginger, Clarissa Explains it All,* and *The Wild Thornberries.*[11]

The *Nickelodeon* network claims to be on "kids' sides," and this notion will be critically explored through an examination of gendered representations in toy commercials aired on the channel. The central purpose of this paper is to explore Banet-Weiser's assertion that *Nickelodeon* is "a key producer of girl power culture."[12] She describes how *Nickelodeon* has taken risks to produce and distribute shows that offer greater visibility, respect, and power to girls while striving not to alienate boys. Yet ironically, *Nickelodeon* positions itself as offering gender-neutral programming, claiming that program decisions are about inclusivity to all kids rather than feminist politics.[13] Further, previous research deduced that commercials on *Nickelodeon* did not coalesce with its branded rebellious and progressive identity.[14]

Specifically, this content analysis investigates gender-role stereotypes, measuring the types of toys, gender portrayals, dominant product users, voiceovers, interactions, settings, and activities in toy commercials. Cognitive, gender, and mass communication theories establish that gender positioning of toys for tweens, elementary school aged children and preadolescents is an outdated marketing strategy. To wit, conventional gender norms are contrary to the progressive mindset of *Nickelodeon*. Results of a content analysis profile how gender identities are being sold to children, concluding that *Nickelodeon* has the continued popularity and dominance in the TV market to be discriminating in its advertising sales.

Theoretical Perspectives and the Construction of Gender

Over the years, research studies have found that males and females are systematically differentiated in television programs and commercials. Males are depicted as "doing" in the public sphere, in a diverse array of professional and working roles. They are characterized as strong, independent, competent, stubborn, and of higher social status when compared to females.[15] While in recent years there are more females working outside of the home and in professional jobs,[16] on-air females are often restricted to "being" in the private sector as wives, mothers, and caretakers. On television, females are depicted as weak, nurturing, stubborn, sexy, subordinate to men, and emotional.

According to gender schema theory, children form knowledge structures for organizing and making sense of a given phenomenon. Gender schemas are frameworks that direct the way we understand what constitutes being male and female. Research suggests that gender-related cognitions can play a salient role in the development of stereotyped preferences, affects, and behaviors.[17] Guiding this content analysis is the concern that gender role stereotypes through culture and communication may contribute to fixed beliefs, as correlational studies have found a relationship between TV viewing habits and gender-related attitudes and behaviors.[18]

Cognitive development approaches further document how children's understanding of gender is "qualitatively *different*" based on age.[19] Piaget's theory of cognitive development proposes four main stages: sensorimotor (birth to two years), preoperational (two to seven years), concrete operational (seven to eleven years), and formal operational (eleven through adulthood). While there are important theoretical and methodological shortcomings with this theory, it is useful in describing age-related patterns and developments.[20]

In terms of the relationship between tweens and gender, as children enter the preoperational stage, their judgments are still perceptually bound to their environment. Children are characterized by centration (focus on one central characteristic at the exclusion of others) and egocentrism (the inability to take into account other perspectives).[21] In this stage, children have begun to form and conform to gender-typed activities, traits, and identities.[22] Concrete operational children can consider several dimensions of a stimulus at a time, but are limited in applying this understanding to abstract examples. Yet they have the motivation, value, and affective component to think outside of these earlier formative and rigid gender schemas. Children in the formal operational stage progress to more complex thought, actively constructing gender based on complex social and personal factors, in addition to accumulated real world and mediated experiences. Thus, researchers agree that gender-schematic processing and cognitive development explains why children come to value and adopt the social role associated with his or her gender label.[23]

If children are searching for cues about gender from their environment to form gendered self-conceptions, findings from cultivation theorists lend salient theoretical understandings of media's impact on viewers. It establishes that people's perceptions of social reality are influenced by media images, characterizations, and portrayals, particularly for moderate and heavy television viewers. Cultivation theory suggests that heavy viewers are more likely to express attitudes and opinions similar to those represented on television when compared to light viewers. Through long-term and ritualistic exposure to the screen, television has a socialization effect. Thus, children's gender role schemas and identities are shaped in part by television content, which is guided by artistic, dramatic, economic, political, and industry concerns rather than developmental, psychological, and social issues.[24]

In integrating these theoretical perspectives, it can be argued that those who spend more time "living" in the world of television are more likely to be influenced by its gendered images, values, portrayals, and stories. It is well documented that media play an ever-growing central role in the lives of children. On average, children watch three hours of TV a day, and more than half of today's children indicate that parents do not set restrictions on the amount and type of programming they can engage in watching.[25] Television, a historically commercialized institution, rather than parents, peers, teachers, and clergy, has become the "central cultural arm of American society."[26] While research has found that infants and toddlers have difficulties imitating and learning from television, 20 percent of children younger than age three have a TV set in their bedroom, and "children younger than age six spend more time watching TV and videos than they do reading (or being read to) or playing outside."[27]

Content analytic research has long deduced that toy advertisements are replete in children's after-school and weekend daytime programming.[28] Toy commercials comprise approximately one-third of all advertisements during this time frame, second to food and candy. Some critics do not see the cultural importance of toys, dismissing them as mere playthings; others argue that parents, rather than the toy industry, are responsible for monitoring what meaning children ascribe to toys. Herein, toys are considered to be cultural artifacts that carry social significance: preparing children for adult roles and concerns; fostering and engaging their imagination, creativity, and knowledge about the world; creating a shared culture with their friends; cultivating personality traits such as independence and power; and preparing them to be capitalistic consumers.[29] Market research indicates that the toy industry is recession-resistant. During the recent economic recession, parents purchased toys and games, scaling back instead on costlier, high-end items and total purchases.[30] The "nag factor,"[31] the unrelentingly requests by children for their parents to purchase advertised products, influences as much as $180 billion of spending during the holiday season. Thus, business executives claim the challenge is in predicting which toys children will desire, rather than which toys parents will purchase.[32]

The Business of Selling Gender

Some may argue that toy manufacturers market products to match children's displayed preference for gendered toys. Previous research has consistently shown that boys and girls to some degree make gender-typed preferences for toys, friends, and in play.[33] Specifically, children tend to respond favorably to gendered content, making gender-typed toy selections as young as eighteen to twenty months old, and by the age of four to five years old avoid toys that may be considered appropriate for the opposite sex.[34] In other words, as this argument goes, it is not the toy industry but biology, parents, children and other social forces that inculcate children's positive responses to gender marketing strategies.

However, tweens have a higher degree of gender flexibility, as they are developmentally primed to think outside of rigid gender-typed characteristics. For example, previous research found that school aged children—particularly boys—who saw nontraditional images were more likely to report that the toy advertised was for boys *and* girls, rather than just boys *or* girls.[35] Similarly, an experiment examining children's responses to gender-role stereotypes in commercials found both gender and age-related responses.[36] With regard to gender, third and fourth grade boys and girls responded positively to ads with both agentic (male stereotype) and communal (female stereotypes) themes and attributes. With regard to age, it was determined that while there were no differences between younger, kindergarteners, and older boys' attitudes, as girls age, they begin to reject traditional communal stereotypes. Additionally, it has been established that children responded positively when viewing ads with higher degrees of gender flexibility as they aged, again corroborating previous research that found that older children were more accepting of a wider range of gender-appropriate activities.[37]

This study exclusively focuses on tweens who are considered to represent an important demographic to the *Nickelodeon* network. Tweens are recognized as one of the most lucrative consumer markets and most apt to watch television programming in the after school hours.[38] While some scholars conceptualize tweens more broadly as between the ages of seven or eight and thirteen or fourteen years old,[39] others offer an average age of eight to twelve.[40] What makes this slightly ambiguous and mixed age range compelling is that it reflects an age delineated marketing category of children in the analytical stage of consumer socialization.[41] During this stage, children shift from perceptual to analytical thought and have a more complex and sophisticated understanding of the marketplace. They are now well positioned to recall advertisements' persuasive intent, be analytical of content from their own point of view, deconstruct gender stereotypes, and benefit from prosocial content.

Additionally, cultivation theory predicts that increased exposure to gender-stereotyped media may influence children's general attitudes about appropriate gender roles and behaviors.[42] It focuses on effects through long term exposure, and while there are some documented variations (e.g., mainstreaming, resonance, genre), *Nickelodeon* has been established as consistently offering greater diversity and visibility of empowered girls, through programs like *Clarissa Explains it All, The Secret World of Alex Mack, The Wild Thornberries,* and *As Told by Ginger*.[43] With *Nickelodeon* dedicated to constructing a different set of gender representations in its original TV programming, and taking account of its success in the marketplace, it is argued that improved and diverse portrayals within toy commercials may have a positive influence on children's gender role socialization.

While the following hypotheses do not make predictions about the effects of televised content or interpretive strategies that children use to make sense of toy commercials, they advance scholarly knowledge about how masculinity and femininity are portrayed in consumer culture. Television advertising plays a role within the wider socialization process, influencing tweens' future gender and social roles.

Gender Portrayals

Content analyses focusing on gender-role stereotypes within commercials have consistently documented the underrepresentation of girls-only when compared to boys-only and boys-and-girls together.[44] Yet in recent years, girls' visibility has increased both in the numbers of girl-only and boys-and-girls together TV commercials.[45] In fact, Debra Merskin, who examined the representation of gender and race on the Turner Cartoon Network concluded, "advertisers are viewing the girl audience as nearly as important as the boy audience."[46] This may reflect the feminine origins of the tween concept as an age stage in the 1940s to reflect girlhood and social ambiguities about girls' maturity, sexuality, puberty, and bodies, as connected to girls' marketplace identities and their increased economic power.[47] Further, a content analysis of toy commercials determined that while there was still progress to be made to achieve gender parity, girls-only commercials outnumbered commercials featuring both boys-only and boys-and-girls together.[48] Herein, it will be established whether this trend of visibility for girls continues, with *Hypothesis 1* and *Hypothesis 2* measuring types of toys, gender portrayal, and product users.

Hypothesis 1: Commercials will most likely feature more girls-only than boys-only or boys-and-girls together.

Hypothesis 2: Commercials will most likely gender position toys when featuring female users and male users than with boy-and-girl users.

Voiceovers

Based on the predominance of content analyses results, the present study should find more boys-only voiceovers when compared to girls-only, boys-and-girls together, and no voiceovers.[49] This study also extends scholarly knowledge to predict a pronounced difference in voiceovers based on toy type. For instance, previous research found that boy-oriented ads contained elements emphasizing action, competition and control, while girl-oriented ads contained elements relating to feelings, nurturance, and passive activity.[50] This being the case, the present study proposes the following hypothesis:

Hypothesis 3: There will be more commercials matching the sex of voiceovers to toy type than neutral voiceovers.

Nature of Interactions, Settings, and Activities

There is a preponderance of evidence showing gender-stereotyped differences in character's activities and interactions.[51] When comparing studies completed over the past two decades, there have been changes in the ways girls have been portrayed over the years. While data collectively suggested that boys still outnumbered girls in competitive interactions, work and outdoor settings, and physical activities, there were more girls featured in active and physical play, in outdoor settings, and playing with boys than found in earlier studies. This content analysis proposes the following hypotheses to document potential changes in gender roles exclusively in toy commercials in this contemporary television programming era:

Hypothesis 4: More commercials will portray girls as cooperative and boys as competitive.

Hypothesis 5: More commercials will portray girls indoors and boys outdoors.

Hypothesis 6: More commercials will portray boys in physical play and girls in productive play.

Methodology

This study analyzed 1,090 toy commercials airing on the *Nickelodeon* network over a two-week period from October 29, 2008 to November 9, 2008, from 2 p.m. to 7 p.m. This time block was selected to correspond with the fourth-quarter sales of toys, when toy manufacturers spend the bulk of their advertising budgets[52] and temporary toy emporiums and workers surge to accommodate the increase in child-related toys bought in this final quarter.[53] One appeal of this sample's time frame is that it predates *Nickelodeon's* synergistic strategies to strengthen and expand its brand identity, exemplified by the rebranding of Viacom cable holdings to *Nick Jr.* and *TeenNick* in 2009. Further, it profiles toy commercials viewed by tweens prior to their strong migration to digital media in an era when *Nickelodeon* was the most important asset to Viacom.[54]

The unit of analysis was each toy commercial shown in the after-school viewing hours, a time period previously established to be popular among children, who spend an average nine hours a week watching TV after school.[55] Programs aired during this time frame also account for some of Nielsen's highest rating points for children's programs, including *SpongeBob Square Pants, The Fairly OddParents,* and *The Adventures of Jimmy Neutron.* Due to the rise of cable, concentration of media ownership, and audience fragmentation, twenty-four hour cable outlets like *Nickelodeon* now dominate the children's television market, making previous broadcast industry practices of "kid vid," Saturday morning programming, obsolete.[56] Thus, weekend daytime programming was also collected during the 2 p.m. to 7 p.m. time frame.

Approximately four-fifths of the commercials repeated throughout the sample. Past research has deduced that repetition is a well-established advertising technique that generates positive effects in terms of increasing ad recall and brand recall.[57] For instance, one experiment reported a positive correlation between children's media exposure to advertised products and increased food and drink requests, inferring that repetition connects to favorable attitudes and purchase requests.[58] Similarly, an investigation of young children's requests for advertised products found that children's familiarity with commercial television was positively associated with the nagging factor.[59] Additionally, an examination of children's requests to *Father Christmas* revealed that children who watched more TV requested a greater number of toys, particularly for branded items, in their letters.[60] Thus, it was deduced that ad repetition is a common feature within continuous television flow that contributes positively to children's comprehension, desires, and purchasing intent. Thus, repetitive commercials were included in this sample not to boost total sample size, but to reflect the natural, aggregate exposure that children would be exposed to when watching live television.

Commercials were coded based on the *type of toy* being advertised, modifying a previously constructed "toy" variable.[61] During data analysis, toys were regrouped to address low frequency counts. Toys were ultimately classified as dolls, action figures, arts and crafts/make believe, animals, games/building, video/electronic games, transportation/construction, sports, and mixed/other. Contrary to the original toy-coding schema, this study accounted for video games and electronics to address both rapidly advancing technology and the inclusion of video games as a toy by the National Retail Federation.[62] Further, game user research documents increased video game popularity among tweens, particularly boys, who spend more time playing than girls.[63] Thus, the inclusion of video games most accurately reflects contemporary toy marketing trends. Mixed/other was intended to account for toys that were not mutually exclusive to one slot or were outliers, based on the variable's previous strong reliability coefficients.[64]

Voiceover was operationalized as the voice (or voices) from an unseen source that described the product and/or encouraged the product purchase.[65] Songs and jingles were not included. Categories established were no voiceover, male voice, female voice, both male and female voice (neutral), and other (including androgynous).

Gender portrayal was analyzed to determine whether commercials represented girls only, boys only, or girls and boys together. Cannot code was indicated for toy commercials that included character dismemberment, or toys featured by characters who could not be identified by gender (e.g., only a character's hands were shown holding up an action figure). The recording instrument also coded for *dominant product user*, to distinguish from the total recognition or frequency of male and female characters as conveyed in gender. This was operationalized as the person handling, consuming, or directly interacting with the advertised product. This could be different than the central character, which may appear most in the commercial.[66]

Using categories based on previous research studies,[67] the *dominant type of interaction* was coded as cooperative, competitive, parallel, or independent. Those coded as cooperative featured characters working and playing together. Competitive commercials showed characters working and playing together, but focused on winning. Parallel interaction featured two or more characters in the scene together, but not interacting with one another. One character present in the commercial was coded as independent. Commercials that included more than one type of interaction, montages, and many schemes were coded as no dominant interaction.

The *dominant setting* was categorized according to previous research as home/indoors (e.g., kitchen, bedroom), home/outdoors (e.g., driveway, backyard), other/indoors (e.g., school, mall), other/outdoors (e.g., soccer field, construction site), limbo (e.g., background), and fantasy/pretend (e.g., does not exist, imagined, dreamt).[68] If there was more than one setting within the commercial, it was coded as no dominant setting. In this study, home/outdoors had low frequency count and was collapsed to create a singular categorical slot labeled outdoors. The category of fantasy/pretend was eliminated, as there was no representation in the toy commercial sample.

Activity considered how characters engaged with the toy, and did not include animated and computer generated added footage. This content analysis design modified a categorical schema from previous research to reflect the type of activities children engaged in.[69] Activity was coded according to any type of play with a toy being advertised, or play, physical play (e.g., athletic such as running, playing ball, skipping), productive play (e.g., task oriented such as homemaking, arts and crafts, building), passive activity (e.g., watching, reading, having conversations), performance (e.g., guitar hero, instrument, dancing), mixed/other, and no characters. Passive play was collapsed into playing with a toy, as there was low frequency count (N=3) in the overall toy commercial sample.

The author and a student research assistant enrolled in an undergraduate college independently coded commercials. Coder training utilized toy commercials airing on the *Cartoon* network and endured until broad based consensus on the measurement of variables was established. Fifteen percent of the data was double-coded to determine reliability for each variable using Krippendorff's Alpha.[70] All reported variables aforementioned above in the recording instrument met Krippendorff's standard of reliability, with alpha levels for each variable having coefficients of 0.80 or above.

Results

In total, there were 1,090 toy commercials examined on *Nickelodeon*. As shown in Table 10.1, dolls and animals constituted one-third (34.8 percent) of the toy commercials, featuring *Barbie*™ dolls, *Polly Pockets*™ dolls, *Bratz*™ dolls, baby dolls, and both plastic and plush animals, such as *My Little Pony*™, *Rescue Pets*™, *Fur Real*™, and *Little Pet Shop*™. Video games/electronics (17.9 percent) and games/building (9.2 percent) constituted approximately one-fourth of the sample, including toys such as *Leap Frog*™, *Legos*™, *Scene It*™ video games, and board games such as *Hungry Hungry Hippos*™, *Twister*™, and *Operation*™. Sports toys (6.0 percent), action figures (6.2 percent), make believe/arts and crafts (8.3 percent) constituted less than one-fifth of the toy commercials featured in the sample. Approximately 5.1 percent of the toys were classified as mixed/other, an unexpected high frequency count based on the coding schema utilized in this study. In-depth analysis of toy commercials classified as "mixed" indicated the majority of the toys did not meet mutually exclusive coding conditions. For example, according to the toy coding schema a *Spy Video Car* was measured as mixed because it was a transportation vehicle and electronic game due to its separate video camera accessory.

Table 10.1 - Frequency of Toys on Nickelodeon

Toys	N	%
Dolls	213	19.5
Video Games and Electronics	195	17.9
Animals	167	15.3
Transportation/ Construction	135	12.4
Game and building	100	9.2
Sport	65	6.2
Action	68	6.0
Make believe	50	4.6
Arts and crafts	41	3.7
Mixed/other	56	5.1
Total	1,091	100

Note: N= Number of toy commercials: %= Percent of toy commercials.

Hypothesis 1 predicted that more girls-only than boys-only will be featured in toy commercials airing on *Nickelodeon*. Frequency counts indicated support for *Hypothesis 1*. Girls-only constituted 37.6 percent of toy commercials, more than one-third of the total sample, compared to boys-only (23.1 percent), boys-and-girls (23.7 percent), and no characters (15.6 percent).

Hypothesis 2 examined the gender positioning of boys and girls in contemporary toy commercials via a cross tabulation of dominant product user by gender (χ^2=835.518, df=24, p=0.000, N=1,090). As shown in Table 10.2, there were distinctions in how female and male users were positioned with toys. Within toys, girls-only were most likely to be the dominant product user with dolls (88.3 percent) and animals (73.1 percent). Boys were most often the dominant product user of action figures (63.2 percent), transportation and construction (47.4 percent), and sports (78.5 percent). Within arts and crafts/make believe toys, boys-only and boys-and-girls together had equal representation (34.1 percent), with slightly less girls-only (31.9 percent) depicted, suggesting gender-neutral positioning of these toys. Video games were most likely to feature boys-only (33.8 percent); approximately one-fourth of the commercials featured girls-only (23.1 percent) as dominant product users. In general, it was determined that *Hypothesis 2* was supported.

Table 10.2 - Toys and dominant product user in toy commercials

Toys	None R%	C%	Boy Users R%	C%	Girl Users R%	C%	Boy and Girl R%	C%	Total R%	C%
Dolls	11.7	14.0	0	0	88.3	43.4	0	0	100	19.5
Action	36.8	14.0	63.2	13.8	0	0	0	0	100	6.2
Arts and Crafts/ Make believe	0	0	34.1	10.0	31.9	6.7	34.1	19.6	100	8.3
Animals	0	0	6.0	3.2	73.1	28.2	21.0	21.0	100	15.3
Games/ Building	11.0	6.1	21.0	6.8	7.0	1.6	61.0	36.5	100	9.2
Video Games	28.7	31.3	33.8	21.2	23.1	10.4	14.4	16.8	100	17.9
Transport/ Construction	36.3	27.4	47.4	20.6	9.6	3.0	6.7	5.4	100	12.4
Sports	0	0	78.5	16.4	16.9	2.5	4.6	1.8	100	6.0
Mix/Other	23.2	7.3	44.6	8.0	32.1	4.2	0	0	100	5.1
Total	16.4	100	28.5	100	39.7	100	15.3	100	100	100

Note: R%= Row percentages; C%= Column percentages; Dominant Product User x Type of Toys (χ^2=835.518, df=24, p=.000, N=1,090).

Hypothesis 3 explored the relationship between type of toy and voiceover (see Table 10.3), and statistically significant chi-square analysis revealed support. There were more commercials matching the sex of voiceovers to toy type than neutral voiceovers. In terms of voiceovers, there were more male voiceovers (51.9 percent) in toy commercials than female voiceovers (43.5 percent). In general, few commercials had neutral or male-and-female voiceovers (1.7 percent). Of the male voiceovers, they were most common in video games and electronics (24.2 percent), transportation/construction (20.3 percent), and games/building (16.3 percent), and least common in doll (1.6 percent) and make believe/arts and crafts (4.9 percent). Female voiceovers were most common in doll (43.0 percent) and animal (27.6 percent) toy commercials, with less than one-tenth of female voiceovers in transportation/construction (4.2 percent), sports (2.3 percent), games/building (0.2 percent), and action (0 percent) toy commercials. Both male and female voiceovers (neutral) were most populous in make believe/arts and crafts toys (83.3 percent), toys deemed to have gender-neutral positioning. To further emphasize the gendered aspect of toy commercials, 95.7 percent of those toy commercials featuring dolls (N=204) and 78.4 percent of those featuring animals (N=131) had female voiceovers, whereas 100 percent of action toys (N=68) and 92.0 percent of game/building toys (N=92) had male voiceovers.

Table 10.3 - Toys and voiceovers

Toys	None R%	C%	Male R%	C%	Female R%	C%	Both (Neutral) R%	C%	Total R%	C%
Dolls	0	0	4.2	1.6	95.8	43.0	0	0	100	19.5
Action	0	0	100	12.0	0	0	0	0	100	6.2
Arts and crafts/ Make believe	20.9	59.4	30.8	4.9	31.9	6.1	16.5	83.3	100	8.3
Animals	0	0	21.6	6.4	78.4	27.6	0	0	100	15.3
Game/ Building	7.0	21.9	92.0	16.3	1.0	.2	0	0	100	9.2
Video games	3.1	18.8	70.3	24.2	25.1	10.3	1.5	16.7	100	17.9
Transport/ Construction	0	0	85.2	20.3	14.8	4.2	0	0	100	12.4
Sports	0	0	83.1	9.5	16.9	2.3	0	0	100	6.0
Mixed/Other	0	0	48.2	4.8	51.8	6.1	0	0	100	5.1
Total	2.9	100	51.9	100	43.5	100	1.7	100	100	100

Note: R%= Row percentages; C%= Column percentages; Voiceovers x Toys (χ^2=813.146, df=24, p=.000, N=1,090).

Hypothesis 4 predicted that more commercials would portray girls as cooperative and more boys as competitive, rather than diversifying their interactions. Significant chi-square analysis revealed support for *Hypothesis 4* in that girls-only (61.6 percent) were more likely to be presented in cooperative interactions than either boys-only (17.7 percent) or boys-and-girls (20.6 percent; see Table 10.4). Also, boys-only (63.2 percent), more than girls-only (0 percent) and boys-and-girls (36.8 percent) were featured in competitive play, supporting *Hypothesis 4*. Interestingly, within gender, approximately one-third (34.1 percent) of boys-only were portrayed as cooperative, yet no girls were shown playing competitively. Yet 17.8 percent of boys-and-girls played competitively; this suggests that girls are more apt to play competitively when engaging with boys, though the majority of boys-and-girls played cooperatively (38.8 percent) or had no dominant interaction style (30.6 percent).

Table 10.4 - Interaction and gender portrayal

Interaction	None		Boys only		Girls only		Both		Total	
	R%	C%	R%	C%	R%	C%	R%	C%	R%	C%
No dominant	59.9	100	4.2	4.8	8.1	5.6	27.8	30.6	100	26.1
Cooperative	0	0	17.7	34.1	61.6	72.9	20.6	38.8	100	44.5
Competitive	0	0	63.2	31.3	0	0	36.8	17.8	100	11.5
Parallel	0	0	6.1	.8	9.1	.7	84.8	10.9	100	3.0
Independent	0	0	44.8	29.0	52.1	20.7	3.1	1.9	100	15.0
Total	15.6	100	23.1	100	37.6	100	23.7	100	100	100

Note: R%= Row percentages; C%= Column percentages; Gender Portrayal x Interaction (χ^2=954.570, df=12, p=.000, N=1,090).

Table 10.5 - Setting and gender portrayal

Setting	None		Boys only		Girls only		Both		Total	
	R%	C%	R%	C%	R%	C%	R%	C%	R%	C%
No dominant	59.9	48.2	11.5	6.3	17.3	5.9	12.2	6.6	100	12.8
Home/indoor	5.8	16.5	9.3	17.9	51.5	61.0	33.4	62.8	100	44.5
Other/indoor	1.4	1.2	40.8	23.0	40.8	14.1	16.9	9.3	100	13.0
Limbo	10.3	7.1	30.8	14.3	30.8	8.8	28.2	12.8	100	10.7
Total	15.6	100	23.1	100	37.6	100	23.7	100	100	100

Note: R%= Row percentages; C%= Column percentages; Gender Portrayal x Setting (χ^2=449.586, df=12, p=.000, N=1,090).

Hypothesis 5 predicted that more commercials would portray girls-only indoors and boys-only would be outdoors, rather than in diversified settings. As shown in Table 10.5, there was partial support for *Hypothesis 5* insofar as within setting, girls-only were more likely to be portrayed in the home (51.5 percent) than either boys-only (9.3 percent) or boys-and-girls (33.4 percent); yet there was equal likelihood of girls-only and boys-only to be presented in "other indoor" settings (40.8 percent). Within outdoor settings, boys-only (46.9 percent) outnumbered girls-only (20.3 percent) by more than a two-to-one ratio, and boys-and-girls by more than a four-to-one ratio (10.6 percent). Within gender, the majority of boys-and-girls together were shown indoors (72.1 percent); of boys-only, they were equally likely to be portrayed indoors (40.9 percent) or outdoors (38.5 percent). When compared to girls-only, with three-fourths featured indoors (75.0 percent), boys-only were featured within a range of settings, suggesting that setting is a gender marker for girls in toy

Susan G. Kahlenberg

commercials. Of interest, frequency analysis indicated that less than one-fifth (19.0 percent) of all toy commercials were featured outdoors, compared to indoors in the home (44.5 percent), other indoor settings (13.0 percent), in no dominant location (12.8 percent), or in limbo (10.7 percent).

Table 10.6 - Activity and gender portrayal

Activity	None R%	C%	Boys only R%	C%	Girls only R%	C%	Both R%	C%	Total R%	C%
Cannot code	88.5	100	1.0	.8	8.3	3.9	2.1	1.6	100	17.6
Play	0	0	27.6	60.7	46.6	62.9	25.8	55.4	100	50.8
Physical	0	0	70.3	20.6	25.7	4.6	4.1	1.2	100	6.8
Productive	0	0	10/8	7.9	57.3	25.9	31.9	22.9	100	17.0
Performance	0	0	26.1	4.8	23.9	2.7	50.0	8.9	100	4.2
Mixed/other	0	0	33.3	5.2	0	0	66.7	10.1	100	3.6
Total	15.6	100	23.1	100	37.6	100	23.7	100	100	

Note: R%= Row percentages; C%= Column percentages; Gender Portrayal x Activity (χ^2=1120.172, df=15, p=.000, N=1,090).

Hypothesis 6 examined the activities that children engaged in while playing, predicting that toy commercials would feature girls in more productive and task oriented activities, whereas boys would be exhibited in more physical activities. Within physical play, the majority of TV characters were boys-only (70.3 percent), versus girls-only (25.7 percent), and boys-and-girls together (4.1 percent; see table 10.6). Within productive play, girls-only (57.3 percent) were more than four times likely to engage in play than boys-only (10.8 percent). These findings indicate support for *Hypothesis 6*. Ultimately, it should be noted that frequency analyses indicated that physical (7.0 percent) and productive (16.8 percent) combined constituted slightly less than one-fourth of all play activities, indicating that the impact of this gender marker in toy commercials was not substantial, compared to the majority of toy commercials that featured children playing with a toy (50.8 percent).

Discussion

Results of this content analysis indicate that toy commercials set forth gender-typed notions in disproportionate ways to the progression afforded to characters documented in the network's television programming.[71] *Nickelodeon*'s business decision to sell commercial space to toy manufacturers seems to defy good marketing strategy, as the network's brand identity is "the renegade, the cool network, the outsider."[72] Yet there is nothing distinct and unique in selling rigid and traditional agentic and communal stereotypes in gender-matched ways, particularly when research on cognitive perspectives of gender development consistently shows that tweens have the cognitive abilities and real world experiences to be open, flexible, and discerning with gendered content.

While the prediction that girls-only would outnumber boys-only was supported, replicating the work of Kahlenberg and Hein, the majority of girls-only were relegated to female oriented toys like dolls and animals. Few girls-only were featured with male oriented toys such as games/building, transportation/construction, and no girls were featured with action figures. In contrast, boys-only were featured with a wider variety of toys, including boy oriented toys like sports, transportation/construction and action, as well as female oriented toys like animals.

Closer examination of toy commercials indicated that boys-only and girls-only were often depicted in stereotypic, gender-typed ways. For instance, boys-only were shown with animal toys culturally associated with power, dominance, speed, and muscularity based on their predatory and hunting status, whereas girls were shown with domestic and nurturing animals, such as kittens, puppies, and bunnies. Girls-only were portrayed with video and electronic toys with traditional feminine gender markings by color, style, and activity. As an example, *Wild Planet's Purse Pals™*, an interactive pet electronic game, featured different domestic pets encased in a stylized purse. "Nibbles the Bunny" *Purse Pal™* is violet-hued and the female voiceover and game packaging emphasized how its owner can feed, groom and play with the animal.

In terms of boys-and-girls together, the highest frequency count was in games/building, animals, and make believe/arts and crafts toy commercials. Although no prediction was made concerning gender and a specific toy type, previous research found that boys-and-girls together were rarely shown with animals (1.2 percent), and were more likely to be with dolls (23.5 percent);[73] this finding was contradicted here, with boys-and-girls more likely to be with animals (21.7 percent) than dolls (1.6 percent). The sample featured only one commercial in repetition, *Bratz Girlfriendz Nite Out Dance Disco™*, with boys and girls dancing together. The bulk of the dolls were for traditional gendered female toys like *Barbie Island Princess™, Little Mommy Real Loving Baby™*, and *Baby So Real™*, dolls associated with appearance, domesticity, and nurturance. Of the animals featuring boys-and-girls together, there were far more gender-neutral marked toys, such as *FurReal Friends Squawkers McCaw Parrot™*, where boys and girls talked, laughed, and pet the bird, explaining the higher frequency count when compared to previous research.

The majority of voiceovers were gender-matched, with girl-oriented toys featuring females (i.e., dolls), boy-oriented toys featuring male voiceovers (i.e., transportation/construction), and gender-neutral toys featuring male and female voiceovers (i.e., arts and crafts). Further, toys were imbued with traditional masculine and feminine attributes. As an example, the deep and loud adult male voiceover for target tagging game *Hyper Dash™* stated, "the faster the speed, the tougher the action," male realms of competition, athleticism, and dominance.

Conversely, the higher pitched adult female voiceover for *Bratz Girlfriendz Night Out™* stated how the dolls have "real eyelashes" and "three different fashions," female oriented realms associated with sociability, beauty, appearance, and fashion.[74] The majority of toys including both male and female voiceovers were featured in gender-neutral ways, with arts and craft/make believe toys, such as *Moon Sand Spin Master™*, and electronic toys like *iDog Speaker™*. As established in *Hypothesis 3*, this newly-established trend indicates that perhaps marketers recognize girls as technology users, rejecting its traditional male orientation.[75]

In terms of interaction, boys-only were shown engaging in varying types of play, including cooperative, independent, and competitive. Conversely, the majority of girls-only were shown cooperatively, taking turns and working together with other girls; no girls were shown in competitive play, as found in previous research.[76] Further, scant numbers of toy commercials featured girls-only and boys-only in parallel interactions, with this type of play dominated by boys-and-girls together.[77] This may give viewers the impression that the toy has universal appeal, even though boys and girls are not interacting with each other, sustaining the notion that children prefer to play in same-sex groupings.[78] However, girls had more visibility overall when taking into account their presence on the screen with boys; this finding coupled with higher frequency counts of girls partaking in "independent" play indicates that girls' presence and visibility in toy commercials continues to improve compared to earlier results.

In terms of setting, more than one-half of the girls were relegated to home settings—kitchens, nurseries, and bedrooms—and domestic, productive, and sedentary play. They were taking care of babies or pets, cooking pretend food concoctions in *Little Tikes Cook-n-Learn Kitchen™*, or creating jeweled bracelet arts and crafts. Other settings—whether indoors or outdoors—seemed to be mere backdrops for traditional feminine activities pertaining to fashion, family, and friendship. In *Garden Girlz Meadow Mansion™*, girls were located in a fantasy outdoor floral garden, yet had the tools to tend, grow and nurture within it. Conversely, boys-only were least likely to be portrayed in home settings. Whether indoors or outdoors, they were playing with toys or games like *Whac-A-Mole Tower™*, *Power Rangers Mega Mission Helmet™*, or *Ai Hogs Heli Laser Battle™* that required skill, training, action, movement, and interactivity, in music studios, construction sites, amusement parks, jungles, race tracks, and laboratories. Thus, boys' play was imbued with adventure, mystery, and action.

The prediction for activity was supported and statistically significant, with boys-only more likely to be portrayed in physical play (e.g., *Spiderman Nerf Dart Tag™*) and girls in productive play (e.g., *Bratz The Movie Making Set™*). However, the total frequency counts were relatively low, with the majority of boys-only and girls-only featured in play that was nondescript. Future research should reconceptualize this variable to address the large number of toys that could not be coded in the sample, as the schema did not allow for more than one type of activity to be coded in each commercial.[79] This will offer a stronger and more nuanced understanding of the activities characters engage in.

In conclusion, it is evident that toy manufacturers capitalize on and benefit from *Nickelodeon*'s progressive and kid-centered reputation to reach a strong, youth-based audience. Toy commercials offer playthings for sale that are strategically and consistently imbued with gender-role stereotypes that may influence children's cognitive, attitudinal, and behavioral tendencies. While contemporary television commercials offered stronger visibility of girls, boys and girls did not have equitable levels of respect in their role portrayals; to wit, settings, activities, and interactions were gender differentiated for boys and girls. Billions of marketing dollars go into constructing toy commercials to ensure they impact children's product and brand-specific attitudes. Findings suggest that the commercial culture on *Nickelodeon* does not strongly contribute to producing girl power products or to empowered viewers in the positive ways afforded to female characters in the corresponding television programs. In the future, commercial content should reflect that tweens watching during after-school hours have more complex play, acceptance of nontraditional gender stereotypes, and tend to recognize advertising persuasive strategies. With television a salient socialization agent in children's lives, it is crucial that in its attempts to sell products it reflect contemporary and age appropriate societal expectations for boys and girls.

Notes

1. The author thanks the Provost's Office at Muhlenberg College for providing funding for student coding via a student research assistantship.

2. Brooks Barnes, "Making Sure Nickelodeon Hangs with the Cool Kids," *New York Times,* October 30, 2010, http://www.nytimes.com/2010/10/31/business/media/31nick.html?ref=nickelodeonnetworks.

3. Jennifer Booton, "Poor Nickelodeon Ratings Push Viacom 1Q Profit Lower," *Fox Business,* February 2, 2012, http://www.foxbusiness.com/industries/2012/02/02/poor-nickelodeon-ratings-push-viacom-1q-profit-lower.

4. Marisa Guthrie, "Nickelodeon vs. Nielsen: Who's to Blame for the Network's Plummeting Ratings," *The Hollywood Reporter,* December 8, 2011, http://www.hollywoodreporter.com/news/nickelodeon-nielsen-ratings-viacom-271100.

5. Tim Molloy, "Disney Channel Knocks Nickelodeon From Top Ratings Perch," *Chicago Tribune,* March 29, 2012, http://www.chicagotribune.com/entertainment/sns-rt-us-disney-nickelodeonbre82s0xh-20120329,0,2571969.story.

6. James U. McNeal, *The Kids Market: Myths and Realities* (New York: Paramount Market, 1999), 16-19.

7. Christine Lagorio, "Resources: Marketing to Kids," *CBS News,* last modified November 1, 2011, http://www.cbsnews.com/stories/2007/05/04/fyi/main2798401.shtml.

8. Committee on Communications, "Children, Adolescents, and Advertising," *Pediatrics* 118, no. 6 (December 2006): 2564, doi 10.1542/peds.2006-2698.

9. Sarah Banet-Weiser, *Kids Rule! Nickelodeon and Consumer Citizenship* (Durham, NC: Duke University Press, 2007); Sarah Banet-Weiser, "The Nickelodeon Brand: Buying and Selling the Audiences," in *Cable Visions: Television Beyond Broadcasting,*

ed. Sarah Banet-Weiser, Cynthia Chris, and Anthony Freitas (New York: New York University Press, 2007), 234-252.

10. Banet-Weiser, *Kids Rule!*, 84-93; Banet-Weiser, "The Nickelodeon Brand," 239-245.

11. Banet-Weiser, *Kids Rule!*, 104-177; Rebecca Hains, "Inventing the Teenage Girl: The Construction of Female Identity in Nickelodeon's *My Life as a Teenage Robot*," *Popular Communication* 5, no. 3 (2007): 191-213; Heather Hendershot, ed., *Nickelodeon Nation* (New York: New York University Press, 2004); Erin L. Ryan, "*Dora the Explorer*: Empowering Preschoolers, Girls, and Latinas," *Journal of Broadcasting and Electronic Media* 54, no. 1 (2010): 54-68.

12. Banet-Weiser, *Kids Rule!*, 105.

13. Banet-Weiser, *Kids Rule!*, 104-105.

14. Susan G. Kahlenberg and Michelle M. Hein, "Progression on *Nickelodeon?* Gender-role Stereotypes in Toy Commercials," *Sex Roles* 62, no. 11/12 (2010): 830-847.

15. Dafna Lemish, *Children and Television: A Global Perspective* (Malden, MA: Blackwell, 2007), 103-105.

16. Nancy Signorielli and Susan G. Kahlenberg, "Television's World of Work in the Nineties," *Journal of Broadcasting and Electronic Media* 45, no. 1 (2001): 4-22.

17. Lisa A. Serbin, Diane Poulin-Dubois, Karen A. Colburne, Maya G. Sen, and Julie A. Eichstedt, "Gender Stereotyping in Infancy: Visual Preferences for and Knowledge of Gender-Stereotyped Toys in the Second Year," *International Journal of Behavioral Development* 25, no. 1 (2001): 7-15; Carol Lynn Martin and Diane Ruble, "Children's Search for Gender Cues: Cognitive Perspectives on Gender Development," *Current Directions in Psychological Science* 13, no. 2 (2004): 67-70.

18. Steven J. Kirsch, *Media and Youth: A Developmental Perspective* (Malden, MA: John Wiley & Sons, 2009).

19. Cynthia Scheibe, "Piaget and Power Rangers: What Can Theories of Developmental Psychology Tell us About Children and Media," in *20 Questions About Youth & the Media*, ed. Sharon R. Mazzarella (New York: Peter Lang, 2007), 65-67.

20. Deborah L. Roedder, "Age Differences in Children's Responses to Television Advertising: An Information-Processing Approach," *Journal of Consumer Research* 8, no. 2 (1981): 144.

21. Deborah Roedder John, "Consumer Socialization of Children: A Retrospective Look at Twenty-five Years of Research," *Journal of Consumer Research* 26, no. 3 (1999): 183-186; Scheibe, "Piaget and Power Rangers," 65-67.

22. Isabelle D. Cherney and Jessica Dempsey, "Young Children's Classification, Stereotyping and Play Behaviour for Gender Neutral and Ambiguous Toys," *Educational Psychology* 30, no. 6 (2010): 651-669.

23. Cherney and Dempsey, "Young Children's Classification"; Martin and Ruble, "Children's Search for Gender Cues."

24. George Gerbner, Larry Gross, Michael Morgan, Nancy Signorielli, and James Shanahan, "Growing Up with Television: Cultivation Processes," in *Media Effects: Advances in Theory and Research*, ed. Jennings Bryant and Dolf Zillmann, 2nd ed. (Mahwah, NJ: Lawrence Erlbaum, 2002), 43-68.

25. Victor C. Strasburger, Barbara J. Wilson, and Amy B. Jordan, *Children, Adolescents, and Media,* 2nd ed. (Thousand Oaks, CA: Sage, 2009), 7.

26. Werner J. Severin and James W. Tankard, Jr., *Communication Theories: Origins, Methods, and Uses in the Mass Media,* 3rd ed. (New York: Longman, 1992), 249.

27. Marina Krcmar, "Assessing the Research on Media, Cognitive Development, and Infants: Can Infants Really Learn from Television and Videos?," *Journal of Children and Media* 4, no. 2 (2010): 119-134; Strasburger, Wilson, and Jordan, *Children, Adolescents, and Media,* 6-7.

28. Daniel Chandler and Merris Griffiths, "Gender-differentiated Production Features in Toy Commercials," *Journal of Broadcasting and Electronic Media* 44, no. 3 (2000): 503-521; Shannon Davis, "Sex Stereotypes in Commercials Targeted Toward Children: A Content Analysis," *Sociological Spectrum* 23, no. 4 (2003): 407-424; Jill K. Maher and Nancy M. Childs, "A Longitudinal Content Analysis of Gender Roles in Children's Television Advertisements: A 27 Year Review," *Journal of Current Issues & Research in Advertising* 25, no. 1 (2003): 71-82; Lois J. Smith, "A Content Analysis of Gender Differences in Children's Advertising," *Journal of Broadcasting and Electronic Media* 38, no. 3 (1994): 323-338.

29. Gary Cross, *Kids Stuff: Toys and the Changing World of American Childhood* (Cambridge, MA: Harvard University Press, 1997); Stephen Kline, *Out of the Garden: Toys, TV, and Children's Culture in the Age of Marketing* (London: Verso, 1993); Ellen Seiter, *Sold Separately: Parents and Children in Consumer Society* (New Brunswick, NJ: Standford University Press, 1993); Brian Sutton-Smith, *Toys as Culture* (New York: Gardner, 1986).

30. Aili McConnon, "Toys: No Must-haves This Holiday Season," *Business Week,* December 1, 2008, http://www.businessweek.com/stories/2008-11-26/toys-no-must-have s-this-holiday-seasonbusinessweek-business-news-stock-market-and-financial-advice; Ben Steverman, "Air Hogs, Sing-a-ma-jigs May Bring Holiday Joy for Toymakers," *Business Week,* September 29, 2010, http://www.businessweek.com/stories/2010-09-29/air-hogs-sing-a-ma-jigs-may-bring-holiday-joy-for-toymakersbusinessweek-business-news-stock-market-and-financial-advice.

31. Holly K.M. Henry and Dina L.G. Borzekowski, "The Nag Factor: A Mixed-methodology Study in the US of Young Children's Requests for Advertised Products," *Journal of Children and Media* 5, no. 3 (2011): 298. In scholarship, the "nag factor" is also referred to as "kid-fluence." For a well articulated discussion of "kid-fluence, see Juliet B. Schor, *Born to Buy: The Commercialized Child and the New Consumer Culture* (New York: Scribner, 2004), 22-25.

32. Larry D. Woodward, "How Marketers Target your Kids," *ABC News,* last modified on December 9, 2009, http://www.abcnews.go.com/Business/marketers-target-kids/story?id=9284270.

33. Aysen Bakir and Kay M. Palan, "How are Children's Attitudes Toward Ads and Brands Affected by Gender-related Content in Advertising?," *Journal of Advertising* 39, no. 1 (2010): 35-48; Cherney and Dempsey, "Young Children's Classification"; Jennifer J. Pike and Nancy A. Jennings, "The Effects of Commercials on Children's Perceptions of Gender Appropriate Toy Use," *Sex Roles* 52, no. 1/2 (2005): 83-91.

34. Cherney and Dempsey, "Young Children's Classification," 652.

35. Pike and Jennings, "Effects of Commercials on Children's Perceptions."

36. Aysen Bakir, Jeffrey G. Blodgett, and Gregory M. Rose, "Children's Responses to Gender-role Stereotyped Advertisements," *Journal of Advertising Research* 48, no. 2 (2008): 255-266.

37. Bakir and Palan, "How are Children's Attitudes Toward Ads."

38. Banet-Weiser, *Kids Rule!*

39. Kevina Cody, "'No Longer, But Not Yet': Tweens and the Mediating of Threshold Selves Through Liminal Consumption," *Journal of Consumer Culture* 12, no. 1 (2012): 47; Daniel Thomas Cook and Susan B. Kaiser, "Betwixt and be Tween: Age Ambiguity and the Sexualization of the Female Consuming Subject," *Journal of Consumer Culture* 4, no. 2 (2004): 204.

40. David L. Siegel, Timothy J. Coffey, and Gregory Livingston, *The Great Tween Buying Machine: Capturing Your Share of the Multimillion Dollar Tween Market* (Chicago: Dearborn Trade Publishing, 2004), 3-4.

41. John, "Consumer Socialization of Children,"186-188.

42. James Shanahan, Nancy Signorielli, and Michael Morgan, "Television and Sex Roles 30 Years Hence: A Retrospective and Current Look From a Cultural Indicators Perspective," Paper presented at the Annual Meeting of the International Communication Association, Montreal, Canada, May 2008.

43. See Banet-Weiser, *Kids Rule!*; Hendershot, *Nickelodeon Nation.*

44. Beverly A. Browne, "Gender Stereotypes in Advertising on Children's Television in the 1990s: A Cross-National Analysis," *Journal of Advertising* 27, no. 1 (1998): 83-96; Chandler and Griffiths, "Gender-differentiated Production Features"; M. Carole Macklin and Richard H. Kolbe, "Sex Role Stereotyping in Children's Advertising: Current and Past Trends," *Journal of Advertising* 13, no. 2 (1984): 34-42; Smith, "Content Analysis of Gender Differences"; Mary Ellen Verna, "The Female Image in Children's TV Commercials," *Journal of Broadcasting* 19, no. 3 (1975): 301-309.

45. Davis, "Sex Stereotypes in Commercials"; Maher and Childs, "Longitudinal Content Analysis of Gender Roles"; Debra Merskin, "Boys Will Be Boys: A Content Analysis of Gender and Race in Children's Advertisements on the Turner Cartoon Network," *Journal of Current Issues & Research in Advertising* 24, no. 1 (Spring 2002): 51-60.

46. Merskin, "Boys Will Be Boys," 55.

47. Cook and Kaiser, "Betwixt and be Tween," 205, 207-212.

48. Kahlenberg and Hein, "Progression on Nickelodeon?"

49. Chandler and Griffiths, "Gender Differentiated Production Features"; Beth A. Hentges, Robert A. Bartsch, and Jo A. Meier, "Gender Representation in Commercials as a Function of Target Audience Age," *Communication Research Reports* 24, no. 1 (2007): 55-62; Fern L. Johnson and Karren Young, "Gendered Voices in Children's Television Advertising," *Critical Studies in Media Communication* 19, no. 4 (2002): 461-480; Macklin and Kolbe, "Sex Role Stereotyping in Children's Advertising"; Maher and Childs, "Longitudinal Content Analysis of Gender Roles"; Thomas W. Whipple and Mary K. McManamon, "Implications of Using Male and Female Voices in Commercials: An Exploratory Study," *Journal of Advertising* 31, no. 2 (2002): 79-91.

50. Johnson and Young, "Gendered Voices in Children's Television Advertising."

51. Davis, "Sex Stereotypes in Commercials"; Kahlenberg and Hein, "Progression on Nickelodeon?"; Mary Strom Larson, "Interactions, Activities and Gender in Children's Television Commercials: A Content Analysis," *Journal of Broadcasting & Electronic Media* 45, no. 1 (2001): 41-56; Smith, "Content Analysis of Gender Differences."

52. Abbey Klaassen and Claire Atkinson, "Kids' Upfront Crawls Along; 6 percent Rise Seen," *Advertising Age* 76, no. 18 (2005): 61.

53. Bruce Horovitz, "Be Ready for Toy Marketers' Christmastime Tactics," *Frank W. Baker,* last modified on November 26, 2006, http://www.frankwbaker.com/holiday_ad _tactics.htm; Anne Kates Smith, "Cherry News for Holiday Shoppers: Price-cutting is Still in Fashion, and Seasonal Hiring Will Increase," *Kiplinger's Personal Finance* (December 2010): 15-16.

54. Barnes, "Making Sure Nickelodeon Hangs."

55. Daisy Whitney, "For Kids TV, Every Day is Saturday," *Advertising Age,* February 21, 2005, 10, http://adage.com/article/special-report-kids/kids-tv-day-saturday /102154.

56. Allison J. Bryant, "How Has the Kids' Industry Evolved?," in *20 Questions About Youth & the Media,* ed. Sharon R. Mazzarella (NY: Peter Lang, 2007), 18-23.

57. C. Chang, "Ad Repetition and Variation in a Competitive Ad Context," paper presented at the Annual Meeting of the International Communication Association, San Diego, CA, May 2003.

58. Lisa L. Chamberlain, Yun Wang, and Thomas N. Robinson, "Does Children's Screen Time Predict Requests for Advertised Products? Cross-sectional and Prospective Analyses," *Archives of Pediatrics and Adolescent Medicine* 160, no. 40 (2006): 363-368.

59. Henry and Borzekowski, "The Nag Factor."

60. Karen J. Pine and Avril Nash, "Dear Santa: The Effects of Television Advertising on Young Children," *International Journal of Behavioral Development* 26, no. 6 (2002): 529-539.

61. Kahlenberg and Hein, "Progression on Nickelodeon?," 837.

62. Kahlenberg and Hein, "Progression on Nickelodeon?," 837; Ylan Q. Mui, "This Year, It's a High-tech Toy Story," *Washington Post,* November 17, 2005, http://www.washingtonpost.com/wpdyn/content/article/2005/11/16/AR2005111602233.h tml.

63. Jeanne B. Funk, "Video Games," in *Children, Adolescents, and the Media,* ed. Victor C. Strasburger, Barbara J. Wilson, and Amy B. Jordan, 2nd ed. (Los Angeles: Sage, 2008), 435-470.

64. Kahlenberg and Hein, "Progression on Nickelodeon?," 837.

65. Browne, "Gender Stereotypes in Advertising," 88.

66. Maher and Childs, "Longitudinal Content Analysis of Gender Roles," 75.

67. Kahlenberg and Hein, "Progression on Nickelodeon?," 837-838; Larson, "Interactions, Activities and Gender," 47.

68. Kahlenberg and Hein, "Progression on Nickelodeon?," 838; Larson, "Interactions, Activities and Gender," 46.

69. Larson, "Interactions, Activities, and Gender, 47; Smith, "Content Analysis Gender Differences," 4, results.

70. Klaus Krippendorff, *Content Analysis: An Introduction to its Methodology* (Beverly Hills, CA: Sage), 1980.

71. See Banet-Weiser, *Kids Rule!;* Haines, "Inventing the Teenage Girl"; Hendershot, *Nickelodeon Nation*; Ryan, "Dora the Explorer."

72. Banet-Weiser, "The Nickelodeon Brand," 250.

73. Kahlenberg and Hein, "Progression on Nickelodeon?," 839.

74. Johnson and Young, "Gendered Voices in Children's Television Advertising."

75. Funk, "Video Games,"436.

76. Kahlenberg and Hein, "Progression on Nickelodeon?," 841.

77. See Larson,"Interactions, Activities, and Gender," 50.

78. Daniel N. Maltz and Ruth A. Borker, "A Cultural Approach to Male-female Miscommunication," in *Language and Gender: A Reader*, ed. Jennifer Coates (Oxford: Blackwell Publishers, 1998), 422.

79. Browne, "Gender Stereotypes in Advertising," coded for varying types of products, whereas this study exclusively focused on toys.

Chapter Eleven

"Stand By, Space Rangers": Interstellar Lessons in Early Cold War Masculinity

Cynthia J. Miller and A. Bowdoin Van Riper

Rocketmen: bold adventurers in space, defenders of democracy, masters of science, and heroes for an age when the universe was full of wonder. Each week, they blasted their way into the living rooms, imaginations, and hearts of children in 1950s America, fighting their battles with Para-Ray guns and Cosmic Vibrators, scanning through walls with Opticon Scillometers, and soaring through the skies with jetpacks on their backs. While long ago replaced by new heroes, their names still resonate in American cultural history: Captain Video, Tom Corbett, Rocky Jones, Commando Cody, and, of course, the interstellar hero whose adventures started it all: Flash Gordon. Long before astronauts like John Glenn, Alan Shepard, and Neil Armstrong were household names; before the "one small step" that left America's national footprint on the Moon; and before the wonders of science fiction became the wonders of science fact, TV's rocketmen showed America's children a thrilling vision of the future.

The rocketmen also taught their young viewers about the roles they would be expected to play in the nearer-future world of their adulthood. They served as exemplars of social, political, and particularly masculine success in a rapidly changing world, thwarting evil, defending democracy, and embodying virtues that advanced the common good. The rocketmen were distinctly Cold War heroes—"Electronic Wizards," "Research Explorers in Time and Space," "Guardians of the Safety of the World"—representing a range of heroic masculinities that emphasized their Atomic Age scientific know-how as much as, and in some cases more than, their combat skills and physical prowess.[1] From the feisty Rocky Jones to the cerebral Captain Z-Ro, the rocketmen served

173

as role models and mentors for their young audiences, and reinforced their teachings through codes, pledges, and Ranger Messages, all designed to create a new generation of Cold War Americans. Fans of *Rod Brown of the Rocket Rangers*, for example, pledged to "never cross orbits with the Rights and Beliefs of others" and "keep my scanner tuned to Learning and remain coupled to my Studies" as they discovered their roles in a globalized future.[2]

Rocketmen series typically featured simple morality tales that functioned as a means of passing on Cold War values and ethics in a futuristic framework, but the masculinity modeled by their characters was complex. Drawing on a range of distinctly American male archetypes, these role models conveyed valued— and sometimes conflicting—masculine-identified traits of conformity and independence, stability and risk-taking, intellect and instinct.[3] Rocketmen embodied patriotism, virtue, and order—father figures, political-military leaders, and Scout leaders, all rolled into one—and served as the ultimate Cold War heroes.

The rocketmen—like heroes of earlier eras—did not struggle alone against evil forces and unknown dangers. They were supported by scientist-allies, by female partners, and, sometimes, by the resources of vast organizations—but above all support came from young male protégés. These cadets and junior space men were a made-for-television version of the teen sidekicks in the comic books and movie serials of the 1940s. Like Robin the Boy Wonder or Captain America's young friend Bucky Barnes, they provided a character with whom young viewers could identify—someone more human-scaled than the seemingly flawless hero—and at the same time, created a space in the narrative where viewers could insert themselves into the adventure.

Reaching toward adulthood in their fictional futures, the young sidekicks joined their mentors in acting as models of adult masculinity for fans— particularly young boys—contemplating their own futures. During the course of their weekly adventures, the rocketmen mentored their young protégés on screen and a generation of eager young fans watching at home. Together, rocketmen and their sidekicks tutored their audiences in what it meant to be an American male, whether military officer, frontier innovator, intellectual gatekeeper, or corporate leader, enabling audience members to experience the consequences and rewards of different strategies for success, in the security of their own living rooms.[4]

The Birth of the Space Hero

Rocketmen were born in the pulp magazines of the late 1920s, and even as they spread to other forms of popular entertainment they retained the marks of their pulp origins. They were uncomplicated, unreflective characters designed to serve the needs of the action-filled stories favored by the pulps' mostly young, mostly male readership. Like the pulps' other hero-figures—ace pilots and jungle explorers, steely-eyed sheriffs and wisecracking detectives—they were drawn in bold, simple strokes and behaved in predictable ways. Their strengths were many and prominent, their weaknesses few and (unless the plot demanded it) carefully hidden. They were strong, smart, brave, and—above all—morally incorruptible.[5] In a fictional world much like that of the already familiar Western genre, where good and bad were both unambiguously defined and prominently labeled, their metaphorical hats were always a bright, shining white.[6]

Buck Rogers and Flash Gordon—comic and film characters who first propelled rocketmen into popular culture in the 1930s—made no attempt to be role models for their fans. They went to the stars for the same reason their counterparts in other pulp genres traveled to the uncharted corners of the Earth: for the adventure. It was only in the aftermath of World War II—when America first confronted its newly central role on Earth and wartime advances in rocketry and atomic power seemed poised to open the road to the stars—that the rocketmen's adventures took on a new sense of purpose and they themselves emerged as mentors. Not coincidentally, it was also then that they made the transition from pulps, comics, and movie screens to television.

Captain Video and his Video Rangers became the vanguards of that transition in 1949, ushering in a host of other series that were among the earliest contributions to science-fiction television.[7] While criticized for its low-budget sets and juvenile simplicity, *Captain Video* ignited the sparks of Space Fever among the country's youthful viewers, a cultural phenomenon that grew in intensity over the next decade, prompting stations and sponsors to scramble for their own rocketmen. ABC's Commander Buzz Corry led his crew on *Space Patrol* (1950); Tom Corbett kept the universe safe on *Tom Corbett, Space Cadet*, on CBS (1950); and a few seasons later, NBC's heroic Commando Cody did the same on *Commando Cody: Sky Marshal of the Universe* (1953). Some rocketmen, like Rocky Jones, began their adventures in syndication (1954) and only held viewers' attention for a season or two, while others, such as Captain Z-Ro, were local heroes who rose to national fame, their exploits continuing for several years. These televised series became so popular that, by 1954, one of the most popular, *Space Patrol*, ranked consistently in the top ten shows broadcast on Saturday.[8]

The rocketmen of 1950s television were champions of truth and justice in a time of rapid postwar social, cultural, and political change. Spanning the galaxy just as American soldiers and diplomats spanned the postwar world, they undertook their weekly adventures in the service of causes greater than themselves. Fearless, loyal, resourceful, and determined, they calmed fears, preserved values, and thwarted enemies—on Earth and throughout the universe—defending humanity and democracy against the forces of evil while fans watched in wonder. The introduction to *Captain Video*, like the opening lines of other space-hero series, set the stage for the futuristic struggle to keep the world safe: "Fighting for law and order, Captain Video operates from a mountain retreat with secret agents at all points of the globe. Possessing scientific secrets and scientific weapons, Captain Video asks no quarter and gives none to the forces of evil. Stand by for *Captain Video and his Video Rangers!*"[9]

To be a rocketman's fan was to adopt the identity that the space heroes modeled each week and passed along to their young protégés on screen and their fans at home—a Cold War identity that united knowledge and imagination, discipline and ingenuity, nation and individual—all wrapped in fantastic science and the promise of a universe waiting to be explored.

Modeling Masculinity

The era of the rocketmen was one in which multiple images of American masculinity coexisted—sometimes uneasily—the result of rapid changes in social, political, and economic conditions. Archetypes of iconic American manhood, from frontier legends to combat heroes, were now joined by another model of masculinity: the Cold War technocrat, defined by his knowledge of science and civics, and his unswerving commitment to the organization that commanded his loyalty and defined his identity.

These archetypes of masculinity and heroism embodied by the rocketmen are deeply rooted in notions of power, success, and American nationalism that have shifted and reconfigured over time in response to changing social, political, and economic conditions. Initially, it was tales of heroic "pioneers"—men who expanded the borders of the new nation ever westward and engaged in a constant struggle with "savages" to establish order in the wilderness—that had initially set the stage for sagas of American moral triumph. As engagement with the West expanded and deepened, so too, did the tales of its heroic figures: in the form of cowboys, rough riders, cavalrymen, and lawmen. The classic Western emphasized a fundamental conflict between civilization and savagery. Embodiments of the untamed Spirit of the West, these heroes of the West were nonetheless charged with taming the wilderness, so that it might be drawn into the civilized realm.[10]

The independent spirit of the cowboy-wanderer could still be found among the rocketmen of 1950s television. These interstellar explorers, whose bravery and initiative could not be confined to the routines and regulations of an increasingly suburbanized Earth, set out to conquer a new frontier: space. By the dawn of the Cold War, however, the inner wildness of the Western hero was most frequently found in the rocketmen's teenage sidekicks who, armed with the natural inquisitiveness of healthy young American boys, skirted regulations, bent rules, innovated, and sometimes defied orders, to save the day and carve out a place for themselves in the adult world.

One such hero-in-the-making was Bobby (Robert Lyden), the eager young rocketman-in-training featured in *Rocky Jones, Space Ranger* (1954). Unlike his highly disciplined mentor, Rocky Jones (Richard Crane), Bobby often strayed from the straight and narrow in the name of initiative. In the episode "Silver

Needle in the Sky," Jones and his crew were held captive by their nemesis, the evil femme fatale Cleolanta (Patsy Parsons), leader of the planet Ophiuchus.[11] When their air supply was cut off, Bobby climbed through the ventilation system in order to save his crewmates. Unable to open the hatch that led to the controls, Bobby took literally the crew's advice to "use his head." In a moment of inspiration, his eyes lit up and he began to bang his head on the door, eventually opening it. He proceeded to pick the lock of the cell door to free his companions and save the mission. While protocols and procedures are highly valued in the military world, the young cadet's pioneering spirit and natural adolescent impulsiveness proved to be his path to success as a rocketman.

Similarly, in *Captain Z-Ro* (1954-1955), the Captain's (Roy Steffens) young assistant Jet (Bruce Haynes) often followed his instincts, rather than his orders, and like his counterpart, Bobby, he sometimes saved the day. When the Captain's time-traveling rocket ship, the *ZX-99*, visited Leonardo da Vinci's (Sydney Walker) studio, Jet's secret attempt to be the first man to fly using da Vinci's ornithopter put his life in jeopardy. More important to human history, however, his empathy for the despondent da Vinci (who believed that all his inventions had been failures and his life's work had all been for naught) led to the artist/inventor's renewed inspiration.

It was the young cadets' curiosity, innovation, and disobedience that helped to establish their roles in these tales of time and space. Their success as junior rocketmen derived not from ready obedience and submission to superior males, but from the shared ingenuity and impulse to explore—to stray outside of traditional boundaries and occasionally break rules—that was their contribution and path to heroism. Just as in tales of the Old West, however, that success was only affirmed through their ultimate willingness to conform.

The lone cowboy persisted as a symbol of American masculinity into the 1940s and beyond, but World War II—particularly the infantry units that bore the brunt of the fighting—gave rise to a new, group-centered model of masculinity. Virtually every unit in the wartime army was a mélange of soldiers from different states, ethnic backgrounds, and peacetime occupations fiercely proud of their particular skills and backgrounds, but united in pursuit of a common goal.[12]

Celebrated in wartime propaganda, this hardscrabble, working-class archetype of American manhood continued to flourish in the postwar era, and blasted off into space in the 1950s. The cast of *Space Patrol* (1950-55)—five brave, uniquely talented men and women, welded by danger into a smoothly functioning unit—recalled those of military "band of brothers" films like *Air Force* (1943) and *Battleground* (1949). Their adventures, though nominally set in the thirtieth century aboard the spaceship *Terra V*, followed the familiar rhythms of wartime dramas set aboard bombers and submarines, with the crew threatened by equipment failures and natural forces, as well as the enemy. *Space Patrol*'s embrace of World War II masculinity was reinforced by the fact that much of its cast and crew—notably Ed Kemmer, who played Commander Buzz Corry—were themselves veterans of the war.

Classic World War II masculinity also flexed its muscles aboard the *Orbit Jet* in *Rocky Jones, Space Ranger* (1954). Despite his narrative status as a Cold War space hero, Jones was a feisty reminder of wartime heroes of an earlier age. Although his dialogue throughout the series' episodes carried mandates for peace, tolerance, and free will, his instincts were those of a fighter, rather than a diplomat. Told that a female navigator fluent in the local language would accompany a mission to Ophiuchus, he retorted: "I'd rather have another pair of fists. That's a language anybody understands."[13]

Winky, the *Orbit Jet's* wry and cynical navigator, was reminiscent of bedraggled wartime working stiffs Willie and Joe, made famous by cartoonist Bill Mauldin in panels drawn for the army newspaper *Stars and Stripes*. His role as the series' "comic relief" made him unique among rocketmen. An able first officer, Winky was, nonetheless, as ready with a wisecrack as his captain is with his fists. His capabilities were often masked by his carefree attitude: He was the first to lobby for vacation, indulging in fantasies of beaches and beautiful women, and generally responded to orders with a wry aside. He boldly offered his opinion to subordinates and superiors alike, in dialogue full of color and slang, more closely resembling a hip teenager than a disciplined space ranger. He was a foot soldier, not a leader, but he was also a mentor. While rocketman Jones inspired their young protégé Bobby's sense of duty and ability, it was Winky who served as the inspiration for the boy's confident ingenuity, modeling adaptation and independence, even as he embodied steadfast devotion to Jones, the *Orbit Jet*, the Space Rangers, and an Earth only subtly coded as postwar America.

The culture of the Cold War—shaped by the need to manage a burgeoning nuclear-arms race, carry on a global ideological struggle, and maintain an expanding military empire—gave rise to a new version of masculinity far removed from those that had been valorized before.[14] The idealized American man was depicted not as a unique individual who confronted the world alone, or one who meshed his unique talents with others' in a "band of brothers" like an infantry squad or bomber crew, but as a "company man"—a member of a tightly integrated corporate hierarchy which had the ability to manipulate technology, create broader political-economic strategies, and promote American-centered conceptions of the common good across a global arena. Stern-faced managers replaced wildcatting innovators, centrally planned strategies pushed aside sparks of ingenuity, and knowledge—of science and technology, history and psychology—took its place alongside strength, bravery, and daring as the mark of a hero. The problems of the Cold War era, the new model of masculinity intimated, were too complex to be solved by brute strength or simple determination. Knowledge of how the world worked, and the power it conferred on those who possessed it, was essential.

Rocketmen, as a group, reflected the new vision of masculinity. The officers of *Rocky Jones, Space Ranger* and *Space Patrol*, and the officers-in-training of *Tom Corbett, Space Cadet*, saw themselves as extensions of the interplanetary organizations they served. Even Flash Gordon—a star athlete turned interplanetary adventurer in the 1930s—became a field agent of the "Galactic Bureau of Investigation" in his 1950s television series. The characters on *Captain Video* and *Captain Z-Ro* replicated the ideal of the tightly integrated hierarchy in miniature, with the title characters commanding networks of loyal followers whose individuality barely registered. Whatever organization they served, the rocketmen were masters of advanced science and technology, and—thanks to their emphasis on diplomacy over war—of politics, history, and practical psychology as well.

Captain Z-Ro, in particular, reflected the valorization of knowledge (and those who possessed it) in 1950s America. A "research explorer in time and space," he used a spaceship of his own design to probe the secrets of the universe, and a time machine to observe key events in world history—intervening, when necessary, to ensure that history unfolded as it should. Captain Z-Ro's approach to the world blended equal measures of action and thought. "Why risk going back in time over 1,500 years just to find out what you already know?" one of his assistants, Tetro, asked in "Attilla the Hun" as the captain prepared to infiltrate the barbarian leader's camp on the eve of a great battle. The swashbuckling scholar's response was simultaneously bold and matter-of-fact: "Because there's something I don't know!"[15] Captain Z-Ro thus conveyed concrete knowledge but also, in both word and deed, the larger Atomic Age message that knowledge was power, and that action, when knowledge was absent or incomplete, could cause disasters that would change the course of history.

Despite their clear conformity to the new Cold War ideal of masculinity, however, the rocketmen also continued to honor the older, more familiar models of earlier eras. Captain Z-Ro—prone to respond to his protégé's questions by declaring: "You've got me, Jet—but there's one sure way to find out! Set the time machine . . ."—had the heart and soul of a pioneer. Rocky Jones could have stepped off the bridge of a World War II destroyer, or led one of George Patton's tank battalions across France, and his navigator Winky mingled the cool competence of a Cold Warrior with the cocky self-assurance of a fighter pilot. This diversity of role models assured viewers that, in the face of rapid social change, familiar ways of characters and ways of being would not simply be discarded. The universe of the rocketmen included and celebrated a range of masculinities—from adventurer to maverick, and foot soldier to intellectual—confirming all as valuable and necessary, even as they reinforced the notion that the new Cold War hero was first among equals.

Mentors in a Cold War World

Televised rocketmen series lacked the high production values of their cinematic counterparts, but they offered their youthful fans something that movie-house heroes could not: intimacy. Thanks to the new medium of television, and its integration into the heart of family life, these fantastic heroes blasted directly into the living rooms of their young audiences, blurring the boundaries between the worlds on either side of the small screen, creating personal relationships with viewers through advice and instruction, and making knowledge of the fantastic "a part of home life rather than any kind of special event."[16] Their mission succeeded far beyond the networks' expectations.[17] A highly elaborated fan culture rapidly emerged, and with it, new forms of futuristic dress, toys, and even conversation. Domestic schedules were rearranged to accommodate programming schedules, and new relationships were formed, as fans formalized their allegiance to their favorite space heroes in official or unofficial fan clubs. If a group of fans had true "spaceman's luck," they might have been left breathless by a visit from their favorite interstellar hero, as he paused at their local store *en route* to his next adventure.

United by their admiration for particular heroes and their sidekicks, fans bonded simultaneously with fellow viewers and with the onscreen figures they idolized. The specificity of the fan culture the rocketmen series engendered devoted fans to wear the uniform and carry the equipment not just of a generic rocketman, but of a specific hero. The Video Rangers who watched *Captain Video* at home saw (and were encouraged by the producers of the show to see) themselves as members of their hero's army just as surely as those who helped him thwart evildoers on screen. The same was true of Captain Midnight's "Secret Squadron," and of the legions of Solar Guard cadets who settled before their black-and-white screens to watch *Tom Corbett*.

These young fans saw themselves reflected on-screen in the cadets, rangers, and junior space men who served as the rocketmen's crews and protégés. The boy heroes of the rocketmen series rendered the new Cold War masculinity accessible and familiar by modeling a version of it overlaid with the mannerisms and enthusiasms of youth. These youthful characters' relationships with their adult rocketman-mentors created the series' central character dynamic, while their ongoing education in the ways of rocketmen gave the action its principal source of week-to-week continuity. The details of their roles varied from show to show: Rocky Jones' cadet Winky—and his counterpart on *Space Patrol*, Cadet Happy—were fully trained junior officers, whereas Bobby played a role closer to cabin boy on the *Orbit Jet*. Jet was nominally Captain Z-Ro's ward, but also functioned as his apprentice: operating equipment while learning the skills of a "research explorer in time and space."[18] All of them, however, served as models for learning to be *American* men of the future, internalizing valued traits, accepting authority, and placing the common good (that of their crew, their planet, or the universe) before themselves.

This modeling was particularly striking in the case of Captain Video (Al Hodge), whose battles against interplanetary villains were also aided by a teenaged assistant (Don Hastings), known only as Video Ranger. Members of the Captain's secret organization were also known as Video Rangers, and the young aide thus stood for all of them. His lack of a distinct personality and his use of a title in lieu of a name made it easy for viewers to project themselves into his place and so into the story. It also, however, made him an idealized vision of Cold War masculinity: defined—even in name—by the organization he served and inseparable from it. Video Ranger himself exhibited very little individuality, never questioning orders or thinking for himself, and playing no role in advancing the narrative.

The heroes of *Tom Corbett, Space Cadet*—Tom and his friends Roger, T. J., and Astro—had greater autonomy, but expressed the same unswerving, unquestioning loyalty. Cadets at the Space Academy, training to be officers in the elite Solar Guard, they prepared for the day when (in the words of the series' voiceover narration) they would "blast through the millions of miles from Earth to far-flung stars and brave the dangers of cosmic frontiers, protecting the liberty of the planets, safeguarding the course of universal peace in the age of the conquest of space." The Guard protected the Solar Alliance, which united the inhabited worlds of the solar system, and were expected to embody its highest ideals as well as defending it, if necessary, with their lives. The cadets' commander and *de facto* mentor, Captain Strong, stressed the magnitude of their responsibility on their first day at the academy: "You hold the future of the Solar Alliance in your hands," he admonished. "There are people to be met and understood. But remember this—you will meet them as men of peace. You'll deal with them in honor and trust. You'll fight only for freedom and for liberty."[19] Personal growth was, therefore, central to the heroes' transformation from cadets into officers. Tom learned to confidently take charge in life-or-death crises, and Roger—initially a cynic who dismissed Strong's speech as "a lot of space gas"—realized that "that stuff about peace and freedom" means something after all.[20] The trio learned, above all, the need to put the needs of others— friends, shipmates, citizens of the Alliance—before one's own: the essential Cold-War act of subordinating self to group.

Younger than Winky, Video Ranger, or Tom Corbett, Jet of *Captain Z-Ro* had yet to learn that lesson. In a world where compliance and self-restraint were coded as "maturity," Jet's character was "young," both chronologically and socially. He was fully capable of carrying out Captain Z-Ro's orders and absorbing his lessons, but lacked the discipline to keep himself focused on others' needs when his own distracted him. Eager and impetuous, he frequently complicated the Captain's missions into the distant past—motivated by a childish desire for fun and excitement rather than by his mentor's selfless determination "to learn from the past . . . to plan for the future."[21] Although the duo's missions often involved intervening in historical events to ensure that they unfold "correctly," Jet typically rushed in where the Captain, cooler and wiser, preferred to first stand back and observe.

The Captain's ongoing education of Jet thus involved teaching him not only about the facts of history and the forces that drive historical events, but also about the need for discipline, patience, and self-restraint. The two forms of education intertwined, throughout the series, with the historical figures the pair visited functioning as object lessons in the importance of such "adult" virtues.

Political leaders who put their people's needs before their own, and revolutionaries who put their lives at risk to advance the cause of freedom loomed large. The episode "King Alfred," for example, began with Jet daydreaming about what he imagined to be the easy life of a nobleman, developed into a time-travel adventure to tenth-century England (where the title character battled invading Danes), and ended with the Captain's stern message that a good king, like Alfred—and, by extension, any responsible leader—lives a life not of luxury and ease, but of sacrifice and tireless work on behalf of his subjects. Jet, good rocketman-in-training that he was, accepted the lesson cheerfully, putting away childish things—at least until the next week's episode.

Underlying all of the rocketmen's mentoring—both of their on-screen protégés and of their fans—was their modeling of the unswerving, uncomplicated loyalty that defined American political culture in the Cold War. The spacefaring heroes demonstrated fierce commitment to the organizations they served, and accepted their authority without question, and even those who—like Captain Video and Captain Z-Ro—operated as free agents displayed similar fidelity to the principles they upheld. In turn, the rocketmen expected the same commitment, and the same unquestioning obedience, from their protégés. Invariably, they received it. Video Ranger's uncomplicated loyalty to his leader and Winky's crisp "Yes sir!" responses to commands would have left them thoroughly at home in an FBI field office or corporate headquarters. Tom Corbett and his fellow space cadets could, but for their uniforms, have been cadets in the newly independent, nuclear-armed Air Force, wielding technology of immense power while earnestly declaring, "Peace is Our Profession." Captain Z-Ro's exploits in the past, Buzz Corry's in outer space, and Rocky Jones' on other worlds—using their mastery of science, technology, history, and politics to defend freedom—not only reflected Cold War culture's valorization of conformity and obedience, but echoed Americans' most idealized visions of their role in the wider world.

As Seen on TV

The series' commercial breaks provided another, more utilitarian, kind of mentoring to youthful fans—guidance on becoming successful domestic consumers—a clear illustration of the ways this early programming may be understood as a "material articulation" of the era's domestic consumerism.[22] These departures from the world of the narrative were crafted, with varying degrees of success, to give the sense of an almost seamless continuity. They utilized the series' sets, stars, and announcer (whose familiar voice already signaled "authority" to the series' young audience members) to blur the distinction between advertising and non-advertising material, facilitating the creation (in children) and reinforcement (in adults) of the ideal domestic consumer. Aspiring Video Rangers were instructed, "Be sure to ask your mom to buy delicious Powerhouse bars," or advised that an ordinary lunch box becomes "extraordinary" when it contains Johnson's Fudge squares. Series tie-in products, such as the Video Rangers' ring, were frequently offered as premiums to reward young viewers for their roles as consumers. Blended into the world of the televised narrative these advertisements made it difficult for young viewers to immediately distinguish between storyline and marketing, the characters becoming that much more "real" in the space of the child's own living room.[23]

In a well-known example from *Captain Video,* the on-screen action shifted to the Video Ranger inside the familiar rocket ship cockpit as the voiceover announcer related: "Off on another dangerous mission for Captain Video, Video Ranger dons one of his most important pieces of equipment—the secret identifying ring." Video Ranger, in a tight close-up, then offered the young rangers in the audience advice: "Rangers, here's why this ring is so important to me and to all video agents: If anyone questions your identity, all you've got to do is show them this ring. . . . [Zoom in on a drawing of the ring, adorned with Captain Video's likeness] Wear it at all times to show that you're on the side of law and order!"[24] With that message, Video Ranger gave his young fans a two-fingered salute and wink, and the screen shifted to an ad for Powerhouse candy bars, during which the youngsters were told that two nickel wrappers and ten cents in coin would earn them their own ring.

Young audiences received similar inducements from other programs, such as an offer from the producers of *Tom Corbett, Space Cadet,* reminding them that it was not too late to use the wrappers from Kraft Caramels to obtain their space cadet membership kits: "Now, here's what you'll get: this handsome space cadet ring, just like Tom and Astro and TJ's; your official space cadet shoulder patch; and your signed membership certificate in the *Tom Corbett* unit."[25]

As televised science fiction series brought new fans to the genre, new productions emerged and space fever swept through American homes, department stores, and supermarkets. Although, as *TV Forecast* proclaimed in an article about *Captain Video,* these series were "produced especially for the modern-minded youngsters who are seeking adventure in front of the family television set." The new wave of science fiction serials propelled the entire family, and domestic life itself, into the electronic age.[26] *Collier's Magazine* reported, "All over the air waves, the Wide Open Spaces are being traded in for the Wide Upper Spaces. The trend may be away from horses and up in the heavens for keeps."[27] And of course, youthful American viewers needed a "new wardrobe, new gear, and a whole new language" to keep up with the new breed of space hero.[28] The cover of the May 10, 1953, issue of *American Weekly* depicted a youthful "space man" proudly clad in his new Atomic Space Suit and helmet, handing down his outmoded cowboy boots and chaps to a dismayed younger brother, and a few months later, the August 1953 issue of *Woman's Day* proclaimed that "a new supersonic generation is putting its cowboy suits in mothballs and encasing itself in space helmets."[29] Mothers became wardrobe and prop masters in order to properly outfit their young rangers. As the housewife's tried-and-true advisor, the magazine offered to help readers faced with these new "space happy" demands develop new domestic skills, with the cover promising "Four Flight-Tested Space Helmets to Make," complete with full-color pictures and two pages of how-to diagrams for creating space helmets "like those seen in Space Patrol and Captain Video." One frustrated mother, perhaps less confident in her abilities, went straight to the producers of Tom Corbett and pleaded with them to market a space helmet for the protection of the family pet—a turtle whose bowl became a makeshift helmet for her two-year-old each time the program aired.[30]

And so, as science fiction series such as Tom Corbett and Captain Video propelled American youth into the space age, their families were carried right along with them. The language of televised space series spread from the sound stage to the living room as youthful viewers traded quips with siblings such as "Plug your jets!" and "Blast me for a Martian mouse!" Adult programming was also infiltrated as comedians and talk-show performers wished viewers "Spaceman's Luck" and urged them to "Blast Your Rockets."[31] Even everyday household objects such as appliances and automobiles took on a space-age look.

The household economy was further affected by products and promotions from the series' numerous sponsors, advertised during the commercial breaks: at breakfast, families ate Kellogg's Corn Flakes, Chex cereals, and "Pep—the solar cereal" (which boasted a picture of Tom Corbett on every box) as the younger members eagerly awaited the enclosed prizes; they snacked on Nestlé's Caramels, Powerhouse bars, and Johnson's Fudge so the wrappers and labels could be exchanged for promotional items; they collected premiums and entered contests for larger prizes, such as Space Patrol's larger-than-life Rocket Club House, awarded to the winner of the "Name the Planet" contest. Even family pets dined on Walter Kendall's "Fives," the multicolored "5-Course Dinner in One!" in allegiance to the sponsor of their young masters' Atomic Age heroes. And for housewives who purchased these products at Market Basket supermarkets, their weekly trips also included a ride for the kids on Exhibit's Space Patrol rides, which were installed at many of the chain's stores.

Booming merchandizing campaigns allowed young fans to join in on the interstellar action, creating what Hugo Gernsback termed the new "third dimensional world of science-fiction"—"toys, games, gadgets, scientific instruments of all kinds, wearing apparel for youngsters, and countless other constantly-evolving, ingenious devices."[32] Supermarkets and department stores alike boasted official series merchandise, such as space suits, cadet uniforms, rocket guns, and other gizmos carefully studied and coveted by their young fans, which were also interwoven into family spending and pastimes in ways that could not be ignored. A 1952 Life magazine photo spread illustrated a dazzling array of items—from cosmic generators to "paralyzers"—bearing the Space Patrol label, predicted to net $40 million in sales that year.[33] Frankie Thomas (who played Tom Corbett) recalled that in addition to eight hardback Tom Corbett novels and a series of comic books, there were 185 separate sale items manufactured bearing the Corbett name. Thomas, who appeared in department stores across the country, observed that "[a]t one point it seemed like the subsidiary rights were getting bigger than the show."[34]

The impact of Corbett and the other rocketmen on domestic economies and patterns of consumption, as well as on the relationships and pastimes of American families, stood as testimony to the heroes' influence on the lives of their audiences. Invited each week into the intimacy of the domestic sphere, Tom Corbett, Commando Cody, Captain Video, and their cohorts reciprocated by reinforcing familial and social norms to their young audiences through modeling behaviors, enacting morality tales, and supporting parents by holding youth to the high standards of a rocketman, as can be observed in the Rocky Jones Space Ranger Code:

> As an official Space Ranger, I pledge
> To obey my parents at all times
> To be kind and courteous to all
> To be brave in the cause of freedom, to help the weak
> To obey the law at all times
> To grow up clean in mind and strong in body [35]

For the series' young fans and their families, the familiar heroes and villains, catchphrases, homemade space helmets, department-store ray guns, secret pictures hidden in boxes of cereal, and all the rest created a continuity between the fantastic worlds on screen and the worlds in which they lived—a world in which real rocketmen were soon to begin their own space adventures. And, even as they did so, fictional rocketmen took on the role, for their young fans, as trusted adult guides to a rapidly emerging future world brimming over with the wonders of the space age and the anxieties of the Cold War—a world that their parents barely understood.

Facing the Future, One Episode at a Time

The rocketmen television series of the 1950s were conceived and produced as space-age contributions to the venerable "boys' adventure" genre. They were fast-paced tales—filled with action, colorful characters, and exotic settings—designed to thrill and excite their audiences (not all of whom were male, and not all of whom were young). The series, however, were more than just entertainment. In between battles with interplanetary villains and near-collisions with meteors, they sought to impart serious messages about values and behavior. The rocketmen themselves, from the earliest *Captain Video* episode, forward, served as archetypes of bravery and heroism in a world now defined by the Cold War. Those with youthful crews and sidekicks had another task, as well, serving as mentors not only to their on-screen charges, but also to the thousands of fans who kept weekly rendezvous with them in their living rooms. They modeled ways of being, specifically *American* ways of being, for the new, uncertain, postwar world.

Each week, children's rocketmen heroes illustrated the perennial value of loyalty, honesty, ethics, obedience, and fairness during the course of their adventures to keep not just the world, but the universe, safe for democracy. Their youthful audiences learned not only by example, but also through the mandates of Ranger Messages and formalized Space Ranger Codes, which banished ambiguities about the meanings of good character and citizenship. For most rocketmen, from the ever-vigilant Captain Video to the fiery Rocky Jones, the mission of the rocketmen was to valorize and extend a way of life that Americans already knew, as they ushered in the Cold War era.

The late 1940s made it clear that the new frontiers of the postwar world, and the ability to defend and spread American values and ideals, demanded mastery of advanced science and technology and an awareness of the complexities of other cultures. The future was uncertain, its shape undefined, but the power to shape it belonged to the knowledgeable. The rocketmen moved with ease and confidence in a fictional, far-future world where space travel was routine, "foreign powers" ruled not just nations but planets, and technology like the Para-Ray Gun and Opticon Scillometer conveyed seemingly magical powers. They showed their young fans a glittering, fantastic future utterly unlike the present, but also presented a model for success in that strange new world. Their own behavior, along with the lessons they imparted to their sidekicks on screen and to fans watching at home, dramatized a new form of masculinity that adapted traditional American values to the demands of the Cold War world.

Notes

1. Voiceover narrations for the adventures of Captain Z-Ro hailed him as a "research explorer in time and space," while opening narration for Captain Video celebrated his role as an "electronic wizard" and "guardian of the safety of the universe."

2. Donald F. Glut and Jim Harmon, *The Great Television Heroes* (Garden City, NY: Doubleday, 1975), 86.

3. For discussion on traditional male archetypes, see M. Elise Marrubio, *Killing the Indian Maiden: Images of Native American Women on Film* (Lexington: University Press of Kentucky, 2006); Robert Bly, *Iron John: A Book About Men* (New York: Da Capo Press, 2004).

4. A number of the rocketman series of the 1950s were performed live, and preserved only on kinescopes, many of which were subsequently lost. *Tom Corbett, Space Cadet; Rocky Jones, Space Ranger; Space Patrol; Flash Gordon*; and *Captain Z-Ro* have been released on DVD, however, and the surviving episodes of *Captain Video* (along with episodes and commercials from other series) are available online. Notable discussions include: Jean-Noel Bassior, *Space Patrol: Missions of Daring in the Name of Early Television* (Jefferson, NC: McFarland, 2005); Allan Asherman, "Rocky Jones: Space Ranger" [2 parts] *Filmfax*, March 1990 and May 1990; Patrick Lucanio and Gary Coville, *Smokin' Rockets: The Romance of Technology in American Film, Radio and Television, 1945-1960* (Jefferson, NC McFarland, 2002). Fan websites such as Ed

Pippin's *Solar Guard Academy* (http://www.solarguard.com) offer a wealth of production data and episode synopses for particular shows.

5. On the pulp science fiction of the 1920s and 1930s, see Mike Ashley, *Time Machines: The Story of Pulp Science Fiction Magazines from the Beginning to 1950* (Liverpool: Liverpool University Press, 2001).

6. Peter Stanfield, *Horse Opera: The Strange History of the 1930s Singing Cowboy* (Urbana and Chicago: University of Illinois Press, 2002).

7. Cynthia J. Miller, "Domesticating Space: Science Fiction Serials Come Home," in *Science Fiction Film, Television, and Adaptation: Across the Screens,* ed. J. P. Telotte, 3-13 (London and New York: Routledge, 2011).

8. Bassior, 238-242.

9. *Classic Sci-Fi TV,* DVD collection (Golden Valley, MN: Mill Creek Entertainment, 2009).

10. Marubbio, 113.

11. *Classic Sci-Fi TV.*

12. Stephen C. Ambrose, *Citizen Soldiers: The U. S. Army from the Normandy Beaches to the Bulge to the Surrender of Germany* (New York: Simon and Schuster, 1997), 273-277; Paul Fussell, *Wartime: Understanding and Behavior in the Second World War* (New York: Oxford University Press, 1989), 79-115. Wartime culture—from glossy Hollywood combat films like *Bataan!* (1943) to cartoonist Bill Mauldin's drawings of GI everymen Willie and Joe—celebrated such bonding, while postwar novels (*The Naked and the Dead,* 1948) and films (*The Sands of Iwo Jima,* 1949) explored its dynamics. For more, see Jeanine C. Basinger, *The World War II Combat Film: Anatomy of a Genre* (Middletown, CT: Wesleyan University Press, 2003); Bill Mauldin, *Up Front* (New York: Henry Holt, 1945).

13. *Classic Sci-Fi TV.*

14. See James Burkhart Gilbert, *Men in the Middle: Searching for Masculinity in the 1950s* (Chicago: University of Chicago Press, 2005); David M. Earle, *All Man! Hemmingway, 1950s Men's Magazines, and the Masculine Persona* (Kent, OH: Kent State University Press, 2009); K. A. Curdileone, *Manhood and American Political Culture in the Cold War: Masculinity, the Vital Center and American Political Culture in the Cold War, 1949-1963* (London: Routledge, 2005).

15. *Classic Sci-Fi TV.*

16. John Ellis, *Visible Fictions: Cinema, Television, Video,* rev. ed. (London: Routledge, 1992), 113.

17. See Miller, "Domesticating Space."

18. *Classic Sci-Fi TV.*

19. *Classic Sci-Fi TV.*

20. *Tom Corbett, Space Cadet,* DVD collection (PR Studios, 2009).

21. *Tom Corbett.*

22. Raymond Williams, *Television* (London: Routledge, 2003), 66-68.

23. See Ellis, *Visible Fictions*; A. Rubin, "Television Use by Children and Adolescents," *Human Communication Research* 5, no. 2 (1979): 109-120; A. Rubin, "Uses and Gratifications," in *Broadcasting Research Methods,* ed. J. Dominick and J. Fletcher (Boston: Allyn and Bacon, 1985).

24. *Classic Sci-Fi TV.*

25. *Classic Sci-Fi TV.*

26. "The Electronic Age of Captain Video," *TV Forecast* (Chicago: Television Forecast, June 10, 1950), 6.

27. Murray Robinson, "Planet Parenthood," *Collier's Magazine*, January 5, 1952, 31.

28. Bassior, 8.

29. "Four Flight-Tested Space Helmets You Can Make," *Women's Day*, August 1953, 25. For more, see Miller, "Domesticating Space."

30. Bassior, 9-10.

31. Frankie Thomas, "Westward The Stars," *American Classic Screen* 4, no. 2 (1980): 50.

32. Hugo Gernsback, "The Science-Fiction Industry: A New Industry in the Making," *Science-Fiction Plus* 1 (May 1953): 2.

33. *Life*, uncredited photograph of Space Patrol merchandise, September 1, 1952, 83.

34. Thomas, 51.

35. *Classic Sci-Fi TV*.

Chapter Twelve

The Avengers and Feminist Identity Development: Learning the Example of Critical Resistance from Cathy Gale

Robin Redmon Wright

Popular culture is "an entry point into social education" and societies "learn early and well from mass media."[1] Growing up in a working class home in Appalachia in the 1960s and 1970s, television was my window to the world. It was a comfort to know that the rest of the world mirrored my own, at least to a certain extent. Although my world was filled with religious dogmatism, work, extreme conservatism, sexism, racism, classism and moral certitude, I didn't realize this at the time, and nothing I watched on TV revealed the truth of my ignorance and oppression. Television programs rarely afforded glimpses behind the curtain of ideology, the dominant hegemony, that kept us all believing in the post-colonial, patriarchal, myopic nationalism making us complicit in our own oppression while increasing the systemic inequality inherent in capitalist societies.

Ultimately, I went to college following a divorce, and became a working, single-mom trying to uncover reality by getting an education. Television, however, remained a passion for me. With no money for vacations, long work days and longer nights studying, TV provided a respite from both work and study—initially. As I advanced in my educational pursuits, however, I began to critically analyze what I watched. My classmates and I formed critical theory study groups to discuss Derrida, Foucault, Lacan, Burke, Saussure, Bahktin, Kristeva, and De Beauvoir, among others. I felt terribly out of place given my background, but I persevered. As a side effect, television became less of a break and more of a center for praxis. Frankly, I began to despair. Where were the feminist models? Where was the resistance? Little did I know at the time that across the pond and half a world away there existed a television character, created when I was just out of diapers, who would rock my world when I saw her for the first time in 2002.

In September 2002, as I strolled through *Barnes & Noble* wondering if I could do sixty hours of coursework required for a Ph.D., while working full time and commuting 136 miles each way to class, I spotted a three-tape VHS set of the old *The Avengers* television program for a mere $9.95. I am a long-time *Avengers* fan, but I didn't recognize the blond woman on the box with John Steed (actor Patrick Macnee): *The Avengers* with a different female lead from Emma Peel (actress Diana Rigg), the playful impish sidekick I knew and had come to love after seeing old episodes in reruns in the 1980s. Who was this blond woman? I was intrigued, mentally energized; this was just what I needed to look forward to while driving home through the dark, desolate countryside.

A Different Kind of Character

*There had never been a woman like that on television before—in fact, there had never been a feminist **creature** before Cathy Gale.*
—Honor Blackman[2]

That unexpected discovery began an obsession that persists to this day. As I watched those Cathy Gale episodes from 1963, I suffered a disorienting disconnect with the female roles I remembered watching as a child. And as a student of feminist theory and history and, having by then earned an MA in English literature, I recognized the uniqueness of the character for the early 1960s. For readers unfamiliar with *The Avengers* or, more specifically, with the 1962-1963 *Avengers* with Honor Blackman as Dr. Catherine (Cathy) Gale in the lead role, I will briefly describe the series and its cultural context.

The outcomes or effects of television "cannot be separated from their context and treated as isolated phenomena to which we are given limited exposure. On the contrary, television's influence is all-pervasive. . . . It shapes the framework of our political discourse."[3] The modern British feminist movement, similar to the US movement, emerged in the decades following World War II. While women's work outside the home was valued—even demanded—during the war, Britain's government sought ways to send women home to have children during the late 1940s and into the 1950s. England lost a significant portion of its population during the war, and a move to "rebuild the family" was stressed by "professionals and politicians" who focused their attention "squarely on the issue of 'adequate mothering' as the surest means to securing future social stability."[4] These concerns were prompted by the "pragmatic problems of the social and geographical dislocation of families as a result of the war."[5] Some experts predicted that by the year 2000, "the population of England and Wales would be reduced to that of London."[6] There was a very real fear that if women stayed in the workplace, or otherwise rejected traditional roles, and did not focus on having and rearing children, then the UK could not retain its status as a world power.

These cultural fears are reflected in the characterizations of women on British television. According to David Gauntlett, "In the 1950s, 1960s, and 1970s, only 20 to 35 percent of characters [on British television] were female. By the mid-1980s, there were more women in leading roles, but still there were twice as many men on screen."[7] In addition to the paucity of female roles, Gauntlett cites several studies conducted in the UK during the 1970s and 1980s that found consistent evidence that "the women's movement had been largely ignored by television with married housewives being the main female role shown."[8] Certainly, as the 1960s dawned, the attitudes of the British government, the media, and others in power, as well as most of the population, were fully entrenched in the idea that women were to focus their attention on home and family.

It was in this environment that Cathy Gale fought her way into British living rooms in 1962. *The Avengers* series began in 1961 on ITV with two male leads; Ian Hendry played Dr. David Keel, the lead role, and Macnee played John Steed, a shady character who worked for some unnamed government spy agency who recruited the medical doctor, Keel, to help him nab the bad guys. But after the first season, Hendry announced his departure in pursuit of a film career. Producers Sidney Newman and Leonard White decided to try to increase the popularity of the show by replacing him with a woman. Since several scripts had already been commissioned for the Ian Hendry-Patrick Macnee team, and this low-budget crime drama had no money for new scripts, the producers had the female replacement, Blackman, read a part written for a man with a name change as the only revision.[9] The result of this cost-cutting measure, combined with the tenacity and unusual talents of Blackman, as Dr. Catherine Gale, was that the character developed with characteristics traditionally thought male, but who was clearly a very beautiful and feminine woman.[10] According to Brian Clemens, one of the writers of the Cathy Gale episodes who went on to become head writer, director and producer of the later seasons, this combination was a "happy accident" that led to the creation of "the first emancipated woman on television."[11]

Of course, while the dialogue was not changed, it was thought too unbelievable to have a female medical doctor. Therefore, to enable her to know about and to have experienced things a doctor who had traveled the world would know and experience, they made her an anthropologist. Still, Dr. Cathy Gale was unique. The producers wanted her to be something of a cross between cultural anthropologist Margaret Mead and Margaret Bourke-White, the famous photographer for *LIFE* magazine who photographed some of the most remote, war-ridden places in the world. Her name was derived from their desire to create a character that would hit audiences like a *gale* force wind. The character had a Ph.D. in anthropology, a black belt in judo, an expertise with firearms, led hunting expeditions in Africa and fought for freedom in Cuba. She also wore black leather and drove motorcycles and sports cars.[12] June Cleaver she was certainly not.

Investigating a Gale Force

From the moment I put the first tape in my VCR, I was captivated. As I watched that first set, and then other DVDs from 1963 bought from Amazon, I tried to reconcile what I was watching with what I remembered from my childhood of watching that snowy screen in my parents' living room. My obsession grew and I discovered there were 1962 episodes not available in the United States. I had to buy them from France and had to buy a Region two DVD player to view them. While I remarried, pursued a doctorate, continued my forty hour workweeks, and mothered four children, I remained fixated on the anomaly that was Cathy Gale. I began to get agitated as I watched. I paced the floor and kept saying to my husband, "If I had only watched these shows growing up instead of *I Dream of Jeanie*!" I began to collect artifacts like written accounts of fan responses, fanzines, and magazine articles. I was consumed with curiosity about the effect the "first feminist female lead"[13] on television must have had on contemporary viewers. According to Andrae, "*The Avengers* refunctioned the patriarchal discourse of the spy genre, transforming woman from an object of male desire into a subject who possessed 'masculine' power and independence."[14] I could not stop wondering how she impacted her fans, and that curiosity eventually became the study I discuss in the rest of the chapter.

Theoretical Framework

I situate this study within a four-sided frame of theoretical perspectives: a Gramscian, political view of popular culture;[15] the concept of "public pedagogy" and "critical public pedagogy" as they are viewed in curriculum theory;[16] critical feminist perspectives on media consumption and the possibility for pockets of resistance within popular culture;[17] and an adult education perspective focusing on how the joys of popular culture can sometimes help learning in adults.[18] The Gramscian view is based on Antonio Gramsci's political work and focuses on the ways people make meaning from popular culture. John Storey explains that we actively participate in culture as we: choose what to consume and reject other cultural products, negotiate the meanings we make while participating in popular culture, assign values to the culture with which we interact, resist elements of the culture with which we interact, resist elements of and meanings within the products we consume, and, at times, are also manipulated by popular culture.[19]

This perspective also investigates how popular culture intersects with and wields *power*.[20] Popular culture is where inequalities of class, gender, race, and sexuality are often made meaningful or brought to consciousness. It can also be where individuals resist and negotiate power relations, and where hegemony is both exercised and resisted.[21]

Theoretical work within current critical curriculum studies views popular culture as sites of "public pedagogy" and informal learning.[22] Popular culture, as viewed through the lens of public pedagogy, teaches audiences how to relate to the world through the ways it represents people and issues and the kinds of discourses it creates and disseminates. Henry Giroux argues that it is through our interactions with popular culture that "identities are continually being transformed and power enacted."[23] Most of this public pedagogy research has focused on how popular culture reproduces hegemonic values and entrenched practices and institutionalized inequalities stemming from racism, sexism, homophobia, xenophobia, machismo and violence.[24] However, there has been little exploration of resistant or "critical" public pedagogies, and that is where I focus my work and this chapter.

The next side is naturally supported by feminist perspectives on popular culture, since I am interested in how feminist identities were developed in contemporary viewers of the Cathy Gale *Avengers*. This literature often posits audiences, not as passive recipients of the "vicious intentions" of patriarchy, but, rather, as "active producers of meaning, interpreting and accommodating media texts to their own daily lives and culture."[25] Audiences may very well use popular culture to shape themselves according to hegemonic ideologies, but Liesbit van Zoonen argues that women may also see "the pleasures popular culture offers" as "potential source[s] of subversion."[26] This view sees female fictional characters not as role models, but as "textual constructions of *possible modes of femininity*" and "symbolic realizations of feminine subject positions with which viewers can identify in fantasy."[27] Judith Butler insists that "various acts of gender create the idea of gender, and without those acts there would be no gender at all. . . . Gender is an identity tenuously constituted in time, instituted in an exterior space through a stylized repetition of acts."[28] In this research, I focused on how participants integrated their fascination with a television character into their adult identity development. Unlike the women in the study cited above, participants in this study *did* position Cathy Gale as a role model. In the cultural/historical moment they encountered Cathy Gale, few role models challenging cultural gender norms were available. Cathy Gale's unique persona enabled participants who held her as a model for sculpting their adult identities to learn ways of performing their feminine/feminist identity that would not have occurred to them without her example.

The fourth side of the theoretical frame is the research into the intersection of adult education and identity development. In an extensive literature review I conducted with Jennifer Sandlin, we outline the various ways the adult education profession has explored popular culture as it relates to adult learning.[29] We found six areas of research and practice in the field: representations of adult learning and adult development in popular media, self-reflexive practices of adult educators who consume popular culture, effective classroom practices involving the popular, analyses of popular culture products and processes as adult education curriculum, the impact of adults' learning from popular culture, and community-based "popular" culture as resistance. In this study, I focus on the self-reflective processes of adult fans and the impact of what is learned from an intense engagement with a popular cultural product or artifact.

Methodology

This research is based on over three years of research and involved two trips to the UK from my home in Texas where I lived at the time. It also involved persistence, perseverance, and tenacity. Since I wanted to hear the stories of women who felt they were impacted by a television character over 40 years earlier, I chose a qualitative design.[30] In the analysis of the transcripts, I used both a constant comparative thematic analysis and elements of narrative analysis, specifically, symbolic conversion analysis.[31] I posted a call for participants on an academic list, on two *Avengers* fan websites, and on flyers that I placed around London. Four participants were referred by British friends. One participant volunteered after I purchased several 1960s magazines featuring Honor Blackman from her on Ebay. In the end, seventeen women agreed to discuss their lives before, during, and after watching the Cathy Gale *Avengers* in the 1960s. Sixteen interviews were conducted during two separate two-week visits to England a year apart, and one interview was conducted in the US. All participants were aged approximately fifty-five to seventy, were British, and were self-selected. Only two were still teenagers when watching *The Avengers*. Interestingly, three were male-to-female transsexuals and were young men when they watched the episodes. I also interviewed two of the screenwriters for the series, Jon Manchip White and Brian Clemens and, ultimately, I interviewed Honor Blackman, the actress who portrayed Cathy Gale.[32] All interviews were audiotaped and transcribed later. With the exception of the actress and writers, all names and identifiers were removed from the transcripts before analysis. Most interviews were conducted in the participants' homes or in public spaces near their homes in London, Brighton, Oxford and other towns and cities.

I also collected and analyzed over seventy-five artifacts dealing with the series (magazine articles, copies of original scripts, fanzines, newspaper clippings, etc.) and spent several days in the archives at the British Film Institute searching for data on audience response and statistics on viewership. I also viewed all forty-four Cathy Gale episodes at least twenty times each as well as the 137.3 surviving original series episodes (1961-1968) to put the Cathy Gale episodes into proper *Avengers* context.[33] For further context, I watched all available episodes of *Danger Man, The Saint,* and *The Prisoner* and a few episodes of *Z-Cars*, paying particular attention to women's roles. Viewing related programs helped locate *The Avengers* within the context of other spy/crime dramas airing on British television at the time. These documents, TV programs and artifacts, along with the interviews with Ms. Blackman and the two screenwriters, helped "ground my investigation in the context of the problem,"[34] and set the stage for understanding the women's stories.

The Powerful Impact of a Television Character

Once I acted Cathy . . . women felt more capable in all sorts of directions.

—Honor Blackman, personal interview, July 2006

Blackman's weekly performance as a fiercely humanitarian woman with a Ph.D., with a black belt in judo, and with character traits that were stereotypically considered to be male, disrupted and made ambiguous the perceived naturalness of a heterogeneous dichotomy of sex and gender that was fully entrenched in British culture as the 1960s dawned.[35] Her performance sent a disruptive gender message to some viewers in that era of severe compulsory heterosexuality and traditional gender norms. She was neither domestic, nor submissive, nor sexual in the way "sexy" women were portrayed in film and television at that time. When she threw large men across the set during live-action taping, she acted gender in a way viewers had never seen from a female actor. The effect of the "happy accident" that Brian Clemens described—of budgetary constraints resulting in a woman being cast in a role written for a man and Honor Blackman's unusual athleticism and professionalism bringing believability to the character—was life-changing for the fans who participated in this study. While individual stories varied, thematic analysis revealed three interrelated themes running through all fan interviews. The women in this study learned to incorporate Cathy Gale's strengths into their identity development; they learned the need for and the value of strong, intelligent, independent feminist role models; and they learned that they could, and most did, reject the traditional gender roles assigned to them by their country, culture, class, families, and religions. The remainder of this chapter is a discussion of that learning, and musings on what it could mean to the study of media and adult learning.

Breaking Bastions and Barriers

Men always said, "women can never be good at it [physical aggression and force]; they're not sufficiently strong." Then if you find somebody who, in fact, can use the aggressor's strength against him, then— well—the last bastion fell.

—Honor Blackman, personal interview, July 2006

James Chapman writes that *The Avengers* producers positioned **both** the "actress and character at the vanguard of modern, liberated femininity,"[36] in their publicity and promotional materials. Dr. Catherine Gale's arrival on the small screen "rocked the existing stereotype of subservient, domesticated TV women."[37] It was 1962 and over a year before Betty Freidan would publish *The Feminine Mystique* in the United States, an event that many scholars mark as the birth of second wave feminism. *The Avengers* was a low-budget crime/spy drama that was filmed on videotape, recorded straight through with one two-minute commercial break, and wrapped for around £4500 an episode.[38] As a result, when Blackman used judo to defend herself in fight scenes, she was using the brown belt she had earned. The press considered it front page news when Blackman knocked out professional wrestler and part-time actor Jackie Paolo while filming the episode entitled, "Mandrake." Newspaper headlines featured Paolo's seven and a half minute loss of consciousness for days.[39] Clad head-to-toe in black leather, Honor Blackman provided an image of an intelligent and educated woman who acted on her convictions, cared about justice and equality, and was able to beat a man in any arena—even in physical battle. That feat, I would argue, is still unequaled on prime-time television. In 1960s Britain, women took notice.

Part of the allure of Cathy Gale's fighting persona was her action wardrobe. Because the costume designer needed to put her in something that would not rip easily, and that would offer some protection from the concrete studio floor when she was rolling around with an 18-stoner, she wore head-to-toe black leather with black leather boots for fight scenes. That leather and those boots became part of British fashion in the 1960s, and the appeal, the participants told me, was that "wearing those boots meant you were tough and could take on anything." Liz and Katie both talked of putting on leather boots even now when they need to feel strong and confident. The boots help them "take on the character" of Cathy Gale when they feel the need to be "confrontational and aggressive." Most of the respondents said that they continue to think actively about the character when they have to confront a variety of difficult situations. They "put on" her posture and defiant manner with their leather. Helen, Rosemary, and Katie said that, even now, they often think to themselves, "What would Cathy do?" when someone attempts to intimidate them. One woman explained, "Cathy, you see, didn't retreat. She was quite feminine, but she didn't retreat when she knew she was right—and she was always right." Camille pointed out with a chuckle, "Blackman was an unusually strong, distinctive woman—hence a real subconscious wobbler for people to handle at the time."

Two of the women I interviewed internalized that message by taking judo lessons in the 1960s and 1970s. While many girls today grow up taking self-defense classes of some sort, in 1962 women in hand-to-hand combat courses were extremely rare. One fanzine reported the effect that Cathy Gale's on-screen martial arts exploits had on her audience:

> Membership rosters swelled dramatically as would-be Cathy Gales jostled with men looking either for her real life counterpart or a chance to defend themselves should they run into one. Correspondents in newspapers chronicled comic scenes in British living rooms as couples who couldn't face the formality of joining a club tried to re-enact *Avengers* scenes with the aid of teach-yourself-judo type publications. The only point of agreement between the two schools of thought was that Cathy Gale had, one way or another, given judo an awful lot of free publicity.[40]

Among the women I interviewed for this study, one had earned a green belt in judo and another achieved the higher ranked brown belt. China, a study participant, explained that her interest in martial arts and resultant black belt in karate "came from watching Cathy do judo." These women explained how empowering it was to be able to physically defend themselves. As one woman told me, "I was not afraid to get out there and do things like my girlfriends were."

Learning that they could physically embody power affected various arenas of their lives. When one participant was told not to pursue a particular career because she was not physically strong enough, she remembered thinking about Honor Blackman, as Cathy, throwing "twelve stone oafs through the air" and said to herself, "I can do this." She did do it, and was able to acquire and maintain a job that required lifting heavy crates and boxes. "It was wonderful," she told me, "because it was like exercising all day. It's why I'm still so thin and healthy!" Most participants were still quite fit and, as Barbara, a tall, thin, retired university tutor put it, "I saw in Cathy Gale the possibility of independence because she was so athletic. I wasn't frightened of being on my own."

These women reconstructed themselves as women who were different from their vision of how women *should* be. They had a defiant tone as they related their stories. They rejected much of what their culture taught them about women because the character of Cathy Gale *performed* a different kind of woman—a woman with what had traditionally been viewed as male traits and abilities—and the fierceness, confidence and aggression. As Liz put it, "I looked at Mum and thought—I don't want to be that. I don't want to spend my life looking after people who don't appreciate it and always feeling . . . timid and afraid to have a thought of my own. I changed." The women began *performing*, in Butler's terms, a revised and reconstructed version of their gender. [41]

Cathy's physicality appealed because it ripped the veil of oppression and submissiveness from these women, but they were equally influenced by the ethic of care that she embodied. It was her commitment to justice and equality, embodied within the physical tigress defending the weak and punishing the wicked, that has had the most lingering and widespread effects on the women I interviewed. Thirteen of the women told me that they do philanthropic and charity work because of both Cathy Gale and Honor Blackman. They admired Cathy as "one of the first women to do more than just talk about doing things to help people and change the bad things in the world." Liz put it like this:

> My mum cared about the people close to her. But she also lived in a small world, if you know what I mean. We didn't have much—perhaps it was that—but she wasn't interested in people starving in Africa or what was happening in places that had once been part of the Empire. I always worried about that. Cathy Gale was the only woman on the telly that was interested as well. I was young and—maybe—idealistic, but I noticed that. She cared about babies in Africa before it was fashionable to do so.

All the participants have followed Honor Blackman's career, in varying degrees, and admire her commitment to activism. However, 13 interviewees specifically described how they have internalized the actor's participation in politics and charities as part of their own identities.

I Am Woman—Hear me Roar!

A "sparkling entertainment," with songs, which takes as its theme women who set about making changes in the way the world saw them and the way they saw the world.
—from the Playbill for *Wayward Women*,
Honor Blackman's One-Woman Show

Another learning theme that arose from this study was the realization that there is a lack of, and a need for, positive and admirable role models for women. The character Cathy Gale and the actress Honor Blackman are both considered role models for the women in this study, but so was the show on which the character/actress appeared: during its heyday twelve million people in the UK were watching *The Avengers* each week. The show was consistently in the weekly Television Audience Measurement [TAM] top twenty most watched television shows.[42] My conversations with women who self-selected for this study and were among those twelve million viewers revealed how they constructed knowledge from popular culture that led to life-altering perspective transformation. Women told stories of their intense appreciation for Cathy as their first role model and related tales of searching for similar models, or being determined to be role models for others, throughout their lives. For each participant in this study, their attraction to Cathy Gale resulted from the fact that the gender identity she performed was unlike anything they had imagined possible before she kicked her way into their living rooms on Saturday nights. Jack Mezirow asserts that imagination is central to the possibility of transformational learning.[43] One must *imagine* something very different from what she has been taught in order to act for change. Yet most people rarely conceive of the kind of dramatic gender/sex/role disruption that Cathy performed in 1962, without first discovering the *concept* in some form of textual, media, or cultural representation. As the women in this study repeated often and insistently, women in 1950s British culture who challenged and resisted gender norms were very rare indeed, and not readily available for consumption. Cathy Gale fed their souls.

Only four of the women identified role models from among their families and communities, and those were conditional role models—a teacher or a community activist whom they admired for a singular trait. Most of the others searched for role models in books, popular culture, or in women outside their familiar spaces. Their comments are reflected in Helen's assertion that, "In my day there just weren't women in my village to admire. No Cathies there. There were the housewives, the blue stockings, and the black garters!" she laughed, "I did NOT want to fit into any of *those* categories!"

The women discussed searching for role models as a learned personal trait that took effort. Many spoke of feminist theorists they had discovered, others female detectives in novels, still others talked about historical figures from Boudicca to Elizabeth I. Each participant came back to the assertion that Cathy Gale—and Honor Blackman herself—was still the most meaningful, lasting and helpful role model in their lives.[44] In her eighties, Blackman is still an activist, acting, active, and commands respect. As she told me, she has stopped riding motorcycles and doesn't fly planes any more, but she still likes a fast car and a challenge. Several of the participants recalled one of Blackman's more recent acts of resistance and dissent when she publicly rejected the monarchy and the concept of imperialism by refusing to accept the Queen's proffered title *Commander of the British Empire* (CBE) in 2003. Seven of the women mentioned this incident with an air of pride. Blackman told one reporter that since she believed England should be a republic, "it would be gross hypocrisy to accept that."[45] Like Cathy Gale, Blackman is an example to them of a principled woman. China emphatically stated, "I wasn't surprised. It's that edge—that fearless edge—she's not afraid of what people think. Not even the queen!" Both the character and the actor have that "fearless edge" that makes them role models and critical public pedagogues.

Fry Your Own Bacon

Cathy was the first character who was allowed to be the intellectual equal of the fellow. I mean, before that, one had sort of blue-stocking ladies, but you'd never had a good-looking, shrewd woman who won over the man. I got huge fan mail from women, because she made women think they could be like her.
—Honor Blackman, personal interview, July 2006

Finally, all the women in this study said that watching Cathy Gale in those early *Avengers* made them realize that they could reject the traditional life-path of "marrying young and having lots of children and being a housewife," as one participant framed it. The three transwomen were equally motivated to construct their post-surgery personas in opposition to what their culture had made them envision as the "proper" role for women. One of the transwomen, Astrid, talked of "painting a picture using the colors drawn from the palette of Cathy Gale" during her transition. China spoke of being worried that after her reassignment, she'd have to "be the wimpy woman—the little washer" in order to pass as female—but not when she reflected on her attraction to the character of Cathy. For China, Cathy's portrayal of a woman who resisted the dominant discourse that taught women that they were the "fairer sex" allowed her to transition and to be a fully feminine, strong and assertive woman.

While Honor Blackman insists that she was not *"fully* aware" of the impact the character would have, she reminisced about women's reactions to Cathy Gale as evidenced by the letters and personal stories fans shared with her: "I

certainly remember housewives who had children and were stuck—or they felt
they were stuck—and then, watching Cathy, they took inspiration to have
another go at life, you know—a career. And having done so, I think they were
quite glad. They hadn't considered, until then, what women were capable of."
The participants in this study could have written the letters Ms. Blackman was
describing. Among the participants was a scientist and university professor who
was told by her teachers and her culture that "girls don't do science," but after
watching *The Avengers* decided that "if Cathy can have a Ph.D. in anthropology
and be smarter than everyone else, I can be good at science and not pretend to be
dumb." There were women who broke off engagements because Cathy helped
them imagine a university education and a career rather than an early marriage
and children. And there were also stories of familial estrangements, emotional
struggles, and painful losses because they chose not to walk the paths their
family and faith had set them on. Family cut them off; friends rejected them;
occasionally, the isolation caused them to try to fit into the mold that had been
constructed for them. Yet, none had stayed in that mold and all of them were
grateful for the powerful lessons they learned from the first feminist on
television. Several told me that they recite a call-and-response mantra when they
feel forces of oppression and find themselves struggling against various forms of
institutionalized patriarchy, sexism and classism; that mantra was always some
version of "What would Cathy do?" and the reliable response was
unquestioningly, "Fight!"

The Aftermath of a Gale Force

*Certainly I had quite a lot of mail from young people who hadn't been
trying very hard and then they decided that, uh, they wanted to be
different, to make a difference, and they learned that they could do that
from Cathy. Which was very gratifying I must say. . . . Then I got some
kinky mail, too!*
                              —Honor Blackman, personal interview, July 2006

Not all responses to Cathy Gale were positive. Many men felt threatened by the
presence of a strong woman, even though she was locked inside the television
set. Blackman confided that she stopped going to parties after the show had been
running just a few weeks because when men had a few drinks they would
challenge her to go outside and fight—confident that they could beat her.
Blackman recalled, "Quite a few men, when they'd had a few drinks, would try
and call me out for a fight . . . and then they liked to try to mock me, because I
really unnerved them." Her husband at the time, Maurice Kaufmann, confided to
a reporter in 1963 that men "seem to resent the way Cathy Gale can take care of
herself. It takes away their male ego. They identify Honor with Cathy Gale so
they take it out on her. And she always rises to the bait and gets aggressive back.
. . . With us, it's the husband stopping the wife having a fight—not the other
way around."[46] Some of the women I spoke with told me that their mothers

disliked the character intensely. She challenged their ideology and their sense of place in the world. Yet the program was extremely popular and, primarily because of Blackman's performance, the show became a cult sensation.

After the 1963 season, Honor Blackman left *The Avengers* to play another accomplished woman—the luscious lesbian pilot, Pussy Galore, in the James Bond film, *Goldfinger*. When discussing her replacement, producers and writers insisted that they needed a women who was less intimidating to men: someone softer, more feminine, and who had "*man appeal.*" It was chance and the secretary recording the conversation's use of a cryptic note to find a replacement with "*m. appeal,*" that gave her successor, Emma Peel, her name.[47] The Gale Force departed and was replaced with Man Appeal. Television has yet to see the likes of Cathy Gale again.

As the quote above indicates, the unusual character of Cathy Gale in the 1962-1963 *Avengers* series created powerful and life-transforming learning experiences for some viewers—but, of course, not all. Certainly for the women who responded to my call for participants, the character created for them an example of a world where women were equal to men—where women were agents of change, executers of justice, and possessors of knowledge—packaged in the body of Pussy Galore in black leather. It was a moment in time that challenged post-colonial, patriarchal hegemony and changed lives by "happy accident." But it provides educators interested in critical public pedagogy with an example of the power of popular culture consumption to facilitate transformative learning.

Critical educators are beginning to recognize the educational power of popular culture in constructing our lives and our worldviews. But those worldviews are, for the most part, being manipulated by the forces of extreme wealth and oligarchy that now control our (popular) culture. Since the late twentieth century, control of US media has shrunk "from fifty competing companies, to five."[48] Moreover, as of 2005, the 118 people on the boards of those conglomerates are directors of a total of 288 other national and multi-national companies.[49] Gramsci argued that in a classed society, the realm of ideology and propaganda is where the fight for ethical treatment of the working class takes place.[50] Critical educators recognize the dialectical relationship between ideological change and material change around issues of social justice and are becoming "less focused on the classroom per se and more directed toward political, cultural, and racial identity, antiracist multicultural education, the politics of whiteness, white supremacy, modes of resistance and popular culture."[51] I argue for the inclusion of gender, socio-economic class, egalitarianism, and nationalism in that list of educational imperatives and that this study indicates how powerfully action can be driven by representations of resistance in popular culture.

Entertaining, engaging stories capture the imagination and endure in audiences' memories, often capturing a cult-like following. Many times, such stories become the narratives that shape cultures. Popular cultural narratives are embedded in our daily lives. They take particular forms and are worked into genres, media and venues that appeal to the entire spectrum of human imaginative tastes. They may be shaped into meta-narratives that become so pervasive in popular culture that they embody our frames of reference. Most contemporary cultural narratives depend on and indeed, are created by, multi-national corporations that mold them into a public pedagogy teaching what Marcuse calls "repressive tolerance" for the oppression and control by corporate/political interests.[52] Not surprisingly, they reinforce a capitalist hegemony of systemic inequality and oppression. We allow ourselves to be dominated by such narratives because they become our common-sense reality. Almost everything produced by the television industry can be held up as an example of those narratives of hegemony. This was certainly the case with the television of my youth. Yet there are a few contrasting television narratives that represent possibilities for resistance to that hegemony. These narratives frequently offer scripts for human interactions and political choices that promote liberty, equality, peace, intellectual growth, and international community and resist the usual themes of consumption, capital, and selfish individuality. Through those counter-narratives we glimpse the possibilities for more inclusive and egalitarian meta-narratives of a just, sustainable, more rewarding peaceful future. Cathy Gale taught me that those resistant narratives are possible. She dispelled the despair that my love of critical analysis initially dumped on my appetite for television drama and replaced it with a determination to study fan learning from other "happy coincidences" that defy conventional roles, and to seek out and investigate intentional challenges to the dominant social, political and global discourses that may be lurking within the pleasures of television fandom.

Notes

1. Elizabeth Pauline Lester, "Finding the Path to Signification: Undressing a Nissan Pathfinder Direct Mail Package," in *Undressing the Ad: Reading Culture in Advertising*, ed. Katherine Toland Frith (New York: Peter Lang, 1998), 20.

2. Dave Rogers, *The Complete Avengers: The Full Story of Britain's Smash Crime-Fighting Team!* (New York: St. Martin's Press, 1989), 2-3.

3. Stephen D. Brookfield, "Media Power and the Development of Media Literacy: An Adult Educational Interpretation," *Harvard Educational Review* 56, no. 2 (1986): 152.

4. Jane Lewis, *Women in Britain Since 1945: Women, Family, Work and the State in the Post-War Years* (Cambridge, MA: Blackwell Publishing, 1992), 11.

5. Lewis, *Women in Britain*, 12.

6. Lewis, *Women in Britain*, 16.

7. David Gauntlett, *Media, Gender and Identity: An Introduction* (London: Routledge, 2002), 43.

8. Gauntlett, *Media, Gender and Identity*, 43.

9. Patrick Macnee, *Blind in One Ear: The Avenger Returns* (San Francisco: Mercury House, 1989), 10-35.

10. Toby Miller, *The Avengers* (London: The British Film Institute, 1997), 1-16.

11. Brian Clemens, interviewed by Robin Redmon Wright, August 24, 2006.

12. Robin Redmon Wright and Jennifer A. Sandlin, "Popular Culture, Public Pedagogy, and Perspective Transformation: *The Avengers* and Adult Learning in Living Rooms," *International Journal of Lifelong Learning* 28, no. 4 (2009): 533-551.

13. Thomas Andrae, "Television's First Feminist: The Avengers and Female Spectatorship," *Discourse: Berkeley Journal for Theoretical Studies in Media and Culture* 18, no. 3 (1996): 115.

14. Andrae, "Television's First Feminist," 116.

15. John Storey, *Cultural Theory and Popular Culture,* 4th ed. (Athens, GA: University of Georgia Press, 2006).

16. Elizabeth Ellsworth, *Places of Learning: Media, Architecture, Pedagogy* (New York: Routledge, 2005); Jennifer A. Sandlin, Brian, D. Schultz, and Jake Burdick, eds., *The Handbook of Public Pedagogy: Education and Learning Beyond Schooling* (New York: Routledge, 2010).

17. Ben Agger, *Cultural Studies as Critical Theory* (London: Falmer Press, 1992); Liesbet Van Zoonen, *Entertaining the Citizen: When Politics and Popular Culture Converge* (New York: Rowman & Littlefield, 2004); Mary Ellen Brown. "Women and Soap Opera: Resistive Readings," in *Critical Readings: Media and Gender,* ed. Cynthia Carter and Linda Steiner (Maidenhead, UK: Open University Press, 2004), 287-306.

18. Robin Redmon Wright and Jennifer A. Sandlin, "Cult TV, Hip Hop, and Vampire Slayers: A Review of the Literature at the Intersection of Adult Education and Popular Culture," *Adult Education Quarterly* 59, no. 2 (2009), 118-141.

19. Storey, *Cultural Theory.*

20. Tony Bennett, *Culture: A Reformer's Science* (London: Sage Publications, 1998).

21. John Hartley, "Twooccing and Joyreading," *Textual Practice* 8, no. 3 (1994), 399-413; Sandlin, Schultz, and Burdick, *Handbook of Public Pedagogy.*

22. Henry Giroux, "Public Pedagogy as Cultural Politics: Stuart Hall and the 'Crisis of Culture,'" *Cultural Studies* 14, no. 2 (2000), 341-360.

23. Giroux, "Public Pedagogy," 345.

24. Peter Mayo, "Public Pedagogy and the Quest for a Substantive Democracy," *Interchange* 33, no. 2 (2002), 193-207.

25. Liesbit van Zoonen, *Feminist Media Studies* (London: Sage Publications, 1994), 149-150.

26. Van Zoonen, *Feminist Media,* 150.

27. Ien Ang, "Melodramatic Identifications: Television Fiction and Women's Fantasy," in *Feminist Television Criticism: A Reader,* ed. Charlotte Brunsdon, Julie D'Acci and Lynn Spigel (Oxford: Clarendon Press, 2003), 162.

28. Judith Butler, *Gender Trouble: Feminism and the Subversion of Identity* (London: Routledge Press, 1990), 140.

29. Wright and Sandlin, "Cult TV, Hip Hop."

30. Robert C. Bogdan and Sari K. Biklen, *Qualitative Research for Education* (Boston: Allyn and Bacon, 2006).

31. Ernest G. Bormann, "Symbolic Convergence Theory: A Communication Formulation," *Journal of Communication* 35, no. 4 (1985), 128-138.

32. I have several beautifully hand-written letters from Ms. Blackman graciously rejecting my requests for an interview with statements like, "I wish you luck in your research, but I no longer discuss The Avengers or James Bond." But I persisted. Eventually, I flew to London, found the office of her manager, talked my way inside, and convinced her of the legitimacy of my request. She, in turn, convinced Ms. Blackman to speak with me.

33. Most of the first season with Ian Hendry was lost because the videotape deteriorated. Only a third of the pilot episode, "Hot Snow," and a couple of other full episodes survive.

34. Sharan B. Merriam, *Qualitative Research and Case Study Applications in Education* (San Francisco: Jossey Bass, 2001), 126.

35. Wright and Sandlin, "Popular Culture."

36. James Chapman, *Saints and Avengers: British Adventure Series of the 1960s* (London: I. B. Tauris Publishers, 2002), 65.

37. Dave Richardson, "Honor Blackman: Leather and Lace," *TV Zone,* February,1996, 41.

38. Miller, *The Avengers*.

39. Miller, *The Avengers*.

40. Dave Rogers, "Cathy Gale vs. The Gong Man," *On Target—The Avengers: The Officially Authorised (sic) Avengers Network Magazine* 2 (1985), 5.

41. Butler, *Gender Trouble*, 1990.

42. "TAM Top 20," *Television Mail*, November 1, 1963.

43. Jack Mezirow and Associates, *Learning as Transformation: Critical Perspectives on a Theory in Progress* (San Francisco: Jossey-Bass, 2000).

44. In 1964 the show was temporarily "banned in England for electoral interference" because the government feared that Honor Blackman's appearance "in a commercial for the Liberal Party," for which she had actively campaigned, would unduly influence the election results. Evidently, Blackman, as well as the character she portrayed, had gained significant influence over the public! See Miller, *The Avengers*, 2-5.

45. S. Galton, "A Question of Honor," *Daily Express Saturday,* January 17, 2004, 11-12.

46. Simon Weaver, "Life with Honor," *TV Times*, November 8, 1963, 14.

47. Miller, *The Avengers*, 7-30.

48. Toby Miller, *Cultural Citizenship: Cosmopolitanism, Consumerism, and Television in a Neoliberal Age* (Philadelphia: Temple University Press, 2007), 16.

49. Miller, *Cultural Citizenship*, 16-17.

50. Antonio Gramsci, *Selections From the Prison Notebooks*, ed. Q. Hoare and G.N. Smith (London: Lawrence and Wishart, 1971).

51. Joe L. Kincheloe, *Critical Pedagogy Primer* (New York: Peter Lang, 2004), 86.

52. Herbert Marcuse, *One Dimensional Man* (Boston: Beacon Press, 1991).

Chapter Thirteen

Juno for Real: Negotiating Teenage Sexuality, Pregnancy, and Love in MTV's *16 and Pregnant/Teen Mom*

Tanja N. Aho

Reality TV shows have become a major site of contestation in which ideas about economic structures, individualized poverty, and family values come into play. Reality TV has become an extremely popular television genre, partly because it mediates a supposedly 'authentic' representation of reality—what John Dovey calls the "subjective-as-authentic mode"[1]—and partly because it offers voyeuristic insights into people's private lives, a theater of intimacy, and, to follow Michel Foucault, a public stage for performance of identities through the open confessional.[2]

MTV's *16 and Pregnant*, as well as its follow-up show *Teen Mom*, constructs a diversified image of oftentimes poor teenage women who struggle to consolidate their self-image with the concept of teenage motherhood.[3] The show follows a schematic narrative in which young women revisit their initial shock, their arguments with their boyfriends, and their struggles with their parent(s), and thus it serves as a cautionary tale about teenage pregnancy. The season finales further cement the moral subtext of the show, in which the young women's active voice is replaced by the "professional" interpretation of Dr. Drew, who admonishes, provokes, and applauds, circumscribing diverse readings of the teenage mothers' experiences for a male-centered, heteronormative reading that polices these young women's bodies and minds and contributes to what Foucault has termed the biopolitics of the nation-state.[4]

The show has also been criticized for valorizing teenage pregnancy, especially through the media attention that some of the show's young mothers garner after moving on to the spin-off docu-soap *Teen Mom*,[5] which is oftentimes accompanied by yellow press attention for these "celebrity temps,"[6] many of whom have started their own fan sites and Facebook pages.[7] The show and its backlash have become emblematic in an OECD developed country[8] that has the highest rate of teenage pregnancy—where three out of ten teenage women will become pregnant before age twenty[9]—and is thus paramount for an understanding of teenage self-identity and television.

Whether or not *16 and Pregnant* lionizes teenage pregnancy, it has become a hugely popular and widely received element of television, which serves today's teenagers as a socializing agent in their quest for self-identity. Not only does the show discuss teenage sexuality, parental relations, pregnancy, birth, and motherhood, the show also purports to demonstrate the volatility of teenage love and the effects teenage pregnancy/parenthood can have on young romance. Finally, in its representation of lower-class families, it oftentimes introduces non-traditional family constructions that range from single parenthood to extended families in which aunts adopt or grandmothers step in. The show is thus central to an understanding of television and its influence on young women and their ideas about self, romance, relationships, motherhood, and responsibility. And while shows such as these are hugely popular—drawing up to two million viewers—they have received scant academic attention.[10] However, as John Fiske claimed in 1978 in *Reading Television*, "an understanding of the way in which television structures and presents its picture of reality can go a long way towards helping us to understand the way in which our society works,"[11] and MTV's teenage drama reality shows *16 and Pregnant* and *Teen Mom* are essential elements of how today's youth constructs its self-understanding and its social positioning in the United States.

Biopolitics, Governmentality, and the 'Technology of the Self'

Reality television—or alternatively, factual television,[12] tabloid TV,[13] or first person media[14]—has become a central site of scholarly contestation centering on the debate of what functions, forms, and effects it has. Key to an understanding of reality television are questions of authenticity, reality, representation, and audience: What type of reality is constructed in these shows, whose view of reality is conveyed, how is reality represented, and how do different audiences engage with these texts? Features of reality TV are, to follow Wendy Helsby,[15] intimacy, immediacy, and interactivity, and, according to many other television scholars, the unscripted nature of the show and non-professionalism of the actors.[16] While many have argued that reality television is cheap and exploits its subjects, others have adopted a more generous reading that sees reality TV as a democratization of television production.

Reality TV has become especially influential in debates surrounding questions of gender, class, and race, and more generally, the postmodern project. Reality TV is oftentimes perceived as a "female" or "feminized" televisual format due to its focus on the pedestrian, trivial, and domestic and, more generally, the private sphere.[17] Not only has reality TV been devalued because of this supposedly feminized concern with quotidian issues, but also because its subject matter oftentimes deviates from the middle-class subject position of much of fictional television productions for a possibly exploitative representation of working- or lower-class U.S.-Americans and women in general. Video diaries and "to camera" monologues exemplify the shifting boundary between, and the constant renegotiations of, the public and the private sphere in reality TV. Furthermore, both *16 and Pregnant* and *Teen Mom* propagate the ostensible rejection of expert opinion for a postmodern focus on the individual and its subjective experience as productive of what Foucault would term knowledges with truth claims. This emphasis on subjective knowledges speaks to a reconfiguration of media and its foundational role in contemporary constructs of the social imaginary inflected by neoliberal and hypercapitalist concerns. Thus, as Beverley Skeggs and Helen Wood argue, critical approaches to reality television have to always consider their placement within systems of power in "which capital extends into the 'private,' in which capital is engaged in the socialization of affective capacities."[18]

While scholars have greatly debated the effects television has on audiences, the public discourse surrounding reality television oftentimes paints viewers as uncritical and unreflective receivers of what is supposedly 'real.' However, as Fiske posited in 1987, these texts—as all other textual productions—are polysemic and are thus read differently by different audiences.[19] Reality TV, just like any other textual production, can potentially be read oppositionally and is always open to negotiation.[20] According to Imogen Tyler, Skeggs and Wood's four-year reality TV audience research project further revealed that "reality participants represent complex figures of identification and dis-identification,"[21] whose evaluation is based on the race, class, and gender background of the audience.[22] As Wood and Skeggs note in 2011, "reality television creates a structure of immanence for viewers through which there is rarely a singular stable 'reading' of a programme, but rather a set of immediate affective moments through which our audiences experience and locate themselves in the unfolding drama,"[23] making a singular or unidirectional reading of reality television not just reductive, but simply untrue. Furthermore, Annette Hill and Marie Gillespie, for example, posit[24] that audiences are less interested in whether or not reality TV really reproduces reality, but are more intrigued by questions of who is acting 'real' and who is performing too stereotypically, thus employing reality television for community building vis-à-vis one's self-positioning to the show and not just viewer self-identification.[25] When discussing reality television productions, we should always keep in mind Fiske's prescient words that "realism is thus defined by the way it makes sense of the real, rather than by what it says the real consists of."[26]

Of course, as both Stuart Hall and John Fiske have pointed out, reality TV is not just reflective of reality, but constitutive of it.[27] Laurie Oulette and James Hay in their 2008 publication, *Better Living through Reality TV: Television and Post-welfare Citizenship,* focus on reality television's linkage to govermentality and citizenship. Their starting point is that reality TV provides guidelines for living which "are not abstract ideologies imposed from above, but highly dispersed and practical techniques for reflecting on, managing, and improving the multiple dimensions of our personal lives with the resources available to us."[28] Shifting the discussion from television's role in constructing individual identities, the authors instead focus on TV's implication in reproducing neoliberal systems of power which center the experience of the individual as a privately empowered and thus functional citizen.

This "entrepreneurial ethic of self-care"[29] propagated by reality television reflects the "rationality of governing that emphasizes self-empowerment as a condition of citizenship,"[30] a form of governmentality that Oulette and Hay derive from Foucault's initial observation of the operations of power within modern societies. In their reading, these modern societies employ regimens of expertise and authority for purposes of social management, legitimizing knowledge that is produced through truth claims within this matrix of power operations. Such regimentation allows not only for the replacement of government through force with governing at a distance, it also legitimates the respect for rules in the name of civil society and the well-being of its subjects. This "governing through freedom"[31] centers not only the rational, but economic self-governing individual who can cultivate herself through what Foucault has labeled the "technology of the self,"[32] of which television becomes a constitutive part. As Oulette and Hay note, reality television has become a "cultural technology that, working outside 'public powers,' governmentalizes by presenting individuals and populations as objects of assessment and intervention, and by soliciting their participation in the cultivation of particular habits, ethics, behaviors, and skills."[33] Paralleling nineteenth- and early twentieth-century professionalization intended to govern the working classes through the establishment of norms of morality and order,[34] the "cultural technology"[35] of television has become "an object of regulation, policy, and programs designed to nurture citizenship and civil society, and an instrument for educating, improving, and shaping subjects."[36] Both *16 and Pregnant* and *Teen Mom* can be understood in this matrix of governmentality, biopolitics, and neoliberal "technology of the self," within which young women and men situate their understandings of pregnancy, mother and fatherhood, romantic love, commitment, and responsibility.

'Maternal TV': MTV's *16 and Pregnant* and *Teen Mom*

16 and Pregnant and *Teen Mom* are both part of what Tyler has labeled "maternal TV": a current trend in televisual representation that has come to center the experience of women in respect to pregnancy, childbirth, and motherhood. However, in contrast to the British equivalent *Underage and Pregnant*, which Tyler analyzes, MTV's shows do not transform "having a baby into a 'class act'";[37] while MTV's shows do feature a number of lower-income families, there are a good number of teenagers who come from middle- and even upper middle-class backgrounds. Therefore, while much of what Tyler observes in respect to British maternal TV, such as the "*scaling* of maternal bodies"[38] or the "coding [of] particular kinds of maternity as desirable or abject,"[39] holds true, the stigmatization of especially lower-class maternity that is the center of *Underage and Pregnant* is less present in MTV's productions. Instead, the "maternal publics"[40] are expanded to include middle and upper middle-class women as well, which shifts the shows' central concern from a fear of working-class motherhood and lower-class reproduction to a warning about young motherhood in general.[41] Nonetheless, the shows do insist on the difficulty of consolidating poverty and motherhood, and emblematically the only teenagers who choose adoption for their child are those who come from extremely precarious family situations in which socioeconomic decisions take precedence over other concerns.[42]

Both *16 and Pregnant* and *Teen Mom* have been airing on MTV since 2009. *Teen Mom* was MTV's most successful show in 2009 and was one of the top three U.S. cable shows that year, attracting an average of 3.3 million viewers,[43] and dubbed by Stephanie Goldberg the "teen mom phenomenon."[44] Both shows are emblematic for a shift in televisual practice that has led to the transformation of MTV itself from the nonstop music video channel of the 1980s to a lifestyle channel catering to the different interests of today's youth. MTV airs dozens of reality TV shows every week and has found great success with this teen-oriented docu-soap format. However, both *16 and Pregnant* and *Teen Mom* deviate from the more traditional docu-soap through their "fun" style: The shows incorporate cartoons, sound effects, and graphics that cater to a very young demographic and 'lighten' the oftentimes heart-breaking and affect-heavy mood of the shows' content.

Most importantly, each homologous episode is narrated by the teenage mother in question,[45] which not only serves reality TV's purpose of immediacy and intimacy, but also establishes an aura of authenticity—and, not to forget, provides a modicum of agency for the young women portrayed, even though questions surrounding scripting, censure, and silencing remain. As Tyler notes throughout her study of maternal TV participants, many of the young women resisted the truncated nature of their representation on the show, and complained about both the reductive nature of cutting and the scripted nature of re-enacting some key scenes of their story[46]—concerns that might apply to MTV's productions as well. Nevertheless, the young women seem to have some authorial control over their portrayal, and are active participants in the construction of their stories and representation.

As already mentioned, the young women come from diverse socioeconomic backgrounds, which do not necessarily correspond to the ease or difficulty with which they cope with their pregnancy and motherhood. While the only teenager of Season one of *16 and Pregnant* who chooses adoption comes from a financially precarious and geographically mobile family, others whose families are equally poor and/or do not conform with the heteronormative nuclear family—in other words, female-headed households in which grandmothers, mothers, and daughters live together, or aunts and/or uncles take on parenting responsibilities, or the boyfriend's family offers the pregnant teenager a home— are able to provide their child with love, care, and support, while others from rather well-off families face loneliness, opposition, and emotional, verbal, and sometimes even physical abuse.[47]

The only factor which unites most of these women is that they come from rural areas. This is oftentimes conveyed through their accents, shots of their towns and/or the countryside where they live—what Tyler, referencing Skeggs and Wood, has titled the "moral subject semiotics," the confluence of "signs, bodies and landscape which compose a familiar assemblage of classed and gendered values."[48] Additionally, the young women in their initial presentation locate themselves geographically, oftentimes referencing the 'small town' in which they live. Teenage motherhood in *16 and Pregnant* is thus not only transformed from a racially and class-inflected "welfare queen" stereotype to a defining feature of "Small Town USA," it is also located in the tradition of local color and social realism, in which the rural is imagined as diametrically opposed or synchronically removed from the assumed "center" of the urban landscape. Inflected by the neoliberal reimagining of individuality, motherhood, and romantic relationships that the late twentieth and early twenty-first century have witnessed, the rural becomes a recalcitrant space of backwardness in which unruly sexuality—the lack of governmentality—coupled with a dearth of information and "civic knowledge" results in the high number of teenage pregnancies that the United States has witnessed.

Governmentality and The 'Ethic of Self-Care' for Young Mothers

As previously noted, reality shows, and among them *16 and Pregnant* and *Teen Mom,* propagate an "entrepreneurial ethic of self-care,"[49] which contributes to a neoliberal form of governmentality that supports the technology of the self through governing through freedom. Both shows cultivate a self-understanding that is based on neoliberal notions of individualism, education, and hard work, but also—more surprisingly—non-heteronormative family values. Next to the obviously moral condemnation of teenage sexuality—albeit even this is limited through the young women's own representation of the naturalness of it and the oftentimes hypocritical nature of their parents' discontent[50]—both shows' driving moral message is the goal of independence for its young mothers. The women come to realize that within a matrix of broken families, unsupportive boyfriends, and false friends, their main goal has to be independence, which can only be achieved through education and the concomitant delayed gratification of personal needs and "teenage fun" such as going out with friends, partying, and personal space/time. Within twenty-first century societal expectations of female employment, college education, and house ownership, as well as the constant rates of early divorce, both shows emphasize that the only way to a stable and successful life is through education, not child-bearing and marriage. Those who do choose to have children first and an education second are punished and come to realize in the end—the ubiquitous refrain of every episode proclaiming that "I should have waited"—that their youth has to be sacrificed for a future-oriented work ethic that prescribes the necessity of a high school diploma or GED, followed by a college education if they ever want to offer their child a "good" life.

In this vein, welfare and government support are highly stigmatized and almost completely omitted. Even though about half or more of the young mothers come from lower-class backgrounds and cannot even afford daycare, they almost unequivocally reject welfare and instead prefer to utilize their extended families for parenting and financial support. Amber in Season one of *Teen Mom*, for example, decides she might have to "go on government" to pay for daycare[51] while she catches up on her GED, as she is not able to access as much familial support as some of the other young mothers. When she informs her cousin of her decision, her cousin is shown to be both shocked and disappointed and tries to find a different solution for Amber so that she does not have to "stoop" to the level of welfare-recipient. A practice that in other countries, such as most of Western and Northern Europe, is considered a normal part of maternity, namely state-supported maternal leave and child support, is here stigmatized as the failure of the individual who does not live up to her civic duties.

While the denigration of state support for young mothers and their responsibility for their regulation of the self become one of the foundational messages of both shows, catering to a neoliberal concern with individualized personhood that ignores systemic ills and societal obstacles, the accompanying message of female independence can be read as empowering to young women. Most of the young women on *16 and Pregnant* end up being abandoned by their boyfriends or consciously choosing to leave them.[52] Oftentimes the young women's mothers—and sometimes fathers—advise them to end their relationships with what Samuel Jay has labeled "deadbeat dads,"[53] warning their daughters of the potential dangers of early marriage or the added stress of caring for a man who acts more like a child than an equal partner.[54] Considering the shows' general pro-life and anti-teenage sex stance, its warnings against marriage and its depiction of failed romantic love—in favor of strong maternal love—is rather surprising. Within the matrix of self-care and self-government, romantic love becomes a burden and the heteronormative institution of marriage a possible obstacle for one's civic duties of maternity and educational success. The most exemplary episode for the need for an ethic of self-care is episode six of Season one of *Teen Mom*, which is even entitled "Standing Up." In this episode all four women make progress in their pursuit of self-governance, but maybe the most pronounced is Amber, who explains at one point after seeing her daughter stand for the first time: "If Leah is learning to stand on her own, maybe I can too."[55]

Most of the young women learn through trial and tribulation that their only path to "happiness" is independence, both from their oftentimes unstable families and especially from their irresponsible partners. Of course there are a number of episodes that complicate this simple reading: some of the young mothers learn that only through acceptance of their own mother's involvement can they reintegrate themselves into the educational landscape; such is the case when Farrah realizes she is dependent on her mother's support, even though she resists her mother's condescending attitude towards her. Some of the young women find out that their boyfriends are the more stable and dependable ones who can be trusted to provide and support for them and their child. Leah of Season two of *16 and Pregnant*, who yearns for a "normal" teenage life, sees her partner Cory stepping up to the challenge, and Catelynn's boyfriend Tyler is probably the best-known example of a supportive and dependable partner, even though the two choose adoption.

Nevertheless, the majority of episodes purports the importance of independence—and especially independence through education—for these young women, who become self-supporting, self-empowered, and self-assured in their role as young mothers. Their quest for motherhood thus becomes a successful feat of independence, and the young mothers locate themselves as ideal citizens through their rejection of state support and their self-governing individuality that is built on education and empowerment.[56]

Biopolitics, Teenage Sexuality, and the Body

Accompanying this turn to individual self-government is the regulation of these young women's bodies and sexuality. Along the lines of Foucault's biopolitics, both shows purport to define what a desirable young woman should look like, and pregnancy is not part of this image. Thus each episode of *16 and Pregnant* begins with shots above the waist, which oftentimes focus on the young woman's desirability as a slim and "beautiful" high school girl. Only at the very end of the opening scene is the camera lowered to reveal what "mars" this young woman's beauty: her big stomach, protruding over low-cut jeans, bulging through stylish t-shirts, or accentuated by a belly piercing. The pregnant stomach becomes the sign of sexual unruliness, moral decay, and carnival pleasures that are illegitimate forms of entertainment for the young female citizen. Some of the women accordingly try to hide their pregnancy by wearing baggy clothes, some drop out of high school to protect themselves from their peers' stares, and some, such as Maci, choose to accelerate their studies to finish high school early because they know that their "belly is a big distraction for the other kids."[57]

A further policing of these young women's bodies is manifested in Amber's physical change. While on *16 and Pregnant* Amber and her partner are both obese and portrayed as indulging in fast food meals while omitting any kind of physical exercise, on the follow-up show, *Teen Mom,* Amber undergoes what seems to be a dangerous weight loss to the health-conscious observer.[58] Following middle-class norms of slimness, Amber seems to desire overcoming her stigmatization as a bad mother and unhealthy woman from *16 and Pregnant* through a drastic refashioning of her physicality, risking her health for a more normative type of beauty. Being one of the few obese women on the entire show, her case is all the more troubling as it seems to leave no room for non-heteronormative female bodies on MTV, especially in light of Amber's eventual imprisonment.[59]

Both the excessive pregnant body and the excessively fat body are constructed as "threats to the social order," in which, according to Fiske, the "pleasures of the individual body constitutes a threat to the body politic."[60] The young, pregnant, and sometimes obese body is the "material form of the body politic,"[61] and the "struggle for control over the meanings and pleasures (and therefore the behaviors) of the body is crucial because the body is where the social is most convincingly represented as the individual and where politics can best disguise itself as human nature."[62] In both shows, sexuality and food consumption are constructed as "bodily pleasures in opposition to morality, discipline, and social control,"[63] the young women defying parents, older relatives, doctors, and mental health professionals with their 'unruly' behavior "threatening to erupt and challenge the patriarchal order,"[64] as Susan Bordo puts it, and which is made manifest in their physicality and speaks to the "politicization of the body in patriarchal capitalism."[65] Both *16 and Pregnant* and *Teen Mom* integrate "apparatuses of social control [that are] accompanied by discursive practices working to control the meanings and behaviors of the body,"[66] which stigmatize teenage sexuality and pregnancy as amoral and possibly catastrophic, and which are incorporated not only on the intratextual level, but also on the metatextual level through public service announcements, commercials, and the season finales with Dr. Drew.

Both *16 and Pregnant* and *Teen Mom* contribute actively to the debate surrounding teenage sexuality, especially in regards to young women's sexual activities. Here again, the shows can be located within a larger framework of biopolitics, which in a neoliberal age convicts young motherhood as unwanted, accidental, and at times disastrous. Most interestingly, abortion is almost never mentioned—as the viewers encounter the young women mostly into their second trimester or later, the early decision of abortion is almost never incorporated.[67] In a few instances the young women discuss their choice either with their parents or their friends, re-living the original conversation, and if abortion is mentioned it is always accompanied by statements that describe the young woman's rejection of a pro-choice position.[68] Both shows thus retain a subtle pro-life message, which in light of the current U.S. legislation and its fierce contestation can be seen as quite problematic.

More importantly, the shows also portray the young women as asexual mothers and/or innocent girls who were "lured" or "tricked" into having intercourse. A number of highly naïve and childish participants, such as Whitney of Season one and Jenelle, Nikkole, Chelsea, Samantha, Leah, and Kailyn of Season two of *16 and Pregnant*,[69] establish these young mothers as accidental care-takers who are still children themselves. Their heterosexual relationships are also reduced to childish infatuation and exploitable adoration, which makes both romantic love and maternal love almost impossible. Instead, the young women are represented as bonding with their children more like younger siblings and not their own offspring. On the other hand, there are a number of young mothers who quickly mature and become the "asexual mother" who sacrifices herself completely for her child, the most prominent example being Maci throughout Season one of *Teen Mom*. Not only does she endure her fiancé's unfaithfulness and neglect of herself and her child, she also develops a deep maternal love for her son Bentley, whom she describes as having not expected to be "so in love" with, even going so far as to criticize those who gave her advice during her pregnancy for leaving out the deep satisfaction and fulfillment of maternal love.[70] Here, motherhood replaces a sexual relationship and viewers are confronted with the realization that there are different types of love that can have a hold on a young woman.[71]

However, whether or not the young women are portrayed as naïve girls or loving mothers, they remain largely asexual. Not only are most intimate interactions with their boyfriends/fiancés eliminated,[72] even most talk about intercourse or sexual intimacies is excluded—except for the ubiquitous moral lesson "I should have waited" that can be heard from all participants. These young mothers' aestheticization even extends to the more physical connections with their child: Only a few young women decide to breast-feed, and even they are shown 'surrendering' after a day or two and switching to formula—even though it is a lot more expensive and many of the young mothers can hardly afford it. Considering the oftentimes stigmatized nature of bodily secretions that are considered "dirty,"[73] breast-feeding becomes an act that "denies the difference between me and not-me and that contaminates the separateness of the body, and therefore its purity as a category,"[74] which is experienced as a threat to the individualized personhood that these young women need to conform to and through which their experience as teenage mothers is read.

The Return of Paternal Professionalism

While both *16 and Pregnant* and *Teen Mom* consist of homologous episodes, there is always one exception within a season: the final show, the finale special, which on *16 and Pregnant* is entitled "Life after Labor" and on *Teen Mom* "Check-up with Dr. Drew." These episodes serve not only as a recap of the past season, but also function to establish a dominant reading of the teen mothers' experience, thus circumscribing oppositional readings and limiting the young women's active voice in the process. Dr. Drew, whose full name is not even given in these episodes,[75] becomes the manifestation of patriarchal capitalism's interest in policing these young women's bodies and minds, and his paternalistic role diminishes the young mothers from active producers of truth claims and subjective knowledge about motherhood to infantilized dependents awash in emotions. Even though the teenage mothers' attempt at self-governance is condescendingly juxtaposed with the 'professional' representing rule, morality, and order, these young women resist their reductionist positioning and talk back to the paternal authority.

As MTV began *16 and Pregnant* in close collaboration with the National Campaign to Prevent Teen and Unplanned Pregnancy,[76] the show's nature as a performative public service announcement becomes the most pronounced in the season finales. The ubiquitous refrain "teenage pregnancy is 100 percent preventable" that had been aired in the commercial breaks of the show and from episode six of Season two of *16 and Pregnant* becomes an embedded part of each episode, even of commercial-free versions, is centered in the season finales and is made manifest through the figure of Dr. Drew. Thus the first words that Dr. Drew speaks to the audience in the season finale of Season two of *16 and Pregnant* are: "One thing you all want to learn about today for sure is prevention,"[77] and he frequently questions the young women as to their contraception choices and makes further announcements along the lines of "I want to reiterate the fact that teen pregnancy is a hundred percent preventable."[78] While some critics of the shows still claim that they lionize teenage pregnancy, two recent studies, one at Indiana University[79] and the other conducted by the National Campaign to Prevent Teen and Unplanned Pregnancy,[80] have shown that MTV's shows can influence the way young women view pregnancy and early motherhood, especially in regards to the difficulty and stress connected with it.[81]

More problematically, the season finales contribute to the individualized portrayal of motherhood concurrent with neoliberal biopolitics. Dr. Drew inserts numerous statistics into the discourse surrounding teenage pregnancy and parenthood in the season finales, which serve to stress the importance of the technology of the self and omit any references to structural issues and systemic ills. Thus, the viewer is informed after the first break that "sadly it's a fact that sons born to teen mothers are more likely to be incarcerated"[82]—this in the context of talking to Jenelle, whose boyfriend has been in and out of jail—and then Dr. Drew proceeds to ask Jenelle how she will avoid her son suffering the same fate. Similarly, when talking to another set of teenage parents, Dr. Drew tells them and the viewers that "it's a sad fact that children born to teen mothers are more likely to grow up poor," following this statistic up with a direct question to the couple: "How are you guys going to try to turn out different?"[83] An even more provocative statistic is provided by Dr. Drew in the season finale of Season one of *Teen Mom*, in which he introduces the loving couple of Catelynn and Tyler, who chose adoption for their child: "And here are some facts you might not know: Children born to teen mothers are more likely to drop out of high school, suffer abuse and neglect, and grow up poor."[84] While these statistics might have been used to underscore the structural difficulties teenage mothers face, the lack of government support and the systemic barriers to successful young parenthood, they are instead employed to underline the individual struggle of teenage mothers in raising a child 'on their own,' within the limits of their self-governance that is supposed to follow the 'ethic of self-care.'

Nevertheless, there are moments in which the young mothers actively speak back to the paternal figure of professionalism, whose power position is underlined by the studio setting in which Dr. Drew's chair is higher than the couch the young women sit on, and in which the shots favor a condescending perspective onto the young mothers. Especially in the season finales of *Teen Mom* do the young women take control of their denotation as objects of analysis and confront Dr. Drew and his heteronormative and truncated readings of their experiences. While all young women resist Dr. Drew's intrusive questions, the 'best-of' cut-backs that are meant to provoke tears and sympathy, and his paternal judgments, Maci is the most pronounced in her rejection of Dr. Drew's claims to truth. Thus when they discuss her failed relationship with Ryan, who is her son Bentley's father, Dr. Drew lays the blame on Maci for not having communicated her wishes enough. Siding with the irresponsible and uninvolved Ryan, Dr. Drew tries to defend the traditional male parenting role and even pushes for the most heteronormative—and, as viewers of the show will understand, disastrous—relationship for them, marriage. However, Maci succeeds at defying his patriarchal truth claim that "he [Ryan] as a man has different feelings" by simply retorting, "I don't agree with that. Different men have different feelings towards their child."[85] And while Maci does not have the social capital of a doctorate to legitimate her claim, her subjective experience, which viewers have been able to share and which has been substantiated by the other young parents on the show, trumps the authoritative claim of Dr. Drew.

These instances of "talking back" to authority on the basis of subjective knowledge are empowering moments for these young women and the viewers alike. While the shows in general contribute to neoliberal forms of governmentality and propagate an ethic of self-care, reinforcing the biopolitics of the nation-state through admonishment and calls for prevention and the policing of women's bodies and minds, there are moments of active agency for the young women involved in which their subjective experience and their truth claims take the upper hand. Unfortunately, these moments are framed by an individualized understanding of parenthood that is part and parcel of today's neoliberal representation of different life stages on television.

Notes

1. John Dovey, *Freakshow: First Person Media and Factual Television* (London: Pluto, 2000).
2. Michel Foucault, *The History of Sexuality*, trans. Robert Hurley (New York: Vintage Books, 1988).
3. This paper is based on the first two seasons of *16 and Pregnant* (more specifically, Season one and part one of Season two, which is divided into two sections) and *Teen Mom*, both of which have seen two further seasons since then, but which have followed approximately the same format/content that the first two seasons already provide.
4. Michel Foucault, *The Birth of Biopolitics: Lectures at the Collège De France, 1978-79*, ed. Michel Senellart, trans. Graham Burchell (Basingstoke: Palgrave Macmillan, 2008); Michel Foucault, *The Will to Knowledge* (London: Penguin, 2006).
5. While *16 and Pregnant* focuses on a different woman in each episode, *Teen Mom* centers on the experience of four women who first starred on *16 and Pregnant* and follows their lives, thus transforming the show into what Helsby has so aptly characterized for the docu-soap, which "combines the observation and interpretation of reality in documentary with the continuing character-centered narrative of soap-opera structured by performance and narrative," Wendy Helsby, *Teaching Reality TV* (Bedfordshire: Auteur, 2010), 18.
6. Scott Feschuk, *Searching for Michael Jackson's Nose and Other Preoccupations of Our Celebrity-mad Culture* (Toronto, ON: McClelland & Stewart, 2003), 105.
7. While the young women's attempt to prolong their Warholian 'fifteen minutes of fame' has been harshly criticized by some, it can also be read as their active involvement in their self-representation outside of the constricting nature of television broadcasting.
8. The Organisation for Economic Co-operation and Development consists of 34 membership states that are for the most part high-income economies situated in North America and Europe, but by now also include Chile, Australia, Japan, South Korea, and Mexico. "OECD—Better Policies for Better Lives," OECD, Organisation for Economic Co-operation and Development, accessed June 21, 2012, http://www.oecd.org/.
9. "Teen Pregnancy," *Centers for Disease Control and Prevention*, CDC, last modified August 2, 2012, http://www.cdc.gov/teenpregnancy/; "The Real Deal," *IYSL: It's Your (Sex) Life*, MTV, accessed November 12, 2012, http://www.itsyoursexlife.com/preventing-pregnancy/the-real-deal/.
10. To my knowledge there are only a few theoretical essays that have undertaken an introductory look at these two shows (Jay; Klein) and a few sociological studies on their viewer impact (Shafer; Wright), and much work remains to be done in this respect. One of the continuing obstacles of a critical discussion of shows such as *16 and Pregnant* and *Teen Mom* is the lack of interest in what is perceived to be pedestrian issues and cheap entertainment. Samuel Jay, "De-racializing 'Deadbeat Dads': Paternal Involvement in MTV's *Teen Mom*," *Flow TV* 12, no. 9 (2010): accessed March 11, 2011, http://flowtv.org/2010/09/de-racializing-deadbeat-dads/; Amanda Ann Klein, "Welfare

Queen Redux: Teen Mom, Class and the Bad Mother," *Flow TV* 13, no. 3 (2010): accessed March 11, 2011, http://flowtv.org/2010/11/welfare-queen-redux/; Autumn Shafer, "'16 and Pregnant': Examining the Role of Transportation and Persuasive Intent in the Effects of an Entertainment-education Narrative," unpublished dissertation, University of North Carolina at Chapel Hill, 2011; Paul J. Wright, Ashley K. Randall, and Analisa Arroyo, "Father–Daughter Communication About Sex Moderates the Association Between Exposure to MTV's *16 and* Pregnant/*Teen Mom* and Female Students' Pregnancy-Risk Behavior," *Sexuality & Culture* 15 (2012).

11. John Fiske and John Hartley, *Reading Television* (London: Methuen, 1978), 17.

12. Richard Kilborn, *Staging the Real: Factual TV Programming in the Age of Big Brother* (Manchester: Manchester University Press, 2003).

13. Kevin Glynn, *Tabloid Culture: Trash Taste, Popular Power, and the Transformation of American Television* (Durham: Duke University Press, 2000).

14. Dovey, *Freakshow*.

15. Wendy Helsby, *Teaching Reality TV* (Bedfordshire: Auteur, 2010).

16. One of the most commonly quoted definitions was first put forward by Richard Kilborn in his 1994 article "How Real Can You Get: Recent Developments in Reality Television": reality programming, for him, includes three major elements: "(a) the recording, 'on the wing', and frequently with the help of lightweight video equipment, of events in the lives of individuals or groups, (b) the attempt to simulate such real-life events through various forms of dramatized reconstruction and (c) the incorporation of this material, in suitably edited form, into an attractively packaged television programme which can be promoted on the strength of its 'reality' credentials." Richard Kilborn, "'How Real Can You Get?' Recent Developments in 'Reality Television,'" *European Journal of Communication* 9, no. 4 (1994): 423.

17. See Glynn, *Tabloid Culture*, 22; Helsby, *Teaching Reality TV*, 1; Elizabeth Johnston, "How Women Really Are: Disturbing Parallels between Reality Television and 18th Century Fiction," in *How Real Is Reality TV?: Essays on Representation and Truth*, ed. David S. Escoffery (Jefferson: McFarland, 2006), 116.

18. Beverley Skeggs and Helen Wood, "The Labor of Transformation and the Circuits of Value 'around' Reality TV," *Continuum: Journal of Media & Cultural Studies* 22, no. 4 (2008): 560.

19. John Fiske, *Television Culture* (London: Methuen, 1987).

20. See Helsby, *Teaching Reality TV*, 40.

21. Imogen Tyler, "Pramface Girls: The Class Politics of 'Maternal TV,'" in *Reality Television and Class*, ed. Helen Wood and Beverley Skeggs (London: Palgrave Macmillan, 2011), 213.

22. Beverley Skeggs, Nancy Thumim, and Helen Wood, "'Oh Goodness, I *am* Watching Reality TV': How Methods Make Class in Multi-Method Audience Research," *European Journal of Cultural Studies* 11, no. 1 (2008): 5-24.

23. Helen Wood and Beverley Skeggs, "Reacting to Reality TV: The Affective Economy of an 'Extended Social/Public Realm,'" in *Real Worlds: The Global Politics of Reality TV*, ed. Marwan M. Kraidy and Katherine Sender (New York: Routledge, 2011), 104.

24. Annette Hill, *Reality TV: Audiences and Popular Factual Television* (New York: Routledge, 2005); Marie Gillespie ed., *Media Audiences* (New York: Open University Press, 2005).

25. Helsby, *Teaching Reality TV*, 39.

26. Fiske, *Television Culture*, 24. One of the most obvious examples of this shift in the reception and understanding of reality television are faux reality shows—so-called mockumentaries—such as *The Office* and *Trailer Park Boys*, in which the techniques of factual television are employed in a completely fictional setting, and in which some of the humor relies on the viewers' understanding of the mixture of these formats.

27. Fiske, *Television Culture*; Stuart Hall, ed., *Representation: Cultural Representations and Signifying Practices* (London, Thousand Oaks, New Delhi: Sage and Open University, 1997).

28. Laurie Oulette and James Hay, *Better Living through Reality TV: Television and Post-welfare Citizenship* (Malden: Blackwell, 2008), 2.

29. Oulette and Hay, *Better Living*, 6.

30. Oulette and Hay, *Better Living*, 7.

31. Oulette and Hay, *Better Living*, 9.

32. Michel Foucault, *The Hermeneutics of the Subject: Lectures at the Collège De France, 1981-82*, ed. Frédéric Gros, trans. Graham Burchell (New York: Palgrave Macmillan, 2005).

33. Foucault, *The Hermeneutics of the Subject*, 13.

34. See Julian Carter, *The Heart of Whiteness: Normal Sexuality and Race in America, 1880-1940* (Durham: Duke University Press, 2007), on the establishment of normativity as a racialized strategy of social control.

35. Oulette and Hay, *Better Living*, 14.

36. Oulette and Hay, *Better Living*, 14.

37. Tyler, "Pramface Girls," 212.

38. Tyler, "Pramface Girls," 220; original italics.

39. Tyler, "Pramface Girls," 220.

40. Tyler, "Pramface Girls," 220.

41. Class markers are diverse and can at times seem misleading; a certain ambiguity about the young women's socioeconomic background is—one might argue purposefully—upheld in both shows. However, visual cues such as the parents' houses and the participants' cars and clothes as well as the toys, etc., acquired for the children provide some contextual information as to the socioeconomic positioning of the respective families. Rurality and/or 'taste,' on the other hand, can be misleading factors in deciding the participants' socioeconomic background. Based on visual markers, about one third of Season one and almost half of Season two of *16 and Pregnant*'s participants would qualify as 'middle class' or, to be less imprecise, as non-poor.

42. Both Catelynn from Season one of *16 and Pregnant* and Lori from Season two come from families that are highly unstable—geographically, financially, and socially, with parents or close family members who have been in and out of jail, have suffered from substance abuse, poverty, and bad health. Both young women are presented as highly mature and aware of the structural features that would harm their children's lives, no matter how much maternal love they would provide them with, and are realistic enough to realize that adoption might be the better choice for their infants. Furthermore, through Catelynn's participation in all seasons of *Teen Mom* viewers become intimately acquainted with the systemic ills that young teenage mothers from precarious backgrounds face. *16 and Pregnant*, "Catelynn," created by Lauren Dolgen, first broadcast July 16, 2009 by MTV; *16 and Pregnant*, "Lori," created by Lauren Dolgen, first broadcast March 16, 2010 by MTV; *Teen Mom*, "Looking for Love," created by Lauren Dolgen, first broadcast December 8, 2009.

43. Tyler, "Pramface Girls," 214.

44. Stephanie Goldberg, "The 'Teen Mom' Phenomenon," *CNN*, September 10, 2010, http://articles.cnn.com/2010-09-10/entertainment/teen.mom.mtv_1_teen-moms-newsstand-show?_s=PM:SHOWBIZ.

45. For *Teen Mom*, which follows only four of the original six teenage mothers, the respective woman portrayed narrates her own sections.

46. Tyler, "Pramface Girls."

47. The most prominent example being Farrah from Season one of *16 and Pregnant* who is also one of the four women on *Teen Mom*. She has had to endure her mother's ubiquitous verbal abuse and, as it is revealed in Season two of *Teen Mom*, also her mother's physical abuse. She is furthermore the only teenage mother who is located in the semi-urban cityscape, Council Bluffs, Iowa, even though shots of urbanness are kept to a minimum. *Sixteen and* Pregnant, "Farrah," created by Lauren Dolgen, first broadcast June 18, 2009 by MTV; *Teen Mom*, Seasons one and two, created by Lauren Dolgen, first broadcast by MTV.

48. Tyler, "Pramface Girls," 210.

49. Oulette and Hay, *Better Living*, 6.

50. Hypocritical in a sense that many of the young women's mothers were teenage mothers themselves. Emblematic here is Samantha, whose mother had her when she was a teenager and who concedes that she should have waited to have procreational sex, but who also stresses the simple fact that "teenagers have sex." *Sixteen and Pregnant*, "Brooke," created by Lauren Dolgen, first broadcast October 26, 2010 by MTV.

51. As Amber says: "I don't want to rely on government assistance, but until I can get a real job it's the only way I can keep Leah away from all the fighting." Daycare here seems to be portrayed as part of the 'socialist evil' within the matrix of neoliberal individualism, as all women reject it and instead try to negotiate their child's care either through personal sacrifice or familial participation. Even in circumstances where daycare would be the easiest and most convenient solution, the young mothers seem to hold an abject fear of daycare, which can only be slowly overcome. Their surprise at the child's welcome acceptance and enjoyment of daycare speaks to the deep-seated angst of these young mothers, whose ideas of motherhood are entrenched in traditional notions of nuclear families with stay-at-home mothers. *Teen Mom*, "Baby Steps," created by Lauren Dolgen, first broadcast January 19, 2009 by MTV.

52. Only a couple of the young mothers become 'selfish party girls' that leave their child with their mother to 'enjoy' their youth—whether or not this is an unconscious reaction to the trauma of young motherhood and/or the ensuing conflicts in the home is never discussed.

53. Samuel Jay, "De-racializing 'Deadbeat Dads.'"

54. For example, Amber's mother, who cannot find much enthusiasm for her daughter's boyfriend and her pregnancy, says: "At least they are not married!" *16 and Pregnant*, "Amber," created by Nicole Dolgen, first broadcast June 25, 2009 by MTV; Lizzie's father furthermore tells his daughter that "I would hate for you to feel like you need to get married because of the baby." *16 and Pregnant*, "Lizzie," created by Nicole Dolgen, first broadcast April 13, 2010 by MTV. Also, the young mothers' self-awareness of traditional gender roles and the new demands and possibilities for women are reflected in many friends' statements, of which Ebony's friend's opinion is emblematic: "You can't just be the perfect little housewife that takes care of the baby all the time." *16 and Pregant*, "Ebony," created by Lauren Dolgen, first broadcast July 2, 2009 by MTV.

55. *Teen Mom*, "Standing Up," created by Lauren Dolgen, first broadcast January 12, 2010 by MTV.

56. Tyler reads the British version *Underage and Pregnant* as a manifestation of the "'fertility anxiety' which haunts middle-class neo-liberal femininity," in which those who abandon their education are harshly judged. Tyler, "Pramface Girls," 220. This kind of middle-class anxiety about lower-class sexuality is also a central tenet of Julian Carter's *The Heart of Whiteness*, in which he discusses the normalization of 'modern American' personhood in the early twentieth century through an elided racialized understanding of sexuality vis-à-vis discourses surrounding heterosexual marriage, reproduction, and eroticism. In a sense MTV's shows do not fit these explanations, as teenage motherhood is not constructed as a class question but as a ubiquitous problem. Both shows furthermore omit any attempt at reconfiguring teenage motherhood as a basis for worthiness, as Tyler's study suggests many lower-class women interpret their experience as seeing their procreation as the only means of attaining value in a neoliberal society that positions them as worthless. Personal worth, on MTV's shows, is always achieved through self-sacrifice, hard work, and education, not good mothering in and of itself. Carter, *The Heart of Whiteness*.

57. *16 and Pregnant*, "Maci," created by Lauren Dolgen, first broadcast June 11, 2009 by MTV.

58. *16 and Pregnant*, "Amber;" *Teen Mom*, Season one and Season two.

59. Amber has become one of the more contested participants of both shows, as she has been portrayed as overwhelmed and emotionally incapable of dealing with her pregnancy and motherhood which manifested both in verbal and physical abuse of her partner Gary as well as her substance abuse which eventually led to her incarceration. However, a more nuanced reading of her character reveals a much more multi-layered persona and thus also numerous ways of reading Amber's experience. She can also be seen as a heroine overcoming her family background through numerous obstacles and against an unsupportive and dependent boyfriend. Amber's case is also one of the few in which the viewer is confronted with more numerous "judgment shots" of dirty laundry, chaos, and a crying baby that seem to tax her psychological and physical capabilities. See Skeggs, Thumim, and Wood, "Oh goodness"; Tyler, "Pramface Girls," 215.

60. John Fiske, *Understanding Popular Culture* (Boston: Unwin Hyman, 1989), 75.

61. Fiske, *Understanding Popular Culture*, 70.

62. Fiske, *Understanding Popular Culture*, 70.

63. Fiske, *Understanding Popular Culture*, 81.

64. Susan Bordo, *Unbearable Weight: Feminism, Western Culture, and the Body* (Berkeley: University of California Press, 1993), 206.

65. Fiske, *Understanding Popular Culture*, 90.

66. Fiske, *Understanding Popular Culture*, 90.

67. An exception here is the special episode of the second part of Season two of *16 and Pregnant*, which aired on December 28, 2010, in which a young woman, Markai, who had already starred in episode 14 of the same season, finds out she is pregnant again shortly after giving birth and has an abortion. *16 and Pregnant*, "No Easy Decision," created by Lauren Dolgen, first broadcast December 8, 2012 by MTV.

68. One woman, Nicole, even goes so far to claim that she is against the morning after pill because she believes it to be equal to abortion, and even after being corrected, remains insistent that she would rather become pregnant again than use it. *16 and*

Pregnant, "Life after Labor Finale Special: Hosted by Dr. Drew," created by Lauren Dolgen, first broadcast December 28, 2010 by MTV.

69. While part one of Season two starred ten women in contrast to the original six of the first season, the increased number of 'naïve' young women on the show might also reflect a shift in the casting choices of the producers, who might have decided to move from the more responsible and mature young women of Season one to a more naïve and child-like cohort in Season two, whose struggles might underline the intended public service announcement-nature of the show more.

70. *Teen Mom*, "Finale Special: Check Up with Dr. Drew," created by Lauren Dolgen, first broadcast February 2, 2010 by MTV.

71. Leah of Season two of *16 and Pregnant* who becomes pregnant with twins makes another interesting statement in regards to different types of love when she contrasts her love for Robbie, who is her ex-boyfriend and probably 'first love,' with her love for Corey, the father of her children. Here, infatuation and the connection between parents are materialized in the two men Leah has feelings for in a comparison of supposedly teenage love and mature love. *16 and Pregnant*, "Leah," created by Lauren Dolgen, first broadcast December 8, 2010 by MTV.

72. Interestingly, the first season final episode of *Teen Mom*, "Unseen Moments," reveals several more intimate moments in which Farrah kisses one of her dates and Catelynn and Tyler snuggle and kiss in their bed, both of which would be unthinkable in the more neutralized episodes. *Teen Mom*, "Unseen Moments," created by Lauren Dolgen, first broadcast February 9, 2010 by MTV.

73. See chapter four, "Offensive Bodies and Carnival Pleasures" in Fiske, *Understanding Popular Culture*, 69-102.

74. Fiske, *Understanding Popular Culture*, 99.

75. TV viewers might also know Dr. Drew from a number of shows that he has hosted, such as his own talk show on HLN, the daytime series *Lifechangers* on The CW, the VH1 show *Celebrity Rehab* with Dr. Drew, or the spinoffs *Sex Rehab* with Dr. Drew and *Celebrity Rehab Presents Sober House*, or from his radio talk show *Loveline*. "Dr. Drew.com," Dr. Drew Pinsky, accessed June 21, 2012, http://www.drdrew.com/.

76. Lauren Dolgen, "Why I Created MTV's '16 and Pregnant,'" CNN, 4 May 2011, accessed June 21, 2012, http://articles.cnn.com/2011-05-04/entertainment/teen.mom.dolgen_1_teen-pregnancy-teen-mom-teen-mothers?_s=PM:SHOWBIZ

77. *16 and Pregnant*, "Life after Labor Finale Special: Hosted by Dr. Drew."

78. *16 and Pregnant*, "Life after Labor Finale Special: Hosted by Dr. Drew."

79. Wright, Randall, and Arroyo, "Father–Daughter Communication."

80. Stephanie Hanes, "Amber Portwood: MTV 'Teen Mom' a Role Model for Better or Worse?" *Christian Science Monitor*, June 11, 2012, http://www.csmonitor.com/The-Culture/Family/Modern-Parenthood/2012/0611/Amber-Portwood-MTV-Teen-Mom-a-role-model-for-better-or-worse.

81. And while there might be many factors playing into the shifting numbers of teen mothers, the CDC recently reported that there has been a 9 percent drop in teenage pregnancy for seventeen- to nineteen-year-olds and an even larger, 12 percent drop in pregnancies of fifteen- to seventeen-year-olds compared to 2009. "Teen Pregnancy," Centers for Disease Control and Prevention, CDC, last modified August 7, 2012, http://www.cdc.gov/teenpregnancy/.

82. *16 and Pregnant*, "Life after Labor Finale Special: Hosted by Dr. Drew."

83. *16 and Pregnant*, "Life after Labor Finale Special: Hosted by Dr. Drew."

84. *Teen Mom*, "Finale Special: Check Up with Dr. Drew."
85. *Teen Mom*, "Finale Special: Check Up with Dr. Drew."

Part Five:

As Not Seen on TV

Chapter Fourteen

Race, Aging, and Gay In/Visibility on U.S. Television

Michael Johnson Jr.

I have always been particularly troubled by the fact that gay men often appear on television in the midst of their youth or perpetually in their early adulthood. The abject invisibility of gay men as "elders/seniors" or the pathologizing hyper-visibility of "older" gay men as stereotypical sexual predators has permeated the televisual landscape.[1] While there is extensive scholarship on the issue of aging, ageism and its sociocultural importance for gay men in a subculture that valorizes youth, little research has been conducted into how this phenomenon is perpetuated and perhaps instigated through the ubiquity of television. Indeed, even less research has successfully explored the intersections of age for gay men of color in terms of televisual invisibility.

The purpose of this chapter is to critically interrogate these issues to determine what the contemporary televisual landscape reveals and what, if any opportunities presage the appearance of characters on networks for queer men of color in the later stages of adulthood. Methodologically, I use textual analysis combined with cultivation theory as a basis for establishing truth claims that construct a theoretical framework through which my analysis is conducted. In this chapter, I argue that despite the increased visibility of gay men on contemporary telenarratives (both on broadcast and cable networks) people of color remain stubbornly less visible, and even within those examples of white gay men who dominate the airwaves, few if any depict men over the age of forty or gay elders over the age of retirement. This invisibility operates a heuristic that pedagogically educates viewers to interpellate gay men as perpetually young or as young adults, thereby rendering middle aged or elders as inconsequential through their conspicuous absence. These representational absences reinforced

227

by the fragmentation of television, operate to exacerbate existing stigmatization of gay men over the age of forty and gay elders through the potent discourses of ageism. Thus this chapter will analyze not only the processes of exclusion but also the resulting consequences that such reinforcement predictably produces through the consumption of the messages conveyed through television.

Queer Sexualities, Aging, and Current Research

Unfortunately, much of the research about aging amongst the queer community is limited, anecdotal and extremely narrow in scope. Generally this research has been concentrated amidst gerontology, psychology, public health, and anthropological disciplines; little if anything exists about queer sexuality and aging on television. Where such research exists, the two issues are universally separated by disciplinary boundaries. Some of the flaws inherent in such microscopic investigation are the focus on identifying barriers to effective care for gay elders to the exclusion of macro-level analyses that identify gay and lesbian elder successes at coping mechanisms and strategies for negotiating ageism and physical deterioration. Even less attention has been directed specifically to the multiple issues faced by gay elders of color who must contend with challenges of ageism, homophobia and racism simultaneously. One important study by Nardi was critiqued by other researchers for failing to include analyses of age as a demographic criteria necessary for a complete study of gay men.[2] There have been studies of working-class gay men,[3] Latino gay men,[4] and Asian American gay men;[5] however, "the masculinities of old[er] gay men make no appearance and in fact . . . the oldest respondent in any of the studies in Nardi's volume was fifty-six."[6] What little research is available notes that "African American respondents, in particular, thought their sexual orientation gave them coping skills that would help them as they entered the aging process."[7] Given the current population trends that illustrate the rapidly growing rate in the population of senior citizens in the US across all demographics, the study of how the media influence the proliferation of discourses about age, race and sexuality will become increasingly more important as time passes.

According to research by Nancy Knauer, today there are an "estimated 1.6 million to 2.4 million gay men and lesbians in the United States who are 65 years of age or older. . . . As of 2008, there were 3.2 million African American seniors, which amounts to between 128,000 and 192,000 African American gay and lesbian elders."[8] Knauer further contends that "when read in conjunction with increasing anecdotal evidence and research conducted by advocacy groups, this existing data strongly suggests that gay and lesbian elders grapple with isolation, financial insecurity, health concerns and the persistent fear that they will experience discriminatory treatment."[9] Moreover, the forces of ageism and homophobia can "combine to render the notion of a gay elder all but unthinkable because elders are not considered to be sexual and gay men and lesbians are, too often, viewed as only sexual."[10] Since 2000, researchers have warned about the high risk of social isolation among gay and lesbian elders.[11] It is therefore with no small sense of irony, that within the Cahill et al. report, not a single word (in its over 130 pages) is mentioned about the discursive forces of the media in making queer elders (of all ethnicities) vulnerable, much less analyzing how those media forces construct the ways in which that vulnerability manifests itself in the risks they identify.[12]

According to a commonly adopted definition, social isolation is not "simply living alone, but refers to a state that can be devastating for seniors in terms of emotional and physical well being. An individual who is socially isolated is cut off from the larger society and unable to access needed social and medical services."[13] This phenomenon is exacerbated because gay and lesbian elders are less likely to have children and often rely on "fictive kinship networks" or "chosen families" for a wide range of support. These families are based on "affinity rather than consanguinity and help compensate for the fact that even today, many gay men and lesbians are estranged or distanced from their families of origin."[14] In many circumstances this familial estrangement is the result of religious belief systems that are found in many African American and Latino/a communities. Thus African American and Latino/a, gay and lesbian elders are even more reliant upon their "chosen families" for support. And the racial divisions within the gay community exacerbate the challenges they face due to the combined factors of racism and ageism.

These divisions and reliance upon "chosen families" are both replicated in and conceivably instigated by constructions by the media through which queer elders and older gay men live their lives. Despite the increased visibility of gay and lesbian people in contemporary society (presaged by popular cultural exemplars in the media), that visibility is nearly universally characterized by whiteness, youth and hegemonic maleness. That visibility belies a very real dilemma for older gay and lesbian people (of all races and ethnicities). Jane Gross noted in a recent *New York Times* article that

> Elderly gay people living in nursing homes or assisted-living centers or receiving home care, increasingly report that they have been disrespected, shunned or mistreated in ways that range from hurtful to deadly, even leading some to commit suicide. Some have seen their partners and friends insulted or isolated. Others live in fear of the day when they are dependent on strangers for the most personal care.[15]

Her conclusion—homophobia directed at the elderly "has many faces." Indeed current research makes abundantly clear that gay elders face major obstacles.

First, is the widespread refusal to acknowledge that seniors remain sexual beings—especially men who, despite living in an era of Viagra™, Cialis™ and Levitra™, exhibit a plethora of evidence that challenges this commonsensical notion. The sociocultural belief that seniors of all sexualities are not interested in sex, should refrain from sex or alternatively are susceptible to sexual abuse belies the data. According to Lindau et al. "studies show that individuals enjoy healthy and active sex lives well past age sixty-five. . . . Among adults ages sixty-five to seventy-four, 53 percent reported that they were sexually active" and that even amongst older Americans ages seventy-five to eighty-five "25 percent responded that they were sexually active."[16] Indeed within this older demographic "over 50 percent reported having sex two or three times a month and almost a quarter (23 percent) reported having sex one or more times a week."[17] Knauer also notes that the "myth of the asexual senior could become the standard against which choices and behavior are evaluated,"[18] as the idea of a sexual senior is socially construed as aberrational, and thus not only is their sexual autonomy endangered but also their identity itself.[19]

Second, gay elders struggle to negotiate the strict confines of hegemonic masculinity valued by American society at large. According to Peter Robinson, "Youth is now the most valued stage in the life cycle"[20] and, according to Michael Mitternauer, "the young have now become society's role models."[21] In 1977 Simone de Beauvoir observed, "society looks upon old age as a kind of shameful secret that is unseemly to mention."[22] Indeed, the parameters by which individuals are assessed as valuable, contributing and important members of society generally begin with age as an unspoken but potently influential criteria. Because of this, "old age confers a loss of power, even for those advantaged by other social locations,"[23] for instance, being an otherwise healthy white, male with wealth is the common construction of gayness perpetuated on television.[24] And according to Margaret Cruikshank, "In our culture, growing old and being old is nowadays constructed as a problem . . . old age is increasingly pathologized in our culture."[25] Thus gay elders who are already competing for power in a social hierarchy that constantly seeks to marginalize their attempts to seize power as a sexual minority, must contend with the additional burden of aging in a society that values youth, and whose values are perpetually broadcast through the media. One need only look at the characters Ted Schmidt and Vick Grassi on the wildly popular Showtime production *Queer As Folk*. Ted is introduced as the "old one" who is constantly rejected by men at gay clubs on the series and eventually falls into an addiction to crystal meth. Meanwhile Vic, a gay elder, suffers from the combination of being perceived as elderly and thus valueless (except to his sister), a perception that is complicated by the pathologizing forces of his HIV positive status. Thus in this example, we see the predictable consequences of aging in the gay community—one either turns to drugs to obtain the popularity denied them or has plastic surgery, suffers the indignity of "pity sex" (as happens with Ted over Seasons one through five) or one dies a slow, marginalized death of invisibility and disease (as happens with Vic in Season four).

As David Eng makes clear, this process of inclusion has occurred within the context of a historical trend in which

gays and lesbians were once decidedly excluded from the normative structures
of family and kinship, today are re-inhabiting them in growing numbers and in
increasingly public and visible ways. . . . Our current moment is marked by the
merging of an increasingly visible and mass-mediated queer consumer lifestyle.
. . . Moreover, recent legal decisions . . . have remade the politics of kinship
into 'families we choose.'[26]

Remarkably, the prior historical efforts to resist mechanisms of state-sanctioned
oppression have yielded to a contemporary desire for state legitimacy and for the
"recognition of same-sex marriage, adoption, custody, inheritance and service in
the military."[27] The path to this historical and political moment has been paved
by corporations' sensitivities to their customers' diverse taste in palatable, but
socially-appearing advancements in modern sensibilities about discourses of
"tolerance" and "diversity" when applied to sexual minorities. Modalities of
"tolerance" have become prominent as domesticated norms of integration and
assimilation in ways that capitalize upon a presumptively universal virtue, so
that its neoliberal application by corporations can be more easily discounted.

Indeed, as Sarah Schulman makes clear, this process of commodification
has larger, more extensive sociocultural meaning than its financially lucrative
component; she states that the "breadth of ideas (about sexuality) permitted into
the popular discourse is extremely narrow" and those ideas are always
accompanied by a rhetoric of "diversity" in which "tolerance" becomes an
"intrinsic component of how dominant-culture people feel about themselves,
how they rationalize their privileges and justify their own sense of objectivity.
. . . Today we face a 'tolerance' defined by the diminishment of the minority and
the heroization of the majority, a 'tolerance' that simply acknowledges that the
minority exists and that claims acknowledgement as an act of generosity."[28]
Because American society values youth so highly and because youthfulness has
become an indispensable component of hegemonic masculinity, some gay elders
are at risk of being perceived by society as even less masculine and seeing
themselves emasculated by the passage of time. Peter Robinson makes clear that
"nowhere in contemporary Western society is this emphasis on youthfulness
more pronounced than in the gay world."[29] The perpetuation of the hyper-sexual,
hyper-masculine image of the gay man has to some degree displaced the
effeminate male stereotype.[30] Nevertheless, gay elders are still held to the same
standards by which society assesses hegemonic masculinity[31] as well as the
stereotypes of hyper-sexuality commonly associated with their gayness,
needlessly reducing their identities to just what they do (or want to do) with their
penises. Yet, being gay involves more than one's sexual object choice; it
encompasses an entire panoply of socially constructed and personally adopted
identity characteristics that extend far beyond the strictly physical, sexual
practices and desires.

Ageism and Gay Identity

Within the gay community, men self-segregate themselves into discrete groups generally distributed along a spectrum defined by age (which as I've already discussed is often inseparable from perceptions of masculinity, and thus attractiveness at its most basic level). Incremental divisions between individuals and groups erect themselves such that gay teens regularly deride the value of gay men in their twenties; gay men in their twenties deride and devalue gay men over the age of thirty and so on. According to Knauer, "the (gay male) body is a form of currency in the free market of desire," and thus the visual perception of vitality associated with youthfulness becomes an intangibly valuable metric by which gay men assess each other. This division of gay men into age cohorts results in a "fractured gay community that is divided by specific social and political experiences into highly compressed generations. Members of the abbreviated generations have difficulty relating to individuals who do not share their common social and political experiences."[32] Ageism commonly refers to a set of beliefs and attitudes that devalues older people and the aging process. This phenomenon is particularly acute in the gay male community, where the gay bar or being in "the gay scene" has historically been an important "meeting place and epicenter" that coincidentally reinforces the primacy of and preference for youth.[33] Gay men are considered older much sooner than in non-gay culture. A cursory look at mass media reveals this fact. "Glossy gay news magazines consistently feature young men on the covers, and gay pornography treats older men as a marginalized fetish."[34] Moreover, the wide variety of television series that include gay characters rarely offers images of gay men over the age of forty, even when those television series occur on explicitly LGBT networks.[35] On Logo, the only LGBT network (on either broadcast or cable), an analysis of its programming reveals that among the thirty-two original, non-news series, none featured a single gay man over forty years old, including ironically, even its animated series.[36]

The age-segregated nature of the gay male community has made intergenerational relationships particularly difficult and is exacerbated by the lack of visibility that subsequently results from the self-segregation that middle-aged and older gay men undertake. Those distancing practices stem from a type of stigma management in which "some gay men protect their own identities by choosing to disidentify with gay men who represent 'visual caricatures'" of gay masculinity.[37] Thus the ageism already extant within gay male communities is further exacerbated by a type of internalized homophobia that equates age with effeminacy, or at least a lack or diminishment of masculinity. This phenomenon becomes a repeated refrain in Kathleen Slevin and Thomas J Linnerman's study, where one participant notes, "I think most men think that. Because most men tie masculinity to their physical prowess. And once they sit in a wheelchair and can't feed themselves anymore, I think they feel very . . . emasculated."[38]

Of course the influence of the media serves to reinforce these complex, self-destructive conditions by rarely offering images of "growing older gracefully," or with the simple inclusion of gay men (of any color) over the age of forty. Those few series where characters are introduced as middle age or older gay elders that depict the "growing older gracefully" phenomenon suffer from some issues that also create the false perception that "grace" means inactivity, lessened sociocultural value, and/or resignation to the social marginalization that results from those perceptions. Moreover, these characters are perpetually relegated to the periphery of the series in "supporting actor" roles and often appear in genre specific series, most fequently comedies. However, some current on-air examples are from different genres including *Smash* (NBC), *Revenge* (ABC), and *Fairly Legal* (USA). Were more telenarratives to include these types of characters, such images may combat the perception of older gay men and gay elders as pursuing an "ongoing effort to imitate an ideal, a pathological condition, struggling to attain an idealized" image of youth. [39]

Ironically, there are extensive resources available to gay *youth* today, that range from advocacy groups for anti-bullying laws (GLSEN) to youth-oriented actives such as alternative proms (GSA) to legal precedents. [40] And yet, a similar range of advocacy resources has not been directed toward improving the conditions of gay elders. Some research suggests that "coping with stigmas of being gay has also taught . . . valuable life lessons about oppression, how to manage it and ideally how to resist it. Gay culture [nonetheless] reinforces youthful and hegemonic masculinity . . . that underscores this obligatory dictate of keeping up appearances." [41] According to Douglas Kimmel, at least one-third of those interviewed in his study "experienced discrimination within the gay community based on age or ethnicity" and that while most of his participants viewed "gay bars, nightclubs and beaches as necessary places to build camaraderie and community" they nonetheless reported "feeling out of place because of their ages." [42] Kimmel notes that "the loss of physical attractiveness and declining physical abilities and health are perhaps the most difficult aspects of aging for gay men" [43] while Raymond Berger observes that some studies of older gay men "show that loneliness is often a problem. But one major survey of gay men showed that older and younger gay men did not differ in self-perceived loneliness." [44] Thus while loneliness is an important problem for gay elders and older gay men, it may not be as severe as gay men of all ages generally understand it to be.

And I contend that one explanation may be the influence of media and its potent reminder of the centrality of a youthful appearance and the consequences that will inevitably ensue should one lose that appearance. The preoccupation with this appearance-based participation within the gay community as a central component of one's self worth, despite the obvious barriers to that participation, continues to function as an important mechanism of an individual's perception of their social value. Some gay men "feel compelled to do everything they can to hide the ravages of their body. They dye their hair, they have facelifts, they wear clothing that they think makes them look younger . . . they do a lot of exercise" but for affluent consumers "especially those who are white, cosmetic surgery offers a way to regain or sustain a more youthful appearance to cover signs of aging and to pass as younger than one's chronological age."[45] Moreover, Graeme Kane notes that the gay male body ideal "involves being both thin and muscular and that this contradictory idea of both weight and muscularity" helps explain the extent that some gay men will go to adapt to (and thus adopt) the prevailing discourses of hegemonic masculinity by which some gay men measure themselves. Kane is the first researcher to note that "it is unclear how such programs [seeking to reduce ageism amongst gay men] would cancel out the effects of the popular television programs the authors identify as the reasons gay men in North America . . . exercise" or pursue any of the appearance management strategies described above.[46] Characters, like Cameron Tucker on *Modern Family*, a white, married, overweight gay male over forty, illustrate Kane's point precisely. Although Cameron doesn't pursue any of the type of appearance management tactics described by Selvin, his failure to do so works as a confirmation of the necessity of those tactics. Cameron's character, and those few characters like him, symbolically operate as a cautionary signifier to young gay viewers. Age is equated with unfit, feminized bodies, safely domesticated and robbed of any visible sexuality or affection, whose contributions and utility are limited to the periphery of telenarrative spaces.

Televisual Historicity, Gay Sexuality, and Race

Television's historical record has demonstrated that it consistently made homosexuality a novel narrative device, to provoke scandal and notoriety for the series or shows in which queer characters and plots appear.[47] Larry Gross makes clear that with the arrival of "network television's first sympathetic portrait of a gay man" on the 1971 episode "Judging Books By Covers" on *All in the Family*, the existing social stigma associated with homosexuality was almost insurmountable for networks.[48] The series ran from 1971 to 1979, ranking number one on the Neilsen ratings for its first five years and features Archie Bunker a WW II veteran whose bigoted views reject any non-WASP characters. As a married, heterosexual man, his centrality to the series foregrounds how the episode's subject matter (controversial for the time) made the homosexuality visible and thus presented the opportunity for a positive portrayal on American television that, according to Gross, was rare for that era. Gross goes on to note that brief forays by typically white, gay, male writers into the subject of gay sexuality often resulted in "one shot appearances on network series," and those appearances were often viciously attacked politically by the "religious right" because of what they perceived were "overly favorable attention to gay people. In fact, gay men were mostly portrayed and used in news and dramatic media in ways that reinforced rather than challenged the prevailing (stereotypical) images."[49] Thus, the early conditions within which gay men (and to a much lesser extent lesbian women) appeared on television was systematically predicated on a logic by which gay characters were defined by their problematic sexuality, confined to stereotypes of the AIDS victim, the predatory sexual molester or the aggressive, butch dyke, often resulting in the alienation by their families and social isolation. These conditions continued with brief appearances of gay characters on *Soap* (ABC, 1977-1981) and *Dynasty* (ABC, 1981-1989).

Today, the corporate variety of "multiculturalism" employed towards sexual minorities has now metamorphosed into a generalized language of anti-prejudice that envisions a utopic, good society to come without addressing any of the material realities of the queer audiences to whom these media conglomerates target. Notably, this version of commodification of queer characters rarely includes men of color, and even less frequently men over the age of forty. Nevertheless, these limited moments of inclusion hallmarked by programs like *Queer Eye for the Straight Guy*, *Will & Grace*, *Boy Meets Boy,* and others, while conforming to these highly constrained versions of gay masculinity, remain valuable even to those men who are not represented. The appeal of queer characters in the images that are created through these telenarratives stems from what Kath Weston describes as feelings of kinship amongst and between sexual minorities,[50] and later which has been articulated by other scholars as a basis for the sociopolitical ostracization and resistance to queer families[51] and the racialization of intimacy in queer communities and the public consciousness.[52] The appeal of these characters stems from viewers' need to see (versions of) themselves depicted in the larger setting offered by mass media vehicles like television. That desire is particularly acute for queer people of color who already are relegated to the periphery of television's heteronormative hegemony. The appeal of queer characters (even those offered to counter public, heteronormative depictions of familial normativity) works to solidify visual solidarity through bonds of shared ostracization and marginalization.

J. M. McPherson's articulation of homophily becomes central to the process of viewer identification, as it describes how queer audiences (and in particular queer viewers of color) can experience shared feelings of communal worth and existence beyond the facticity of daily life, when seen through mass media vehicles like television. Television functions as a mechanism that provides regular confirmation and reassurance that sexual (and racial) minorities not only exist, but also possess commonly shared bonds of affinity developed through the operation of social stigmatization and marginalization. Extensive communication research makes clear that media can also shape an individual's concept of themselves in relation to others while also shaping one's perceptions of cultural values and norms by which television characters may serve as proxy.[53] Capitalizing upon the scholarship about homophily originally articulated by Livaditi et al.,

> this 'sense of belonging' can be broken into two categories: Firstly, viewers are able to place themselves in a specific social and economic context, either by comparison with different groups or by identification with their own. Secondly,

viewers are able to discuss with other viewers what they watched on television, and thus be able to place themselves in a community of viewers and interact with others.[54]

Therefore the appeal to audiences of rudimentary and identifiable queer characters in their media diet also stems from the extensive research on homophily as an organizing principle that structures social relationships in which individuals form homophilous relationships.[55] Research by Jaye Derrick and Gabriel Shira illustrates that individuals find a sense of belonging with their favorite series and this knowledge is a well known phenomena within the media industry.[56] Television supplies a ready-made commodity in the form of characters of color in neatly packaged narratives who appear, speak, behave and perform their queer identities in highly choreographed and persuasive ways that appeal to their targeted audiences.

Queer characters who appear in these telenarratives conform to a very specific type of paradigmatic, visual appeal. They generally are measured by the degree to which they deviate from the white, heteronormative, nuclear family model historically central and indispensable to the ideals of U.S. culture. Even those queer characters who display phenotypically white characteristics remain safely identifiable as in opposition to those ideals; thus their identity is always reduced to their sexuality. Moreover, as queer characters of color are already estranged from the telenarrative historical record, their presence is even more palpably felt, however limited their time on screen or vivid their presence may appear in a given series.[57] One example would be the appearance of *Noah's Arc* on the Logo Channel from 2005 to 2006 and the subsequent film *Noah's Arc: Jumping The Broom* in 2008: "It is not, however, an 'outdated notion' that our status as a sexual minority revolves around the differences and nonconformity of our sex lives. And this fact is particularly true for ethnic sexual minorities already suffering under the weight of prejudices directed towards them based on ethnicity."[58] Therefore, their appeal to viewers is always deliberately positioned in relation to the powerful discursive forces of social palatability by which their telenarrative actions, behaviors, dialogue and appearance are regulated.

The racialization of queer characters is especially subject to these forces, because while their appeal must not alienate heterosexual viewers, they must simultaneously encourage the active commodification by queer audiences. And even within that queer demographic of viewers is embedded its own racial politics of ostracization, which finds itself expressed in the very limited numbers of men and women of color performatively appearing in queer roles.[59] The notion that telenarratives in the media market "offer queer social citizenship, and therefore political voice, tend to overestimate the so-called benefits by not accounting for those who remain invisible and silenced or unable to enter the commodified realm of gay visibility."[60] Television's tangibility as a commodity possesses and embodies Rosemary Hennessy's "reification of the erotic" through character depictions of sexual desire, language, dialogue, actions and plots. The content of telenarratives operates as a type of commentary on those who buy into the messages they produce because it's not the *product that is being purchased but rather it is the message* that is conveyed by the telenarratives being consumed. Many telenarrative series condense same sex desire into a cultural signifier as a commodity that remains securely fetishized.[61] The popularity of Showtime's *The L Word* for heterosexual men illustrates how the titillation of girl-on-girl pairings replicate the centrality of the male gaze to the consumption of the series as a fetishized commodity.

Television's influence affords LGBTQ viewers an opportunity to see themselves depicted and imbues meaning into those depictions which resonates with LGBTQ identities. But the opportunity costs may be higher than the value accrued. Jaime Hovey rhetorically asks, "Are we happy . . . to be called out as consumers of idealized images of ourselves, and do such images insert us into mainstream culture, if only in fantasy, in a way we long to see?"[62] The inclusion of racial minorities operates within a framework of authenticity common to telenarratives. That framework depends on the fragile logic of racial stereotypes that has a familiarity with target audiences who consume these telenarratives with an appetite cultivated over time. Sarah Schulman makes clear that the inclusion of racial minorities, by switching the paradigm, "masquerades as 'progressive' because it defies stereotypes, but actually it obscures the real racial dynamics"[63] that already exist in the television industry at large and in the society that consumes those images. Less research exists about the emergence of gay men of color on television, and even less about gay men of color in late adulthood. However, some research has shown that a history exists that displays the figures of black men as perpetually virile, sexually aggressive predators,[64] along with the "Latin lover" stereotypes[65] of Latino men, that remains a potent reminder of the hyper-sexuality of gay men of color. An analysis of data provided by the *Gay & Lesbian Alliance Against Defamation* reveals an important, but one-dimensional version of facts, about the invisibility of gay men of color on television. Of eighty-three LGBT characters on both broadcast and cable series during the 2011 to 2012 timeframe, only ten were men of color and none of these characters were over the age of forty.[66] Extending this analysis further, over the past seven years during which GLAAD has collected data, one finds even more alarming statistics.

From 2005 to 2011, there were a total of 395 LGBT characters on both cable (241) and broadcast (154) series. Of that total, gay men dominated, comprising 127 characters on cable and 102 characters on broadcast series. Yet, they represented at most 6 percent, 3 percent and 2 percent of African American, Latino and Asian-Pacific Islander categories, respectively. When analyzed for age (meaning over forty), the numbers drop to less than 1 percent for gay white men and near zero for gay men of color. When examined against the 3094 total characters on broadcast programs *alone* over the same five year period of time, despite gay white men's dominance, the numerical representation of sexual minorities is astonishingly anemic and even more so for queer characters of color (of any gender).

Viewers tend to feel similar to characters who are like themselves in terms of demographic characteristics such as gender, race and age. Hoffner and Buchanan argue that "some degree of similarity to media characters seems to promote a desire to be like them, possibly because certain similarities signal that it is both possible and appropriate for the viewer to become like the character in additional ways."[67] I argue that the same is true in terms of sexuality. This shared sense of similarity can be construed a number of ways for sexual minorities. But Hoffner and Buchanan note that "one of the reasons that people give for watching . . . television is that the characters' experiences suggest useful ways for the viewer to deal with their own problems."[68] According to the "drench hypothesis," even one salient role model who exhibits appealing traits can have a strong impact on audience members who are drawn to that character.[69] Thus recurring characters have enormous potential to affect the attitudes, values and behaviors of the audience.[70]

It is through that process of selection that audiences thereby express affinity for and adopt the "meanings, pleasures and social identities" promulgated for their consumption, often times originating from characters (and the actors who portray them) who look, act, speak, believe, and behave nothing like them. For audiences who are both financial and cultural consumers of the messages produced for and about them but not by them, their ability to obtain recognition implicates claims by those viewers who pursue "full membership" into American society through their media consumption practices. Gay men, as a target demographic of telenarrative marketers, possess both the social currency and financial power to influence the producers of those commodities. If gay men, as conspicuous consumers of the images and the messages conveyed to them, are to adopt practices that render older gay men and gay elders intelligible within the discursive system of ageism, they must begin to demand more accurate, comprehensive portrayals of themselves across the larger spectrum of chronological ages. Moreover, they must reject media messages that irresponsibly perpetuate the creeping inevitability of social irrelevancy that accompanies aging and that has remained stubbornly commonsensical to many gay men.

Notes

1. Larry Gross, *Up From Invisibility* (New York: Columbia University Press, 2001).

2. Julie Jones and Steven Pugh, "Ageing Gay Men: Lessons From the Sociology of Embodiment," *Men and Masculinities* 7, no. 3 (2005): 248-260.

3. David Barrett, "Masculinity Among Working Class Gay Males," in *Gay Masculinities*, ed. Peter M. Nardi (Thousand Oaks: Sage Publications, 2000), 176-205.

4. Larry Cantu, "Entre Hombres/Between Men: Latino Masculinities and Homosexualities," in *Gay Masculinities*, ed. Peter M. Nardi (Thousand Oaks: Sage Publications, 2000), 224-246.

5. Chong-Suk Han, "They Don't Want To Cruise Your Type: Gay Men of Color and the Racial Politics of Exclusion," *Social Identities* 12, no. 1 (2007): 51-67.

6. Kathleen Slevin and Thomas J. Linnerman, "Old Gay Men's Bodies and Masculinities," *Men and Masculinities* 12, no. 4 (2010): 487.

7. MetLife, "Still Out, Still Aging: The MetLife Study of Lesbian, Gay, Bisexual, and Transgender Baby Boomers," *MetLife Insurance*, March 14, 2010.

8. Nancy J. Knauer, *Gay and Lesbian Elders: History, Law, and Identity Politics in the United States* (Ashgate Publishing, 2011), 33 and 49.

9. Knauer, *Gay and Lesbian Elders*, 31.

10. Knauer, *Gay and Lesbian Elders*, 31.

11. Sean Cahill, Ken South, and Jane Spade, "Outing Age: Public Policy Issues Affecting Gay, Lesbian, Bisexual and Transgender Elders," *The Policy Institute of the National Gay and Lesbian Task Force* (2000).

12. Cahill, "Outing Age."

13. Knauer, *Gay and Lesbian Elders*, 86.

14. Kath Weston, *Families We Choose: Lesbians, Gays, Kinship* (Columbia University Press, 1997).

15. Jane Gross, "Aging and Gay, and Facing Prejudice in Twilight," *New York Times*, October 9, 2007, http://www.nytimes.com/2007/10/09/us/09aged.html?pagewanted=all.

16. Stacey Tessler Lindau et al., "A Study of Sexuality and Health Among Older Adults in the United States," *New England Journal of Medicine* 357, no. 8 (2007): 762.

17. Lindau et al., "A Study of Sexuality," 768.

18. Knauer, *Gay and Lesbian Elders*, 61.

19. Knauer, *Gay and Lesbian Elders*, 61.

20. Peter Robinson, "The Influence of Ageism on Relations Between Old and Young Gay Men," in *Out Here: Gay and Lesbian Perspectives VI*, ed. Yorick Smaal and Graham Willett (Monash University Publishing, 2011), 223-236.

21. Michael Mitternauer, *A History of Youth* (Oxford: Blackwell Publishers, 1992).

22. Simone de Bueavoir, *Old Age* (Harmondsworth: Penguin Books, 1977).

23. Tony M. Calasanti and Kathleen F. Slevin, *Gender, Social Inequalities and Aging* (Walnut Creek: AltaMira Press, 2001).

24. Ron Becker, *Gay TV and Straight America* (Camden: Rutgers University Press, 2006).

25. Margaret Cruikshank, *Learning To Be Old: Gender, Culture and Aging* (Lanham: Rowman and Littlefield, 2003).

26. David L. Eng, *The Feeling of Kinship: Queer Liberalism and the Racialization of Intimacy* (Durham, NC: Duke University Press, 2010), 3.

27. David L. Eng, *The Feeling of Kinship*, 3.

28. Sarah Schulman, "The Making of a Market Niche," *The Harvard Gay & Lesbian Review* 5, no. 1 (1998): 17.

29. Peter Robinson, *The Changing World of Gay Men* (New York: Palgrave Macmillan, 2008).

30. Christopher Pullen, "Heroic Gay Characters in Popular Film: Tragic Determination and the Everyday," *Continuum: Journal of Media & Cultural Studies* 25, no. 3 (2011): 397-413.

31. Susan Bordo, *The Male Body: A New Look At Men In Both Public and Private* (New York: Farrar, Straus & Giroux, 1999).

32. Knauer, *Gay and Lesbian Elders*, 68.

33. Knauer, *Gay and Lesbian Elders*, 70-71.

34. Slevin and Linnerman, "Old Gay Men's," 448.

35. Michael Johnson Jr., "The Channel for Gay America? A Cultural Criticism of The Logo Channel's Commercial Success on American Cable Television" (master's thesis, Tampa: University of South Florida, 2008).

36. *The A-List: Dallas, The A-List: New York, Alien Boot Camp, The Arrangement, The Big Gay Sketch Show, Bump!, The Cho Show, Coming Out Stories, Curl Girls, Exes and Ohs, First Comes Love, Gimme Sugar, Jacob and Joshua: Nemesis Rising, Jeffery & Cole Casserole, Noah's Arc, Open Bar, Pretty Hurts, Real Gay, Real Momentum, Rick & Steve: The Happiest Gay Couple in All the World, The Ride: Seven Days to End AIDS, Round Trip Ticket, RuPaul's Drag Race, RuPaul's Drag U, Setup Squad, Shirts & Skins, Sordid Lives: The Series, Transamerican Love Story, TransGeneration, TripOut, U.S. of ANT,* and *Wisecrack.*

37. Anthony Frietas, Susan Kaiser, Davis Joan Chandler, Davis Caroll Hall, Jung-Won Kim, and Tania Hammidi, "Appearance Management As Border Construction: Least Favorite Clothing, Group Distancing and Identity Not!" *Sociological Inquiry* 67, no. 3 (1997): 323-335.

38. Slevin and Linnerman, "Old Gay Men's," 501.

39. Judith Butler, *Bodies That Matter: On the Discursive Limits of Sex* (New York: Routledge, 1993).

40. Those precedents include court cases which have helped secure the right of public school students to be free from anti-gay harassment (Nabozny v. Podlesny 1996); to recognizing the right of public high school students under the Federal Equal Access Act to organize GSAs in their schools (East High Gay/Straight Alliance v. Board of Education of Salt Lake City School District 1999).

41. Slevin and Linnerman,"Old Gay Men's," 500.

42. Douglas C. Kimmel and Dawn Lundy Martin, *Midlife and Aging In Gay America: Proceedings of the SAGE Conference* (New York: Harrington Park Press, 2001), 42-43.

43. Kimmel and Martin, "Midlife and Aging In Gay America," 46.

44. Raymond Mark Berger, *Gay and Gray: The Older Homosexual Man* (New York: Harrington Park Press, 1996), 60-61.

45. Slevin and Linnerman,"Old Gay Men's," 500-501.

46. Graeme Kane, "Unmasking The Gay Male Body Ideal: A Critical Analysis of the Dominant Research on Gay Men's Body Image Issues," *Gay & Lesbian Issues and Psychology Review* 5, no. 1 (2009): 28.

47. Rodger Streitmatter, *From 'Perverts' to 'Fab Five': The Media's Changing Depiction of Gay Men and Lesbians* (New York: Routledge, 2009).

48. Gross, *Up From Invisibility*, 81.

49. Gross, *Up From Invisibility*, 82.

50. Weston, *Families We Choose,* 102.

51. Mary Bernstein and Renate Reimann, eds., *Queer Families, Queer Politics* (Columbia Univesity Press, 2001).

52. Eng, *The Feeling of Kinship.*

53. Robert Abelman, *The Televiewing Audience: The Art & Science of Watching TV* (Cresskill: Hampton Press, 2002); Tim Bergling, *Reeling In The Years: Gay Men's Perspectives on Age and Ageism* (New York: Harrington Park Press, 2004); Dustin Goltz,

"Investigating Queer Future Meanings," *Qualitative Inquiry* 15, no. 3 (2009): 561-586; Eric Louw, *The Media and Cultural Production* (Thousand Oaks: Sage Publications, 2011); Maurice McGinley, "Television's Job-To-Be-Done," *How I Got My Kink* (blog), May 10, 2012, http://howigotmykink.blogspot.com/2012/05/televisions-job-to-be-done-image-source.html; Toby Miller, *Cultural Citizenship: Cosmopolitanism, Consumerism, and Television in a Neoliberal Age* (Philadelphia: Temple University Press, 2007); Jason Mittell, "Narrative Complexity and Contemporary American Television," *The Velvet Light Trap* 58 (Fall 2006): 30-40; David Morely, *Televisions, Audiences and Cultural Studies* (London and New York: Routledge, 1992); Alan M. Rubin, "The Uses-And-Gratification Perspective of Media Effects," in *Media Effects: Advances in Theory and Research*, ed. Jennings Bryant and Dolf Zillmann, 2nd ed. (Mahwah: Erlbaum, 2002), 525-548; Theo Sonneckus, "Consumption as Citizenship, The Media, and The Making Of A Gay Niche Market," *LitNet.com* (March 3, 2008), http://www.litnet.co.za/cgi-bin/giga.cgi?cmd=cause_dir_news_item&news_id=33813&cause_id=1270.

54. Julia Livaditi, Konstantina Vassilopoulou, et al. "Needs and Gratification for Interactive TV Applications: Implication for Designers," Proceedings of the 36th Hawaii International Conference on System Sciences, 2003.

55. J. Miller McPherson and James M. Cook, "Birds of a Feather: Homophily in Social Networks," *Annual Review of Sociology* 27 (2001): 415-444.

56. Jaye Derrick and Gabriel Shira, "Social Surrogacy: How Favored Television Programs Provide the Experience of Belonging," *Journal of Experimental Social Psychology* 45, no. 2 (2009): 352-362.

57. Darnell M. Hunt, *Channeling Blackness: Studies on Television and Race in America* (Oxford University Press, 2004).

58. Michael Johnson Jr., "Noah's Arc: Where Do We Go From Here," in *Queers In American Popular Culture*, ed. Jim Elledge (Santa Barbara, CA: Praeger, 2010), 45.

59. Jose Esteban Munoz, "Queer Minstrels for the Straight Eye: Race as Surplus in Gay TV," *GLQ: A Journal of Lesbian and Gay Studies* 11, no. 2 (2005): 101-102.

60. Sonnekus, "Consumption as Citizenship."

61. Rosemary Hennessy, *Profit and Pleasure: Sexual Identities in Late Capitalism* (New York: Routledge, 2000).

62. Jaime Hovey, "Queer Change Agents," in *Media Queered: Visibility and its Discontents*, ed. Kevin G. Barnhurst (New York: Peter Lang Publishing, 2007), 164.

63. Sarah Schulman, *Stagestruck: Theater, AIDS, and The Marketing Of Gay America* (Durham: Duke University Press, 1998), 89.

64. Guy Mark Foster, "Desire and the "Big Black Sex Cop': Race and the Politics of Sexual Intimacy in HBO's Six Feet Under," in *The New Queer Aesthetic on Television*, ed. James Keller (Jefferson: McFarland & Company, 2005), 99-112; Dariek Scott, "Jungle Fever? Black Gay Identity Politics, White Dick and the Utopian Bedroom," *GLQ: A Journal of Lesbian and Gay Studies* 1, no. 3 (1994): 299-321; Kobena Mercer, "Just Looking for Trouble: Robert Mapplethorpe and Fantasies of Race," in *Dangerous Liasons: Gender, Nation and Postcolonial Perspectives*, ed. Anne McClintock, Aamir Mufti and Ella Shohat (Minneapolis, MN: University of Minnesota Press, 1997).

65. Jesus Salvador Treviño, "Latino Portrayals in Film and Television," *Jump Cut: A Review of Contemporary Media* 30 (March 1985): 14-16.

66. GLAAD, "Where We Are On TV," *Gay & Lesbian Alliance Against Defamation: Words & Images Matter,* Septemeber 2011, http://www.glaad.org/publicatio ns/whereweareontv11.

67. Cynthia Hoffner and Martha Buchanan, "Young Adults' Wishful Identification with Television Characters: The Role of Perceived Similarity and Character Attributes," *Media Psychology* 7 (2005): 328.

68. Hoffner and Buchanan, "Young Adults' Wishful Identification," 329.

69. Bradley S. Greenberg, "Some Uncommon Images and the Drench Hypothesis," in *Television As A Social Issue*, ed. Stuart Oskamp (Newbury Park: Sage, 1988), 88-102.

70. Michael J. Papa, Arvind Shinghai, Sweety Law, Saumya Pant, Suruchi Sood, Everett M. Rogers, and Corrine L. Shefner-Roberts, "Entertainment-Education and Social Change: An Analysis of Parasocial Interaction, Social Learning, Collective Efficacy and Paradoxical Communication," *Journal of Communication* 50, no. 4 (2000): 31-55.

Chapter Fifteen

Eighty is Still Eighty, But Everyone Else Needs to Look Twenty-Five: The Fascination with Betty White Despite Our Obsession with Youth

Deborah A. Macey

Betty White has been a mainstay in the television industry since its inception. She might best be known for her work on *Password* (1961-1975), *The Mary Tyler Moore Show* (1970-1977), and *Golden Girls* (1985-1992). More recently White's career has seen a resurgence, starting with her 2009 supporting role in *The Proposal* with Sandra Bullock and Ryan Reynolds. After *The Proposal*, her success continued with a Super Bowl Snickers commercial, a new sitcom, guest roles on *Community* (2009-present) and *The Middle* (2009-present), and a ground-swell Facebook campaign in 2010 demanding White host *Saturday Night Live* (*SNL*, 1975-present).

In 2010 White was scheduled to appear in only the pilot episode of *Hot in Cleveland* (2010-present), but was asked to stay on as a lead character for the remainder of the first season. *Hot in Cleveland* was recently picked up for its fourth season and White remains one of the four principal leads. White earned her sixth Emmy for her *SNL* performance, which was arguably the best show of that season, bringing back the powerhouse of female *SNL* cast members over the years for the Mother's Day episode.[1] During 2010-2011, White received a Screen Actors Guild Lifetime Achievement Award, promoted two books, *If You Ask Me: (And of Course You Won't)* and *Betty & Friends: My Life at the Zoo*, and starred in another film, *You Again*, with Kristen Bell, Jamie Lee Curtis, and Sigourney Weaver. In January of 2012, Betty White celebrated her ninetieth birthday with a star-studded, ninety minute, NBC special,[2] followed by a new reality series, which she hosts, *Betty White's Off Their Rockers*.[3] White also received a Best Reality Host Emmy nomination for her work on *Off Their Rockers* in 2012. White's star power continues to rise, and the fan adoration is cosmic.

The Women's Media Center's comments regarding White's 2010 Snickers commercial did not fit this adoration. In the article critiquing Super Bowl commercials, Jehmu Greene and Shelby Knox stated, "Snickers rags on older people by comparing lagging players to Betty White and Abe Vigoda and then slamming them into the ground,"[4] implying that the culture disregards its seniors. Certainly the literal visual presentation might have suggested that, and when the same commercial with Roseanne Barr being pummeled by a log aired, it felt like feminism, and in particular, outspoken women were being pummeled. However, Roseanne Barr and Betty White do not carry the same star presence. Barr's fan base is not as widespread as White's, and Greene and Knox failed to acknowledge the great love and respect people have for White; rarely is there a negative comment written about her. This chapter investigates this Betty White fascination by exploring Richard Dyer's[5] theory on star texts and their importance to the cultural zeitgeist; by applying Todd Gitlin's[6] discussions of recombinant television to the archetypal characters of the iron maiden, the sex object, the mother, and the child that are pervasive in media[7] and in White's career; and by examining White's embodiment of these archetypes and the cultural meaning in these representations.

How Stars Function

Dyer asserts that stars are socially influential and work to manage the contradictions of the dominant ideology.[8] Dyer describes ideology as a system of ideas that are collectively held by individuals in order to make sense of their world.[9] Stuart Hall argues that for one ideology to be dominant, others must be marginalized; however, the dominant ideology is never a closed system and stars both challenge and reinforce prevailing cultural norms.[10] Stars negotiate the boundaries of dominant cultural ideology and serve both subversive and patriarchal functions.[11]

The emergence of a particular star coincides with cultural and societal needs and desires within a particular moment in time.[12] For example Dyer describes Marilyn Monore's stardom as a sexual icon emerging around the same time as *The Kinsey Reports, Playboy,* and *The Feminine Mystique* were published and widely distributed.[13] Dyer asserts that Monroe became a star because she embodied the sexual tensions of that time.[14]

Recombinant Television

In his book, *Inside Prime Time*, Gitlin discusses what he calls "The Triumph of the Synthetic" in television production.[15] Gitlin claims that network executives have an extreme aversion to risk and therefore take the safest route in program development. Gitlin states, "the safest, easiest formula is that nothing succeeds like success."[16] Similarly, Bernard Gendron agrees with Adorno's criticism of jazz and other popular music as interchangeable parts that are easily reusable, replaceable, and reproducible, void of any real artistic depth.[17] Common practice must then involve recycling prepackaged formulas to avoid or reduce financial risk and fill airtime. Included in these synthetic re-productions are spin-offs, copies, and recombinants.[18] Spin-offs capitalize on the appeal of a successfully established television series by developing a new series around a popular character from the former, "spinning" this character off and expanding independent storylines. Spin-offs are character driven, and television producers and advertisers believe they assume less risk by developing a series around an already recognizable character. Whether spin-offs actually are more lucrative than newly developed programming has not been proven systematically, but those in the business who believe "the single most important factor in series success is the appeal of its major characters"[19] bank on the triumph of the spin-off.

While the spin-off employs the use of a successful character, copies reproduce a particular formula. Television professionals regard almost all programming as imitations of something else.[20] Gitlin concludes, "The entire history of art is rife with imitation,"[21] and television and "the present-day culture industry has erected an apparatus for the mass production of self-imitating artifacts."[22] Gitlin asserts that writing for television is more of a craft than an art. In the mass-produced culture industries, including books, popular music, and movies, "imitation runs rampant, but in television the process was raised to self-parody by the economics of competition."[23] Networks would copy nearly any series that achieved success: think *Law & Order*, *CSI*, or even the *Real Housewives* franchise. While there is some caché in being first, once this imitation becomes parody of itself, the genre or formula would lose its appeal. Gitlin suggests that the "jiggle" genre, with *Charlie's Angels* as the genre's originator, is a prime example of the downside to rampant imitations.[24] Another difficulty of the copy involves determining what the appeal of the formula is and reproducing it in the right balance. While television producers continue to copy other successful series, Gitlin asserts:

> More clones end up in speedy demise than network executives like to think. Television audiences spot a copy when it is hurled right between their eyes. Clones beg for comparison and usually suffer by it. But they are easy to conceive, they do not stretch the imagination, and they keep the assembly line moving.[25]

In only slight contrast to the clone or copy, Gitlin describes the recombinant as a recombination of elements to create something "new." One element of the recombinant series includes character recombination. The benefit of recombinant programming is that while the series may very well be a copy, the recombination of characters or formula often passes as novel.[26] For example, my work regarding *Golden Girls*, *Living Single* and *Sex and the City* reveals striking similarities among characters and storylines.[27] At first glance, these shows appear to be about very different people: older white women in suburban Miami, Florida; twenty-something African American women in Brooklyn, New York; and thirty-something, white, professional women in Manhattan, respectively. In addition these recombinant series were seen as groundbreaking: *Golden Girls* for its prominence of older women in primetime; *Living Single* as a part of Fox's narrowcasting strategy, reaching African American audiences with Black actors and producers; and *Sex and the City* for its frank and explicit discussion of sex by and about women. Despite this variance, *Golden Girls,' Living Single*, and *Sex and the City* contained analogous archetypal characters of the iron maiden, the sex object, the child, and the mother.

Recombinant television serves as a sort of industry shorthand that facilitates pitching, production, casting, and audience following.[28] Gitlin confirms

> recombinant talk is splendidly practical, too, providing signposts for rapid recognition, speeding up meetings, streamlining discussion about cultural goods that might otherwise seem elusive, unwieldy, hard to peg. Meetings have to be brisk, for the mass-cultural assembly line has to keep moving.[29]

One can imagine the pitch for *Living Single* sounding something like, "This show will be the young, hip, edgy, urban version of *Golden Girls/Designing Women* with Queen Latifah as the lead." The casting pitch for the role of Dorothy in *Golden Girls* called for a "Bea Arthur-esque" type.[30] Who could play Bea Arthur-esque better than Bea Arthur herself? The need to cut costs and reduce risks drives the use of recombinants. Think of the prominent working-class buffoon character in *King of Queens* (1998-2007), *According to Jim* (2001-2009), *Still Standing* (2002-2006), *Yes, Dear* (2000-2006), *Everybody Loves Raymond* (1996-2005), or even long-running animated shows such as *The Simpsons* (1989-present) and *King of the Hill* (1997-2010). In his discussion of the working-class buffoon character, Richard Butsch asserts that the prevalence of this character "illustrates ideological hegemony, the dominance of values in mainstream culture that justify and help to maintain status quo," depicting working-class men as incompetent and in need of supervision, thus legitimizing their lower class status.[31] In addition, gender and class expectations are also reinforced within these series as the likeable, but inept partner and/or father figure, is incapable of cleaning up after himself or looking after children, thus maintaining women's position as the natural guardian of the private sphere while constructing the female partner as the neurotic, nagging, domestic shrew who bullies her husband like a domineering tyrant.

Beyond practicality, Gitlin and Susan Sontag assert that recombinant thinking deeply pervades Western culture and thought.[32] Gitlin explains that capitalism needs novelty, or at least the perception of novel, for the continuous consumption of consumer products. He warns, however, that

> The inseparable economic and cultural pressure for novelty must co-exist with a pressure toward constancy . . . manufacturers want to deploy their repertory of the tried-and-true in such a way as to generate novelty without risk. The fusion of these pressures is what produces the recombinant style, which collects the old in new packages and hopes for a magical synthesis.[33]

Recombinant thinking does not have to be negative. Sontag notes that this type of thinking allows one to categorize and compare one experience with, and as a variation of, another.[34] Arthur Koestler argues that this type of thinking, applying one idea in an alternative context, produces much of the creative scholarship in academia. He states, "the creative act . . . does not create something out of nothing: it uncovers, reshuffles, combines, synthesizes already existing facts, ideas, faculties and skills."[35] Gitlin, however, reminds us "that recombination as such brings forth a hundred or a thousand banalities for each new synthesis, and in the process degenerates into mechanical juxtaposition to suit the rhythm of consumption and fashion in a consumer society."[36] Gitlin makes it seem as if successful recombinants are rare. However, given the culture in which American television is created (including the vast array of cable channels, many of which rely on a mix of syndicated and first run programming), it seems instead we should expect this kind of recombinant fusion, and often. Betty White is an example of an actress who embodies this phenomenon, playing characters representing multiple female archetypes.

Recombinant Archetypes of the Iron Maiden, the Sex Object, the Child, and the Mother

Television producers revamp tried and true hits essentially by re-employing similar characters and genres, while updating them to prevailing social and cultural values of the time. Scholars suggest this is done because of the time pressure not only to pitch shows to executives, create scripts, and cast actors, but also to connect with viewers to attract and maintain large coveted audiences to sell to advertisers.[37] While Butsch offers an exploration of the working-class male buffoon character, my previous research examines four archetypal characters, the iron maiden, the sex object, the child, and the mother, prevalent in media and particularly television sitcoms with four female leads. Applying Carl Jung's work on archetypes,[38] Julia T. Wood's discussion of stereotypes of women in the workforce,[39] and Jean Shinoda Bolen[40] and Christine Downing's[41] discussions on how characteristics of mythological goddesses manifest themselves in real women's lives, I connect the archetypal characters of the iron maiden, the sex object, the child, and the mother with the mythological goddess of Artemis, Aphrodite, Persephone, and Demeter, respectively, demonstrating their long-term prevalence in Western culture.[42] Betty White's ninety years has nothing on the ancient Greek goddesses. These representations are ingrained in our psyches; Betty White simply re-embodies them through her roles.

The iron maiden character (Artemis) is cynical, competitive, sometimes abrasive and mean-spirited, and often antagonistic toward men. Her viewpoints might be considered feminist or just plain bitchy. Although she may desire a romantic partnership, she is independent and/or finds romantic love impractical and/or incompatible with her career ambitions and independent needs. The child archetype (Persephone) is eager to please, passive, and compliant. She is prudent and conventional, and is seen as prim, puerile, and simple. The child is portrayed as dumb and immature, although sometimes she makes surprisingly profound statements, as children sometimes do. She is naïve and her comments are usually silly or ridiculous. The child believes deeply in the romantic love of fairytales at the expensive of reality. She desires romantic love above most other goals. The sex object character (Aphrodite) is sensual and superficial, taking great pride in her appearance and sexual experiences. She derives power from sexuality and her ability to be desired and/or adored by others.[43]

The mother archetype (Demeter) is the most difficult to define. The mother character is usually the center of the group or the star vehicle of the show. In general, this maternal character seeks psychological wellness for herself and the other characters, performing much of the emotional work for the group. However, when this archetypal character was intersected by age and nationality, as with Sophia Petrillo of *Golden Girls*, this mother archetype was reduced to the eccentric old lady and ethnic mother stereotype. The most defining characteristic of the archetypal mother character proved to be her storytelling ability. For example, Sophia Petrilla of *Golden Girls* was often telling stories from the old country that began with "Picture this, Sicily 1925 . . . ," whereas Khadijah James of *Living Single* and *Sex and the City*'s Carrie Bradshaw are both journalists.[44]

More important than simply describing the archetypes within the series involves understanding how the archetypal characters function within the series and how their corresponding discourses are either privileged or ridiculed. The archetypes function in an ideological way, producing and contributing to cultural and competing discourses that are privileged, neutralized, or derided within the narratives. At best the iron maiden functions to bring forth a feminist perspective as Dorothy of *Golden Girls* often does. At times when the iron maiden's discourse is disparaged, she is seen as a cautionary feminist tale and/or simply cantankerous, as Bonnie Dow describes Murphy Brown[45] and as I argue of Maxine Shaw in *Living Single*. The sex object, when not reduced to self-absorption, like Regine Hunter of *Living Single*, or debauchery, like Samantha Jones of *Sex and the City*, can be seen as a powerful character in that she unabashedly owns her sexuality, pleasure, and beauty. The child, while typically seen as frivolous and simple-minded, when privileged can carry a traditional, and at times regressive point of view, like that of Charlotte York from *Sex and the City*. The mother archetypal character varies the most and can range from eccentric old woman, as is the case with Sophia Petrillo, neutral observer, as with Carrie Bradshaw, to strong Black feminist, as with Khadijah James.[46] This chapter describes White's embodiment of these archetypal characters throughout her career and what her performances contribute to the cultural discourse.

In her most prominent roles, Betty White has played the sex object archetype (as Sue Ann Nivens on *The Mary Tyler Moore Show*), the child archetype (as Rose Nyland in *Golden Girls*), and currently plays the mother archetype (as Elka Ostrowsky in *Hot in Cleveland*). With a fake sweetness and aggressive sex drive, White's Sue Ann Nivens was the "Happy Homemaker," at Mary's station, WJM. In her first appearance, Sue Ann has an affair with Lars Lindstrom, the husband of Phyllis Lindstrom (played by Cloris Leachman). Phyllis confronts Sue Ann about the affair on the Happy Homemaker set and ruins Sue Ann's soufflé. Kicking the high oven door closed with her leg in an efficient and somewhat provactive manner, Sue Ann checks the soufflé. Initially Sue Ann refuses to give up Lars. Desperate to save her marriage, Phyllis begs Mary to help. Mary, knowing that the rumors of an affair are not the right image for the "Happy Homemaker," threatens Sue Ann, "either Lars or your show." This is an easy decision for the vain Sue Ann, who earlier stopped production because she needed a third camera for her soufflé. Sue Ann claims her decision to remain the "Happy Homemaker" is not for herself "but for those ladies who need me."[47]

Throughout her time on *The Mary Tyler Moore Show*, Sue Ann's vanity and sexual exploits continue. Sue Ann is constantly trying to bed Lou Grant (played by Ed Asner), the news producer at WJM. Lou tries to avoid Sue Ann's advances while she touches and talks with him inappropriately, and it isn't until Season six, episode eighteen, that Lou drunkenly and regrettably gives in to Sue Ann's advances.[48] In addition to Sue Ann's sexual exploits, she see herself in competition with other women. For example Sue Ann feels threatened by a young woman who she believes is trying to take her job. Sue Ann claims the young woman is sleeping with the program manager at the station. When Mary questions why this affair would necessarily mean the young woman will steal Sue Ann's job, Sue Ann admits with a wry smile, "How do you think I got it?"[49]

In this 1970s sitcom, Sue Ann's sexual exploits are quite scandalous, but the sex object comes out in other ways as well. Sue Ann sees herself as superior to the others in the series. She often offers advice condescendingly and/or provides tips that don't work, only to prove she is better in her appearance and maintaining the home than the others on the show. While Sue Ann is no Samantha of *Sex and the City*, she is the very memorable sex object of this series, delivering many double entrendres and sexual one-liners, similar to Blanche Devereaux of *Golden Girls*.

Betty White was actually offered the part of Blanche, the sex object, in *Golden Girls*, but didn't want to play such an analogous character (to Sue Ann), so she switched roles with Rue McClanahan to play the role of Rose Nyland, the naïve child archetype.[50] Rose, the Minnesota native, represents the child archetype in *Golden Girls*. Rose tries to see the bright side of everything and looks for the good in people. She likes to be helpful, even though the other characters find her exasperating with her long-winded, usually pointless, stories of St. Olaf, the small, droll Minnesota town where Rose grew up, married, and raised her children before moving to Miami. In Season one, episode twenty, Blanche takes a class where she is sexually harassed by her instructor. While Dorothy, the iron maiden of this series, recounts a sexual harassment story that takes the issue from the personal to the political, Rose, the child archetype, tells a much less politically charged sexual harassment story. Rose narrates, "Nils Felander attempted to harass me repeatedly." Blanche asks, "What do you mean attempted?" Rose continues,

> He worked at Lars Erickson, a drugstore and tackle shop [in St. Olaf]. He was a soda jerk. Now that I think about it, he was the town jerk. Every Saturday afternoon, I'd go in and have a sundae. Well . . . Nils would arrange the ice cream scoops in an obscene way.

Blanche and Dorothy roll their eyes at Rose and her story, but Rose resumes, "I could never prove it because by the time I would take it home to show my father . . . the evidence had melted. To this day every time I pass an ice cream parlor or a tackle shop, I blush." This exchange demonstrates the ridiculousness of Rose, her story, and her hometown as well as the disenchantment others have in Rose's stories and her storytelling ability.[51]

The disenchantment is often verbalized by the other characters who regularly tell Rose to "shut up." This abrasive verbal silencing reduces much of Rose's discourse. In Season two, episode eight, Rose, Dorothy, and Blanche become stranded on an island during their vacation. When they realize they are going to be rescued, Rose merrily acknowledges how special it is that they were all together. Blanche and Dorothy, tired of Rose's "Pollyanna" ways, exclaim in unison, "Shut up Rose!" To this, Rose replies, "I'm glad everything is back to normal."[52]

Rose does not develop much throughout the series; the ridicule of her and her St. Olaf stories become a significant, expected, and exaggerated part of the show through the finale. As a result, Rose's childlike stupidity pervades the series. In Season three, episode six, Rose volunteers with the Sunshine Cadets, a girls' organization similar to Girl Scouts. As Rose enters the home in her yellow Sunshine Cadet uniform, she informs Blanche and Dorothy that she is "concerned about nuclear war." Dorothy mocks, "And just yesterday her biggest concern was, is Bubbles, the chimp, traveling with Michael Jackson against his will." Rose's concern with nuclear war stems from letters several of her young cadets wrote about the fear they have of the devastation it could cause. Dorothy acknowledges, "This is not so uncommon. Kids hear about nuclear war on T.V. They read it in the papers. It's part of their lives. They can't help but think about it." Rose decides to write a letter to Gorbachev and Reagan because she "always believed you can fix a problem no matter how big it is, if you just put your mind to it."[53]

Later in the episode, a Russian ambassador visits to tell Rose, "Premier Gorbachev read Rose's letter and would like to meet with her. He was quite moved by her letter. He wished to extend an invitation to her and her family to visit Moscow and discuss nuclear disarmament and world peace." Immediately before the press conference Rose is supposed to attend, Dorothy and Blanche discover that Gorbachev believes that Rose is a child "based on her letter, we figure nine or ten." To save themselves the embarrassment, they decide to let one of the Sunshine cadets read the letter, but Rose decides she cannot let that happen because "a Sunshine cadet never lies." Upset by these events, Rose states, "this is the worst day of my life . . . I made a total fool of myself in front of the press. I'm the laughing stock of the entire country. What am I going to tell my mother?" Dorothy responds, "your mother is from St. Olaf, she'll understand." Rose continues to berate herself, "I'm just stupid. I'm a dimwitted, dumb, simple-minded, Grade A, Minnesota chucklehead." While Blanche and Dorothy try to console Rose, they do not disagree. The episode ends with Dorothy saying, "it's a shame more people don't think like nine-year-olds."[54] If this episode focused on Dorothy, the iron maiden of the series, and nuclear disarmament, it most likely would have developed a more political stance. However, because the episode involves Rose, the real issue is reduced to a joke about Rose's naïveté.

On *Hot in Cleveland* White again switched from her past archetypes (the sex object in *The Mary Tyler Moore Show* and child archetype in *Golden Girls*) to portray the mother figure. Admittedly, White's character, Elka Ostrowsky, is hardly maternal, as her first line in the series is, "Why are you renting to prostitutes?"[55] describing the other three lead characters Melanie Moretti (played by Valerie Bertinelli), Joy Scroggs (Jane Leeves), and Victoria Chase (Wendie Malick). Elka is defined as the mother archetype because of her age and the fact that "she's a caretaker that comes with the house."[56] In many ways this role parallels Sophia Petrillo, the mother archetype from *Golden Girls,* including her acerbic wit and old country ethnicity.[57] Like Sophia, Elka is the eccentric old woman/ethnic mother stereotype, this time outfitted in colorful tracksuits and dispensing terse advice and guilt. In the first exchange among Elka and the other lead characters, Elka states, "I've been the caretaker of this house for fifty years, but you can kick me out." Hemming, Melanie suggests she would not kick Elka out, to which Elka responds, "No worries, if you can escape the Nazis, you can handle anything."[58] When the mother archetype is intersected by age, feminine/motherly expectations are no longer compulsory. Age allows these characters (Sophia, Elka) to say what they want.[59] In fact, their sarcastic comments are excused, and almost expected, because of their age.

While *Hot in Cleveland* is clearly a recombinant of *Golden Girls*, there are differences that point to cultural shifts, particularly in how society views age. When *Golden Girls* began in 1985, Bea Arthur was sixty-three years old, playing Dorothy, a late fifty-something. While it is unclear how old Blanche is in the series, Rue McClanahan was fifty-one. Estelle Getty who plays Dorothy's mother, Sophia, was actually a couple months younger than Bea Arthur. Betty White, the oldest, and only still living actress from the series, was also sixty-three, four months older than Arthur, playing Rose in her mid-fifties. Sophia, Blanche, and Rose are widowed; Dorothy is divorced after thirty-eight years of marriage. By the end of the series all are grandmothers and look grandmotherly throughout the series.

This stands in stark contrast to the lead characters in *Hot in Cleveland*. While *Golden Girls* was lauded for its representations of older women in primetime, *Hot in Cleveland* feigns to be about challenging unrealistic expectations of age and beauty, especially those beauty norms in Los Angeles that, according to the series, don't exist in Cleveland. While White celebrates her age, the other characters still seem bound by impossible standards of youth and feminine beauty as they play women who are ten years younger than the actors' real-life ages. Jane Leeves and Valerie Bertinelli are in their early fifties and Wendie Malick is in her early sixties. Yet the synopsis from the Internet Movie Database reads, "Three forty-something best friends from Los Angeles are flying to Paris when their plane makes an emergency landing in Cleveland. Realizing that all the norms from Los Angeles don't apply anymore, they decide to celebrate a city that values real women and stay where they're still considered hot."[60]

A visual comparison of the women in the two series reveals very different looking women. Joy (the iron maiden), Melanie (the child) and Victoria (the sex object) of *Hot in Cleveland* are not only not grandmotherly, they balk at the idea of becoming a grandmother. This is significant because in *Golden Girls* only the vain and self-absorbed sex object Blanche had a similar response to being a grandmother, while on *Hot in Cleveland* all of the characters have a shared sense of vanity. Culture's obsession with youth requires us to focus on our appearance in an increasingly narcissistic world.[61] In the pilot episode, Melanie is giddy about her first date in twenty-five years. Elka tells Melanie that she's "too old to act like this." Joy defends Melanie, "She's not old. Forty is the new thirty." Then Victoria chimes in, "And fifty is the new forty." Then Elka asks curiously and excitedly, "What's eighty?" Joy curtly responds, "It's still eighty."[62]

After discovering her date is married, Melanie sadly says, "I just wanted to feel young and stupid, now I just feel stupid, stupid and old." Joy tries to console, "You're not old, forty is the new twenty-five." Victoria questions, "I thought forty was the new thirty?" To which Joy responds, "Well if we're going to make crap up, I'd rather be twenty-five."[63] The women of *Hot in Cleveland*, despite their real-life ages, represent the compulsory societal expectations for women, now women over fifty (and sixty), to look half their age. So despite their desire to represent women who will not conform to the narrow beauty norms of Los Angeles, Melanie, Joy, and Victoria end up reinforcing these impossible youth and beauty standards. White might be popular as an unapologetic eighty-plus-year old, especially among young people, but nonetheless society's focus on youth is alive and well. Indeed fifty is the new twenty-five!

TV Land, a Viacom cable network that initially aired only classic television reruns, is the ideal network for a series such as *Hot in Cleveland*. *Hot in Cleveland*, one of TV Land's first newly scripted series to air on the network, blends perfectly the old with the new. A recombinant series, with long-time veteran television actors like Jane Leeves from *Fraiser*, Wendie Malick from *Just Shoot Me!*, and Valerie Bertinelli from *One Day at a Time*, not to mention the golden girl of television, Betty White, brings together the classic with the novel, or at least the perception of novel. A network which once embraced the old (reruns), now is consciously aping its own programming, an intertextuality that reinforces the recombinant nature of the series.

This intertextuality fits well with TV Land's branding. *Hot in Cleveland* employs the four archetypes television viewers have seen in many series, such as *Designing Women*, *Golden Girls*, *Living Single*, and *Sex and the City* among others. Jane Leeves, as Joy, plays the crotchety iron maiden with little feminist import. Wendie Malick is the vain, self-obsessed former soap opera star, the sex object, Victoria, not a stretch from her role as Nina Van Horn in *Just Shoot Me!* Valerie Bertinelli as the Pollyanna child archetype of the series is reminiscent of the good daughter, Barbara, in *One Day at a Time*. Because of her age, Betty White plays the mother archetype, the eccentric old woman who says whatever is on her mind. The similarities among archetypes in various series are no accident and are important to understanding our culture, not only because of their prevalent re-productions, but also because the variations among these representations point to significant cultural differences in society. If television serves as our modern story-teller, it makes sense that producers would evoke such powerful and ingrained cultural archetypes not only to entertain audiences, but also to portray the dominant ideologies of the time.

White's role in *Hot in Cleveland* differs from her previous archetypal roles as the sex object in *The Mary Tyler Moore Show* and the child in *Golden Girls*. When compared to *Golden Girls*, *Hot in Cleveland* lacks the progressive perspective that Bea Arthur as Dorothy was able to convey within the series. Leeves/Joy's iron maiden is simply not the feminist icon that Arthur/Dorothy was. This lack of an outspoken feminist point of view reflects a post-feminist cultural shift.[64]

As with any recombinant series, *Hot in Cleveland* is updated to reflect prevailing cultural norms. Again when compared to *Golden Girls*, representations of age are quite different. With the largest population cohort in U.S. history reaching retirement age, it makes sense that age and aging would be significant issues within the series. However, despite a premise to the contrary, the representations of age in *Hot in Cleveland* instead reflect on society's obsession with youth.

Conclusion

While Betty White's stardom defies society's obsession with youth, her continuous and growing popularity is linked to portraying deeply-rooted cultural archetypes that have appeared not only in sitcoms throughout television history, but are also ingrained in our psyches as manifestations of three mythical goddesses: Aphrodite the sex object (*The Mary Tyler Moore Show*'s Sue Ann Nivens), Persephone the child (*Golden Girls*'s Rose Nyland), and Demeter the mother (*Hot in Cleveland*'s Elka Ostrowsky). It is interesting to note that White has not played Artemis (the iron maiden), the archetype who would be seen as the most feminist. While White's star persona has pushed boundaries sexually as Sue Ann Nivens in a 1970s sitcom and even today with her bawdy risqué comments as herself and Elka Ostrowsky, White has not threatened status quo patriarchy, unlike Bea Arthur and Roseanne Barr.[65] We see White as the sweet, optimistic, if at times eccentric, old woman, who we all wish were our grandmother. At ninety, White demonstrates that you can still be happy and healthy, and best of all working, because with the economic uncertainty of our times, Baby Boomers might be forced to work well beyond retirement age.

White and her various roles challenge and reinforce cultural tensions. At a time when societal expectations of gender, age, and economics are increasingly in flux, White's embodiment of ancient goddesses maintain traditional roles for women. With an aging Baby Boomer population focused on youth, White offers a positive alternative to embrace aging and the idea of growing old gracefully. White demonstrates not only how it is possible, but also how it is desirable to continue working well beyond retirement age. There is no denying White's popularity; however, without broader representations of women, especially portryals of women of a certain age, eighty (or ninety) is still eighty for Betty White, but the rest of us might need to look, act and work as if we were twenty-five.

Notes

1. *Saturday Night Live*, "Betty White/JayZ," produced by Lorne Michaels, first broadcast May 8, 2010 by NBC.

2. *Betty White's 90th Birthday: A Tribute to America's Golden Girl*, directed by Gary Halvorson, first broadcast January 16, 2012 by NBC.

3. *Betty White's Off Their Rockers*, "Parachute Drop," directed by Russell Arch and Tim Gibbons, first broadcast January 9, 2012 by NBC.

4. Jehmu Greene and Shelby Knox, *Super Bowl Sexism, by the Numbers*, February 8, 2010,http://www.huffingtonpost.com/jehmu-greene/super-bowl-sexism-bythe_b_454249.html.

5. Richard Dyer, *Stars* (London: British Film Institute, 2004).

6. Todd Gitlin, *Inside Prime Time* (New York: Pantheon, 1983).

7. Deborah A. Macey, "Ancient Archetypes in Modern Media," in *Media Depictions of Brides, Wives, and Mothers*, ed. Alena Amato Ruggerio (Lanham, MD: Lexington Books, 2012), 49-62. For a more in-depth analysis see Deborah A. Macey, *Ancient Archetypes in Modern Media: A Comparative Analysis of Golden Girls, Living Single, and Sex and the City*. PhD diss., University of Oregon, 2008.

8. Dyer, *Stars*.

9. Dyer, *Stars*.

10. Stuart Hall, "Encoding/Decoding," in *Media and Cultural Studies: Key Works*, ed. Meenakshi Gigi Durham and Douglas M. Kellner, rev. ed. (Malden, MA: Blackwell Publishing, 2006), 163-173; Dyer, *Stars*.

11. Dyer, *Stars*.

12. Dyer, *Stars*.

13. Richard Dyer, "Monroe and Sexuality" in *Heavenly Bodies: Film Stars and Society* (New York: St. Martin's Press, 1986), 19-66.

14. Dyer, "Monroe and Sexuality."

15. Gitlin, *Inside Prime Time*, 63.

16. Gitlin, *Inside Prime Time*, 63.

17. Bernard Gendron, "Theodor Adorno Meets The Cadillacs," in *Studies in Entertainment: Critical Approaches to Mass Culture*, ed. Tania Modleski (Bloomington, IN: Indiana University Press, 1986), 18-37.

18. Gitlin, *Inside Prime Time*.

19. Gitlin, *Inside Prime Time*, 67.

20. Gitlin, *Inside Prime Time*, 67.

21. Gitlin, *Inside Prime Time*, 70.

22. Gitlin, *Inside Prime Time*, 71.

23. Gitlin, *Inside Prime Time*, 71.

24. Gitlin, *Inside Prime Time*, 71.

25. Gitlin, *Inside Prime Time*, 75.

26. Gitlin, *Inside Prime Time*, 75.

27. Macey, "Ancient Archetypes," 49-62.

28. Richard Butsch, "Ralph, Fred, Archie, and Homer: Why Television Keeps Recreating the White Male Working Class Buffoon," in *Gender, Race, and Class in Media: A Text-Reader*, ed. Gail Dines and Jean Humez (Thousand Oaks, CA: Sage Publications), 575-585.

29. Gitlin, *Inside Prime Time*, 77.

30. *"Golden Girls*: Trivia," *IMDB.com*, http://www.imdb.com/title/tt0088526/trivia.

31. Butsch, "Ralph, Fred, Archie, and Homer," 576.

32. Gitlin, *Inside Prime Time*.

33. Gitlin, *Inside Prime Time*, 77-78.

34. Susan Sontag, "Seminar on Television," New York: Institute for the Humanities, 1981.

35. Arthur Koestler, *The Act of Creation* (London: Picador, 1975).

36. Gitlin, *Inside Prime Time*, 78.

37. Gitlin, *Inside Prime Time*; Butsch, "Ralph, Fred, Archie, and Homer."

38. Carl Jung, *The Archetypes and the Collective Unconscious* (Princeton, NJ: Princeton University Press, 1959).

39. Julia T. Wood, *Gendered Lives: Communication, Gender, and Culture*, 9th ed. (Boston: Wadsworth Cengage Learning, 2011).

40. Jean Shinoda Bolen, *Goddesses in Everywoman: A New Psychology of Women* (New York: Harper & Row, 1984).

41. Christine Downing, *The Goddess: Mythological Images of the Feminine* (New York: The Continuum Publishing Company, 1981).

42. Macey, "Ancient Archetypes," 49-62.

43. Macey, "Ancient Archetypes," 49-62; Bolen, *Goddesses in Everywoman.*

44. Macey, "Ancient Archetypes," 49-62; Bolen, *Goddesses in Everywoman.*

45. Bonnie Dow, *Prime-Time Feminism: Television, Media Culture, and the Women's Movement Since 1970* (Philadelphia: University of Pennsylvania Press, 1996).

46. Macey, "Ancient Archetypes," 49-62.

47. *The Mary Tyler Moore Show*, "The Lars Affair," directed by Jay Sandrich, first broadcast September 15, 1973 by CBS.

48. *The Mary Tyler Moore Show*, "Once I Had a Secret Love," directed by Jay Sandrich, first broadcast January 17, 1976 by CBS.

49. *The Mary Tyler Moore Show*, "A New Sue Ann," directed by Jay Sandrich, first broadcast October 26, 1974 by CBS.

50. "Betty White," *IMDB.com*, http://www.imdb.com/name/nm0924508/bio.

51. *Golden Girls*, "Adult Education," directed by Jack Shea, first broadcast February 22, 1986 by NBC.

52. *Golden Girls*, "Vacation," directed by Terry Hughes, first broadcast November 29, 1986 by NBC.

53. *Golden Girls*, "Letter to Gorbachev," directed by Terry Hughes, first broadcast October 31, 1987 by NBC.

54. *Golden Girls*, "Letter to Gorbachev."

55. *Hot in Cleveland*, "Pilot," directed by Micahel Lembeck, first broadcast June 16, 2010 by TVLand.

56. *Hot in Cleveland*, "Pilot."

57. Sophia is a Sicilian and Elka is Polish.

58. *Hot in Cleveland*, "Pilot."

59. Macey, "Ancient Archetypes," 49-62.

60. "Hot in Cleveland," *IMDB.com*, http://www.imdb.com/title/tt1583607/.

61. Facebook and Twitter are just two examples of the way technology has contributed to society's narcissism.

62. *Hot in Cleveland*, "Pilot."

63. *Hot in Cleveland*, "Pilot."

64. This can also be seen in *Sex and the City*, as Miranda, the iron maiden archetype, is neutralized by Carrie's unbiased journalistic position. The meaning of post-feminism is debated in the literature, but here it represents a world that has benefited from gender politics, but no longer needs them. This cultural shift can be seen as regressive and a backlash against feminist ideals.

65. Even as an outspoken animal rights advocate, White does not challenge animal food industries; she is not even a vegetarian according to an interview with Monica Rizzo, "Lunch with Betty White," *People*, May 7, 2012, 50.

Bibliography

Abel, John D. "The Family and Child Television Viewing." *Journal of Marriage and the Family* 38, no. 2 (1976): 331-35.

Abelman, Robert. *The Televiewing Audience: The Art & Science of Watching TV.* Cresskill, NJ: Hampton Press, 2002.

Adalian, Josef. "Bravo Nabs Popular TV Website." *Variety.* Last modified March 13, 2007. http://www.variety.com/article/VR1117961063?refCatId=14.

Adaval, Rashmi, and Robert S. Wyer Jr.. "The Role of Narratives in Consumer Information Processing." *Journal of Consumer Psychology* 7, no. 3 (1998): 207-45.

Agger, Ben. *Cultural Studies as Critical Theory.* London: Falmer Press, 1992.

Akass, Kim. "Mother Knows Best: Ruth and Representations of Mothering in *Six Feet Under.*" In *Six Feet Under: TV to Die For*, edited by Kim Akass and Janet McCabe, 110-121. London: I.B. Tauris, 2005.

Akass, Kim, and Janet McCabe. "Beyond the Bada Bing!: Negotiating Female Narrative Authority in *The Sopranos.*" In *This Thing of Ours: Investigating The Sopranos*, edited by David Lavery, 146-161. New York: Columbia UP, 2002.

——, eds. *Reading Six Feet Under: TV to Die For.* London: I.B. Tauris, 2005.

Albada, Kelly F. "The Public and Private Dialogue About the American Family on Television." *Journal of Communication* 50, no. 4 (2000): 79-109.

Allen, Amy. "'Mommy Wars' Redux: A False Conflict." *New York Times.* May 27, 2012. http://opinionator.blogs.nytimes.com/2012/05/27/the-mommy-wars-redux-a-false-conflict.

Alvarez, Mildred M., Aletha C. Huston, John C. Wright, and Dennis D. Kerkman. "Gender Differences in Visual Attention to Television Form and Content." *Journal of Applied Developmental Psychology* 9, no. 4 (1988): 459-475.

Ambrose, Stephen C. *Citizen Soldiers: The U. S. Army from the Normandy Beaches to the Bulge to the Surrender of Germany.* New York: Simon and Schuster, 1997.

Anderson, Benedict. *Imagined Communities: Reflections on the Origin and Spread of Nationalism.* London: Verso, 1983.

Anderson, Steven. "History TV and Popular Memory." In *Television Histories: Shaping Collective Memory in the Media Age*, edited by Gary R. Edgerton and Peter C. Rollins, 19-36. Lexington, KY: The University Press of Kentucky, 2001.

Andrae, Thomas. "Television's First Feminist: The Avengers and Female Spectatorship." *Discourse: Berkeley Journal for Theoretical Studies in Media and Culture* 18, no. 3 (1996): 112-136.

Andrejevic, Marc. *Reality TV: The Work of Being Watched.* New York: Rowman & Littlefield Publishers, Inc., 2004.

——. "Watching Television without Pity: The Productivity of Online Fans." *Television & New Media* 9, no. 1 (2008): 24-46.

Andriani, Lynn. "'What to Expect' Readies for a Rebirth." *Publishers Weekly* 255, no. 11 (2008): 8.

Ang, Ien. "Melodramatic Identifications: Television Fiction and Women's Fantasy." In *Feminist Television Criticism: A Reader,* edited by Charlotte Brunsdon, Julie D'Acci, and Lynn Spigel, 155-166. Oxford: Clarendon Press, 2003.

——. *Watching Dallas: Soap Opera and the Melodramatic Imagination.* London: Routledge, 1989.

Asherman, Allan. "Rocky Jones: Space Ranger." *Filmfax,* March 1990 and May 1990.

Ashley, Mike. *Time Machines: The Story of Pulp Science Fiction Magazines from the Beginning to 1950.* Liverpool: Liverpool University Press, 2001.

Austin, Erica W. "Exploring the Effects of Active Parental Mediation of Television Content." *Journal of Broadcasting and Electronic Media* 37, no. 2 (1993): 147-158.

Austin, Erica W., and C. Leigh Nelson. "Influences of Ethnicity, Family Communication, and Media on Adolescents' Socialization to U.S. Politics." *Journal of Broadcasting and Electronic Media* 37, no. 4 (1993): 419-35.

Bakir, Aysen, Jeffrey G. Blodgett, and Gregory M. Rose. "Children's Responses to Gender-role Stereotyped Advertisements." *Journal of Advertising Research* 48, no. 2 (2008): 255-266. doi: 10.2501/S002184990808029X.

Bakir, Aysen, and Kay M. Palan. "How are Children's Attitudes Toward Ads and Brands Affected by Gender-related Content in Advertising?" *Journal of Advertising* 39, no. 1 (2010): 35-48. doi: 10.2753/JOA0091-3367390103.

Ball, Alan, and Alan Poul, eds. *Six Feet Under: Better Living Through Death.* New York: Pocket Books, 2003.

Bandura, Albert. *Social Learning Theory.* Upon Saddle River, NJ: Prentice-Hall, 1977.

——. *Social Foundations of Thought and Action: A Social Cognitive Theory.* Englewood Cliffs, NJ: Prentice-Hall, 1986.

——. Social Cognitive Theory and Exercise of Control over HIV Infection." In *Preventing AIDS: Theories and Methods of Behavioral Interventions,* edited by Ralph J. DiClemente and John L. Peterson, 25-59. New York: Plenum, 1994.

——. "Social Cognitive Theory of Mass Communication." *Media Psychology* 3, no. 3 (2001): 265-99.

Bandura, Albert, Dorothea Ross, and Sheila A. Ross. "Transmission of Aggression through Imitation of Aggressive Models." *Journal of Abnormal and Social Psychology* 63, no. 3 (1961): 575-82.

Banet-Weiser, Sarah. *Kids Rule! Nickelodeon and Consumer Citizenship.* Durham, NC: Duke University Press, 2007.

——. "The Nickelodeon Brand: Buying and Selling the Audiences." In *Cable Visions: Television Beyond Broadcasting,* edited by Sarah Banet-Weiser, Cynthia Chris, and Anthony Freitas, 234-252. New York: New York University Press, 2007.

Barbato, Carole A., Elizabeth E. Graham, and Elizabeth M. Perse. "Communicating in the Family: An Examination of the Relationship of Family Communication Climate and Interpersonal Communication Motives." *Journal of Family Communication* 3, no. 3 (2003): 123-48.

Barnard, Malcolm. *Fashion as Communication,* 2nd ed. London and New York: Routledge, 2002.

Barnes, Brooks. "Making Sure Nickelodeon Hangs with the Cool Kids." *New York Times*. October 30, 2010. http://www.nytimes.com/2010/10/31/business/media/31ni ck.html?ref=nickelodeonnetworks.

Barrett, David. "Masculinity Among Working Class Gay Males." In *Gay Masculinities*, edited by Peter M. Nardi, 176-205. Thousand Oaks, CA: Sage Publications, 2000.

Barthes, Roland. *Mythologies*. New York: Farrar, Straus and Giroux, 1972.

——. *Image–Music–Text*. New York: Noonday Press, 1977.

Baruh, Lemi. "Publicized Intimacies on Reality Television: An Analysis of Voyeuristic Content and Its Contribution to the Appeal of Reality Programming." *Journal of Broadcasting & Electronic Media* 53, no. 2 (2009): 190–210.

Basinger, Jeanine C. *The World War II Combat Film: Anatomy of a Genre*. Middletown, CT: Wesleyan University Press, 2003.

Bassior, Jean-Noel. *Space Patrol: Missions of Daring in the Name of Early Television*. Jefferson, NC: McFarland, 2005.

Baym, Nancy. *Tune in, Log on: Soaps, Fandom, and Online Community*. Thousand Oaks, CA: Sage, 2000.

Beck, Cheryl Tatano. "Pentadic Cartography: Mapping Birth Trauma Narratives." *Qualitative Health Research* 16, no. 4 (2006): 453-66.

Becker, Ron. *Gay TV and Straight America*. Camden, NJ: Rutgers University Press, 2006.

Bell, Catherine. *Ritual Theory, Ritual Practice*. New York: Oxford University Press, 2009.

Bennett, Tony. *Culture: A Reformer's Science*. London: Sage Publications, 1998.

Benjamin, Walter. "On the Image of Proust." In *Walter Benjamin Selected Writings: Volume 2, Part 1, 1927-1930*, edited by Michael W. Jennings, Howard Eiland, and Gary Smith, 237-247. Cambridge, MA: Harvard University Press, 2005.

Berger, Raymond M. *Gay and Gray: The Older Homosexual Man*. New York: Harrington Park Press, 1996.

Bergling, Tim. *Reeling In The Years: Gay Men's Perspectives on Age and Ageism*. New York: Harrington Park Press, 2004.

Bernstein, Mary, and Renate Reimann, eds. *Queer Families, Queer Politics*. New York: Columbia Univesity Press, 2001.

Besser, Avi, and Beatriz Priel. "Trait Vulnerability and Coping Strategies in the Transition to Motherhood." *Current Psychology* 22, no. 1 (2003): 57-72.

Bilandzic, Helena, and Rick W. Busselle. "Transportation and Transportability in the Cultivation of Genre-Consistent Attitudes and Estimates." *Journal of Communication* 58, no. 3 (2008): 508-29.

Bly, Robert. *Iron John: A Book About Men*. New York: Da Capo Press, 2004.

Bochner, Arthur P. "It's About Time: Narrative and the Divided Self." *Qualitative Inquiry* 3, no. 4 (1997): 418-38.

——. "Narrative's Virtues." *Qualitative Inquiry* 7, no. 2 (2001): 131-57.

Bogdan, Robert C., and Sari K. Biklen. *Qualitative Research for Education*. Boston: Allyn and Bacon, 2006.

Bolen, Jean Shinoda. *Goddesses in Everywoman: A New Psychology of Women*. New York: Harper & Row, 1984.

Booton, Jennifer. "Poor Nickelodeon Ratings Push Viacom 1Q Profit Lower." *Fox Business*, February 2, 2012. http://www.foxbusiness.com/industries/2012/02/02/ poor-nickelodeon-ratings-push-viacom-1q-profit-lower.

Bormann, Ernest G. "Symbolic Convergence Theory: A Communication Formulation." *Journal of Communication* 35, no. 4 (1985): 128-138.

Bordo, Susan. *Unbearable Weight: Feminism, Western Culture, and the Body.* Berkeley, CA: University of California Press, 1993.

——. *The Male Body: A New Look At Men In Both Public and Private.* New York: Farrar, Straus & Giroux, 1999.

Bourdieu, Pierre. "Forms of Capital." In *Handbook of Theory of Research for the Sociology of Education,* edited by John G. Richardson, 241-258. New York: Greenwood Press, 1986.

Boyatzis, Richard E. *Transforming Qualitative Information.* Thousand Oaks, CA: Sage Publications, 1998.

Boym, Svetlana. *The Future of Nostalgia.* New York: Basic Books, 2001.

Bradley, Patricia. *Mass Media and the Shaping of American Feminism, 1963-1975.* Jackson, MS: University Press of Mississippi, 2003.

Briggs, Matt. *Television, Audiences and Everyday Life: Issues in Media and Cultural Studies.* Maidenhead, Berkshire, England: Open University Press, 2009.

Brookfield, Stephen D. "Media Power and the Development of Media Literacy: An Adult Educational Interpretation." *Harvard Educational Review* 56, no. 2 (1986): 151-170.

Brooks, Dwight, and Lisa Hebert. "Gender, Race, and Media Representation." In *Handbook of Gender and Communication,* edited by Bonnie Dow and Julia T. Wood, 297-317. Thousand Oaks, CA: Sage, 2006.

Brown, Mary Ellen. "Women and Soap Opera: Resistive Readings." In *Critical Readings: Media and Gender,* edited by Cynthia Carter and Linda Steiner, 287-306. Maidenhead, UK: Open University Press, 2004.

Browne, Beverly A. "Gender Stereotypes in Advertising on Children's Television in the 1990s: A Cross-National Analysis." *Journal of Advertising* 27, no. 1 (1998): 83-96.

Brubaker, Sarah J., and Christie Wright. "Identity Transformation and Family Caregiving: Narratives of African American Teen Mothers." *Journal of Marriage and Family* 68, no. 5 (2006): 1214-1228.

Brunsdon, Charlotte, Julie D'Acci, and Lynn Spigel. "Introduction." In *Feminist Television Critism,* ed. Charlotte Brunsdon, Julie D'Acci, and Lynn Spigel, 1-19. Oxford: Clarendon Press, 1997.

Bruner, Jerome. *Acts of Meaning: Four Lectures on Mind and Culture.* Cambridge, MA: Harvard University Press, 1990.

Bryant, J. Allison. "How Has the Kids' Industry Evolved?" In *20 Questions About Youth & the Media,* edited by Sharon R. Mazzarella, 13-28. New York: Peter Lang, 2007.

Bryant, Jennings, Rodney A. Carveth, and Dan Brown. "Television Viewing and Anxiety: An Experimental Investigation." *Journal of Communication* 31, no. 1 (1981): 106-19.

Butler, Judith. *Gender Trouble: Feminism and the Subversion of Identity.* London: Routledge Press, 1990.

——. *Bodies That Matter: On the Discursive Limits of Sex.* New York: Routledge, 1993.

Butsch, Richard. "Ralph, Fred, Archie, and Homer: Why Television Keeps Re-creating the White Male Working Class Buffoon." In *Gender, Race, and Class in Media: A Text-Reader,* edited by Gail Dines and Jean Humez, 575-585. Thousand Oaks, CA: Sage Publications.

Byrne, Julie. *O God of Players: The Story of the Immaculata Mighty Macs*. New York: Columbia University Press, 2003.

Cahill, Sean, Ken South, and Jane Spade. *Outing Age: Public Policy Issues Affecting Gay, Lesbian, Bisexual and Transgender Elders*. The Political Institute of the National Gay and Lesbian Task Force, 2000. http://www.thetaskforce.org/download s/reports/reports/OutingAge.pdf.

Calasanti, Tony M. and Kathleen F. Slevin. *Gender, Social Inequalities and Aging*. Walnut Creek, CA: AltaMira Press, 2001.

Campbell, Richard, Christopher R. Martin, and Bettina Fabos. *Media and Culture: An Introduction to Mass Communications*. Boston: Bedford/St. Martin's, 2010.

Cantu, Larry. "Entre Hombres/Between Men: Latino Masculinities and Homosexualities." In *Gay Masculinities*, edited by Peter M. Nardi, 224-246. Thousand Oaks, CA: Sage Publications, 2000.

Caplan, David. "Kourtney Kardashian Agonized Over Whether to Keep Her Baby." *People*. August 19, 2009. http://www.people.com/people/article/0,,20298807,00.htm l.

Cardwell, Sarah. "Is Quality Television Any Good? Generic Distinctions, Evaluations and the Troubling Matter of Critical Judgment." In *Quality TV: Contemporary American Television and Beyond*, edited by Janet McCabe and Kim Akass, 19-34. London: I.B. Tauris, 2007.

Carnes, Mark C. *Secret Ritual and Manhood in Victorian America*. New Haven, CT: Yale University Press, 1989.

Carter, Julian. *The Heart of Whiteness: Normal Sexuality and Race in America, 1880-1940*. Durham, NC: Duke University Press, 2007.

Carveth, Rodney, and Alison Alexander. "Soap Opera Viewing Motivations and the Cultivation Process." *Journal of Broadcasting and Electronic Media* 29, no. 3 (1985): 259-73.

Cassidy, Lisa. "Is Carmela Soprano a Feminist?: Carmela's Care Ethics." In *The Sopranos and Philosophy: I Kill Therefore I Am*, edited by Richard Greene and Peter Vernezze, 97-107. Chicago: Open Court, 2004.

Caughley, John L. *Imaginary Social Worlds: A Cultural Approach*. Lincoln, NE: University of Nebraska Press, 1984.

Caughlin, John P. "Family Communication Standards: What Counts as Excellent Family Communication and How Are Such Standards Associated with Family Satisfaction?" *Human Communication Research* 29, no. 1 (2003): 5-40.

Chaffee, Steven H., and Albert R. Tims. "Interpersonal Factors in Adolescent Television Use." *Journal of Social Issues* 32, no. 4 (1976): 98-115.

Chaffee, Steven H., Jack M. McLeod, and Charles K. Atkin. "Parental Influences on Adolescent Media Use." *American Behavioral Scientist* 14, no. 3 (1971): 323-40.

Chamberlain, Lisa L., Yun Wang, and Thomas N. Robinson. "Does Children's Screen Time Predict Requests for Advertised Products? Cross-sectional and Prospective Analyses." *Archives of Pediatrics and Adolescent Medicine* 160, no. 40 (2006): 363-368.

Champagne, Christine. "Rattles and Ratings." *Advocate*, no. 788 (1999): 107.

Chandler, Daniel, and Merris Griffiths. "Gender-differentiated Production Features in Toy Commercials." *Journal of Broadcasting and Electronic Media* 44, no. 3 (2000): 503-521.

Chang, Chingching. "Ad Repetition and Variation in a Competitive Ad Context." Paper presented at the Annual Meeting of the International Communication Association, San Diego, CA, May 2003.

Chapman, James. *Saints and Avengers: British Adventure Series of the 1960s.* London: I. B. Tauris Publishers, 2002.

Cherney, Isabelle D., and Jessica Dempsey. "Young Children's Classification, Stereotyping and Play Behaviour for Gender Neutral and Ambiguous Toys." *Educational Psychology* 30, no. 6 (2010): 651-669. doi:10.1080/01443410.2010.498 416.

Chism, Denise M. *The High-Risk Pregnancy Sourcebook.* Los Angeles, CA: Lowell House, 1997.

Cody, Kevina. "'No Longer, But Not Yet': Tweens and the Mediating of Threshold Selves Through Liminal Consumption." *Journal of Consumer Culture* 12, no. 1 (2012): 41-65. doi: 10.1177/14695405/12438155.

Cohen, Jonathan. "Defining Identification: A Theoretical Look at the Identification of Audiences with Media Characters." *Mass Communication and Society* 4, no. 3 (2001): 245-64.

Committee on Communications. "Children, Adolescents, and Advertising." *Pediatrics* 118, no. 6 (2006): 2563-2569. doi: 10.1542/peds.2006-2698.

Connerton, Paul. *How Societies Remember.* Cambridge, MA: Cambridge University Press, 1989.

Cook, Daniel Thomas, and Susan B. Kaiser. "Betwixt and be Tween: Age Ambiguity and the Sexualization of the Female Consuming Subject." *Journal of Consumer Culture* 4, no. 2 (2004): 203-227. doi: 10.1177/1469540504043682.

Cooke-Jackson, Angela, and Elizabeth Hansen. "Appalachian Culture and Reality TV: The Ethical Dilemma of Stereotyping Others." *Journal of Mass Media Ethics* 23, no. 3 (2008): 183-200.

Cox, Nicole, and Jennifer Proffitt. "The Housewives' Guide to Better Living: Promoting Consumption on Bravo's The Real Housewives." *Communication, Culture & Critique* 5, no. 2 (2012): 295–312.

Cross, Gary. *Kids Stuff: Toys and the Changing World of American Childhood.* Cambridge, MA: Harvard University Press, 1997.

Cruikshank, Margaret. *Learning To Be Old: Gender, Culture and Aging.* Lanham, MD: Rowman and Littlefield, 2003.

Curdileone, Kyle A. *Manhood and American Political Culture in the Cold War: Masculinity, the Vital Center and American Political Culture in the Cold War, 1949-1963.* London: Routledge, 2005.

Datta, Ayona. "'This is Special Humour:' Visual Narratives of Polish Masculinities in London's Building Sites." In *After 2004: Polish Migration to the UK in the "New" European Union,* edited by Kathy Burrell, 189-210. London: Ashgate, 2009.

Davidson, Diana. "'A Mother Like You': Pregnancy, the Maternal, and Nostalgia." In *Analyzing Mad Men: Critical Essays on the Television Series,* edited by Scott F. Stoddart, 136-54. Jefferson, NC: McFarland and Co., Inc.

Davis, Fred. *Fashion, Culture, and Identity.* Chicago: University of Chicago Press, 1992.

Davis, Shannon. "Sex Stereotypes in Commercials Targeted Toward Children: A Content Analysis." *Sociological Spectrum* 23, no. 4 (2003): 407-424. doi: 10.1080/027321 70390225331.

Dayan, Daniel, and Elihu Katz. *Media Events: The Live Broadcasting of History.* Cambridge, MA: Harvard University Press, 1992.

De Beauvoir, Simone. *Old Age.* Harmondsworth: Penguin Books, 1977.

De Certeau, Michel. *The Practice of Everyday Life.* Berkeley, CA: University of California Press, 1988.

Decker, Phillip J., and Barry R. Nathan. *Behavior Model Training: Principles and Training.* New York: Praeger, 1985.

Declercq, Eugene R., Carol Sakala, Maureen P. Corry, and Sandra Applebaum. "Listening to Mothers II: Report of the Second National U.S. Survey of Women's Childbearing Experiences." New York: Childbirth Connection, 2006. Accessed November 10, 2012. http://www.childbirthconnection.org/pdfs/LTMII_report.pdf.

Deleuze, Gilles, and Félix Guattari. *Anti-Oedipus: Capitalism and Schizophrenia.* Minneapolis: University of Minnesota Press, 1983.

Deleuze, Gilles, and Félix Guattari. *A Thousand Plateaus: Capitalism and Schizophrenia.* Minneapolis: University of Minnesota Press, 1987.

DeNora, Tia. *Music in Everyday Life.* Cambridge, MA: Cambridge University Press, 2000.

Derrick, Jaye, and Gabriel Shira. "Social Surrogacy: How Favored Television Programs Provide the Experience of Belonging." *Journal of Experimental Social Psychology* 45, no. 2 (2009): 352-362.

Deuze, Mark. "Ethnic Media, Community Media and Participatory Culture." *Journalism* 7, no. 3 (2006): 262-280. doi: 10.1177/1464884906065512.

"The Dinner Party by Judy Chicago." Brooklyn Museum, 2004-11. http://www.brooklynmuseum.org/exhibitions/dinner_party.

Doane, Mary Ann. "Information, Crisis, Catastrophe." *Logics of Television: Essays in Cultural Criticism,* edited by Patricia Mellencamp, 222-239. Bloomington, IN: Indiana University Press, 1990.

Dolgen, Lauren. "Why I Created MTV's 'Sixteen and Pregnant.'" *CNN.* May 4, 2011. http://articles.cnn.com/2011-05-04/entertainment/teen.mom.dolgen_1_teenpregnancy-teen-mom-teen-mothers?_s=PM:SHOWBIZ.

Dorr, Aimee. "II. Television and Affective Development and Functioning: Maybe this Decade." *Journal of Broadcasting* 25, no. 4 (1981): 335-45.

Douglas, Susan J. *Where the Girls Are: Growing Up Female with the Mass Media.* New York: Random House, 1994.

Douglas, Susan J., and Meredith W. Michaels. *The Mommy Myth: The Idealization of Motherhood and How It Has Undermined Women.* New York: Free Press, 2004.

Dovey, John. *Freakshow: First Person Media and Factual Television.* London: Pluto, 2000.

Dow, Bonnie J. *Prime-Time Feminism: Television, Media, Culture, and the Women's Movement Since 1970.* Philadelphia: University of Pennsylvania Press, 1996.

Downing, Christine. *The Goddess: Mythological Images of the Feminine.* New York: The Continuum Publishing Company, 1981.

Dumlao, Rebecca. "Tapping into Critical Thinking: Viewer Interpretations of a Television Conflict." *Studies in Media and Information Literacy Education* 3 (2003). doi: 10.3138/sim.3.1.001.

Durham, Meenakshi Gigi. "Constructing the 'New Ethnicities': Media, Sexuality, and Diaspora Identity in the Lives of South Asian Immigrant Girls." *Critical Studies in Media Communication* 21, no. 2 (June 2004): 140-161. doi: 10.1080/073931804100 01688047.

Dyer, Richard. "Monroe and Sexuality." In *Heavenly Bodies: Film Stars and Society*, 19-66. New York: St. Martin's Press, 1986.

——. *Stars*. London: British Film Institute, 2004.

Earle, David M. *All Man! Hemmingway, 1950s Men's Magazines, and the Masculine Persona*. Kent, OH: Kent State University Press, 2009.

Edwards, Leigh. "Reality TV and the American Family." In *The Tube Has Spoken: Reality TV and History*, edited by Julie Taddeo and Ken Dvorak, 123-44. Lexington, KY: The University Press of Kentucky, 2011.

"The Electronic Age of Captain Video." *TV Forecast*. June 10, 1950, 6.

Ellis, John. *Visible Fictions: Cinema, Television, Video*. Revised ed. London: Routledge, 1992.

Ellsworth, Elizabeth. *Places of Learning: Media, Architecture, Pedagogy*. New York: Routledge, 2005.

Eng, David L. *The Feeling of Kinship: Queer Liberalism and the Racialization of Intimacy*. Durham, NC: Duke University Press, 2010.

Engelhardt, Tom. *The End of Victory Culture: Cold War America and the Disillusioning of a Generation*. New York: Basic Books, 1995.

Eron, Leonard D. "Age Trends in the Development of Aggression, Sex Typing, and Related Television Habits." *Developmental Psychology* 19, no. 1 (1983): 71-77.

Esmalian, Ani. "Lamar Odom's New Manager: Mama Kris Jenner." *Holly Scoop*, October 13. http://www.hollyscoop.com/lamar-odom/lamar-odoms-new-manager-mama-kris-jenner_25399.aspx.

Eyal, Keren. "Measuring Identification with Media Characters." Paper presented at the annual meeting of the National Communication Association, Miami Beach, Florida, November 2003.

Fairclough, Norman. "Critical Analysis of a Media Discourse." In *Media Studies: A Reader*, edited by Paul Marris and Sue Thornham, 308-325. New York: New York University Press, 2000.

Feasey, Rebecca. *Masculinity and Popular Television*. Great Britain: Edinburgh Press, 2008.

Fernandez, Sofia. "E!'s 'Keeping Up With the Kardashians' Hits Ratings High." *Hollywood Reporter*, September 9, 2011. http://www.hollywoodreporter.com/live-feed/es-keeping-up-kardashians-hits-231695.

Feschuk, Scott. *Searching for Michael Jackson's Nose and Other Preoccupations of Our Celebrity-mad Culture*. Toronto, ON: McClelland & Stewart, 2003.

Feuer, Jane. "HBO and the Concept of Quality TV." In *Quality TV: Contemporary American Television and Beyond*, edited by Janet McCabe and Kim Akass, 145-157. London: I.B. Tauris, 2007.

Fisher, Walter R. "Narration as Human Communication Paradigm: The Case of Public Moral Argument." *Communication Monographs* 51, no. 1 (1984): 1-22.

——. "The Narrative Paradigm: An Elaboration." *Communication Monographs* 52, no. 4 (1985): 347-67.

——. "Clarifying the Narrative Paradigm." *Communication Monographs* 56, no. 1 (1989): 55-58.

Fiske, John. *Television Culture*. London: Methuen, 1987.

——. *Understanding Popular Culture*. Boston: Unwin Hyman, 1989.

——. "The Codes of Television." In *Media Studies: A Reader*, edited by Paul Marris and Sue Thornham, 220-230. New York: New York University Press, 2000.

——. *Reading the Popular*. 2nd ed. New York: Routledge, 2011.

Fiske, John, and John Hartley. *Reading Television*. London: Methuen, 1978.

Fitzpatrick, Mary Anne, and L. David Ritchie. "Communication Schemata within the Family: Multiple Perspectives on Family Interaction." *Human Communication Research* 20, no. 3 (1994): 275-301.

Foster, Guy M. "Desire and the "Big Black Sex Cop': Race and the Politics of Sexual Intimacy in HBO's Six Feet Under." In *The New Queer Aesthetic on Television*, edited by James Keller, 99-112. Jefferson, IA: McFarland & Company, 2005.

Foucault, Michel. *Archaelogy of Knowledge*. London: Ravistock, 1972.

——. *The History of Sexuality*. Translated by Robert Hurley. New York: Vintage Books, 1988.

——. *The Hermeneutics of the Subject: Lectures at the Collège De France, 1981-82*. Edited by Frédéric Gros. Translated by Graham Burchell. New York: Palgrave Macmillan, 2005.

——. *The Will to Knowledge*. London: Penguin, 2006.

——. *The Birth of Biopolitics: Lectures at the Collège De France, 1978-79*. Edited by Michel Senellart. Translated by Graham Burchell. Basingstoke: Palgrave Macmillan, 2008.

"Four Flight-Tested Space Helmets You Can Make." *Women's Day*. August 1953, 25.

Frank, Arthur. *The Wounded Storyteller*. Chicago: The University of Chicago Press, 1995.

Freud, Sigmund. *The Ego and the Id*. Translated by Joan Riviere. London: Hogarth Press and Institute of Psycho-Analysis, 1927.

——. *Dream Psychology*. New York: MacMillan, 1990.

Frietas, Anthony, Susan Kaiser, Davis Joan Chandler, Davis Caroll Hall, Jung-Won Kim, and Tania Hammidi. "Appearance Management As Border Construction: Least Favorite Clothing, Group Distancing and Identity Not!" *Sociological Inquiry* 67, no. 3 (1997): 323-335.

Funk, Jeanne B. "Video Games." In *Children, Adolescents, and the Media*. Edited by Victor C. Strasburger, Barbara J. Wilson, and Amy B. Jordan, 2nd ed., 435-470. Los Angeles: Sage, 2008.

Fussell, Paul. *The Boys' Crusade: The American Infantry in Northwest Europe. 1944-1945*. New York: Modern Library, 2003.

Fussell, Paul. *Wartime: Understanding and Behavior in the Second World War*. New York: Oxford University Press, 1989.

Galton, S. "A Question of Honor." *Daily Express Saturday*. January 17, 2004, 11-12.

Ganong, Lawrence H., and Marilyn Coleman. "Effect of Family Structure on Family Attitudes and Expectations." *Family Relations* 33, no. 3 (1984): 425-32.

Gauntlett, David. *Media, Gender and Identity: An Introduction*. London: Routledge, 2002.

Gauntlett, David, and Annette Hill. *TV Living: Television, Culture and Everyday Life*. London: Routledge, 1999.

Gendron, Bernard. "Theodor Adorno Meets The Cadillacs." In *Studies in Entertainment: Critical Approaches to Mass Culture*, edited by Tania Modleski, 18-37. Bloomington, IN: Indiana University Press, 1986.

Gerbner, George. "On Defining Communications: Still Another View." *Journal of Communication* 16, no. 2 (1966): 99-103.

——. "Toward 'Cultural Indicators':The Analysis of Mass Mediated Public Message Systems." *AV Communication Review* 17, no. 2 (1969): 137-48.

——. "Cultural Indicators: The Third Voice." In *Communications, Technology, and Social Policy*, edited by George Gerbner, Larry Gross, and William H. Melody, 555-73. New York: Wiley, 1973.

Gerbner, George, and Larry Gross. "Living with Television: The Violence Profile." *Journal of Communication* 26 (1976): 173-99.

Gerbner, George, Larry Gross, Michael Morgan, and Nancy Signorielli. "The 'Mainstreaming of America': Violence Profile No. 11." *Journal of Communication* 30, no. 3 (1980): 10-29.

Gerbner, George, Larry Gross, Michael Morgan, Nancy Signorielli, and James Shanahan. "Growing Up with Television: Cultivation Processes." In *Media Effects: Advances in Theory and Research*. 2nd ed., edited by Jennings Bryant and Dolf Zillmann, 43-68. Mahwah, NJ: Lawrence Erlbaum, 2002.

Gerhard, Jane. "Judy Chicago and the Practice of 1970s Feminism." *Feminist Studies* 37, no. 3 (2011): 591-618.

Gernsback, Hugo. "The Science-Fiction Industry: A New Industry in the Making." *Science-Fiction Plus* 1 (May 1953): 1-2.

Gilbert, James Burkhart. *Men in the Middle: Searching for Masculinity in the 1950s.* Chicago: University of Chicago Press, 2005.

Gillespie, Marie, ed. *Media Audiences*. New York: Open University Press, 2005.

Gillis, Stacy, and Joanne Hollows, eds. *Feminism, Domesticity and Popular Culture.* New York: Routledge, 2011.

Giroux, Henry. "Public Pedagogy as Cultural Politics: Stuart Hall and the 'Crisis of Culture.'" *Cultural Studies* 14, no. 2 (2000): 341-360.

Gitlin, Todd. *Inside Prime Time.* New York: Pantheon, 1983.

——. *Watching Television: A Pantheon Guide to Popular Culture.* New York: Pantheon Books, 1985.

GLAAD. "Where We Are On TV." *Gay & Lesbian Alliance Against Defamation: Words & Images Matter.* Septemeber 2011. http://www.glaad.org/publications/whereweare ontv11.

Glut, Donald F., and Jim Harmon. *The Great Television Heroes.* Garden City, NY: Doubleday, 1975.

Glynn, Kevin. *Tabloid Culture: Trash Taste, Popular Power, and the Transformation of American Television.* Durham: Duke University Press, 2000.

Goldberg, Stephanie. "The 'Teen Mom' Phenomenon." *CNN.* Last modified September 10, 2010. http://articles.cnn.com/2010-09-10/entertainment/teen.mom.mtv_1_teen-moms-newsstand-show?_s=PM:SHOWBIZ.

——. "Kim Kardashian, Kris Humphries: Are you surprised?" *CNN.com.* Last modified November 1, 2011. http://www.cnn.com/2011/11/01/showbiz/celebrity-news-gossip/kim-kardashian-kris-humphries-divorce/index.html.

Goltz, Dustin. "Investigating Queer Future Meanings." *Qualitative Inquiry* 15, no. 3 (2009): 561-586.

Gorton, Kristyn. "'Why I Love Carmela Soprano': Ambivalence, the Domestic and Televisual Therapy." *Feminism & Psychology* 19, no. 1 (2009): 128-31.

——. "Domestic Desire: Older Women in *Six Feet Under* and Brothers & Sisters." In *Feminism, Domesticity and Popular Culture*, edited by Stacy Gillis and Joanne Hollows, 93-106. New York: Routledge, 2011.

Gramsci, Antonio. *Selections From the Prison Notebooks*, edited by Q. Hoare and G.N. Smith. London: Lawrence and Wishart, 1971.

Gray, Jennifer B. "Interpersonal Communication and the Illness Experience in the Sex and the City Breast Cancer Narrative." *Communication Quarterly* 55, no. 4 (2007): 397-414.

Gray, Jonathan, Cornel Sandvoss, and C. Lee Harrington, eds. *Fandom: Identities and Communities in a Mediated World*. New York: NYU Press, 2007.

Green, Melanie C., and Timothy C. Brock. "The Role of Transportation in the Persuasiveness of Public Narratives." *Journal of Personality and Social Psychology* 79, no. 5 (2000): 701-21.

Greenberg, Bradley S. "Some Uncommon Images and the Drench Hypothesis." In *Television As A Social Issue*, edited by Stuart Oskamp, 88-102. Newbury Park, CA: Sage, 1988.

Greene, Jehmu, and Shelby Knox. *Super Bowl Sexism, by the Numbers*. February 8, 2010, http://www.huffingtonpost.com/jehmu-greene/super-bowl-sexism-bythe_b_454249.html.

Gross, Jane. "Aging and Gay, and Facing Prejudice in Twilight." *New York Times*, October 9, 2007. http://www.nytimes.com/2007/10/09/us/09aged.html?pagewant ed=all.

Gross, Larry. *Up From Invisibility*. New York: Columbia University Press, 2001.

Guthrie, Marisa. "Nickelodeon vs. Nielsen: Who's to Blame for the Network's Plummeting Ratings." *The Hollywood Reporter*. Last modified December 8, 2011. http://www.hollywoodreporter.com/news/nickelodeon-nielsen-ratings-viacom27110 0.

Hains, Rebecca C. "Inventing the Teenage Girl: The Construction of Female Identity in Nickelodeon's *My Life as a Teenage Robot*." *Popular Communication* 5, no. 3 (2007): 191-213. doi: 10.1080/15405700701384855.

Hall, Alice. "Perceptions of the Authenticity of Reality Programs and Their Relationships to Audience Involvement, Enjoyment, and Perceived Learning." *Journal of Broadcasting & Electronic Media* 53, no. 4 (2009): 515-31.

Hall, Stuart ed. *Representation: Cultural Representations and Signifying Practices*. London, Thousand Oaks, New Delhi: Sage and Open University, 1997.

——. "Encoding/Decoding." In *Media and Cultural Studies: Key Works*, edited by Meenakshi Gigi Durham and Douglas M. Kellner, rev. ed., 163-173. Malden, MA: Blackwell Publishing, 2001.

Han, Chong-suk. "They Don't Want To Cruise Your Type: Gay Men of Color and the Racial Politics of Exclusion." *Social Identities* 12, no. 1 (2007): 51-67.

Handfield, Bronny, Sue Turnbull, and Robin J. Bell. "What Do Obstetricians Think About Media Influences on Their Patients?" *Australian & New Zealand Journal of Obstetrics & Gynaecology* 46, no. 5 (2006): 379-83.

Hanes, Stephanie. "Amber Portwood: MTV 'Teen Mom' a Role Model for Better or Worse?" *Christian Science Monitor*. Last modified June 11, 2012. http://www.csmonitor.com/The-Culture/Family/ModernParenthood/2012/0611/Amber-Portwood-MTV-Teen-Mom-a-role-model-for-better-or-worse.

Harrington, C. Lee, and Denise Bielby. *Soap Fans: Pursuing Pleasure and Making Meaning in Everyday Life*. Philadelphia: Temple University Press, 1995.

Hartley, John. "Twoocing and Joyreading." *Textual Practice* 8, no. 3 (1994): 399-413.

Hawkins, Robert P., Suzanne Pingree, and Ilya Adler. "Searching for Cognitive Processes in the Cultivation Effect." *Human Communication Research* 13, no. 4 (1987): 553-77.

Heath, Stephen. "Representing Television." In *Logics of Television: Essays in Cultural Criticism*, edited by Patricia Mellencamp, 267-302. Bloomington, IN: Indiana University Press, 1990.

Heintz-Knowles, Katharine E. "Balancing Acts: Work-Family Issues on Prime-Time TV." In *Television and the American Family*. 2nd ed., edited by Jennings Bryant and J. Alison Bryant, 177-206. Mahwah, NJ: Erlbaum, 2001.

Helsby, Wendy. *Teaching Reality TV*. Bedfordshire: Auteur, 2010.

Hendershot, Heather, ed. *Nickelodeon Nation*. New York: New York University Press, 2004.

Hennessy, Rosemary. *Profit and Pleasure: Sexual Identities in Late Capitalism*. New York: Routledge, 2000.

Henry, Holly K.M., and Dina L.G. Borzekowski. "The Nag Factor: A Mixed-methodology Study in the US of Young Children's Requests for Advertised Products." *Journal of Children and Media* 5, no. 3 (2011): 298-317. doi: 10.1080/17482798.2011.584380.

Hentges, Beth A., Robert A. Bartsch, and Jo A. Meier. "Gender Representation in Commercials as a Function of Target Audience Age." *Communication Research Reports* 24, no. 1 (2007): 55-62. doi: 10.1080/08824090601128174.

Hesmondhalgh, David. "Audiences and Everyday Aesthetics: Talking About Good and Bad Music." *European Journal of Cultural Studies* 10, no. 4 (2007): 507-27.

Hill, Annette. "Fearful and Safe: Audience Response to British Reality Programming." *Television & New Media* 1, no. 2 (2000): 193-213.

——. *Reality TV: Audiences and Popular Factual Television*. New York: Routledge, 2005.

——. "Big Brother: The Real Audience." In *Television: The Critical View*, edited by Horace Newcomb, 7th ed., 471-485. New York: Oxford University Press, 2007.

Hoffner, Cynthia, and Joanne Cantor. "Perceiving and Responding to Mass Media Characters." In *Responding to the Screen: Reception and Reaction Processes*, edited by Jennings Bryant and Dolf Zillmann, 63-101. Hillsdale, NJ: Erlbaum, 1991.

Hoffner, Cynthia, and Martha Buchanan. "Young Adults' Wishful Identification With Television Characters: The Role of Percieved Similarity and Character Attributes." *Media Psychology* 7 (2005): 325-351.

Holmes, Su. "'All You've Got to Worry About is the Task, Having a Cup of Tea, and Doing a Bit of Sunbathing': Approaching Celebrity in *Big Brother*." In *Understanding Reality Television*, edited by Su Holmes and Deborah Jermyn, 111-35. New York: Routledge, 2004.

Horovitz, Bruce. "Be Ready for Toy Marketers' Christmastime Tactics." *Frank W. Baker.* Last modified on November 26, 2006. http://www.frankwbaker.com/holiday _ad_tactics.htm.

Horrocks, Roger. *Male Myths and Icons.* New York: St. Martin's Press, 1995.

Hovey, Jaime. "Queer Change Agents." In *Media Queered: Visibility and its Discontents,* edited by Kevin G. Barnhurst, 161-164. New York: Peter Lang Publishing, 2007.

Huang, Li-Ning. "Family Communication Patterns and Personality Characteristics." *Communication Quarterly* 47, no. 2 (1999): 230-33.

Huesmann, L. Rowell, Leonard D. Eron, Monroe M. Lefkowitz, and Leopold O. Walder. "Stability of Aggression over Time and Generations." *Developmental Psychology* 20, no. 6 (1984): 1120-34.

Hunt, Darnell M. *Channeling Blackness: Studies on Television and Race in America.* Oxford University Press, 2004.

Huyssen, Andreas. *Twilight Memories: Marking Time in a Culture of Amnesia.* New York: Routledge, 1995.

Hyden, Lars-Christer. "Illness and Narrative." *Sociology of Health and Illness* 19, no. 1 (1997): 48-69.

Jay, Samuel. "De-racializing 'Deadbeat Dads': Paternal Involvement in MTV's *Teen Mom.*" *Flow TV* 12, no. 9 (2010). http://flowtv.org/2010/09/de-racializing-deadbeat-dads/.

Jenkins, Henry. *Textual Poachers: Television Fans and Participatory Culture.* New York: Routledge, 1992.

——. *Convergence Culture: Where Old and New Media Collide.* New York: New York University Press, 2006.

Jensen, Jeff. "Naked Ambition." *Entertainment Weekly,* September 3, 2010, 42-46.

Jhally, Sut, and Jackson Katz. "Big Trouble, Little Pond: Reflections on the Meaning of the Campus Pond Rapes." *Umass,* Winter, 2001, 26-31.

John, Deborah R. "Consumer Socialization of Children: A Retrospective Look at Twenty-five Years of Research." *Journal of Consumer Research* 26, no. 3 (1999): 183-213.

Johnson, Fern L., and Karren Young. "Gendered Voices in Children's Television Advertising." *Critical Studies in Media Communication* 19, no. 4 (2002): 461-480.

Johnson, Jr., Michael. "The Channel for Gay America? A Cultural Criticism of The Logo Channel's Commercial Success on American Cable Television." Master's Thesis. Tampa: University of South Florida, 2008.

——. "Noah's Arc: Where Do We Go From Here." In *Queers In American Popular Culture,* edited by Jim Elledge, 35-46. Santa Barbara, CA: Praeger, 2010.

Johnston, Elizabeth. "How Women Really Are: Disturbing Parallels between Reality Television and 18th Century Fiction." In *How Real Is Reality TV?: Essays on Representation and Truth,* edited by David S. Escoffery, 115-32. Jefferson: McFarland, 2006.

Jones, Julie, and Steven Pugh. "Ageing Gay Men: Lessons From the Sociology of Embodiment ." *Men and Masculinities* 7, no. 3 (2005): 248-260.

Jung, Carl. *The Archetypes and the Collective Unconscious.* Princeton, NJ: Princeton University Press, 1959.

Jung, John. "How Useful is the Concept of Role Model? A Critical Analysis." *Journal of Social Behavior and Personality* 1, no. 4 (1986): 525-36.

Kane, Graeme. "Unmasking The Gay Male Body Ideal: A Critical Analysis of the Dominant Research on Gay Men's Body Image Issues." *Gay & Lesbian Issues and Psychology Review* 5, no. 1 (2009): 20-33.

Kahlenberg, Susan G., and Michelle M. Hein. "Progression on *Nickelodeon*? Gender-role Stereotypes in Toy Commercials." *Sex Roles* 62, no. 11/12 (2010): 830-847. doi: 10.1007/s11199-009-9653-1.

Karim, Karim H. *The Media of Diaspora*. London: Routledge, 2003.

Katriel, Tamar, and Thomas Farrell. "Scrapbooks as Cultural Texts: An American Art of Memory." *Text & Performance Quarterly* 11, no. 1 (1991): 1-17.

Kilborn, Richard. "'How Real Can You Get?' Recent Developments in 'Reality Television.'" *European Journal of Communication* 9, no. 4 (1994): 421-39. doi: 10.1177/0267323194009004003.

——. *Staging the Real: Factual TV Programming in the Age of Big Brother*. Manchester: Manchester University Press, 2003.

Kimmel, Douglas C., and Dawn L. Martin. *Midlife and Aging In Gay America: Proceedings of the SAGE Conference*. New York: Harrington Park Press, 2001.

Kincheloe, Joe L. *Critical Pedagogy Primer*. New York: Peter Lang, 2004.

King, Russell, and Nancy Wood. *Media and Migration: Constructions of Mobility and Difference*. London: Routledge, 2001.

Kirsch, Steven J. *Media and Youth: A Developmental Perspective*. Malden, MA: John Wiley & Sons, 2009.

Klaassen, Abbey, and Claire Atkinson. "Kids' Upfront Crawls Along; 6% Rise Seen." *Advertising Age* 76, no. 18 (2005): 61.

Klein, Amanda Ann. "Welfare Queen Redux: Teen Mom, Class and the Bad Mother." *Flow TV* 13, no. 3 (2010). http://flowtv.org/2010/11/welfare-queen-redux/.

Kline, Kimberly N. "Midwife Attended Births in Prime-Time Television: Craziness, Controlling Bitches, and Ultimate Capitulation." *Women and Language* 30, no. 1 (2007): 20-29.

Kline, Stephen. *Out of the Garden: Toys, TV, and Children's Culture in the Age of Marketing*. London: Verso, 1993.

——. "The Play of the Market: On the Internationalization of Children's Culture. *Theory, Culture, & Society* 12 (1995): 103-129.

Knauer, Nancy J. *Gay and Lesbian Elders: History, Law, and Identity Politics in the United States*. Burlington, VT: Ashgate Publishing, 2011.

Koerner, Ascan F., and Mary Anne Fitzpatrick. "Toward a Theory of Family Communication." *Communication Theory* 12, no. 1 (2002): 70-91.

Koestler, Arthur. *The Act of Creation*. London: Picador, 1975.

Krcmar, Marina. "The Contribution of Family Communication Patterns to Children's Interpretations of Television Violence." *Journal of Broadcasting and Electronic Media* 42, no. 2 (1998): 250-54.

——. "Assessing the Research on Media, Cognitive Development, and Infants: Can Infants Really Learn from Television and Videos?" *Journal of Children and Media* 4, no. 2 (2010): 119-134.

Krippendorff, Klaus. *Content Analysis: An Introduction to its Methodology*. Beverly Hills, CA: Sage, 1980.

Kruger, Lou-Marie. "Narrating Motherhood: The Transformative Potential of Individual Stories." *South African Journal of Psychology* 33, no. 4 (2003): 198-204.

Lagorio, Christine. "Resources: Marketing to Kids." *CBS News*. Last modified November 1, 2011. http://www.cbsnews.com/stories/2007/05/04/fyi/main2798401.shtml.

Lahman, Maria K. E. "Dreams of My Daughter: An Ectopic Pregnancy." *Qualitative Health Research* 19, no. 2 (2009): 272-78.

Larson, Mary Strom. "Interactions, Activities and Gender in Children's Television Commercials: A Content Analysis." *Journal of Broadcasting & Electronic Media* 45, no. 1 (2001): 41-56.

Lavery, David, ed. *This Thing of Ours: Investigating The Sopranos*. New York: Columbia UP, 2002.

——, ed. *Reading The Sopranos: Hit TV from HBO*. London: I.B. Tauris, 2006.

——. "Read Any Good Television Lately? Television Companion Books and Quality TV." In *Quality TV: Contemporary American Television and Beyond*, edited by Janet McCabe and Kim Akass, 228-236. London: I.B. Tauris, 2007.

Lawson, Mark. "Mark Lawson Talks to David Chase." In *Quality TV: Contemporary American Television and Beyond*, edited by Janet McCabe and Kim Akass, 185-220. London: I.B. Tauris, 2007.

Lee, Shu-Yueh. "The Power of Beauty in Reality Plastic Surgery Shows: Romance, Career, and Happiness." *Communication, Culture & Critique* 2 (2009): 503-19.

Lembo, Ron. *Thinking Through Television*. Cambridge: Cambridge University Press, 2000.

Lemish, Dafna. *Children and Television: A Global Perspective*. Malden, MA: Blackwell, 2007.

Lester, Elizabeth P. "Finding the Path to Signification: Undressing a Nissan Pathfinder Direct Mail Package." In *Undressing the Ad: Reading Culture in Advertising*, edited by Katherine Toland Frith, 19-34. New York: Peter Lang, 1998.

Lewis, Jane. *Women in Britain Since 1945: Women, Family, Work and the State in the Post-War Years*. Cambridge, MA: Blackwell Publishing, 1992.

Lindau, Stacey Tessler, L. Phillip Schumm, Edward O. Laumann, Wendy Levinson, Colm A. O'Muircheartaigh, and Linda J. Waite. "A Study of Sexuality and Health Among Older Adults in the United States." *New England Journal of Medicine* 357, no. 8 (2007): 762-774.

Lindlof, Thomas R., and Bryan C. Taylor. *Qualitative Communication Research Methods*. 2nd ed. Thousand Oaks, CA: Sage, 2002.

Livaditi, Julia, Konstantina Vassilopoulou, Christos Luogos, and Konstantinos Chorianopolous. "Needs and Gratification for Interactive TV Applications: Implication for Designers." Proceedings of the 36th Hawaii International Conference on System Sciences. The IEEE Computer Society, 2003.

Louw, Eric. *The Media and Cultural Production*. Thousand Oaks, CA: Sage Publications, 2011.

Lucanio, Patrick, and Gary Coville. *Smokin' Rockets: The Romance of Technology in American Film, Radio and Television, 1945-1960*. Jefferson, NC: McFarland, 2002.

Luke, Barbara. "The Changing Patterns of Multiple Births in the United States: Maternal and Infant Characteristics, 1973-1990." *Obstetrics and Gynegology* 84, no. 1 (1994): 101-106.

Luke, Barbara, and Tamara Eberlein. *When You're Expecting Twins, Triplets, or Quads*. New York: Harper Collins, 2004.

Lull, James. "Family Communication Patterns and the Social Uses of Television." *Communication Research* 7, no. 3 (1980): 319-34.

MacCoby, Eleanor E., and William C. Wilson. "Identification and Observational Learning from Films." *Journal of Abnormal and Social Psychology* 55, no. 1 (1957): 76-87.

Macey, Deborah A. *Ancient Archetypes in Modern Media: A Comparative Analysis of Golden Girls, Living Single, and Sex and the City.* PhD dissertation, University of Oregon, 2008.

——. "Ancient Archetypes in Modern Media." In *Media Depictions of Brides, Wives, and Mothers*, edited by Alena Amato Ruggerio, 49-62. Lanham, MD: Lexington Books, 2012.

Macklin, M. Carole, and Richard H. Kolbe. "Sex Role Stereotyping in Children's Advertising: Current and Past Trends." *Journal of Advertising* 13, no. 2 (1984): 34-42.

Macnee, Patrick. *Blind in One Ear: The Avenger Returns.* San Francisco: Mercury House, 1989.

Maher, Jill K., and Nancy M. Childs. "A Longitudinal Content Analysis of Gender Roles in Children's Television Advertisements: A 27 Year Review." *Journal of Current Issues & Research in Advertising* 25, no. 1 (2003): 71-82.

Maltz, Daniel N., and Ruth A. Borker. "A Cultural Approach to Male-female Miscommunication." In *Language and Gender: A Reader*, edited by Jennifer Coates, 417-434. Oxford: Blackwell Publishers, 1998.

Manchester, William. *Goodbye Darkness: A Memoir of the Pacific War.* Boston: Little, Brown, 1980.

Marcuse, Herbert. *One Dimensional Man,* Boston: Beacon Press, 1991.

Marrubio, M. Elise. *Killing the Indian Maiden: Images of Native American Women on Film.* Lexington: University Press of Kentucky, 2006.

Marshall, S. L. A. *Men against Fire: The Problem of Battle Command.* 1947. Norman: University of Oklahoma Press, 2000.

Martin, Carol Lynn, and Diane Ruble. "Children's Search for Gender Cues: Cognitive Perspectives on Gender Development." *Current Directions in Psychological Science* 13, no. 2 (2004): 67-70.

Matheson, Richard. "Clothes Make the Man." *Worlds Beyond* 1, no. 3 (1951): 84.

Mauldin, Bill. *Up Front.* New York: Henry Holt, 1945.

Mayo, Peter. "Public Pedagogy and the Quest for a Substantive Democracy." *Interchange* 33, no. 2 (2002): 193-207.

Mazierska, Ewa. *Polish Postcommunist Cinema.* Bern: Peter Lang Publishing, 2007.

McCabe, Janet. "'Like, Whatever': Claire, Female Identity, and Growing Up Dysfunctional." In *Six Feet Under: TV to Die For*, edited by Kim Akass and Janet McCabe, 121-134. London: I.B. Tauris, 2005.

McCabe, Janet, and Kim Akass. "What has Carmela Ever Done for Feminism?: Carmela Soprano and the Post-Feminist Dilemma." In *Reading The Sopranos: Hit TV from HBO*, ed. David Lavery. London: I.B. Tauris, 2006.

——, eds. *Quality TV: Contemporary American Television and Beyond.* London: I.B. Tauris, 2007.

McClain, Amanda. *American Ideal: How American Idol Constructs Celebrity, Collective Identity, and American Discourses.* Lanham, MD: Lexington Books, 2011.

McConnon, Aili. "Toys: No Must-haves This Holiday Season." *Business Week*, December 1, 2008. Accessed October 16, 2011. http://www.businessweek.com/stori es/2008-11-26/toys-no-must-haves-this-holiday-seasonbusinessweek-business-news-stock-market-and-financial-advice.

McDermott-Perez, Lisa. *Preemie Parents: Recovering from Baby's Premature Birth*. Westport, CT: Praeger, 2007.

McGinley, Maurice. "Television's Job-To-Be-Done." *How I Got My Kink* (blog), May 10, 2012. http://howigotmykink.blogspot.com/2012/05/televisions-job-to-be-done-image-source.html.

McLeod, Jack M., and Steven H. Chaffee. "The Construction of Social Reality." In *The Social Influence Process*, edited by James T. Tedeschi, 50-59. Chicago: Aldine-Atherton, 1972.

McMurria, John. "Desperate Citizens and Good Samaritans: Neoliberalism and Makeover Reality TV." *Television & New Media* 9, no. 4 (2008): 305-32.

McPherson, J. Miller, and James M. Cook. "Birds of a Feather: Homophily in Social Networks." *Annual Review of Sociology* 27, (2001): 415-444.

McNeal, James U. *The Kids Market: Myths and Realities*. New York: Paramount Market, 1999.

Mendes, Elizabeth, Lydia Saad, and Kyley McGeeney. "Stay-at-Home Moms Report More Depression, Sadness, Anger, But Low-Income Stay-at-Home Moms Struggle the Most." *Gallup*, May 18, 2012. http://www.gallup.com/poll/154685/stay-home-moms-report-depression-sadness-anger.aspx.

Mercer, Kobena. "Just Looking for Trouble: Robert Mapplethorpe and Fantasies of Race." In *Dangerous Liasons: Gender, Nation and Postcolonial Perspectives*, edited by Anne McClintock, Aamir Mufti, and Ella Shohat, 240-252. Minneapolis, MN: University of Minnesota Press, 1997.

Merkin, Daphne. "The Wild Bunch," *The New York Times*, December 4, 2010, http://tma gazine.blogs.nytimes.com/2010/12/04/the-wild-bunch.

Merriam, Sharan B. *Qualitative Research and Case Study Applications in Education*. San Francisco: Jossey Bass, 2001.

Merskin, Debra. "Boys Will Be Boys: A Content Analysis of Gender and Race in Children's Advertisements on the Turner Cartoon Network." *Journal of Current Issues & Research in Advertising* 24, no. 1 (2002): 51-60.

Mertler, Craig A., and C. M. Charles. *Introduction to Educational Research*. 5th ed. Boston, MA: Pearson Education, 2005.

MetLife. "Still Out, Still Aging: The MetLife Study of Lesbian, Gay, Bisexual, and Transgender Baby Boomers." *MetLife Insurance*. March 2010. http://www.metlife.c om/assets/cao/mmi/publications/studies/2010/mmi-still-out-still-aging.pdf.

Mezirow, Jack, and Associates. *Learning as Transformation: Critical Perspectives on a Theory in Progress*. San Francisco: Jossey-Bass, 2000.

Miller, Cynthia J. "Domesticating Space: Science Fiction Serials Come Home." In *Science Fiction Film, Television, and Adaptation: Across the Screens*, edited by J. P. Telotte, 3-13. London and New York: Routledge, 2011.

Miller, Toby. *The Avengers*. London: The British Film Institute, 1997.

——. *Cultural Citizenship: Cosmopolitanism, Consumerism, and Television in a Neoliberal Age*. Philadelphia: Temple University Press, 2007.

Miner, Madonne M. "'Like a Natural Woman': Nature, Technology, and Birthing Bodies in Murphy Brown." *Frontiers: A Journal of Women Studies* 16, no. 1 (1996): 1-17.

Mittell, Jason. "Narrative Complexity and Contemporary American Television." *The Velvet Light Trap* 58 (Fall 2006): 30-40.

Mitternauer, Michael. *A History of Youth.* Oxford: Blackwell Publishers, 1992.

Molloy, Tim. "Disney Channel Knocks Nickelodeon From Top Ratings Perch." *Chicago Tribune.* March 29, 2012. http://www.chicagotribune.com/entertainment/sns-rt-us-disney-nickelodeonbre82s0xh-20120329,0,2571969.story.

Moore, Roy L., and George P. Moschis. "The Role of Family Communication in Consumer Learning." *Journal of Communication* 31, no. 4 (1981): 42-51.

Morgan, Michael, and Heather Harr-Mazar. *Television and Adolescents' Family Life Expectations.* Unpublished manuscript. 1980. The Annenberg School of Communications, University of Pennsylvania, Philadelphia.

Morley, David. *Family Television: Cultural Power and Domestic Leisure.* New York: Routledge, 1986.

———. *Televisions, Audiences and Cultural Studies.* London and New York: Routledge, 1992.

———. *Home Identities: Media, Mobility and Identity.* New York, Routledge, 2000.

Morris, Theresa, and Katherine McInerney. "Media Representations of Pregnancy and Childbirth: An Analysis of Reality Television Programs in the United States." *Birth: Issues in Perinatal Care* 37, no. 2 (2010): 134-40.

Moyer-Guse, Emily, and Robin L. Nabi. "Explaining the Effects of Narrative in an Entertainment Television Program: Overcoming Resistance to Persuasion." *Human Communication Research* 36, no. 1 (2010): 26-52.

Mui, Ylan Q. "This Year, It's a High-tech Toy Story." *Washington Post.* November 17, 2005. http://www.washingtonpost.com/wpdyn/content/article/2005/11/16/AR20051 1602233.html.

Munoz, Jose Esteban. "Queer Minstrels for the Straight Eye: Race as Surplus in Gay TV." *GLQ: A Journal of Lesbian and Gay Studies* 11, no. 2 (2005): 101-102.

National Institute of Mental Health. *Television and Behavior: Ten Years of Scientific Progress and Implications for the Eighties, Vol 1. Summary Report.* (DHHS Publication No. ADM 82-1195). Washington, DC: U.S. Government Printing Office, 1982.

Nelson, Robin. "Quality TV Drama: Estimations and Influences Through Time and Space." In *Quality TV: Contemporary American Television and Beyond,* edited by Janet McCabe and Kim Akass, 38-51. London: I.B. Tauris, 2007.

Newcomb, Horace. "Reflections on TV, *The Most Popular Art.*" In *Thinking Outside the Box: A Contemporary Television Genre Reader,* edited by Gary R. Edgerton and Brian G. Rose. Lexington, KY: University of Kentucky Press, 2005.

———, ed. *Television: The Critical View.* 7th ed. New York: Oxford University Press, 2006.

Niederdeppe, Jeff, Erika Franklin Fowler, Kenneth Goldstein, and James Pribble. "Does Local Television News Coverage Cultivate Fatalistic Beliefs About Cancer Prevention?" *Journal of Communication* 60, no. 2 (2010): 230-53.

Nora, Pierre. *Realms of Memory: Rethinking the French Past.* New York: Columbia University Press, 1997-2000.

"OECD—Better Policies for Better Lives." *OECD, Organisation for Economic Co-operation and Development.* Accessed June 21, 2012. http://www.oecd.org/.

O'Guinn, Thomas C., and L. J. Shrum. "The Role of Television in the Construction of Consumer Reality." *Journal of Consumer Research* 23, no. 4 (1997): 278-94.

O'Leary, Kevin. "Sisters Torn Apart." *US Weekly,* August 23, 2010, 42-47.

Oulette, Laurie, and James Hay. *Better Living through Reality TV: Television and Post-welfare Citizenship*. Malden: Blackwell, 2008.

Owens, Charles R., and Frank R. Ascione. "Effects of the Model's Age, Perceived Similarity and Familiarity on Children's Donating." *Journal of Genetic Psychology* 151, no. 3 (1991): 341-57.

Papa, Michael J., Arvind Shinghai, Sweety Law, Saumya Pant, Suruchi Sood, Everett M. Rogers, and Corrine L. Shefner-Roberts. "Entertainment-Education and Social Change: An Analysis of Parasocial Interaction, Social Learning, Collective Efficacy and Paradoxical Communication." *Journal of Communication* 50, no.4 (2000): 31-55.

Paré, Elizabeth R., and Heather E. Dillaway. "'Staying at Home' versus 'Working': A Call for Broader Conceptualizations of Parenthood and Paid Work." *Michigan Family Review* 10, no. 1 (2005): 66-87.

Pike, Jennifer J., and Nancy A. Jennings. "The Effects of Commercials on Children's Perceptions of Gender Appropriate Toy Use." *Sex Roles* 52, no. 1/2 (2005): 83-91. doi: 10.1007/s11199-005-1195-6.

Pine, Karen J., and Avril Nash. "Dear Santa: The Effects of Television Advertising on Young Children." *International Journal of Behavioral Development* 26, no. 6 (2002): 529-539. doi: 10/1080/0165025014300081.

Pleiss, Mary K., and John F. Feldhusen. "Mentors, Role Models, and Heroes in the Lives of Gifted Children." *Educational Psychologist* 30, no. 3 (1995): 159-69.

Pozner, Jennifer. *Reality Bites Back*. Berkeley, CA: Seal Press, 2010.

Press, Andrea. *Women Watching Television: Gender, Class, and Generation in the American Television Experience*. Philadelphia: University of Pennsylvania Press, 1991.

Pullen, Christopher. "Heroic Gay Characters in Popular Film: Tragic Determination and the Everyday." *Continuum: Journal of Media & Cultural Studies* 25, no. 3 (2011): 397-413.

Radway, Janice. *Reading the Romance*. Chapel Hill: University of North Carolina Press, 1984.

"The Real Deal." *IYSL: It's Your (Sex) Life*. MTV. Accessed November 12, 2012. http://www.itsyoursexlife.com/preventing-pregnancy/the-real-deal/.

Reeves, Byron B., and Mark M. Miller. "A Multidimensional Measure of Children's Identification with Television Characters." *Journal of Broadcasting* 22, no. 1 (1978): 21-86.

Richardson, Dave. "Honor Blackman: Leather and Lace." *TV Zone*. February, 1996.

Ridley-Johnson, Robyn, June E. Chance, and Harris Cooper. "Correlates of Children's Television Viewing: Expectancies, Age, and Sex." *Journal of Applied Developmental Psychology* 5, no. 3 (1984): 225-35.

Ritchie, L. David. "Family Communication Patterns: An Epistemic Analysis and Conceptual Reinterpretation." *Communication Research* 18, no. 4 (1991): 548-65.

Ritchie, L. David, and Mary Anne Fitzpatrick. "Family Communication Patterns: Measuring Intrapersonal Perceptions of Interpersonal Relationships." *Communication Research* 17, no. 4 (1990), 523-44.

Rizzo, Monica. "Lunch with Betty White." *People*, May 7, 2012, 50.

Robinson, James D., and Thomas Skill. "Five Decades of Families on Television: From the 1950s through the 1990s." In *Television and the American Family*. 2nd ed.

Edited by Jennings Bryant and J. Alison Bryant, 139-62. Mahwah, NJ: Erlbaum, 2001.

Robinson, Murray. "Planet Parenthood." *Collier's Magazine.* January 5, 1952.

Robinson, Peter. *The Changing World of Gay Men.* New York: Palgrave Macmillan, 2008.

——. "The Influence of Ageism on Relations Between Old and Young Gay Men." In *Out Here: Gay and Lesbian Perspectives VI*, edited by Yorick Smaal and Graham Willett, 223-236. Clayton, Victoria: Monash University Publishing, 2011.

Roedder, Deborah L. "Age Differences in Children's Responses to Television Advertising: An Information-Processing Approach." *Journal of Consumer Research* 8, no. 2 (1981): 144-153.

Rogers, Dave. "Cathy Gale vs. The Gong Man." *On Target—The Avengers: The Officially Authorised [sic] Avengers Network Magazine* 2 (1985): 3-7.

——. *The Complete Avengers: The Full Story of Britain's Smash Crime-Fighting Team!* New York: St. Martin's Press, 1989.

Romer, Daniel, Kathleen Hall Jamieson, and Sean Aday. "Television News and the Cultivation of Fear of Crime." *Journal of Communication* 53, no. 1 (2003): 88-104.

Rubin, Alan M. "Television Use by Children and Adolescents." *Human Communication Research* 5, no. 2 (1979): 109–120.

Rubin, Alan M. "Uses and Gratifications." In *Broadcasting Research Methods*, edited by Joseph R. Dominick and James E. Fletcher. Boston: Allyn and Bacon, 1985.

——. "The Uses-And-Gratification Perspective of Media Effects." In *Media Effects: Advances in Theory and Research.* Edited by Jennings Bryant and Dolf Zillman, 2nd ed., 525-548. Mahwah: Erlbaum, 2002.

Rucker, Allen. *The Sopranos Family Cookbook: As Complied by Artie Bucco.* New York: Warner Books, 2002.

——. *Entertaining with the Sopranos: As Compiled by Carmela Soprano.* New York: Warner Books, 2006.

Ryan, Erin L. "*Dora the Explorer*: Empowering Preschoolers, Girls, and Latinas." *Journal of Broadcasting and Electronic Media* 54, no. 1 (2010): 54-68. doi:10.1080/08838150903550394.

Rydzewska, Joanna. "'Great Britain, Great Expectations': The Representation of Polish Migration to Great Britain in Londyńczycy / *Londoners.*" *Critical Studies in Television* 6, no. 2 (2011): 127-140.

Sandlin, Jennifer A., Brian D. Shultz, and Jake Burdick, eds. *The Handbook of Public Pedagogy: Education and Learning Beyond Schooling.* New York: Routledge, 2010.

Saphir, Melissa N., and Steven H. Chaffee. "Adolescents' Contributions to Family Communication Patterns." *Human Communication Research* 28, no. 1 (2002): 86-108.

Sayeau, Ashley. "Americanitis: Self-help and the American Dream in *Six Feet Under.*" In *Six Feet Under: TV to Die For*, edited by Kim Akass and Janet McCabe, 94-104. London: I.B. Tauris, 2005.

Schaefer, Charles E. *How to Influence Children.* New York: Van Nostrand Reinhold, 1978.

Scheibe, Cynthia. "Piaget and Power Rangers: What Can Theories of Developmental Psychology Tell us About Children and Media." In *20 Questions About Youth & the Media*, edited by Sharon R. Mazzarella, 61-72. New York: Peter Lang, 2007.

Schor, Juliet B. *Born to Buy: The Commercialized Child and the New Consumer Culture*. New York: Scribner, 2004.

Schulman, Sarah. *Stagestruck: Theater, AIDS, and The Marketing Of Gay America*. Durham, NC: Duke University Press, 1998.

———. "The Making of a Market Niche." *The Harvard Gay & Lesbian Review* 5, no.1 (1998): 17.

Scott, Dariek. "Jungle Fever? Black Gay Identity Politics, White Dick and the Utopian Bedroom." *GLQ: A Journal of Lesbian and Gay Studies* 1, no. 3 (1994): 299-321.

Seiter, Ellen. *Sold Separately: Parents and Children in Consumer Society*. New Brunswick, NJ: Stanford University Press, 1993.

Sennett, Richard. "Street and Office: Two Sources of Identity." In *On the Edge: Living with Global Capitalism*, edited by Will Hutton and Anthony Giddens, 175-190. London: Jonathan Cape, 2000.

Serbin, Lisa A., Diane Poulin-Dubois, Karen A. Colburne, Maya G. Sen, and Julie A. Eichstedt. "Gender Stereotyping in Infancy: Visual Preferences for and Knowledge of Gender-Stereotyped Toys in the Second Year." *International Journal of Behavioral Development* 25, no. 1 (2001): 7-15. doi: 10.1080/01650230042000078.

Severin, Werner J., and James W. Tankard, Jr. *Communication Theories: Origins, Methods, and Uses in the Mass Media*, 3rd ed. New York: Longman, 1992.

Shafer, Autumn. "'16 and Pregnant': Examining the Role of Transportation and Persuasive Intent in the Effects of an Entertainment-education Narrative." Unpublished dissertation, University of North Carolina at Chapel Hill, 2011.

Shanahan, James, Nancy Signorielli, and Michael Morgan. "Television and Sex Roles 30 Years Hence: A Retrospective and Current Look From a Cultural Indicators Perspective." Presentation at the Annual Meeting of the International Communication Association, Montreal, Canada, May 2008.

Sharf, Barbara, and Marsha Vanderford. "Illness Narrative and the Social Construction of Health." In *Handbook of Health Communication*, edited by Teresa L. Thompson, Alicia M. Dorsey, Katherine I. Miller, and Roxanne Parrott, 9-34. Mahwah, NJ: Lawrence Earlbaum, 2003.

Shelton, Nikki, and Sally Johnson. "'I Think Motherhood for Me Was a Bit Like a Double-Edged Sword': The Narratives of Older Mothers." *Journal of Community & Applied Social Psychology* 16, no. 4 (2006): 316-30.

Shoemaker, Deanna. "Mamafesto! Why Superheroes Wear Capes." *Text & Performance Quarterly* 31, no. 2 (April 2011): 190-202.

Shrum, L. J. "Psychological Processes Underlying Cultivation Effects: Further Tests of Construct Accessibility." *Human Communication Research* 22, no. 4 (1996): 482-509.

Shrum, L. J., Robert S. Wyer, and Thomas C. O'Guinn. "The Effects of Television Consumption on Social Perceptions: The Use of Priming Procedures to Investigate Psychological Processes." *Journal of Consumer Research* 24, no. 4 (1998): 447-58.

Siegel, David L., Timothy J. Coffey, and Gregory Livingston. *The Great Tween Buying Machine: Capturing Your Share of the Multimillion Dollar Tween Market*. Chicago: Dearborn Trade Publishing, 2004.

Signorielli, Nancy, and Susan G. Kahlenberg. "Television's World of Work in the Nineties." *Journal of Broadcasting and Electronic Media* 45, no. 1 (2001): 4-22.

Signorielli, Nancy, and Michael Morgan. *Cultivation Analysis: New Directions in Media Effects Research*. Newbury Park, CA: Sage, 1990.

——. "Television and the Family: The Cultivation Perspective." In *Television and the American Family*. 2nd ed., edited by Jennings Bryant and J. Alison Bryant, 333-51. Mahwah, NJ: Erlbaum, 2001.

Sillars, Malcolm, and Bruce Gronbeck. *Communication Criticism: Rhetoric, Social Codes, Cultural Studies*. Prospect Heights, Ill.: Waveland Press, 2001.

Skeggs, Beverley, and Helen Wood. "The Labor of Transformation and the Circuits of Value 'around' Reality TV." *Continuum: Journal of Media & Cultural Studies* 22, no. 4 (2008): 559-72.

Skeggs, Beverley, Nancy Thumim, and Helen Wood. "Oh Goodness, I *am* watching Reality TV": How Methods Make Class in Multi-Method Audience Research." *European Journal of Cultural Studies* 11, no. 1 (2008): 5-24.

Skill, Thomas, and James D. Robinson. "Four Decades of Family on Television: A Demographic Profile, 1950-1989." *Journal of Broadcasting and Electronic Media* 38, no. 4 (1994): 449-64.

Sledge, E. B. *With the Old Breed at Peleliu and Okinawa*. Novato, CA: Presidio Press, 1981.

Slevin, Kathleen F., and Thomas J. Linnerman. "Old Gay Men's Bodies and Masculinities." *Men and Masculinities* 12, no. 4 (2010): 483-507.

Smith, Anne K. "Cheery News for Holiday Shoppers: Price-cutting is Still in Fashion, and Seasonal Hiring Will Increase." *Kiplinger's Personal Finance* (December 2010): 15-16.

Smith, Jonathan Z. *To Take Place: Toward Theory in Ritual*. Chicago: The University of Chicago Press, 1987.

Smith, Lois J. "A Content Analysis of Gender Differences in Children's Advertising." *Journal of Broadcasting and Electronic Media* 38, no. 3 (1994): 323-338.

"Smith Voices." *Smith Alumnae Quarterly* 98, no. 4 (2012): 3.

Sneegas, James E., and Tamyra A. Plank. "Gender Differences in Pre-adolescent Reactance to Age-Categorized Television Advisory Labels." *Journal of Broadcasting and Electronic Media* 42, no. 4 (1998): 423-34.

Sonnekus, Theo. "Consumption as Citizenship, The Media, and The Making Of A Gay Niche Market." *LitNet.com*. March 3, 2008. http://www.litnet.co.za/cgi-bin/giga.cgi?cmd=cause_dir_news_item&news_id=33813&cause_id=1270.

Sontag, Susan. "Seminar on Television." New York: Institute for the Humanities, 1981.

"Sopranos Creator Takes on Angry Fans." *Entertainment Weekly*, October 17, 2007, http://www.ew.com/ew/article/0,,20152845_2,00.html.

Spigel, Lynn. *Make Room for TV: Television and the Family Ideal in Postwar America*. Chicago: University of Chicago Press, 1992.

Stage, Christine W., and Marifran Mattson. "Ethnographic Interviewing as Contextualized Conversation." In *Expressions of Ethnography: A Novel Approach to Qualitative Methods*, edited by Robin P. Clair, 97-105. Albany, NY: State University of New York Press, 2003.

Stanfield, Peter. *Horse Opera: The Strange History of the 1930s Singing Cowboy*. Urbana and Chicago: University of Illinois Press, 2002.

Steinberg, Neil. *Hatless Jack: The President, the Fedora, and the History of an American Style*. New York: Plume, 2004.

Steverman, Ben. "Air Hogs, Sing-a-ma-jigs May Bring Holiday Joy for Toymakers." *Business Week*, September 29, 2010. http://www.businessweek.com/stories/2010-

09-29/air-hogs-sing-a-ma-jigs-may-bring-holiday-joy-for-toymakersbusinessweek-business-news-stock-market-and-financial-advice.

Storey, John. *Cultural Theory and Popular Culture*. 4th ed. Athens, GA: University of Georgia Press, 2006.

Strasburger, Victor C., Barbara J. Wilson, and Amy B. Jordan. *Children, Adolescents, and the Media*, 2nd ed. Thousand Oaks, CA: Sage, 2009.

Streitmatter, Rodger. *From 'Perverts' to 'Fab Five': The Media's Changing Depiction of Gay Men and Lesbians*. New York: Routledge, 2009.

Sturken, Marita. *Tangled Memories: The Vietnam War, the AIDS Epidemic, and the Politics of Remembering*. Berkeley: University of California Press, 1997.

Sutton-Smith, Brian. *Toys as Culture*. New York: Gardner, 1986.

Swan, Karen. "Social Learning from Saturday Morning Cartoons." In *Social Learning from Broadcast Television*, edited by Karen Swan, Carla Meskill, and Steven DeMaio, 87-112. Cresskill, NJ: Hampton, 1998.

Task Force on Television Management, Nielsen Media Research. "Independent Task Force on Television Measurement Report." Last modified March 21, 2005. http://www.everyonecounts.tv/news/documents/taskforcereport.pdf.

"Teen Pregnancy." *Centers for Disease Control and Prevention*. CDC. Last Modified August 7, 2012. http://www.cdc.gov/teenpregnancy.

Temple, Bogusia. "Diaspora, Diaspora Space and Polish Women." *Women's Studies International Forum* 22, no. 1 (1999): 17-24.

Terdiman, Richard. *Present Past: Modernity and the Memory Crisis*. Ithaca, NY: Cornell University Press, 1993.

Thomas, Frankie. "Westward The Stars." *American Classic Screen* 4, no. 2 (1980): 47-52.

Tichi, Cecelia. *Electronic Hearth: Creating an American Television Culture*. New York: Oxford University Press, 1992.

Treviño, Jesus Salvador. "Latino Portrayals in Film and Television." *Jump Cut: A Review of Contemporary Media* 30 (March 1985): 14-16.

Tuchman, Gaye, Arlene Daniels, and James Benet, eds. *Hearth and Home: Images of Women in Mass Media*. New York: Oxford University Press, 1978.

Turner, Graeme, and Jinna Tay, eds. *Television Studies After TV: Understanding Television in the Post-Broadcast Era*. New York: Routledge, 2009.

Tyler, Imogen. "Pramface Girls: The Class Politics of 'Maternal TV.'" In *Reality Television and Class*, edited by Helen Wood and Beverley Skeggs, 210-24. London: Palgrave Macmillan, 2011.

Van der Voort, T. H. A. *Television Violence: A Child's Eye View*. Amsterdam: North Holland, 1986.

Van Evra, Judith P. *Television and Child Development*. 3rd ed. Mahwah, NJ: Erlbaum, 2004.

Van Leeuwen, Theo. *Introducing Social Semiotics*. London and New York: Routledge, 2005.

Van Zoonen, Liesbet. *Feminist Media Studies*. London: Sage Publications, 1994.

——. *Entertaining the Citizen: When Politics and Popular Culture Converge*. New York: Rowman and Littlefield, 2004.

Verna, Mary Ellen. "The Female Image in Children's TV Commercials." *Journal of Broadcasting* 19, no. 3 (1975): 301-309.

Vizziello, Graziella Fava, Maria Elisa Antonioli, Valentina Cocci, and Roberta Invernizzi. "From Pregnancy to Motherhood: The Structure of Representative and Narrative Change." *Infant Mental Health Journal* 14, no. 1 (1993): 4-16.

Wartella, Ellen, and Nancy Jennings. "New Members of the Family: The Digital Revolution in the Home." *Journal of Family Communication* 1, no. 1 (2001): 59-69.

Weaver, Simon. "Life with Honor." *TV Times*. November 8, 1963.

Weber, Bill. "We Need Better TV Role Models for Kids." *Television Week*, June 28, 2004.

Weber, Max. *The Protestant Ethic and the Spirit of Capitalism*. Los Angeles: Roxbury Publishing Company, 1996.

Weiss, Audrey J., and Barbara J. Wilson. "Children's Cognitive and Emotional Responses to the Portrayal of Negative Emotions in Family-Formatted Situation Comedies." *Human Communication Research* 24, no. 4 (1998): 584-609.

Weston, Kath. *Families We Choose: Lesbians, Gays, Kinship*. New York: Columbia University Press, 1997.

Wheeler, Katrina-Kasey. "'Kourtney & Kim Take New York' debuts with huge ratings -- 3 million viewers." *Examiner*, January 25. http://www.examiner.com/tv-in-national/kourtney-kim-take-new-york-debuts-with-huge-ratings-3-million-viewers.

Whipple, Thomas W., and Mary K. McManamon. "Implications of Using Male and Females Voices in Commercials: An Exploratory Study." *Journal of Advertising* 31, no. 2 (2002): 79-91.

Whitney, Daisy. "For Kids TV, Every Day is Saturday." *Advertising Age* (February 21, 2005), 10. http://adage.com/article/special-report-kids/kids-tv-day-saturday/102154/.

Williams, Raymond. *Television*. London: Routledge, 2003.

Wilson, Barbara J. "The Mass Media and Family Communication." In *Handbook of Family Communication*, edited by Anita L. Vangelisti, 563-591. Mahwah, NJ: Erlbaum, 2004.

Wilson, Brian, and Robert Sparks. "'It's Gotta be the Shoes': Youth, Race, and Sneaker Commercials." *Sociology of Sport Journal* 13, no. 4 (1996): 398-427.

Wilson, Eric. "Kim Kardashian Inc." *The New York Times*. November 17, 2010, http://www.nytimes.com /2010/11/18/fashion/18KIM.html?emc=eta1.

Wood, Helen, and Beverley Skeggs. "Reacting to Reality TV: The Affective Economy of an 'Extended Social/Public Realm.'" In *Real Worlds: The Global Politics of Reality TV*, edited by Marwan M. Kraidy and Katherine Sender. 93-107. New York: Routledge, 2011.

Wood, Julia. *Gendered Lives: Communication, Gender, and Culture*. 9th ed. Boston: Wadsworth Cengage Learning, 2011.

Woodward, Larry D. "How Marketers Target Your Kids. *ABC News*. Last modified on December 9, 2009. http://www.abcnews.go.com/Business/marketers-target-kids/story?id=9284270.

Wright, Paul J., Ashley K. Randall, and Analisa Arroyo. "Father–Daughter Communication About Sex Moderates the Association Between Exposure to MTV's *16 and Pregnant/Teen Mom* and Female Students' Pregnancy-Risk Behavior." *Sexuality & Culture* 15 (2012). doi: 10.1007/s12119-012-9137-2.

Wright, Robin Redmon, and Jennifer A. Sandlin. "Cult TV, Hip Hop, and Vampire Slayers: A Review of the Literature at the Intersection of Adult Education and Popular Culture." *Adult Education Quarterly* 59, no. 2 (2009): 118-141.

Wright, Robin Redmon, and   Jennifer A. Sandlin. "Popular Culture, Public Pedagogy, and Perspective Transformation: *The Avengers* and Adult Learning in Living Rooms." *International Journal of Lifelong Learning* 28, no. 4 (2009): 533-551.

Young, Diony. "Childbirth Education, the Internet, and Reality Television: Challenges Ahead." *Birth: Issues in Perinatal Care* 37, no.2 (2002): 87-89.

Index

About the Contributors

Tanja N. Aho is currently working on several projects that range from representations of class and poverty on television to notions of citizenship and belonging in women's literature to the Finnish-American radical theater of the twentieth century. She is a graduate student at both the University of Erlangen-Nuremberg in Germany and the University at Buffalo, SUNY, where she teaches classes in global gender studies, American studies, and African American studies.

Andrée E. C. Betancourt is an independent interdisciplinary scholar and multimedia artist who has worked in the film and entertainment industry. Betancourt received her doctoral degree in communication studies from Louisiana State University, and she was awarded a Graduate School Dissertation Fellowship for "Under Construction: Recollecting the Museum of the Moving Image," a study that demonstrates ways in which we recollect our memories and ourselves through museum-going and technologies of reproduction. She conceived and directed *Agridulce*, a performance about magical realism, family recipes, and los Días de los Muertos (the Days of the Dead), for the LSU HopKins Black Box theatre. Betancourt taught courses across the communication discipline during her doctoral program and as an adjunct faculty member at the University of South Alabama in the Department of Communication. She received her B.A. degree in psychology from Smith College, and her M.A. degree in film studies from University College Dublin. Currently a freelance writer and editor for a national consulting firm in the D.C. area, she has worked for numerous arts and cultural institutions in the United States and Europe. Her recent scholarship explores intersections among memory, collecting, and images (traditional and digital, moving and still), and www.DreBetancourt.net features samples from her portfolio.

Amy C. Duvall is an M.A. student in communication at the University of Arkansas.

Jennifer G. Hall, Ph.D., is a 2010 graduate of Purdue University with a concentration in health communication. She currently works as a long-term lecturer at Purdue and continues to study how narrative accounts of pregnancy and childbirth impact women's lived experiences.

Michael Johnson Jr. is a Ph.D. candidate, American studies, at Washington State University. Michael earned his M.L.A. in social and political thought from the University of South Florida as well as his M.S. in information studies from Florida State University. He was the 2008–2009 Ronald E. McNair Fellow at WSU and currently serves as the Area Chair for Gender and Sexual Identity for the SWTX Regional Popular Culture/American Culture Association and as an associate editor for the *NeoAmericanist*. His primary research/interest areas include critical media studies at the intersections of queer and ethnoracial representation in U.S. corporate television networks, employing political economic analyses; interrogating Foucauldian effects of "naturalizing" forces on queer sex acts; and the intersections of ethnicity and socio-political queer activism.

Susan G. Kahlenberg has been a member of the faculty at Muhlenberg College since 1998. Her research focuses on the relationships among media institutions, images, and effects. Using content analysis methodology, she explores how media messages are produced, the types of images that are represented in the media, and the impact of these messages. She examines characterizations on fictionally based television programming and daytime TV commercials, to deduce the extent that gender-role stereotypes may serve to sustain the social order. See http://www.muhlenberg.edu/main/academics/mediacom/community/faculty/kahlenberg.html.

Amanda S. McClain is the arts and communications coordinator and an assistant professor of communication at Holy Family University, in Philadelphia, PA. McClain earned her doctorate in mass media and communication from Temple University. Her first book, *American Ideal: How American Idol Constructs Celebrity, Collective Identity, and American Discourses*, was published by Lexington Books in 2011. McClain's research interests include reality TV, social media, celebrity, communication theory, narrative, and media representations of women.

Brian McKernan is a doctoral candidate in the Sociology Department at University at Albany, State University of New York. He is also a visiting lecturer at Mount Holyoke College. His research adopts a cultural sociology framework to examine the roles of mass media and popular culture in civil society. Brian's current research examines the social construction of video games in different types of media outlets. He is also conducting research on celebrity's multiple discourses in civil society and is involved in a project with

Ronald Jacobs that explores the treatment of American television in non-American newspapers.

Cynthia J. Miller is a cultural anthropologist, specializing in popular culture and visual media. Her work has appeared in edited volumes and journals across the disciplines. She is the editor of *Too Bold for the Box Office: The Mockumentary from Big Screen to Small* (2012), and co-editor of *Cadets, Rangers, and Junior Space Men: Televised "Rocketman" Series of the 1950s and Their Fans* (with A. Bowdoin Van Riper, 2012), *Undead in the West: Vampires, Zombies, Mummies and Ghosts on the Cinematic Frontier* (with A. Bowdoin Van Riper, 2012), and *Steaming into a Victorian Future: A Steampunk Anthology* (with Julie Anne Taddeo, 2012). Cynthia also serves on the editorial board of the *Encyclopedia of Women and Popular Culture* and is series editor for Scarecrow Press's *Film and History* series.

Marcelina Piotrowski is a doctoral student in the Faculty of Education in the University of British Columbia. Her program of research examines the cultural politics of documentary cinema, and particularly environmental film and video. Her current research examines short, online political documentary films that focus on socio-cultural aspects of oil and pipelines, and the role these have in mapping cosmopolitan subjects.

Leah A. Rosenberg holds a joint position as visiting assistant professor at the University of Missouri, Columbia for the departments of Sociology and Communication. She holds a Ph.D. from Emory University in the Graduate Institute of Liberal Arts, an M.A. from Emory in liberal arts and an M.A. from the University of California, Irvine in social relations. Her dissertation, "Mourning News: Grief, Memory, and Television Viewership of 9/11," examines the connection between news consumption, catastrophes, and individual memory.

David Staton is a freelance writer, multi-media producer and graduate student at the University of Oregon's School of Journalism and Mass Communication. He has an M.A. in art history from State University of New York Purchase College and a B.A. in journalism from the University of New Mexico.

Ellen E. Stiffler is an instructor of communication at Henderson State University in Arkadelphia, Arkansas. She has an M.A. in Communication from the University of Arkansas, Fayetteville.

A. Bowdoin Van Riper is an independent scholar whose work focuses on the history of modern science and technology and images of science and technology in popular culture. His work has appeared in *Film & History, New Scientist, Journal of Popular Film and Television,* and collections such as *Icons of Evolution* (ed. Brian Regal, 2008), *Sounds of the Future* (ed. Mathew J.

Bartowiak, 2009), and *Too Bold for the Box Office* (ed. Cynthia J. Miller, 2012). He is the author, most recently, of *A Biographical Encyclopedia of Scientists and Inventors in American Film and TV since 1930* (2011) and co-editor, with Cynthia J. Miller, of *1950s "Rocketman" TV Series and their Fans: Cadets, Rangers, and Junior Spacemen* (2012) and *Undead in the West: Vampires, Mummies, Zombies and Ghosts on the Cinematic Frontier* (2012).

Lynne M. Webb, Ph.D., University of Oregon, is a professor in interpersonal and family communication at the University of Arkansas, Fayetteville. Webb has published over fifty articles including work in the *Journal of Applied Communication Research, Communication Education, Journal of Family Communication, Health Communication, Women's Studies in Communication, Communication Research Reports, Southern Communication Journal,* as well as other journals and edited volumes. Her vita lists over one hundred conference presentations and/or papers, including seventy since joining the Arkansas faculty: eight were top papers in her divisions. She is the recipient of twelve small grants ranging from $2,000 to $10,050 and two additional research awards from the Southern States Communication Association. She has been the book review editor for the *Journal of Family Communication* as well as the special issue editor of two issues of the *Journal of Applied Communication Research* and one issue of the *Southern Communication Journal.* She has served as associate editor for nine journals as well as ad hoc reviewer for an additional nine journals. Dr. Webb has served on the governing boards of four professional associations and as chair of three units in the National Communication Association. She is a past president of the Southern States Communication Association.

Robin Redmon Wright is currently an assistant professor of adult education at Penn State, Harrisburg. She holds both a B.A. and an M.A. in English literature from the University of Tennessee and a Ph.D. in educational human resource development from Texas A&M University. Her research interests reflect a critical perspective on the intersection of popular culture and informal adult learning and identity development, feminist identity development, and critical theory as it is applied to adult learning, educational access, and socio-economic class. Recent publications include articles in the *International Journal of Lifelong Education, Adult Education Quarterly, Journal of Transformational Education, Journal of Studies in International Education, Journal of Curriculum and Pedagogy, Routledge Handbook of Public Pedagogy,* and *New Directions in Adult and Continuing Education.*

Jingsi Christina Wu is an assistant professor of media studies at Hofstra University. She received her Ph.D. from the joint program of sociology and communication at SUNY Albany. Dr. Wu uses a variety of perspectives and research approaches from media studies, cultural sociology, and political communication to study the convergence of popular culture and politics, how entertainment experiences contribute to civic engagement, how people behave in new media environments, such as massively multi-player online games, and how citizens use the social media to connect with others and organize their civic voices. Interested in both the U.S. media and the mass media in China, where Dr. Wu is from, she is also delving into cross-cultural comparisons.

About the Editors

Deborah A. Macey holds a Ph.D. from the University of Oregon. She is a visiting assistant professor at Saint Louis University, where she teaches courses in human communication and media studies. Her research interests focus on the intersections of gender, race, and class in popular culture representations, particularly television. As a lifetime member of the Organization for the Study of Communication, Language, and Gender, she frequently presents at its annual conference, among others including Women and Society, National Communication Association, and International Communication Association. Her work has appeared in *Media Depictions of Brides, Wives, and Mothers* (Lexington), *International Encyclopedia of Communication* (Blackwell), and *Human Studies: A Journal for Philosophy and the Social Sciences*.

Kathleen M. Ryan spent more than twenty years in network and local news production, and she continues to work as an active multimedia director and producer. Ryan's research interests include news labor and content, as well as oral history and visual communication. She has been recognized for excellence in both her professional and academic work, including an award of merit from the Broadcast Education Association for the film *Backstretch*; research honors from the International Communication Association and Association for Education in Journalism and Mass Communication, a Chris Award as co-producer for *Saving Faces*, and numerous other national and regional broadcast awards including a New England Emmy nomination. Ryan holds a Ph.D. in communication and society from University of Oregon, an M.A. in broadcast journalism from University of Southern California, and a B.A. in political science from University of California, Santa Barbara.